THE REBELS:

A BROTHERHOOD OF

OUTLAW BIKERS

Daniel R. Wolf

THE REBELS:

A Brotherhood of Outlaw Bikers

UNIVERSITY OF TORONTO PRESS

Toronto Buffalo London

© University of Toronto Press 1991
Toronto Buffalo London
Printed in Canada
Reprinted 1991
Reprinted in paperback 1992, 1995
ISBN 0-8020-2724-5 (cloth)
ISBN 0-8020-7363-8 (paper)

Printed on acid-free paper

Canadian Cataloguing in Publication Data

Wolf, Daniel R., 1948-
The Rebels: a brotherhood of outlaw bikers

Includes bibliographical references and index.
ISBN 0-8020-2724-5 (bound)
ISBN 0-8020-7363-8 (pbk.)

1. Rebels Motorcycle Club. 2. Motorcycle gangs - Alberta.
3. Motorcycle gangs - Canada. 4. Subculture.
5. Deviant behaviour. I. Title.

HV6491.C3W64 1991   302.3'4   C90-095849-9

The research funding for this book was provided by the following awards:
Canada Council Doctoral Fellowship;
Izaak Walton Killam Memorial Scholarship;
Canada Mortgage and Housing Corporation Graduate Fellowship;
and Province of Alberta Dissertation Fellowship.

This book has been published with the help of a grant
from the Social Science Federation of Canada,
using funds provided by the Social Sciences and
Humanities Research Council of Canada,
and with assistance from the Canada Council
and the Ontario Arts Council under their block grant programs.

Photo on front cover: courtesy *Edmonton Journal*

To those Rebels who, like myself,

are a little older now,

but are still riding,

still riding in the wind

Contents

Acknowledgments

I would like to thank Dr David E. Young as my mentor in psychological anthropology, a fine and respected man who was always there as both a friend and scholar. A number of colleagues have read the manuscript at various stages and offered helpful comments and criticisms. Among them I would especially like to mention Dr Robert Stebbins, Dr David Smith, Dr Desmond Ellis, Dr Robert Prus, Dr Ruth Gruhn, Dr Regna Darnell, Dr Tony Fisher, Dr David Bai, Dr Thomas Fleming, Dr Richard Wills, Dr Louis Watson, Dr Augustine Brannigan, Dr William Shaffir, Dr Richard Brymer, and the whiz-kid of biotelemetry, Dean Charles. There were many law-enforcement officers who recognized that my mandate was neither to condemn nor to glorify bikers, but to explain the world of outlaw bikerdom from an insider's perspective. Among those who both accepted and helped were Detective Andy D. Van Dusen (Intelligence unit, Calgary city police), Corporal Randy Marchand (Motorcycle coordinator, RCMP), Staff Sergeant Paul J. Shrive (Chief Instructor, Ontario Provincial Police), Detective Harvey Empter (Intelligence, Edmonton city police), Detective Brendan A. Kapuscinski (Special Strike Force, Calgary city police), and long-time buddy of mine Constable Phillip Haggart (Calgary city police). Deep and special thanks are due to Dr Patricia A. McCormack, who contributed hours of her superb editorial skills along with countless ideas and suggestions while we sat on the couch with her Alaskan Malamutes and munched on her unsurpassed blueberry pancakes. Finally, there is Iris, companion, who shared that which only she and I will ever know about, and without whom ... as an old saying goes.

Voodoo, Jim, and Tramp outside the Rebel club bar

'I can't walk, but I can still ride': Caveman riding with his broken leg in a cast and his crutches strapped to his 'sissy' backrest

The face of determination: Steve, the Rebels' sergeant at arms, continued to ride with the help of a prosthesis after losing his left leg in an accident.

The funeral run of a Rebel (July 1988): The Rebels pay final tribute to a lost brother (courtesy of *Edmonton Journal*).

Shakedown: The RCMP intercept members of the King's Crew MC on their way to join the Rebels at Coronation, Alberta (courtesy of *The Western Report*).

OPPOSITE

Living the biker fantasy

Hanging tough: Two Grim Reapers compete in a tire-pull contest at a 'field-day' for the Rebels, Grim Reapers, and Hell's Angels.

Blues and his 'hog': A personal statement forged in chrome and steel

Sandra, Coyote's ol' lady and companion on a moonlight mile

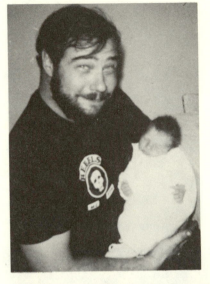

Some Rebels are fathers:
Wee Albert and his
newborn daughter Karen

Family life:
Trevor with his
three-year-old daughter
Rheanna

Part One

FREEDOM AND PROTEST: THE SEDUCTIVE WORLD OF BIKING

1

Introduction:
Entering the World
of the Outlaw

All the world likes an outlaw. For some damn reason they
remember 'em.

(Jesse James)

A midnight run shatters the night air. Thirty Harley-Davidson motorcycles stretch out for a quarter-mile, thundering down the highway.
The pack moves in tight formation, advancing as a column of staggered twos. Veteran riders make sure there are fifteen yards between
themselves and the bikes they are riding behind, three yards and a
45-degree angle between themselves and the bikes they are riding
beside. Thirty men ride in boots and jeans, leathers and cut-off
denim jackets, beards and long hair, tattoos and earrings, buck
knives and chain belts. Each rider follows the grimacing skull on the
back patch of the rider in front of him. Some ride with their ol'
ladies, 'jamming in the wind' with a laid-back coolness bordering on
arrogance, a combination of speed, grace, and power. The lead biker
snaps his wrist to full throttle and the supercharged V-twin engines
heat up and pound out the challenge. Each biker is locked into the
tunnel vision of his own world. He feels the heavy metal vibrations in
every joint of his body, but he can no longer hear the rumble of his
own machine, just a collective roar. Headlamps slice open just
enough darkness to let the sculptured metal of extended front ends
slide through. Cool blackness clips over high-rise handlebars, whips
their faces, then quickly swallows the red glare of tail-lights. A grey
blur of pavement that represents instant oblivion passes six inches
beneath the soles of their boots. At a hundred miles an hour the

inflections of the road surface disappear, eye sockets are pushed back, and tears flow. Riders hurtle down the highway, in total control of their own destinies, wrapped in the freedom of high sensation. They are the Rebels: Caveman, Blues, Tiny, Wee Albert, Gerry, Slim, Tramp, Danny, Onion, Jim, Raunch, Ken, Voodoo, Larry, Killer, Whimpy, Clayton, Steve, Indian, Armand, Crash, Big Mike, Smooth Ed, Yesnoski, Snake, Dale the Butcher, Saint, and Terrible Tom.

Outlaw motorcycle clubs originated on the American west coast following the Second World War. With names such as the Booze Fighters and their parent club the 13 Rebels, the Galloping Gooses, Satan's Sinners, and the Winos, they rapidly spread across the United States and into Canada in the early 1950s; Canada's first outlaw club was the Canadian Lancers in Toronto, Ontario. Today outlaw motorcycle clubs are an international social phenomenon. As of 1990 the outlaw club subculture had spread into eleven other countries, including the European nations of Great Britain, West Germany, France, Switzerland, Austria, Belgium, Denmark, and the Netherlands in the mid-sixties and early seventies, and then into Australia, New Zealand, and Brazil in the mid-seventies and early eighties.

What is or is not considered deviant by society, and how society reacts to that deviance, always involves the process of social definition. Technically, the label 'outlaw motorcycle club' designates a club that is not registered with the American Motorcycle Association (AMA) or the Canadian Motorcycle Association (CMA), which are the respective governing bodies for the sport of motorcycling in the United States and Canada. The AMA and CMA are themselves affiliated with the Fédération Internationale Motorcycliste (FIM), the international coordinating body for motorcycling whose headquarters are located in Paris, France. A motorcycle club that is registered with the AMA or CMA obtains a club charter from those parent bodies that allows the club and its members to participate in or sponsor sanctioned motorcycle events – mainly racing competitions. AMA or CMA registration further aligns the club with the legal and judicial elements of the host society; some clubs will go one step further and incorporate themselves as 'registered societies' with the local state or provincial authorities. Non-registered clubs are labelled 'outlaw' and considered as the 1 per cent deviant fringe that continues to tarnish the public image of both motorcycles and motorcyclists. For its part, the outlaw-biker community graciously accepted the AMA's 'one percenter' label as a means of identifying a 'righteous outlaw.' Today, many outlaw club members wear 1% badges as a supplement to their club colours; or, as Sonny Barger, president of the Hell's Angels, first did in the sixties, they make a very personal and uncompromising statement on where they stand on the issue of being an outlaw by having the 1% logo tattooed on their shoulders.

Historically, the initial and most dramatic definition of outlaw clubs occurred in response to the world's first motorcycle riot in the rural town of Hollister, California, on 4 July 1947. Approximately five hundred non-affiliated bikers disrupted an AMA-sponsored Gypsy Tour and competition events involving 2500 affiliated bikers by drinking and racing in the streets of the host town of Hollister. The ineffective efforts of a numerically insufficient seven-man police force, in conjunction with the sometimes provocative vigilante tactics of indignant local residents, caused the motorcyclists to coalesce as a mob. At the height of the riot, bikers rode their motorcycles into bars and restaurants and through traffic lights, tossed bottles out of upper-floor windows, and got rid of the beer they had been drinking in the streets (indecent exposure). The unruly behaviour lasted for approximately thirty-six hours, from July 4th to 5th; the world's first motorcycle riot ended with the departure of many of the partyers on the evening of the first day and the arrival on the second of an auxiliary police force of thirty-two officers.

The national exposure that was given the Hollister incident by *Life* magazine and others resulted in the stigmatization of an image: the motorcyclist as deviant. *Life*'s account started a mass-media chain reaction that saw the Hollister incident grow considerably in its sensationalistic portrayal, and, as a result, the image of the motorcyclist as deviant become more defined and immutable. In 1949, Frank Rooney wrote a short narrative entitled 'Cyclist Raid,' based on *Life*'s one-hundred-and-fifteen-word documentary. In 1951, 'Cyclist Raid' was published in *Harper's* magazine. The *Harper's* serial was read by Stanley Kramer, a Hollywood producer, who immortalized the 'motorcycle riot' in the movie *The Wild One*, released in 1953. The anti-hero image of the motorcyclist was cast in the person of Marlon Brando, while Lee Marvin personified the motorcyclist as villain. Interestingly enough, the striped shirt that Lee Marvin wore in the movie was later bought by a member of the Hell's Angels

Motorcycle Club (MC) – a symbolic indication of events to come. The movie was to titillate the North American media with its 'factual' account of a 'menacing element of modern youth':

> A little bit of the surface of contemporary American life is scratched in Stanley Kramer's 'The Wild One' ... and underneath is opened an ugly, debauched and frightening view of a small, but particularly significant and menacing element of modern youth ...
> The subject of its examination is a swarm of youthful motorcyclists who ride through the country in wolf-pack fashion and terrorize the people of one small town ... These 'wild ones' resent discipline and show an aggressive contempt for common decency and the police. Reckless and vandalistic, they live for sensations, nothing more – save perhaps the supreme sensation of defying the normal world. (Crowther, *New York Times*, 31 December 1953)

> Audiences who like their facts dished up with realism, no matter how painful, might pay attention to 'The Wild One' – a picture that is factual ... It displays a group of hoodlums, motorcyclists who ride around the country with a contempt for the law and a fondness for annoying people, who take over a small town ... a slice of contemporary Americana at its worst. (Hartung, *Commonweal*, 3 February 1954)

The above 'factual' accounts were based on viewing a Stanley Kramer movie production whose script was written by John Paxton; Paxton's script was based on Kramer's reading of Frank Rooney's serialized story in *Harper's* magazine; Rooney's short story was in turn based on his reading of *Life*'s one-hundred-and-fifteen-word report – complete with photo – which itself was originally construed by adding four major distortions to a brief press-wire release.

By contemporary standards the amount of property damage and civic duress incurred in Hollister was minimal. In actuality there were only thirty-eight arrests (out of approximately three or four thousand bikers), fighting was mostly confined to the bikers, and no one was killed, maimed, or even gang-kissed. 'Wino Willie' Forkner is a biker who has ridden Harleys since he was a teenager in the 1930s. He had returned from the Second World War after fighting the

Japanese as a waist gunner and engineer for the American Seventh Air Force. He attended the Hollister incident as a charter member of the Booze Fighters MC:

> The worst thing that happened was that a bunch of guys wanted to break Red Daldren out of jail. I was in a bar and somebody came in and said there were about 500 bikers ready to break him out, and I thought, 'Shit, that's all we need, something like that.' So I ran down to where the crowd was assembling and told 'em, 'Hell, old Red's drunk and he needs a good night's sleep. Leave him stay – he'll be out in the morning.' Then I turned around and went back to the bar, and damned if the cops didn't come and nail me for inciting a riot [the charges were dropped] ... but no big bad things happened. There were a few broken windows that we paid for. ('Wino Willie' Faukner, interview in *Easyriders*, September 1986: 107)

However, as *Life* was to point out twenty-five years after the Hollister riot, the significance of the media chain reaction was its very real consequences: '*The Wild One* became a milestone in movie history, launching the cult of gang violence in films. It also helped create an image of motorcycling that non-violent bike riders have been trying to live down for a quarter of a century now' (*Life*, September 1972: 32). After the Hollister incident and, more to the point, after the movie, the AMA issued its now famous statement about 1 per cent of the motorcycling public, specifically clubs like the Booze Fighters, being a deviant criminal fringe element.

There is a tendency to view the Hollister motorcycle riot and its subsequent national media coverage as the genesis of the 'outlaw biker' – it was the birth of an image. In effect, the outlaw biker image that was created served as a frame of reference for many young and restless rebels who copied the celluloid vision in search of both a thrill and a cause. Historically, outlaw motorcycle clubs have operated in the shadows of several different media stereotypes, all of which have been variations on the theme of 'social menace.' In the 1950s bikers were depicted as social rebels and deviants; in the sixties and seventies the clubs were seen as subcultures of violence and drugs. The contemporary image adds a spectre of organized crime. In 1984 the Criminal Intelligence Service of Canada (CISC) declared that outlaw motorcycle gangs had become as much of an organized-crime threat to Canada as the traditional Mafia. According to the CISC report, outlaw clubs 'are involved in practically all major crime activities from murder to white-collar crime.' At the annual meeting of Canadian police chiefs in 1985, outlaw motorcycle clubs were again acknowledged as the number-one concern in the area of organized crime; media headlines carried the claim: 'Bikers more powerful than Mafia' (Canadian Press release, *Edmonton Journal*, 15 August 1985: A12). How law-enforcement agencies have come to view outlaw motorcycle clubs is summarized in the following profile contained in an application for a search warrant made out by a member of the City of Calgary police department's Special Strike Force:

> Outlaw Motorcycle Gangs have over the years evolved into highly sophisticated 'organized crime' bodies, involved in drug manufacture/distribution/trafficking, prostitution, 'gun running,' fencing of stolen property and strong arm debt collection.
>
> Law enforcement agencies across Canada have recognized that outlaw motorcycle gangs as 'organized crime' bodies pose the single most serious threat to the country.
>
> An outlaw motorcycle gang is 'Any group of motorcycle enthusiasts who have voluntarily made a commitment to band together and abide by their organization's rigorous rules enforced by violence, who engage in activities that bring them and their club into serious conflict with society and the law.'
>
> It is their involvement as a group in criminal activities and anti-social behaviour which sets them apart from other organized groups. (Detective Brendan Alexander Kapuscinski, City of Calgary police force, 'Application for Warrant to Search and Seize,' 1988: 2)

'If the Cops are the Good Guys,' writes the representative of an American federal law-enforcement training centre, 'then it's hard to imagine a more archetypal Bad Guy than the outlaw motorcyclist!' (Ayoob, 1982: 26). North Americans typically react with an interesting mixture of apprehension and fascination to the fearsome images of aggression, revolt, anarchy, and criminal abandon that are used to portray outlaw-biker gangs.

Ironically, the appeal of outlaw clubs to their members is very different from what the public understands. Outlaw bikers view themselves as nothing less than frontier heroes, living out the 'freedom ethic' that they feel the rest of society has largely abandoned. They acknowledge that they are antisocial, but only to the extent that they seek to gain their own unique experiences and express their individuality through their motorcycles. Their 'hogs' become personal charms against the regimented world of the 'citizen.' They view their club as collective leverage that they can use against an establishment that threatens to crush those who find conventional society inhibiting and destructive of individual character. In an interesting twist of stereotypes the citizen becomes the bad guy, or at least weak, and the outlaw becomes the hero. Bikers make much of the point that the differential treatment – harassment – accorded outlaw clubs by law-enforcement agencies runs counter to the basic principles of self-determination. They protest that a truly democratic society should be able to tolerate diversity and accommodate an awareness that drifting away from society's conventions is very different from opting out of society's laws. Somewhere between the convenient stereotype of 'criminal deviants' used by the police and the stylized self-conscious image outlaws have of themselves as 'frontier heroes' lies the story of real people.

The Rebels Motorcycle Club is an outlaw club. It began in 1969 as a small club of motorcycle enthusiasts who rode their Harley-Davidsons on the streets of Edmonton, Alberta, a mid-sized Canadian city with a population of approximately 700,000 people. Today (1990), the Rebels MC is a federation of four clubs – located in the provinces of Alberta and Saskatchewan – that maintains informal social and political ties with the Hell's Angels MC. Becoming a Rebel means being part of a tightly knit voluntary association that operates as a secret society within an organizational framework that includes a political structure, a financial base, a geographical territory, a chain of command, a constitution, an elaborate set of rules, and internal mechanisms for enforcing justice and compliance from within.

At its best a veteran club will operate with the internal discipline and precision of a paramilitary organization, which is completely necessary if it hopes to beat the odds and survive. These men close their world to the outside, turning to each other for help and guidance. They protect themselves with a rigid code of silence that cloaks their world in secrecy. Thus, despite the fact that outlaw motorcycle clubs are found in every major urban centre in Canada and the United States – there are approximately 900 clubs – *the subculture had remained ethnographically unexplored.*

As a doctoral graduate student in anthropology at the University of Alberta, Edmonton, I wanted to study the 'Harley tribe.' It was my intent to obtain an insider's perspective on the emotions and the mechanics that underlie the outlaw bikers' creation of a subcultural alternative. My interest in outlaw motorcycle clubs was not entirely theoretical; it was also a personal challenge. Brought up on the streets of a lower-class neighbourhood, I saw my best friend – with whom I broke into abandoned buildings as a kid – sent to prison for grand theft auto, and then shot down in an attempted armed robbery. Rather than be crushed like that, I worked in meat-packing plants and factories for thirteen hours a day and put myself through university. I also bought myself a British-made Norton motorcycle. My Norton Commando became a 'magic carpet ride' of thrills and excitement that I rode with lean women who were equally hungry to get their share. But it was more than that. I rode my motorcycle in anger; for me it became a show of contempt and a way of defying the privileged middle class that had put me down and had kept my parents 'in their place.' I felt that the Establishment had done me no favours and that I owed it even less. At that time I saw outlaw bikers as a reflection of my own dark side. I made them the embodiment of my own youthful rebellion and resentment. In retrospect, I believe that it was this aspect of my non-academic background – the fact that I had learned to ride and beat the streets – that made it possible for me to contemplate such a study, and eventually to ride with the Rebels.

At the time of beginning my fieldwork I had been riding British-made motorcycles for three years and had talked briefly to members of the King's Crew MC in Calgary. But this was not enough to comprehend the outlaw-biker community or to study it. My impression of outlaw bikers was narrow and incomplete and, in that sense, almost as misleading as the stereotype held by most 'citizens.' I was physically close to the scene, but far removed from a balanced understanding; that understanding would only come from 'being there.'

I customized my Norton, donned some biker clothing, and set off to do some fieldwork. My first attempts at contacting an outlaw club were near disasters. In Calgary, I met several members of the King's Crew MC in a motorcycle shop and expressed an interest in 'hanging around.' But I lacked patience and pushed the situation by asking too many questions. A deviant society, especially one that walks on the wild side of illegal activities, will have its own information network for checking out strangers. I found out quickly that outsiders, even bikers, do not rush into a club, and that anyone who doesn't show the proper restraint will be shut out. That was mistake number one. Days later, I carelessly got into an argument with a club 'striker,' a probationary member, that led to blows in a bar-room skirmish. He flattened my nose and began choking me. Unable to get air down my throat and breathing only blood through my nostrils, I managed a body punch that luckily found his solar plexus and loosened his grip. I then grabbed one of his hands and pulled back on the thumb till I heard the joint break. Mistake number two. It was time to move on. I packed my sleeping-bag on my Norton and headed west for Vancouver with some vague and ridiculous notion of meeting up with the Satan's Angels, now a chapter of the Hell's Angels.

Riding into Burnaby (Greater Vancouver) I discovered that an outlaw biker has to learn a whole new set of rules for dealing with the law. I had decided to modify my public identity in order to facilitate participant observation of a deviant group; I could not expect any favours from legal authorities and I would have to learn how to cope with what might be termed differential treatment – bikers use the term 'harassment' – on the part of police officers. I saw the flashing red light in my rear-view mirror moments before I heard the siren. I had been looking for the Admiral Hotel, a bar where the Satan's Angels hung out. I started to gear down when I noticed that the RCMP (Royal Canadian Mounted Police) cruiser was only three feet from my rear tire. I continued to slow down and hoped that he knew what he was doing. I pulled into the parking lot behind the Admiral bar, got off my bike, and turned around to approach the officer. As I reached for my wallet he immediately ordered me to turn around and put my hands behind my head. I froze in what was probably 90 per cent uncertainty and 10 per cent defiance. When I didn't move he unlatched the holster that held his pistol; he gripped the weapon and then reached inside his car and grabbed the radio mike to call for a backup. Within moments a second cruiser was on the scene. He lined me up with the car's headlights, turned on the high beams, and then began the standard shakedown. Upon request I produced my operator's licence, vehicle registration, and insurance, and was then asked where I was from, what club I rode with, if I had a criminal record, and if I had ever been in trouble with the law before. As I answered the questions, wondering what kind of trouble I was in now, a third cruiser pulled up, turned on its bright lights, and two more officers joined in. At that time some of my identification read 'Daniel' and some read 'Danny,' which prompted a series of questions about aliases and a radio check about outstanding arrest warrants and vehicle registration. When this failed to produce any evidence against me, I was asked if I was carrying any weapons or drugs. The answer to both questions was 'no' and the whole situation began to seem absurd. I was being put on stage under the spotlights of three police cruisers in a back alley drama directed by five RCMP officers. Meanwhile, the Satan's Angels that I'd come to meet were relaxing and having some cool beers in the bar across the alley. I began to laugh at the irony, which was mistake number three. 'Put your hands up against that wall!' yelled a constable who was angered by my apparent disdain for the law. One officer searched through the pockets of my leathers and jeans while another rummaged through the leather saddle-bags on my bike. After the bike and body search, I asked the officers if motorcycle clubs were a major problem in their area. I was told they weren't, 'but some guys figure they're king shit when you pull them over, and you've got to remember that no matter how tough you are, there's always someone tougher!' I was then asked how long I was staying, and I replied that it depended on my financial situation. I answered straightforwardly and stated that I was carrying credit cards and a little more than three hundred dollars, as the police already knew – having counted it. Only then did one of the officers explain: 'When he asked you how long you're staying, what he's saying is that this road leads to Harvey Avenue, which leads to the highway out of town!'

I had sewn a secret pocket into the sleeve of my leather jacket. It contained a letter from the Canada Council (SSHRC) addressed to the RCMP that identified myself and my research. The officers failed to find it, and I wasn't about to reveal it. My research goal was to find out and experience what happens within the outlaw-biker scene, not be told what happens from the outside. Three days earlier I had talked to a Vancouver city police officer who knew me as a researcher: 'I'll save you a whole lot of trouble, maybe even your neck, and explain this whole biker thing to you,' he said. 'They're all just psychologically unstable. That's all you have to know; otherwise none of it makes any sense.'

'Those cops [at the Admiral Hotel] were setting you up,' Steve, the Rebels MC sergeant at arms, would explain some months later. 'They were just waiting for you to make a stupid move and they've got you by the balls. They could have beaten the shit outta you, and you'd have five cops as witnesses. Well, it would've been tough shit for you!' I learned that one does not play the role of Jesse James when being pulled over by 'the man,' especially on a 'club run,' or motorcycle tour, where police can make a shakedown last up to two hours. One learns to avoid all eye contact and restrict all verbal responses to a monosyllabic 'no' or 'yes.' Over the next few years I got lots of practice; that first summer I was pulled over and interrogated fifteen times – on only one of these occasions was I actually charged with an offence, a speeding violation.

While touring through the British Columbia interior I joined up with three members of the Tribesmen MC from Squamish, BC, whom I met at a Penticton hamburger stand. From the Tribesmen I learned that gaining entry into a club would take time. The time factor meant that my best chance of success lay in studying the Rebels in the familiar confines of my own back yard in Edmonton. 'You don't make friends with members of a club,' cautioned Lance of the Tribesmen. 'You let them make friends with you.' Lance pointed out that in order to ride with a club I would have to be accepted by all the members, get to know some of the members personally, and at least one member well enough that he would be willing to sponsor me and take responsibility for my actions. A critical suggestion emphatically made by all three Tribesmen was 'Get yourself a hog [Harley-Davidson]!'

These first experiences 'in the field' made it clear that I couldn't study any club I wanted, at any time that suited me. There was a good reason for this, as I discovered later. Restricting contacts with non-club members was a key to club survival. With time I realized that maintaining strict boundaries is a central theme that underlies all aspects of club life. This fact presented a major ethical dilemma. I could not do a study if I explained my research goal at the outset. However, an 'undercover' strategy contravened a fundamental ethical tenet in which I believed, that no research should be carried out without the informants' full awareness. I devised an alternative strategy that satisfied myself, my thesis committee, and the guidelines that the University of Alberta had set down for ethical research. The plan was that initially I would attempt to establish contact with the

Rebels as a biker who also happened to be a university – anthropology – student. If I were successful in achieving sufficient rapport and mutual trust with club members, I would officially ask the Rebels MC for permission to conduct a study. The bottom line was that it would be the Rebel club members I rode with who would make the final decision as to whether or not the study would go beyond my personal files.

This strategy was not without risks. Outlaw clubs are aware that they are under constant police surveillance, often by special police units, such as the RCMP's E-squad in Vancouver or the City of Calgary's Strike Force. I learned that the Edmonton Rebels suspected that a biker who had recently attempted to gain entry into their club as a 'striker' was an agent of the RCMP. After repeated attempts, the police have long since discovered that infiltrating an outlaw club is a long, arduous, and risky process when it is being done for 'professional' reasons. 'Infiltration of the gangs is difficult. "They have an internal discipline that makes it dangerous," said a police officer. "It's an area we have trouble infiltrating. The conditions of initiation make it almost impossible ..." "They are scary," said one police intelligence officer, who asked not to be identified. "We've had two or three informants killed, found tied to trees up north with bullet holes in them"' (Canadian Press release, *Edmonton Journal*, 29 September 1979).

In the United States the FBI had gone so far as to have several agents start up their own club in order to bypass the striker (probation) period that screens out bogus bikers. The Edmonton police play a wide variety of angles in order to update their information on the Rebels. On one occasion, two plain-clothes officers wore media badges at a biker rally protesting mandatory helmet legislation in order to move freely among the club members and take pictures. If the Rebels discovered my research motive before I was ready to tell them, it would have been difficult to communicate any good intentions, scientific or otherwise. There existed the distinct possibility that more than just the study would have been terminated prematurely. I lived with that possibility for three years.

I fine-tuned my image before I approached the Rebels. This was going to be my final make-it-or-forget-it attempt. I purchased an old 1955 Harley-Davidson FL, a 'panhead,' which I customized but later sold in favour of a mechanically more reliable 1972 Electraglide, a 'shovelhead.' I had grown shoulder-length hair and a heavy beard. I bought a Harley-Davidson leather jacket and vest, wore studded leather wristbands and a shark's-tooth pendant, and sported a cut-off denim jacket with assorted Harley-Davidson pins and patches, all symbolic of the outlaw-biker world-view. While I was still very nervous about approaching the Rebels, I had become more comfortable with myself. My public image expressed what I now felt was my personal character. There was no pretension. As far as I was concerned, I was a genuine biker who was intrigued with the notion of riding with an outlaw club.

I discovered that I was a lot more apprehensive than I thought as I sat at the opposite end of the Kingsway Motor Inn and watched the Rebels down their drinks. The loud thunder of heavy-metal rock music would make initiating a delicate introduction difficult if not impossible; and there were no individual faces or features to be made out in the smoky haze, only a series of Rebel skull patches draped over leather jackets in a corner of the bar that outsiders seemed to warily avoid. It was like a scene out of a western movie: hard-faced outlaws in the bar, downing doubles while waiting for the stagecoach to arrive. I decided to go outside and devise an approach strategy, including how I would react if one of the Rebels turned to me and simply said, 'Who invited you?' I had thought through five different approaches when Wee Albert of the Rebels MC came out of the bar to do a security check on the 'Rebel iron' in the parking lot. He saw me leaning on my bike and came over to check me out. For some time Wee Albert and I stood in the parking lot and talked about motorcycles, riding in the wind, and the Harley tradition. He showed me some of the more impressive Rebel choppers and detailed the jobs of customizing that members of the club had done to their machines. He then checked out my 'hog,' gave a grunt of approval, and invited me to come in and join the Rebels at their tables. Drinking at the club bar on a regular basis gave me the opportunity to get to know the Rebels and gave them an opportunity to size me up and check me out on neutral ground. I had made the first of a long sequence of border crossings that all bikers go through if they hope to get close to a club.

Wee Albert became a good buddy of mine, and he sponsored my participation in club runs and at club parties. In addition to my having a sponsor, my presence had to be voted on by the membership as a whole at their weekly Wednesday meeting. If two of the twenty-five members voted 'no,' then I wasn't around. The number of close friends that I had in the club increased and I was gradually drawn into the Rebel brotherhood. Measured in terms of social networking, brotherhood meant being part of a high frequency of interpersonal contacts that were activated over a wide range of social situations. Among the activities that I took part in were drinking and carousing in the club bar, assisting members in the chopping (customizing) and repair of motorcycles, loaning and borrowing money, shooting pool and 'bullshitting' at the clubhouse, exchanging motorcycle parts along with technical information and gossip at a motorcycle shop owned by two club members, going on a duck hunt and on fishing trips, making casual visits and receiving dinner invitations to members' homes, general partying and riding together, providing emotional support, and, when necessary, standing shoulder-to-shoulder in the face of physical threat. Brotherhood, I came to learn, is the foundation of the outlaw-club community. It establishes among members a sense of moral, emotional, and material interdependence; feelings of commitment arise out of a sense of sharing a common fate. The enduring emotion of brotherhood is comradeship. To a 'patch holder' (club member) brotherhood means being there when needed; its most dramatic expression occurs when brothers defend each other from outside threats. I vividly remember sitting with the Rebels in the Kingsway Motor Inn bar, trying to sober up quickly while I mentally acted out what I thought would be my best martial-arts moves. I looked down at my hand; I had sprained my thumb the night before while sparring in karate. My right hand was black, blue, swollen, and useless. I watched nervously as sixty-five members of the Canadian Airborne Regiment strutted into the bar. Their walk said that they were looking for us and a brawl. I came to view brotherhood as both a privilege and a tremendous personal responsibility.

I watched my own identity change as the result of experiences I had on my own as a biker and those I shared with club members. These often involved the process of public identification, or labelling, and other reactions by outsiders. I learned that a lone biker on the highway is vulnerable. I was run off the road three times over a four-year period. On one of those occasions I was forced off a mountain road into the side of a cliff and nearly catapulted into oblivion. Another lesson was that an outlaw biker has to be ready for 'the heat to come down' at the most unexpected times. For instance, while I was washing my bike at a car wash, the owner phoned the police about a suspicious-looking biker. The police came, searched my bike, and I was arrested and charged with carrying a concealed and illegal weapon – a switch-blade. I felt sure that I would have a criminal record long before, and maybe instead of, a PhD. Fortunately, I discovered that a good lawyer, who is 'owed a favour' by the crown prosecutor, can get the charges dropped – in this case, three minutes prior to the start of the trial. I learned that a police officer will follow an outlaw biker for five miles to give him a ticket for doing 35 mph in a 30-mph zone. A biker could be given a ticket for a balding tire or because his custom handlebars were one-half of an inch too high above the motorcycle's seat. I recall being turned down by insurance companies for vehicle coverage, refused admittance to private camp-grounds, and kicked off a public beach by Penticton police who thought we intended to incite a riot. I found that associating with outlaw patch holders could be an invitation to danger. While riding with the club, I and some patch holders were pulled over by a cruiser and warned that members of the Highway Kings MC were out gunning for Rebels with shotguns. None of these situations could have been acted out in a detached manner. My involvement demanded the intensity of a highly emotional reaction. Each encounter was an escalation towards an outlaw-biker identity. My record of personal encounters with citizens and the police, especially those that were threatening, enabled me to understand and articulate the biker's perspective on drifting away from the Establishment and being drawn into the club. Sometimes, as I watched the faces of the Rebels, I could see the hardening of an attitude – 'us-against-the-world.'

Gradually my status changed from being a 'biker' with a familiar face to being a 'friend of the club.' There were no formal announcements. Tiny just yelled across at me one afternoon while we were starting up our bikes, 'Hey! "Coyote!" No way I'm riding beside you. Some farmer is going to shoot our asses off and then say he was shooting at varmints.' This was a reference to the coyote skin I had taken to wearing over my helmet. Wee Albert looked at me, grinned, and said 'That's it, "Coyote." From now on that'll be your club name.' Most of the patch holders had club names, such as Spider or Greaser. These names are reminders of club association. More important, they separate the individual from his past, giving him the opportunity to build a new persona in terms of group-valued traits.

Pseudonyms give members an aura; they draw upon a collective power. They are no longer just Rick, Allan, or Bill; they are Blues, Terrible Tom, and Caveman; they are outlaw bikers!

As a 'friend of the club' I took part informally in political rhetoric concerning the club's future, such as debates concerning the hot issue of club expansion. This position of trust with the Rebels brought me into contact with other outlaw clubs such as the King's Crew of Calgary, the Spokesmen of Saskatoon, the Bounty Hunters of Victoria, the Gypsy Wheelers of White Rock, and the Warlords of Edmonton. Through these inter-club contacts I became familiar with the political relationships of conflict and alliance that exist among outlaw clubs. Meeting members of different clubs also provided me with the comparative data I needed to isolate those aspects of behaviour and organization that were shared by all clubs, and helped to explain how some clubs were different and why. My long-term association with the Rebels gave me a valuable historical perspective that included insights into the developmental sequence of clubs. I was able to describe how new clubs form, why few emergent clubs beat the odds and survive, and how a chosen few clubs achieved long-term success and expansion while all that remains of other clubs is their colours hanging upside down as trophies on the wall of a rival's clubhouse.

If the Rebels had at any time refused permission for the study, I would have destroyed all the data I had collected and closed the investigation. The fact that I had established myself as a friend of the club was no reason for the members to agree to become scientific units of analysis. Rejection of the study appeared more and more imminent as I grew to sense and share members' distrust of outsiders. I had come to appreciate some of the multifaceted advantages of having a negative public stereotype – however unrealistic. When outsiders look at an outlaw biker they do not see an individual, all they see is the club patch that he wears on the back of his leathers. The negative image that comes with the Rebel skull patch discourages unnecessary intrusions by outsiders. 'That way I'm not bothered,' explained Steve of the Rebels, 'and I don't have to tell the guy "Fuck off, cunt!"' The patch becomes part of the biker's threat display; it effectively keeps violence to a minimum by warding off those outsiders who might otherwise choose to test the mettle of the bikers. For the majority of outsiders, the prospect of having to initiate even the briefest of encounters with an outlaw biker brings forth emotions ranging from uneasiness to sheer dread. Ironically, the more I got to know the members and the greater the bonds of trust and brotherhood, the less I expected that they would approve of the study. 'The best public relations for us,' according to Indian of the Rebels, 'is no public relations!' I found it increasingly difficult to live with the fact that the closer I came to my destination of knowing the Rebels, the further distant became my goal of doing an ethnographic study.

One night, during a three-week Rebel run to the west coast, I was sharing a beer with Tiny while sitting on the porch of the Bounty Hunters' clubhouse. We were watching officers of the Victoria police force who were watching us from their cruisers in the street and from a nearby hotel – binoculars between closed curtains. 'You know, Coyote,' grumbled a 6-foot, 275-pound Tiny in a very personable tone, 'I've talked with some of the guys and we think that you should strike [enter probationary membership] for the club. The way I see it, it shouldn't take you more than a year to earn your colours [club patch].' The pressure was now on and building for me to make a move that would bring me even closer to the club. I had made a commitment to myself that under no circumstances would I attempt to become a full-fledged member without first revealing my desire to do a study on the club. It was time to disengage. It was time for me to sell my study to the Rebels, but I was at a loss as to what to say. I had been a brother through good times and bad, thick and thin; but to distance myself from the Rebels by announcing a study done for outsiders of a way of life I had shared with them against the world seemed nothing short of a betrayal. Entering the field as a biker and maintaining relations of trust and friendship during the course of fieldwork prevented my leaving the field with my notes. I had accomplished what I had hoped to during my fieldwork, but at this point there was no way out. There was no formula for disengagement of the field project. As far as I was concerned I had lost a three-year gamble.

Weeks of personal frustration and near-depression later, I had an incredible stroke of luck. Wee Albert, who took great pleasure in talking about 'what it means to be a Rebel and a brother,' approached me and said, 'Being an anthropologist you study people, right? Well, have you ever thought of maybe doing a study on the club? Chances are it probably wouldn't carry [club approval], but maybe. I'd like to see it happen.' I told Wee Albert that I'd consider it and approach the executive members with the proposal. The door of disengagement was open; Wee Albert had provided me with an honourable way out. Whether or not it would be a successful disengagement – the approval of an ethnography – remained to be seen.

I first talked to Ken and Steve about the prospect of 'doing an anthropological study.' Ken, president, and Steve, sergeant at arms, were both friends of mine and well-respected club officers, but their most positive response was a shrug of the shoulders and 'We'll see.' Ken decided to bring up the proposed study at a meeting of the club executive. The officers of the club discussed the proposal among themselves and determined that no harm would be done if they presented it one week later to the general membership at a club meeting. For me it was the longest night of the year as I waited for the decision. The issue was hotly debated, a vote was held, and the study approved. Why? Granting me permission for the study was done as a 'personal favour': 'You have come into favour with a lot of the members and been nothing but good to the club. All in all you've been a pretty righteous friend of the club. But there was a lot of opposition to your study, especially from guys like T.T. [Terrible Tom] and Blues. The way I see it the vote went the way it did because you were asking us a favour. You didn't come in promising us the moon, you know, money from books and that sort of thing. You promised us nothing so we did it as a personal favour' (Wee Albert). Any offers of economic remuneration on my part would have been interpreted as an insult; the Rebels were doing me a favour. I strongly suspect that any researcher who buys his or her way into a closed society – with promises of money or royalties – will garner information that is at best forced, at worst fabricated. However, I did give the 'victims' of the four-and-one-half-hour questionnaire a twenty-six-ounce bottle of Alberta Springs (Old Time Sipping Whisky) and a Harley-Davidson beer mug. 'Fair return' for the club as a whole was a bound copy of my thesis, which found a home in the Rebels' clubhouse.

I continued to ride with the Rebels for another year and a half, during which time I carried out formal data-gathering procedures. These included extensive open-ended interviews with a number of Rebel patch holders and ended with the administration of a four-hour-long structured questionnaire to six members. Interestingly enough, Blues, a Rebel who was both a friend and a staunch opponent of the study, was one of the six. 'The club is all I have. It means everything to me. It's with me all the time. I feel leery about talking to anybody about it. If I wasn't 100 per cent for you I wouldn't be here. If you'd been asking these questions three years ago [when I initially made contact with the Rebels MC], well no fucking way! We've been burned before, but never again!' Blues's trust and vote of confidence brought me a tremendous degree of personal satisfaction.

The theoretical framework and methodological approach that I use in this book are based on a cognitive definition of culture. Culture is here defined as the rules and categories of meaning and action that are used by individuals to both interpret and generate appropriate behaviour. I therefore view the outlaw-biker subculture as a human experience. It is a system of meaning in which I, as an anthropologist, had to involve myself in order to develop an adequate explanation of what was being observed. That is, in order to understand the biker subculture, or any culture for that matter, one must first try to understand it as it is experienced by the bikers themselves. Only then can one comprehend both the meaning of being an outlaw and how that meaning is constructed and comes to be shared by bikers. Only by first seeing the world through the eyes of the outlaws can we then go on to render intelligible the decisions that they make and the behaviours they engage in. Those meanings, decisions, and behaviours may lead you to applaud outlaw bikers as heroes. Alternatively, they may lead you to condemn them as villains. Labelling them as heroes or villains is a subsequent value judgment that the reader has the option of making. That value judgment is quite separate from first knowing outlaw bikers – my job as an ethnographer.

In order to operationalize this theoretical position of capturing an insider's perspective, I adopted a research methodology that closely resembles that of a symbolic interactionist. That is, within the overall framework of participant observation I emphasize analysis that is proximate – events are described in terms of variables that are close to the immediate situation in which the actors find themselves; processual – events are viewed as an emerging step-by-step reality whose completion requires actors to meet a series of contingencies; and phenomenological – events are explained in a manner that pays serious attention to how the actors experience them (Lofland, 1969: 296–7). By blending the methodological strategy of participant observation with the perspective of symbolic interactionism (Visano, 1989: 3, 29), I hope to replicate for the reader the experienced natural world as it unfolds for the outlaw biker.

Aside from the fact that this study could not have been completed in any other manner, the significance of approaching the Rebels as a biker not an anthropologist was that I was able to take full advantage of the reciprocal relationship between participation and observation. Combining participation and observation is the most effective way of achieving an understanding of a culture as it is experienced and lived by its participants. Through observation, I was in a position to elicit and deduce those categories of meaning and rules of action that constituted members' cultural repertoires, that is, what one must know to be a biker. Through participation, I was able to test the validity of my own formulations by either predicting or generating what members considered acceptable behaviour, that is, how to convert biker knowledge into appropriate biker behaviour. The rationale for my becoming a biker reflects 'a bedrock assumption held historically by fieldworkers that "experience" underlies all understanding of social life' (Maanen, 1988: 3). The effectiveness of this strategy in gaining access to, and understanding, outlaw-biker culture is perhaps best conveyed by witnessing some of the difficulties and limitations that have occurred when a fieldworker assumes a more marginal role. Lincoln Keiser, who published *The Vice Lords*, an ethnography of a Chicago street gang, made it known to gang members that he was an anthropologist. He gained entry by offering 'to share any royalties [from his book] with the group' (Keiser, 1970: 226–35). Keiser's approach put him in a position wherein he 'was always an outsider' who 'could never fully participate' (ibid.). As an outsider Keiser 'did not understand the significance of most actions and many words' and 'did not act properly in certain social situations.' Finally, Keiser 'was never completely sure if Vice Lords sensed my reactions, and in turn reacted to them. Thus I was not always certain if my feelings ... of distaste ... affected the events I was trying to observe' (ibid.). Keiser recognizes the obvious limitations his marginal participation had for even being exposed to, let alone understanding, the culture he set out to describe.

The emic quality – insider's perspective – of *The Rebels* is largely due to the fact that my entry into the outlaw-biker community was not artificial, nor was my participation feigned. To the Rebels I was Coyote; to me the Rebels were friends and brothers. In my work with the Rebels I was never afforded the luxury of not having to perform or not being able to understand the rules of the outlaw game. Riding with the Rebels meant that I either learned, understood, and performed as well as any other biker who wanted to be a friend of the club, or I left the scene. When I made a mistake, I paid for it. As one novice biker who 'wasn't able to cut it' was told by Tramp of the Rebels, 'We aren't into babysitting wanna-be bikers.'

In addition to participant observation, I made extensive use of key informants in order to construct a historical and comparative framework. Prior to his becoming a Rebel, Wee Albert was a member of the Golden West MC, a Canadian Motorcycle Association chartered club operating in Calgary. Wee Albert's association with both an outlaw and a chartered club provided some insightful dimensions of both similarity and contrast. A historical perspective on how outlaw clubs have changed since the late fifties and early sixties was provided by Ace, who had been a long-standing sergeant at arms of one of Canada's original outlaw clubs, the Canadian Lancers – now the Black Diamond Riders MC of Toronto. Another comparative dimension was added to the study when I met Gypsy, a former road captain of the Satan's Choice MC. Gypsy was on a one-year 'leave of absence' from the Choice. There was a warrant for his arrest outstanding in Ontario and he had come out west to Edmonton to find work and 'let things cool down.' Gypsy had been to jail twice already. He had grown tired of checking off the days of a calendar inside a cell and of being shot at during periods of club territorial warfare. I found Gypsy a place where he could hide out, and he became interested in one of the two women that I was living with at the time. In return Gypsy provided me with details on how the Satan's Choice, a club that engaged in organized crime (motorcycle theft and drug dealing), differed from the Rebels, a club that committed criminal offences (mainly drug use and assorted minor misdemeanours), but whose members were not professional criminals. Gypsy eventually reverted back to being Don. He married and subsequently settled in Calgary, trying his hand at several different careers. The last time Don wrote me he was a professional wrestler working for Calgary's Stampede Wrestling.

I was extremely fortunate to have a female as a steady companion throughout the course of my fieldwork. Sandra – an anthropology undergraduate student – became my 'ol' lady' in the outlaw-biker subculture. She interacted with the women of the club and gathered information on the role of women and the woman's perspective to which I would not otherwise have had access. I specifically designed the chapter entitled 'Women and the Outlaws' to go beyond the description of male or female roles to approach the broader, more illuminating topic of gender studies – how and why being masculine and being feminine are interrelated. Specifically, male and female gender identities are dealt with as distinct, but always interconnected and interdependent, phenomena. Within this context, the study discloses why women are attracted to the club, how they are integrated, why they occupy different statuses among themselves, what critical roles they play, and, paradoxically, why they pose the ultimate threat to the brotherhood. In truth, I was inspired to write this section by Dr Patricia A. McCormack, a colleague who has been studying and teaching about gender relations at the University of Alberta. The process of this successful collaboration led to my asking her to contribute her astute editing skills and ideas to the rest of the book.

Having direct access to all aspects of club life was critical to the theoretical component of my study: studying the reconciliation of identity and diversity in an outlaw motorcycle club. While rarely seen by outsiders, internal differences are very much a part of the reality of club existence. After I got past the surface-level uniformity that outsiders see, it became evident that I was dealing with twenty-five distinct individuals, each of whom had his own version of 'what the Rebels are all about.'

I approach the phenomenon of individual variation as something that is very real and not to be ignored, averaged out, or transcended. It will become obvious to the reader that the Rebels MC does not operate like a mechanical model according to Aristotelian logic. The Rebels simply cannot be described in terms of a singular set of norms and values that all members have equally internalized, or a code of behaviour that all members uniformly adhere to. Inside the Rebels community are incompatible values, different group goals, distinct personal goals, conflicting impulses, and outright contradictions. These are the 'facts' of social existence with which any group has to deal. Furthermore, differences between Rebels were not always solved through some form of synthesis or reconciliation. Oppositions and internal conflicts often remained self-contradictory, tense, and unresolved. The strength of the Rebels was their ability to take these conflicts in stride. The club was resilient. It was able to return to a state of operational equilibrium after absorbing an instance of conflict; and it was able to accommodate this variation and conflict and still maintain its basic elements and relationships of brotherhood. As far as I was concerned, the Rebels' ability to accommodate diversity was as much a secret to their success as was their ability to command uncompromising commitment. Interestingly enough, variation was often converted into an asset. When handled properly, individual variation provided an internal dynamic for change and gave the Rebels the ideational and behavioural flexibility to deal with a wide variety of social circumstances.

Throughout this book I try to show the nature of these differences and the way they are accepted and accommodated, negotiated and compromised, or suppressed and camouflaged. I was particularly interested in discovering how internal variation was handled by an organization whose attraction for its members was based on a strong corporate identity (a sense of shared goals and common purpose) and which also required the cohesion of a paramilitary unit in order to survive. What I found was that the Rebels assume different faces, depending on the circumstances. In some situations, such as political decision making inside the guarded confines of the clubhouse, factions engage in political lobbying and heated exchanges precede the democratic resolution of differences of opinion. 'You don't always get your way,' according to Raunch of the Rebels, 'but you always get your say.' Diverse opinions are encouraged and become the basis of political rhetoric that leads to change and adaptation. In other situations, such as the club bar where members are on a public stage, uniformity is required, and differences – a sign of weakness to hostile outsiders – are camouflaged. 'The club is like a safe,' confided Wee Albert while we sipped some Canadian Club whisky, 'There's a lot of loose change on the inside. But when the tumblers fall in place and the doors to that safe open, look out! 'Cause the Rebels come out as one!'

For all their toughness, the Rebels are vulnerable to police action, and I wanted to be sure that my work could not be used against them. My lengthy association with the club gave me a good idea as to when vested interests of the club conflicted with the host society. At no time was any information that could damage the group passed on to any person or agency. While I did receive outside support for my study in the form of a Canada Council (SSHRC) doctoral fellowship and an Isaac Walton Killam Memorial Scholarship, I made sure that I was under no obligation to turn over field notes or other data to any of the sponsors. No data were provided to the above sponsors or any other organization – academic, legal, or otherwise – that were not also made accessible to the general community as a whole, including the Rebels MC. However, even public information can be dangerous to one's informants, so I was careful to make sure that nothing that I wrote would contain details that would result in someone being issued a subpoena. Here too, unfortunately, I found out that even the best-intentioned technique is never perfect or completely foolproof.

A few years after I'd stopped riding with the Rebels, the City of Calgary police brought a member of the Rebels' Calgary chapter to court (1987) in an attempt to revoke his Firearms Acquisition Certificate. A member of the Calgary police force claimed the status of 'expert witness' and acted as a witness for the crown prosecutor. 'Expert witness' means that the individual is considered capable of offering the court an 'informed opinion' on a judicial matter by virtue of his overall knowledge and familiarity with the situation. When the lawyer for the defendant asked on what grounds the police officer could claim any knowledge of the Rebels, the officer was able to justify his eligibility as an 'expert witness' by virtue of having read my thesis. The Calgary Rebel eventually won his court case and retained his legal right to possess firearms; however, he came up to Edmonton to settle a score with me. I agreed to meet the Calgary Rebel in a downtown Edmonton bar. My anxiety level heightened when I entered the smoky bar and one of the Rebels frisked me to see if I was 'packing.' Apparently, the Calgary Rebels had seen me with a couple of Calgary police officers and thought that I had professional ties with the City of Calgary Strike Force. It was another between-a-rock-and-a-hard-place irony, for several members of the Calgary police force were leery about cooperating with me because they felt that I had membership ties with the Rebels and that I was 'pumping them for information': 'Hey, why ask *us* about the Rebels? Why don't you tell us what's going on?!' After several rounds of beer while watching strippers perform I was able to convince the Rebel that he had been compromised unintentionally. But, understandably, he was still very upset; and he and several other club members turned against the publication of an ethnography of the Rebels: 'No way that you're going to publish that book!' The Rebels of today are not the Rebels of the eighties that granted permission for the study; nor do they feel any obligations to the past; least of all do they want to have their delicate political interactions with the Grim Reapers MC and Hell's Angels MC discussed publicly. It was an interesting ethical complication; and a dangerous personal complication. However, these were not the brothers with whom I had made my original pact, and I have decided to go ahead and publish *The Rebels: A Brotherhood of Outlaw Bikers*. 'That could be very dangerous,' warned one police sergeant who was a member of the Calgary Strike Force. 'Any one of those guys could do you in on his own simply by calling in a favour owed them by some punk on the street. There would be no connection; no one's the wiser.'

The issue of confidentiality is a delicate but major point of contention that has to be settled before one leaves the field. Respecting the confidentiality of one's informants is a particularly delicate matter if one is dealing with a deviant or criminal subculture that is subject to police surveillance. I did not disguise the Rebels Motorcycle Club. Anonymity is not an issue for them; they have none. The Rebels, then and now, are a high-profile club. When I rode with the Rebels they had already gained national notoriety and extensive media coverage through a number of incidents, such as their brawl with members of the Canadian Airborne Regiment and their confrontation (along with members of the Hell's Angels, King's Crew, and Satan's Angels) with three hundred police officers in Coronation, Alberta, the largest police action of its kind in Canada. Anonymity for the club members as individuals was a matter of personal choice. I asked Rebel patch holders to decide for themselves on their personal identities. In subsequent publications readers were introduced to the Rebels under a combination of first names, such as Ken, and club names, such as Blues. Most of the names are real, some are fictitious; only the Rebels will know for sure.

Similarly, I do not disguise myself or my involvement with the Rebels during the course of my fieldwork. I chose to write portions of this ethnography in a first-person experiential style as opposed to a more traditional third-person matter-of-fact voice. Ethnography is more than description, it is also interpretation (Agar, 1986). The 'social facts' that appear in an ethnography, including the 'natives' point of view,' are not simply points of information that have been objectively recorded. Ultimately, social facts are 'human fabrications' made by the ethnographer (Maanen, 1988: 93) and are several steps removed from behavioural reality. Social facts derive from the personal fieldwork experience of the ethnographer, who develops them in terms of his selective recordings and editing, and who interprets them within his particular analytical framework. What we read in an ethnography is not social reality itself, but social reality exposed to our mode of questioning, observing, and recording. An ethnographer who removes himself – the 'I' – from the ethnography only creates the illusion of objectivity. When I relate aspects of Rebel life and the outlaw-biker perspective in the first person, my intention is not to support or profess, but to describe the outlaw-biker lifestyle as 'I' experienced it. The use of the first person and a narrative style to describe events is meant to transport the reader into the back-stage reality of Rebel life, just as I had been when I did the study. This book is written to give the reader the opportunity to become actively involved in the process of interpretation and understanding. The reader should come away with a deeper sense of the problems posed by the research enterprise itself, and of the circumstances surrounding how the data came to be known and analysed.

The book is divided into five parts. The first part looks at why young men turn to a man-machine relationship in order to fulfil their quest for personal identity and how they make that machine, a Harley-Davidson motorcycle, the centre-piece of their lifestyle. Part two traces the journey from 'citizen' to 'outlaw.' It provides a social profile of prospective bikers and reveals the motivating forces and psychological pay-offs that urge a man though the lengthy – from six months to three years – procedures of learning, testing, selection, and ritualized incorporation that comprise the group-socialization process. Perhaps the richest settings for discovering the ground rules and dominant themes of a society are those wherein novices are instructed in appropriate behaviour. With that in mind, a chapter is devoted to each of the four progressive stages that culminate in a man being integrated into the club as a member: biker, friend of the club, striker, and initiate. The third part first describes the gender relationships that exist between women and the outlaws, and then goes on to detail the non-membership but critically supportive roles played by women associated with the club. Part four portrays life in an outlaw's world, and takes the reader inside the three major areas of operation that form the cornerstones of outlaw-club life: the clubhouse, the club bar, and the club run. The concluding part reveals how outlaw clubs cope with some fundamental problems of subcultural existence in order to make it all work. Separate chapters devoted to the dynamics of economics, political organization, and territorial defence describe how outlaw clubs emerge, operate, and sometimes survive.

The Rebels are shown as real people with a legitimate and oper-able world. This kind of *authenticity* requires more than sensational-but-isolated facts taken out of context; it *demands a total picture* that includes all aspects of club life. To accomplish this goal I integrate the ethnographic detail of people, scenes, and events into a com-posite portrait of the outlaw-biker lifestyle. I am a psychological anthropologist; as such, I found the interpretive framework that best explains the world of the outlaw biker to be one that focuses on their personal and collective search for identity and community. However, whenever it was possible I let the Rebels and other bikers speak for themselves and give their own reasons for action; for it is, above all else, their world. Both in their actions and in their words the Rebels are often eloquent spokesmen for their way of life.

Biker:
Building an Identity

It's my bike. It's my dream. There's very little else that's as
important to me.

(Voodoo, Rebels MC)

Becoming a biker constitutes a search for identity. At the least, it
leads to a mechanical pastime and high-speed thrills; at the most, it
can lead to the creation of a meaningful lifestyle. The outlaw biker is
a product of urban industrial society. A survey of the socio-economic
background of bikers furthermore indicates that becoming a biker is
a class-specific response to the general problem of self-actualization.
Whether outlaw bikers are loners or club patch holders, they tend to
come from the lower working class. None of the Rebels or any of the
bikers with whom I associated during my ten years as an active biker
originated in the upper-middle or upper class, and few held professional, managerial, or administrative positions. Police profiles of
outlaw clubs confirm a lower-working class origin. Exceptions are
rare. Like myself, most of the Rebels were the sons of men who
laboured. The exceptions were four members with a rural farming
background who had moved to the inner city. As a group these
bikers showed a striking occupational inheritance from their fathers.
While one Rebel MC club member was an IBM technician and two
collaborated as owners of a motorcycle shop, the remainder were
skilled and non-skilled manual labourers (see chapter 10). My own
experience was typical. My father was a Canadian Pacific Railway
blacksmith and my mother was a janitress. My first adult jobs were

cleaning up and moving carcasses for a Canada Packers slaughterhouse, then shovelling graded rock and unloading shingles at an IKO asphalt plant.

Why does the lower working class produce candidates for a biker subculture? The answer lies in the culture of the streets and in the workplace. It is a modern-day urban setting that lacks symbols and activities around which to build a personal identity, and is largely devoid of meaningful collective endeavours around which to build a sense of community. Often the only identity available to a manual labourer is that of a cog in an impersonal machine. He begins each day by 'punching in' his number to an assembly line, his work task is not his decision but that of a management whose face he never sees, the pace of his work is decided by a machine, and there is no variation in the grinding monotony of petty tasks unless the machinery breaks down. The same pattern repeats itself day after day with no prospect of change. He simply sweats a lot and leaves a little of himself behind at the factory each day. While he receives a paycheque, he finds himself short-changed in meaning. Whether you call it 'alienation' or label it 'anomie,' he is deprived of adequate psychological pay-off in the way of life-expanding experiences and identity-confirming ritual. Isolation from meaningful social participation and the subsequent psychological experience of inadequate identity fulfilment may result in a personal search for self-authenticity. If the labourer is a young man in search of himself, he will find nothing in his self-image at work that will excite him; he had best look elsewhere. Men who are chained to these circumstances share a compelling desire to escape.

Since he does not have the same opportunity to build a satisfying sense of self around a career that the professional does, the male labourer may turn to his leisure time in order to develop and act out a self-concept that is 'the real me.' In the hours after work, he can select his own meaningful experiences, such as bar-room socializing or sporting events, that provide him with everything from diversion and relaxation to intrigue and excitement. A biker is a man who has turned to a machine to find himself. He has learned how to find both meaning and pleasure in the man-machine relationship, and he uses his motorcycle to create peak emotional experiences that are worth living for. Wee Albert recounted how his leisure time as a biker provided sanctuary for his identity: 'When I get to the plant in the morning I lock my colours away in my locker. Then I do what I'm told for the next eight or ten hours. I repair fittings and replace pipe [as a pipefitter]. Clayton calls it "turd herding." But when that shift's over, fuck it! I ride away. I do what I want to do. I say what I want to say. I walk the way I want to walk. As far as I'm concerned that's the real me. That's what keeps me going, keeps me alive. The trick is to make sure that the job and all the hassles at home don't kill it.'

For individuals like Wee Albert, 'free time' spent as a biker means more than just social and emotional gratification. It involves a spiritual rebirth, if only for some guarded precious moments. As far as Wee Albert is concerned, he has beaten the system by regaining the dignity of personal decision making. He controls the machine, and he writes the rules. His bike is his 'two-wheeled freedom.' He uses his motorcycle to create an arena wherein he is a hero, a theatre where he can be larger than life. Speed seasoned by danger satisfies his quest for 'thrills' or peak experiences, and the highly machismo image and tradition of the motorcycle revitalize his self-image and engage his search for a personal identity.

A social-psychological denominator common to all humanity is the utilization of aspects of the material world as extensions of their personalities. Bikers, like other North Americans, are certainly no exception to this rule. Like members of all other cultures, they use their possessions to create an identity, personal quality, or social position that they feel they embody or would aspire to. It is in this sense that one's vehicle is never merely one's mode of transportation. Regardless of what *Consumer Report* says, a car is not just a machine that takes you from one place to the other. It is a concrete statement of your taste, your personality, and your lifestyle. Historically, the motorcycle has constituted a symbolic affront to a basically four-wheeled culture. Relative to the automobile, it is an impractical, dangerous, loud and gregarious, conspicuous yet not prestigious vehicle. The motorcycle represents a departure from the rational, secure, and sensible. As a border marker between acceptance of the status quo and the lionization of a subculture, the motorcycle was as efficacious in the early 1900s as it is today. In a 1909 article entitled 'The Rise of the Motorcycle,' printed in *Harper's Weekly*, the author laments: 'They would ride in city or open country with their mufflers cut out, or in numerous cases absolutely devoid of muffling attachment. In some instances it was the rider's desire for noise, or to bring attention to the fact that he owned a motorcycle; in other instances it was the owner's desire for more power; but whichever the case, this offence in principle and in conjunction with that of unsuitable attire has done more to retard the advancement of motorcycling in general than all other arguments combined.'

The theme of 'offence in principle' and 'unsuitable attire' received a more contemporary articulation in 'Myth of the Motorcycle Hog,' an essay by Robert Hughes in *Time* magazine (1971): 'Has any means of transportation ever suffered a worse drubbing than the motorcycle? In the 17 years since Stanley Kramer put Marlon Brando astride a Triumph in *The Wild One* (1953), big bikes and those who ride them have been made into apocalyptic images of aggression and revolt – Greasy Rider on an iron horse with 74 cu. in. lungs and ape-hanger bars, booming down the freeway to rape John Doe's daughter behind the white clapboard bank: swastikas, burnt rubber, crab lice and filthy denim ... As an object to provoke linked reactions of desire and outrage, the motorcycle has few equals – provided it is big enough ... Anti-social? Indeed Yes.'

The outlaw biker lifestyle constitutes a lower-working-class bohemian subculture. The ideological foundation of the subculture accurately reflects the lower-working-class origins of its participants. A man who enters this subculture in search of an identity looks to the outlaw-biker tradition to provide him with long-standing values, behaviours, and symbols. What he will find are heroes and role models, a personal legacy that is consistent with what he discovered on the streets about the complete man. He will adopt attitudes and learn behaviours that gravitate around lower-class focal concerns with independence, freedom, self-reliance, toughness, impulsiveness, and masculinity, all of which will be embodied in a highly romanticized image of the anti-hero.

The concepts of socio-economic status and lower-class alienation provide a useful overall framework for understanding where outlaw bikers come from (epidemiology). However, becoming a Rebel cannot be explained simply as the inevitable result of these background considerations. Only a tiny fraction of that small portion of lower-working-class youths who take up motorcycling ever become outlaw bikers. In order to isolate the necessary and sufficient causes (etiology) of becoming an outlaw biker, it is essential to focus in on variables that are immediate to the reality in which these people live and act. We must be able to understand their world from their perspective if we hope to be able to make sense of – not necessarily

TABLE 1
Four stages in becoming a member or 'patch holder' of an outlaw
motorcycle club

Transitional stage	Behaviour involved	Individual's relationship to club
1. Biker	Degree of shared knowledge and acceptance of behaviour and values associated with motorcycling	*Categorical relationship*: sense of collectivity; no interaction with club/member is implied
2. Friend of club	Formation of affective bonds with members	*Interpersonal ties*: member of group social network
3. Striker/Prospect	Probationary period	*Institutional ties*: member of formal group network
4. Initiate	Ritualized incorporation	*Institutional ties*: member of formal group network
5. Patch holder	Membership	*Institutional ties*: member of formal group network

agree with – the decisions they make. Only by entering the everyday life of the biker and capturing his experiences can we come to appreciate how long and truly problematic the whole process of becoming an outlaw is.

Becoming a member of an outlaw motorcycle club requires a lengthy period of socialization – from six months to three years – that includes the processes of learning, testing, selection, and ritualized incorporation. These socialization processes are organized in terms of four distinct and cumulative stages that the bikers themselves recognize: (1) biker, (2) friend of the club, (3) striker or prospect, and (4) initiate. The transitional stages involved in becoming a member of an outlaw club, the behaviour associated with each stage, and the commensurate change in the man's relationship to the club are outlined in table 1. The transition from citizen to outlaw biker involves crossing a series of borders that lead away from the mainstream of conventionality into the outlaw-biker community. These borders are best viewed as a succession of dependencies and decisions, each of which may or may not set up the conditions necessary for crossing the succeeding border. Becoming an outlaw biker is not inevitable, nor is it an all-or-nothing proposition; it is a gradual process of cumulative decisions. These decisions reflect a growing commitment towards a biker self-image that in turn fosters a gradual transition of cultural consciousness. A citizen who initially decides to become a novice biker may eventually cross enough social borders that an outlaw biker emerges on the other side. If at some point he chooses to align his fortunes with those of an outlaw club, the members will judge whether or not he is a 'righteous biker' who has the potential to become their 'brother.'

BIKER RAGS: INTRODUCING A LIFESTYLE

A young man is intrigued by some 'cool-looking dude puttin' down the street on his scooter.' Out of curiosity he picks up a biker magazine from a grocery-store shelf. Affectionately labelled 'biker rags,' these magazines introduce the outsider or 'wanna-be biker' to the world of the outlaw. Afterwards, these magazines continue to act as socializing agents for individual bikers and a source of information for the outlaw community as a whole. They play a very prominent role in ensuring that a tradition of biking is reproduced and that new bikers are recruited. *Easyriders*, *Supercycle*, *Outlaw Biker*, *Chopper*, and *Biker Lifestyle* are the major publications whose target readers are the outlaw fraternity.

The main attractions these biker rags provide are features about and photographs of bikers, their motorcycles – Harleys only – and their women, 'leading the only lifestyle worth living.' In articles like 'Partyin' and Stompin' at Sturgis,' the novice will see and read about how bikers dress, socialize, and have 'good times.' Letters to the editor and editorials express biker viewpoints and concerns. Prose, poetry, fiction, and humour portray how bikers visualize themselves and perceive outsiders. Articles such as 'The Court/Police System – A Web They Want You Locked Into' and 'Feds Are Tryin' to Outlaw Your Bike!' single out their enemies and the threats to their lifestyle. Features such as 'Final Tribute to Brothers Lost' share sentiments for fallen brethren, while reference materials like 'Legal Comments in Everyday Language' and 'ABATE, a National Organization of Street Bikers' outline strategies for coping with shared problems.

As biking becomes a focal point for his identity, a man will gradually accumulate more and more of the obvious symbols of his growing commitment. Numerous businesses that cater to the outlaw-biker lifestyle use the magazines to market all the hardware, mechanical data, memorabilia, and symbolic paraphernalia in which a biker might care to indulge. Companies like Jammer Cycle Products or Drag Specialities will mail order all the high-performance parts and accessories he needs for customizing his Harley. The wealth of symbolism that this subculture provides is by no means confined to the motorcycle or the garage. Either 2 Wheeler's M/C Shop or Righteous Products will supply a biker and his ol' lady with items such as leather jackets, 'bad ass' biker boots, a Harley-motif tank top and T-shirt ('Bikers Have More Fun Than People'), Harley history books and manuals, biker wallet, chain belt and buckle, patches, rings and pendants, a Harley eagle wall-clock, Harley-Davidson-motif panties ('Contents 100% Guaranteed') and bras ('Genuine Harley-Davidson Parts'), Harley-Davidson coffee cup, lighters, and ash trays, and finally, the 'man-sized bitchin' beer mug' whose 'design is an absolutely perfect reproduction of the old, original Harley oil can.' If he has any money left over after touring through the ads, the man might take up an invitation from the Hell's Angels to send in a $10 donation for their Defense Fund and receive a 'Hell's Angels Are Americans' T-shirt (not to be worn while disputing a traffic ticket in court).

The glossy pages of *Easyriders, Supercycle*, and *Biker Lifestyle* provide the cornerstones of a new biker's consciousness of himself as part of a collective identity. Those who ride are given legends to admire and a tradition to articulate. They need this collective consciousness to stabilize their convictions and to insulate themselves from the negative stereotypes and prejudices that come from the citizen or 'straight society.' For example, a Vancouver police officer once offered to help me understand bikers: 'I could save you a lot of time and trouble and explain this whole biker thing to you,' he said. 'They're all just psychologically unstable. That's all you have to know, otherwise none of it makes any sense.'

In fact, biker magazines make it possible for a man to construct a biker identity and develop a sense of loyalty to that image without having met another biker. The novice is exposed to biker norms and values, and he is given a vicarious glimpse of the behavioural patterns that constitute the outlaw lifestyle. The stability of his identity may rest on psychological factors alone without external social factors of affirmation, such as group interaction. However, even those solo bikers who are 'loners' believe they belong to a brotherhood. For example, after they ran a feature on the funeral of a member of the Brother Speed MC, the editors of *Easyriders* (June 1977) received letters that were variations on the following theme: '... your "In The Wind at a Brother's Funeral" ... made me proud to be part of the greatest brotherhood of all time' (Chopper Dan).

HOGS VS RICEBURNERS: CHOOSING A MOTORCYCLE

To some, a Harley is just another motorcycle. To a biker a
Harley is magical, for only a true biker can bring a Harley
to life, and in return, only a Harley can bring life to a biker.
(Lawman, a biker from Texas)

An outsider might consider Harleys and Hondas as simply different brands of motorcycles. The prospective biker must come to view them as symbolic opposites. As far as the outlaw biker is concerned, there is only one motorcycle, the Harley-Davidson 'hog.' There is no entry into the outlaw-biker fraternity for those who ride anything else, particularly 'Jap crap.' Japanese two-wheelers made by Honda, Kawasaki, Suzuki, and Yamaha are not considered motorcycles, but 'riceburners.' A man who 'drives' such a machine is not taken seriously as a biker; he is a 'ricer.' All outlaw bikers are members of a Harley-Davidson cult, and they allow no room for compromise: 'Harley is the best, fuck the rest.' A biker will tell you that 'Harley-Davidson is more than a machine, it's a way of life' and 'Until you've ridden on a Harley you haven't been on a motorcycle.'

A man who has just purchased a new 1991 Harley-Davidson Heritage Softail FLST has bought himself a motorcycle that represents eighty-eight years of legends and glory. He will talk about the motorcycle, its era of production, and the factory that built it with the same degree of interest, knowledge, and reverence that a member of the British nobility would talk about his ancestry. He will tell you that the earliest ancestor of his bike was 'The Silent Grey Fellow.' The Silent Grey Fellow, complete with its single-cylinder 25-cu.-in. motor – capable of 3 horsepower – and 'soup can' carburettor that required continual manual adjustment, was the first motorcycle to emerge out of the Harley-Davidson ten-foot-by-fifteen-foot clapboard shack in Milwaukee, Wisconsin, in 1903. It was the same year that Henry Ford introduced the Model T and the Wright brothers succeeded at powered flight. He will talk of how Harleys were first used successfully by the army in 1916 along the Mexican border in pursuit of the bandit Pancho Villa, how army scouts armed with submachine-guns did reconnaissance and dispatch work on them in two world wars, and how law-enforcement officers have adopted Harleys as the 'police motorcycle' since the 1920s.

Today's Harley-Davidson motorcycles are duplicating the splendid record made by their predecessors in World War I. The hard-riding scouts who lead the advance of the armoured divisions to reconnoiter, spot mines, traps and ambushes, report on road conditions and enemy movements know that the staunch and sturdy construction of their mounts will not let them down. They know that in Harley-Davidsons reliability and dependability are inbuilt qualities that make them equal to any task that may be assigned to them. All the exacting care and skill of determined loyal workers – all the resources and experience of the Harley-Davidson organization – are enlisted to give freedom's fighters the best in motorcycles. That we pledge until complete victory has been won.' (Harley-Davidson Motor Co. advertisement circa 1943; as replicated in *Easyriders* magazine's book *Earlyriders* [Malibu, Calif. 1977], 74)

A biker will love Harley-Davidson trivia and enjoy nothing more than quoting or listening to significant dates in the evolution of 'his' motorcycle company. He will tell you that hydraulic tappets were introduced to motorcycling in the panhead model and that in 1965 the Duo-Glide became the first Electra-Glide with the addition of an electric starter, and so on. But no matter how many of the improvements and changes he mentions, he will always come back to the same basic point: all Harleys share a common blood-line. He will talk proudly of the common denominator of all Harley machinery since 1909, the V-twin engine, and point out the time-honoured traditional styling that makes his Harley the descendant of the venerable 1936 Knucklehead. Place his 1991 Heritage beside a 1949 panhead and you will be struck by the amazing sameness of basic properties and appearance. The manufacturing principle is a simple one: preserve the classic beauty and form of the past by using technology of the future. In effect, a Harley-Davidson motorcycle constitutes a biker's claim to a heritage. It provides him with a highly romanticized structure of traditions and values, his personal roots in an adventurous past. A true biker will make the machine's legacy of glory and heroes part of his personal heritage.

The Harley-Davidson tradition of producing the world's largest, most powerful, and most valuable motorcycle crystallizes in the form of a stereotype: 'Red-blooded, hairy-chested he-men ride Harley-Davidsons.' The media have always chosen the Harley to portray an anti-hero folk image, from Jimmy Dean and Marlon Brando to Elvis Presley and Peter (Easyrider) Fonda. If the attitude was 'Don't tread on me,' and the look was that of leather jackets, turned-up collars, engineer boots, and switch-blades, then the bike had to be a Harley. Choosing the Harley-Davidson as the vehicle of the social rebel began with the early 'gypsies,' touring bikers of the thirties, and persists in the outlaws of today. The folklore that surrounds the Harley-Davidson motorcycle enables the outlaw-biker community to establish historical roots with tales of glory. Contemporary outlaw bikers continue to use the prestige and power of the Harley to define themselves as the élite of motorcycling.

We're an all-Harley club. There was a time when we'd tolerate strikers having British bikes. But that was on the understanding that they'd get their act together and get themselves a hog. They could always give the Triumph or Norton to their ol' lady. But the Japanese shit, forget it! We don't like having Jap crap on the same parking lot as us. In the whole concept of outlaw motorcycle clubs the Harley-Davidson has always been the supreme bike. Any Joe on the street can ride a Yamaha or Honda, and that don't make him nothing. As far as we're concerned he might as well be driving a car. You know, he's just not there. But if he's on a Harley, you might have something there. (Steve, Rebels MC)

As far as outlaw clubs are concerned, ownership of a Harley is not sufficient in itself to make one a biker, but it is the necessary and only place to start.

Outlaw bikers consider the Japanese motorcycle to be the motorcycle of the Establishment. Japanese manufacturers changed forever the image of the motorcycle by making it socially respectable, mechanically dependable, and financially affordable. Respectability was achieved by an advertising campaign that whitewashed the motorcyclist's image of any predilections for crime or social deviance. The first and largest Japanese manufacturer made extensive use of the slogan 'You Meet the Nicest People on a Honda.' Perhaps more to the point was one of their advertisements in *National Geographic* that featured a middle-class family barbecue, complete with green lawn, white picket fence, and a cherry-red motorcycle. The caption read: 'Honda. The motorcycle for people who think they hate motorcycles.' Dependability resulted from innovative technology and engineering that made the motorcycle easy to operate and maintain, and that introduced frills and comfort features, such as computerized cruise control, push-button adjustment of the suspension system, AM/FM stereo, auto-reverse cassette player and intercom, a four-speaker surround-sound system, an electronic travel computer for elapsed time and average speed, and automatic transmission. Affordability was brought about by a marketing strategy of selling motorcycles at rock-bottom prices in order to eliminate competition – 'dumping' according to an International Trade Commission ruling in 1983.

Realizing that there was little future in a business that catered to social outcasts, the Japanese emasculated the motorcycle as a border marker in order to sell it to Mr and Ms Average North American. Anyone can buy and handle one, even those who lack the mechanical skill, personal dedication, and commitment that are the hallmarks of the true biker. The Japanese motorcycle does not allow a biker to make a statement about personal freedom or macho self-reliance and daring. Such a motorcycle could not become one of life's priorities because there is no 'price' to be paid. Outlaw bikers develop a sectarian contempt for the ricer, whom they consider as different from them 'as night is from day.' For the biker, his bike is a mode of personal transformation, the focal point of his identity. He sees the ricer as someone for whom the motorcycle is strictly a mode of transportation. The biker finds meaning in life through his motorcycle. It is not a casual hobby sport, but rather a cult-like dedication whose devotees 'Live to Ride, Ride to Live.' 'The life of a biker is riding. His bike is his first obligation no matter what else is wrong. If he has ten dollars to his name and his bike needs an oil change, then his bike gets an oil change. If I need a pair of shoes and the bike needs a tire, I'll bum a pair of shoes off one of my brothers and I'll go out and buy a tire for my bike. If my bike needs five dollars' worth of gas and I want a beer, I'll put five dollars' worth of gas in my bike and worry about where I'm going to find the beer later. A biker is a biker. To me he lives and thinks bikes twenty-four hours a day' (Caveman, Rebels MC). For bikers, life without a Harley would be mere existence. The hog is the basis of their lifestyle. Bikers see the ricer as someone who has about as much personal regard for his motorcycle as he does for his Maytag washer.

The American outlaw biker's dislike of Japanese machinery often takes on political overtones. For example, he may be prone to blame much of American unemployment on the influx of Japanese products. One biker T-shirt carries the statement 'Hungry? Out of Work? Eat Your Riceburner'; a bumper sticker reads 'Honda, Suzuki, Yamaha, Kawasaki, from the People Who Brought You Pearl Harbor.' When Harley riders get together at major gatherings, such as the annual runs to Sturgis in the Black Hills of Dakota or Daytona Beach in Florida, they often engage in a little 'Honda bashing.' A few Japanese bikes are assembled and bikers line up to pay a quarter – donated to a local charity – to take their turn at customizing the Japanese machinery with a sledge-hammer. Waiting in line for his turn is a bearded biker whose T-shirt has a picture of a hand grenade with the caption 'Honda Repair Kit.' In November 1989, the magazine *Supercycle* featured a new contest: 'Win A Chance To Bomb A Honda.' Two months earlier *V-Twin* magazine had done a feature on the annual 'Milwaukee Honda Drop,' where 'two 100-foot high cranes, sporting massive American flags (one was an H-D flag, same difference), were haulin' foreign makes into the heavens to see if they could fly' (September 1989: 88). While Canadian bikers don't cloak the issue in red, white, and blue politics, they are equally adamant about maintaining the border between real bikers and people who ride Jap crap. I once asked Blues (Rebels MC) what he would do if he was stuck downtown and he had the choice of riding a Yamaha or taking the bus home. 'If I was wearing my colours, I'd say, "Fuck it! I'll walk!" But if I wasn't wearing my colours, I guess I'd take the bus.'

To add insult to injury, Japanese manufacturers picked up traditional Harley-Davidson styling cues and further encroached upon Harley's position in the market-place by selling imitations of Harley's custom-look motorcycles. Bikers view a threat to the Harley-Davidson company as a threat to their lifestyle: 'You are about to be denied one more of your freedoms,' warns Steve Lorio of *Supercycle*, 'the right to own and possess a new Harley ... courtesy of your friends from Japan' (April 1983: 60). Steve Lorio's warning was well grounded; as late as 1985 the Harley-Davidson Motor Co. was in dire financial straits and came within seven days of filing for bankruptcy. However, Harley management was able to turn things around. They introduced an internal program known as concurrent development under which representatives from engineering, styling, marketing, and manufacturing work together in new-product development teams. Harley-Davidson then went public – traded on the New York Stock Exchange – in mid-1986 at around $14 (U.S.) a share; the share price dropped to $7.37 before the end of that year, but has hit new highs ever since and reached $52 as of June 1990. Today the Harley-Davidson Motor Co. represents a well-made-in-America success story. Understandably, outlaw bikers react to these imitators with predictable bitterness and disdain: 'So what if Honda and Yamaha have V-twins. The [Honda] Shadow and [Yamaha] Virago are like female impersonators; they're fucking transvestites made by Japanese queers. No matter how good a transvestite looks on the outside, it hasn't got the parts that you want, and no real man is going to want to ride one!'

Ironically, today's biker is likely to start his biking career with a Japanese riceburner and not a Harley hog. Harley-Davidson does not make low-cost, mid-range power motorcycles. To the novice buying his first motorcycle, purchasing a brand-new 1991 Harley FLHTC for $18,999 Canadian is just a fantasy. I started out in the early seventies with a used Norton Commando. But, thanks to shrewd Japanese marketing, the once-proud British motorcycle industry of Norton, Triumph, and Birmingham Small Arms (BSA) no longer exists. 'I was a wanna-be for three years riding a little whiz-banger Jap bike in high school,' reminisced Blues, a hard-core Harley fanatic, 'but I saved my money and scored a used Harley. It needed a lot of work but I did most of the work myself with some help from friends who rode Harleys.'

CHOPPING: PERSONALIZING THE MACHO MACHINE

> For a real biker that motorcycle is an extension of himself
> and taking it away leaves a hole in his life big enough to
> drive a Mac truck through.
>   (Gerry, Rebels MC)

The transition from novice motorcyclist to 'righteous biker' involves a man coming to view his motorcycle as an extension of himself. The customized motorcycle is a concrete reference point for the biker's identity; it is his personal statement in chrome and steel as to what he is all about. If he is persistent, the novice will gradually acquire the mechanical skills and experience that characterize the proficiency of the independent biker. He will learn how to mate together individual pieces of powerful machinery into a systematic harmony of artistic form and mechanical function. Eventually the man may attempt to build a 'chopper,' the ultimate challenge in customizing and the symbolic trademark of the outlaw biker. How he can improve either the beauty or power of his Harley will never stray far from his mind. He will continue to search through biker magazines, dealer catalogues, his own mind, and those of his brothers for parts and ideas that will inspire. The process of building an image by seeking perfection in his machine becomes a constant in the life of a committed biker. An overall pattern of increasing commitment begins to emerge, one in which the biker invests progressively larger amounts of himself and which in turn makes the motorcycle increasingly more important as a focal point of his life.

The novice rider who has just left his Harley-Davidson dealer with a brand-new 1991 Low Rider FXRS will not feel the need, nor will he have the capability or, at a cost of $14,000 Cdn, the money, to make any radical changes. However, the biker who sees the motorcycle as a personal symbol of himself will still want to make his motorcycle look as unique as he feels he is. In the initial stages of customizing (personalizing) his machine, the biker can make a number of elementary cosmetic-for-character changes that involve simple bolton operations using common tools. He might dress up his Low Rider with a chromed battery cover, large chromed foot-pegs, braided-steel clutch cable and oil lines, and some pony-express-styled leather saddle-bags for his gear. He may decide to improve his 'ride' by replacing the drag-type bars that come from the factory with pull-back risers that move the bars back for a different look and a more comfortable feel. A few more miles and a few bucks down the road he may indulge himself by replacing all the stock engine nuts, bolts, washers, and studs with their acorn-style equivalents that are finished in 24-ct gold. While these types of modifications don't require tremendous finesse with a wrench, they allow for a degree of personalization and can turn a good-looking Harley into a great-looking hog.

A biker wants more than chrome-cool looks: 'chrome don't get yah home.' He wants the strength, reliability, and sound of a strong motor. As he becomes more mechanically proficient, the biker will progress to the second phase of customizing and begin to experiment with power-for-strength modifications. The biker improves upon what is already the motorcycle industry's largest production engine, the Harley-Davidson V-twin Evolution engine, which displaces upwards of 80 cubic inches (1340 cc). He can turn his Low Rider into a 'power putt' by adding a 'stroker kit' that will increase engine displacement by enlarging the cylinder bore and extending the piston stroke. To get a fast gear-shift along with maximum performance and durability out of his 'stroked' V-twin engine he can put 'tall gears' – with their larger gear ratios – into his transmission. He can bolt on a Dell'Orto racing carburettor for quicker response, add a hot-drag camshaft for more mid-range and top-end power, and then install a competition clutch that can withstand the power transfer of his 'power-jumped' motor.

These and other possible modifications involve mechanical competency and a sound understanding of how the basic power plant of a motorcycle interrelates with the rest of the machine. Modifying a portion of the machine without first understanding the whole of the machine, however, is an invitation to an expensive disaster. For example, my stock 1971 Harley-Davidson FLH (74 cu. in.) has an engine compression ratio of 8.5 to 1. A typical stroker piston would increase that ratio to 9.5 to 1. This modification would certainly make my bike run faster, but only until the excessive compression destroyed the rod assembly. The proper strategy would be to keep the compression constant at 8.5 to 1 by adding a stroker flywheel plate that was one-half as thick as the piston-stroke increase; for example, if I increased the piston stroke by 1/4 inch then I would run a stroker plate of 1/8 inch. This would allow me to increase my engine displacement from 74 to 80 cu. in. without destroying the rod assembly, and would add the convenience of my being able to start the engine on a cold Canadian morning (the lower the compression ratio the easier it is to kick the engine over). Sometimes the stroker motor won't fit back into the frame after you've made the modifications and you have to cut the frame and weld in a 1/2-inch spacer for extra clearance. Even if you have enough room to slip the engine back into the frame, you may not have that same smug smile on your face when you later discover that there still isn't enough room to remove the rear piston head and you have to pull the whole *%!*&^!! engine out of the frame to repair a lousy head gasket. There are literally hundreds of things that have to be changed and balanced that you can do wrong or just entirely forget to do. That's why you keep your ears open when the brothers rap about the experiences they've had modifying their hogs. If you are persistent and willing to experiment and learn, the scenario of you swearing obscenities at your motorcycle in the garage will change to you talking to it as you cruise down the highway. By installing good-looking high-performance parts, the biker ensures himself that not only does he have beauty, he has lots of beast.

Chopping is the last stage and the ultimate challenge in personalizing a motorcycle. The biker not only rebuilds the entire machine; he virtually redesigns it. When a biker spends a couple of thousand dollars on a used Harley FL at a police auction with the intention of doing a 'chop job,' he has bought into his share of hassles, grief, and broken knuckles and the frustration of hours of hard work and inevitable mistakes. The practical side of chopping is that it allows a biker to turn a used and inexpensive 'rat bike' (poor condition) into a symbol of power and status. Even a hog that has been totalled in an accident, the classic 'basket case,' can be resurrected back to its king-of-the-road status. A true biker will gaze at an old Harley with misty eyes, regardless of its condition; he will see an opportunity to restore and therefore become part of a long-standing and revered tradition: 'Old Harleys don't die, they just get rebuilt.' A visitor to the clubhouse of an outlaw club would see a variety of Harley-Davidson models that represent past eras of production. While each would have been customized, a biker could easily identify different eras of production by the design style of the engine head. There would be a few of the new 'evolution' engines, or blockheads (1983–present); the vast majority of the bikes would be shovelheads (1963–84); there would likely be a few panheads (1948–65), perhaps a knucklehead (1936–47), and possibly an old flathead (1929–74). 'Harleys are like good whisky,' mused Tramp of the Rebels, 'both get better with time.'

Square one in chopping is a fridge full of beer and the biker sitting on a milk crate in the garage staring at all the metal parts in boxes; his tools are on the shelves and he's wondering where to begin. There are a few common elements that act as guiding principles. First and foremost, a chopper is lean; a righteous chop job will reduce the motorcycle to the bare necessities and portray an image of raw power. If he is working on an FLH touring model, the biker will strip away all the accessories that cause outsiders to recognize it as a police motorcycle (chopper fanatics will refer to it as a 'garbage wagon'). Gone are non-essential items such as rollbars, windshield, and fibreglass luggage bags. Other stock items are replaced by smaller streamlined custom parts, such as a small 'coffin' (shaped) gas tank, a 'bobbed' or shortened rear fender, a thin front wheel, a diminutive 'pillion pad' for the passenger seat, and a tapered solo seat for himself that gives the impression that he is straddling the motor. The stripped-down chopper's imposing look of raw machine is backed up by its greater power-to-weight ratio.

The other critical feature of a chopper is that it has an extended front end. The biker lengthens the wheelbase and raises the front end by installing front forks that are anywhere from two to twenty inches over stock. In order to accommodate the extended forks without raising the front end too high, a section will have to be chopped, or cut out, of the neck of the frame. A miscalculation of the angle of rake (angle of the forks) will put excessive pressure on the juncture of the fork and frame, and could cause the bike to break in half at 80 miles per hour. The biker may use 'dog bones,' steel struts that raise the handlebars, in combination with 'ape hangers,' long handlebars that extend backward, to ensure that he can reach the hand controls while riding in a laid-back position. He will bolt on 'highway pegs,' up-front extra foot-pegs, and then install forward-positioned custom shift and brake assemblies, so that he will be able to relax and rest his feet in a forward position. A 'sissy bar,' or backrest, supports his back and completes the rider profile that is the trademark of the outlaw biker, one of laid-back-in-the-wind cool.

The final and most personal mark of biker sophistication is a moulding and custom paint job. The biker can give his motorcycle a smooth, sculptured look by applying coats of bondo or moulding around the gas tank and neck area of the bike. Voodoo of the Rebels moulded the front of his gas tank into the shape of a skull. The custom paint job that follows moulding is the one area of building a chopper where a biker doesn't have to compromise with the laws of physics. The biker can be as wild or conservative as his personal style, from basic black or multicoloured pastels to flame jobs and intricate murals. A biker knows that even if he does an impeccable job on the sanding, lacing, patterning, striping, and spraying, a custom paint job, by its very nature, is more susceptible to wear than a factory baked-on enamel paint job. He makes this sacrifice in order to leave his unmistakable signature on the machine: 'This is *my* hog and you aren't going to see anything else like it!' One particularly vivid paint job had a white base and featured a human skeleton overlaid in fog; on top of that was a group of vultures; the bike's name was Lost Soul. Not surprisingly, the colour that predominates in the world of outlaw bikerdom is basic black, which in our culture portrays a mystique of mystery and power.

Many of the decisions that a biker makes while chopping his hog will reflect a solidifying of his outlaw-biker attitude, especially if his choices fly in the face of what the motorcycle industry would consider standard safety features and technological advancements, and what outsiders consider common-sense comfort features. For example, he will have to choose between having a 'springer' front end that uses an antiquated system of cushioning the ride with external springs, and a 'glide' front end with hydraulic shock absorbers that has been used in modern production motorcycles since 1949. If the biker chooses the brute strength and 'boss looks' of the sculptured steel springer over the comfortable-riding but plain-looking glide front end, he makes a strong statement that will be understood within the outlaw community. Along with the choice of forks goes the choice of frames. A biker who runs with a springer front end will also likely choose the smooth classic lines of a rigid frame – affectionately referred to as a 'hard tail' – that has no rear shock absorbers, as opposed to a 'juice' frame that compromises bone-clean looks for the comfort of rear shocks. Fellow bikers again will appreciate the sacrifice that this choice entails: 'Hard tails are for hard asses.' Some of the decisions will involve taking risks; most chopper fanatics run their scooters without front fenders or signal lights. The 'paybacks' a biker faces for taking these risks will vary from having to eat mud when it rains – if he runs his chopper without a front fender – to having his bike ticketed and confiscated as an unsafe vehicle if the handlebars are 1/2 inch too high above the level of the seat.

Customizing is an exercise in identity construction. A biker builds a very personal bond between himself and a mechanical reality that he designs, creates, and then maintains. When the biker modifies his motorcycle he becomes involved on a first-hand basis with the myths and symbols of the outlaw-biker culture, and these in turn provide him with a focus for his own life. However, this particular man-machine relationship goes beyond the biker simply using the motorcycle as a symbolic extension of himself like he would his leather jacket. A true biker will push the relationship much further and try to make the motorcycle a part of himself, and vice versa. A biker cares about his motorcycle and this caring leads to a form of identification with what he is doing. When the man-machine identification is complete the motorcycle becomes a material reflection of his spiritual reality. Outwardly the biker shapes chrome and steel, inwardly he shapes the self he wants to be. A tremendous sense of personal satisfaction, almost serenity, is a biker's reward when, after he resets the points and replaces the plugs, the motor-cycle rumbles to life at just the right number of rpm's. At this point in the relationship, the art of knuckle-busting mechanics has not only taught him to care about what he does, it has also taught him to care about who he is.

In the world of outlaw bikerdom, simply owning and riding a chopper means nothing in the way of status or recognition if you did none of the work; it means everything if you did all of the work. If you happened to pull up beside a group of outlaw patch holders at a service station while straddling a 'righteous chop job,' one of the first questions they would ask you is 'Who did the work?' If all you did was screw on the licence plate, they still might take a moment to admire the bike, but you, at very best, will be ignored. Club bikers take their motorcycles seriously with an attitude that is both highly personal and professional; conversely, they take a dim view of an individual who would flaunt the symbol of their lifestyle without having earned it. Alternatively, if the question 'Who did the work?' causes you to feel a rush of personal pride and you respond, 'Me and

Harley-Davidson,' the doors of communication will be opened. The club bikers will recognize you as a knowledgeable and competent guy, someone worth knowing – not just a stud.

Customizing becomes a major part of a biker's ongoing attempt to find, communicate, and share meaning in what might otherwise be, to him, a meaningless world. Some of the meaning he builds into his machine will be universal and understood by all bikers; some he will share alone with brothers; some will remain part of his own private world.

IN THE WIND: THE GENERATION OF PEAK EXPERIENCES

A new biker quickly discovers the charisma of being 'in the wind.' Riding his motorcycle, the biker is able to transcend the mundane and ordinary in his search for identity. On his very first ride he will learn that he can use the motorcycle to create his own private drama of speed, excitement, and danger. As the miles roll by, the biker will learn how to use his motorcycle to generate a variety of peak experiences and ultimate sensations. 'Riding in the wind' will become the ultimate, the 'it' experience. More and more the biker will turn to his hog in order to express a wide range of emotions – from ventures into lonely introspection to episodes of raw hate at high speeds. With time, riding will come to act as his personal rite of passage to self-discovery. Gradually, those moments he spends on his motor-cycle and the perspective on life that he creates while riding will become his most meaningful frame of reference and come to dominate the major decisions that affect his life.

There is an immediacy to a motorcycle that is not found with a car. You are part of the scene, not just a passive passenger passing through the scenery waiting to get somewhere. On a motorcycle you feel an overwhelming sense of presence with your surroundings and you make things happen. The motorcycle in motion becomes part of the biker's body image. When the rider snaps his wrist the bike leaps forward in powerful immediate response. He feels the mechanical changes as he works his right wrist and his left foot. He does not steer a motorcycle into a turn; he leans into the corner using his centre of gravity and the posture of his upper body to guide the lean angle of the tires. The machine demands all of him. His every movement is in relation to the motorcycle; he blends himself with the power of the machine as a single synchronized unit. 'When I'm on my bike I feel good. I feel free. It's just me and my bike, two against the world. You know the freedom. You get 700 pounds of hot throbbing iron between your legs ... when I twist open that throttle I know she's going somewhere' (Tramp, Rebels MC). The basis of a motorcycle acting as a stimulant goes beyond symbolism and imagination; it is very much a gut-level physiological response. Acceleration causes nerves to react in muscles all over the body. Signals are sent through the spinal cord that increase muscle tone and the body's overall state of arousal. The central nervous system then converts this heightened state of arousal into a number of emotions, ranging from fear to pleasure (Marsh and Collett, 1987).

Arousal enables you to act. Once aroused, you can use the energy released by adrenalin to act out the emotion. The experienced biker uses the motorcycle as a mechanical medium for expressing the full spectrum of his emotional self. On a soft summer afternoon, when his lady presses her thighs to his hips, the motorcycle takes them on a ride of sensual motion. The free-flight sensation of the wind in his face, the gliding body motion, and the constancy of the motor's vibration enable the biker to lose himself in the tranquillity of introspection. 'When I'm riding my bike it's my mind that travels,' reminisced a mellow Voodoo. 'My mind can go anywhere it wants.' The internal dialogue that he engages in while riding may lead to insights into the origins of his attitudes and behaviours and, perhaps, inner peace of mind. On a motorcycle feeling, experience, and thought are united. The rider is wholly at one with his world. Alternatively, the biker will use the motorcycle to express the assertive, the aggressive, and the competitive parts of his psychological make-up. After arguing with his lady or being harassed on the job, he can anthropomorphize; the motorcycle becomes an animal that is alive with his anger and howls his rage. If the biker feels that he has been used, manipulated, or twisted by some institution, the motorcycle will return to him a sense of strength and potency.

The psychological impact of what I would call *Positive Biking* derives from its ability to restore the attitude of self-control. The biker converts 'jammin' in the wind' into a private ritual that restores his courage to be himself. Riding his hog is a concrete dramatization of the biker image of freedom and masculinity that he is trying to emulate. These are qualities that the outside world may force him to compromise in the name of other commitments – such as a job – that offer little in the way of an identity pay-off. He may have to compromise values that have become personally critical, and he may have to suppress what he feels is truly himself. But when he power rides his motorcycle the compromises and contradictions disappear. 'My Harley is my way of getting away from it all,' Wee Albert once commented while sharing a brew after we had done some 'serious puttin.' 'If it weren't for my hog I'd probably go insane.' There is no conflict or deceit while riding his bike; he is doing what really matters to him. The assertive aggressiveness of riding generates self-confidence and inner strength. 'When I handle that piece of Milwaukee iron it feels like I could handle anything' (Slim). The biker uses the control of power, the execution of skill, and the exhilaration of speed to break down the constrictions and inhibitions that have numbed his mind. The biker creates and repairs his self-image while riding. The dreams and fantasies that he engages in while acting out the powerful biker persona open him up to the potentials of his life. They allow him to see that everyday reality itself is a human construct, one that he can both control and change. Just as the experience of power can re-energize the spirit, the escape to solitude can restore objectivity. In a moment of philosophical reflection, Blues of the Rebels revealed: 'Yeah, I'll ride my bike a lot when I'm on a downer, or just uptight. It doesn't change anything, but it clears my head. It lets me see things for what they are.' While hard and visible circumstances define our reality, this ability to mentally transcend one's immediate circumstances is the essence of hope. The sensation of controlled power helps silence inner doubts; it works against a self-image of being a passive functionary whose life is a matter of fate or circumstance. Controlling power encourages people to believe that they are the key to cause and effect and to take full responsibility for their lives; this is the key to effective decision making in life. By itself riding is an elixir that the biker uses to change the base metal of life into gold. Simply by engaging in an activity that he feels is 'the real me,' the biker makes a statement about his being an individual who has the freedom to choose his own destiny. This is the psychological core of those elusive and hard-to-define sensations that a biker will sometimes refer to as 'two-wheeled freedom.'

When a man rides a motorcycle he crosses a border that represents a divergence from those values that underlie the rational, secure, and sensible things of established middle-class society. 'Jamming' is a defiance of the inner voice of caution that wants only to save its own skin and warns against any risks and all pains. The citizen who is satisfied with the conventional identity he has achieved within the system is likely to condemn riding as irritatingly gregarious, an irrationally dangerous way of getting kicks. An outlaw biker is often a man who feels that he has been cheated, used, or denied by society. He comes to view riding as an act of liberating defiance that removes, or at least temporarily suspends, the mass-conditioned repressions that patterned his parents and threaten to curb his impulse towards freedom and pleasure.

For both the citizen and the biker, the most salient border marker of riding is the threat of death. The death toll for motorcyclists, calculated on a mileage basis by the U.S. Department of Transport (1967), is four times that of car/truck operators. While motorcyclists make up only 1.4 per cent of all vehicle registrations, they are involved in double that percentage (2.8) of all motor-vehicle fatalities. In an accident situation the motorcycle is highly vulnerable and offers the rider nothing in the way of protection. According to Transport Canada (1980), 75 per cent of all motorcycle accidents result in personal injury. American Department of Transport authorities (1979) raise this figure to 93 per cent. 'In the event of a crash,' according to a Manitoba Safety Committee report (1986), 'a motorcyclist is five times as likely to face death as a motorist.'

Outlaw bikers are not ignorant of these statistics, nor do they consider themselves impervious to the dangers involved in motorcycling. However, their collective image is one that disdains timidness and refuses to give any hint of fear or self-doubt. Riding a hog is an area where they have an edge, and they certainly don't want to give outsiders the impression that they are hedging their bets. They scoff at the riders who deck themselves out in multicoloured leather outfits, complete with a high-tech wraparound Bell helmet and face-shield. To outsiders these riders look safe and respectable; to hard-core bikers they look 'chickenshit.' In the spirit of the outlaw image the biker faces the elements with a cut-off Levi jacket or a leather vest, jeans, cowboy boots, shortie riding gloves, shades, and, if he happens to be riding in one of the twelve American states that doesn't require them, without a helmet (mandatory in all Canadian provinces and territories). In inclement weather he will add a leather jacket and maybe some riding chaps, but as Wee Albert pointed out, 'the pretty yellow and orange rain suits are strictly for candy asses who ride riceburners.' The outlaws consider their face-it-head-on-and-tough-it-out approach towards danger and discomfort to be another line of demarcation between themselves and the citizen.

Bikers face their vulnerability with a cavalier attitude, a style they feel has a lot to do with the courage to face risks and endure uncertainty. But they do get angry about the distinct possibility that their demise may result from the negligence of some citizen. Statistics lend credibility to the bikers' viewpoint. Figures released by Transport Canada (1980) and the American Department of Transport (1980) indicate that over 70 per cent of all collisions involving motorcycles are caused by car/truck drivers. 'Bikers should expect the worst from the drivers of other vehicles on the road,' according to John Wiley, the chairman of the Manitoba Safety Committee (1986). 'People just don't extend the same courtesy to a motorcyclist as they grant a car.' Over a five-year period Rebel patch holders were involved in four major accidents. One brother had his back broken, another had his leg amputated, a third suffered a broken leg, arms, and collar-bone, and a fourth brother died. Three of the four accidents were caused by car drivers, of whom two were impaired and the third ran a stop sign.

Outlaw bikers come to view the citizen who drives a 'cage' as a major threat to their existence, and they bitterly resent the 'respectable' citizen who pleads, 'But officer, I just never saw the motorcycle.' Furthermore, they have little confidence in a criminal-justice system that fails to level adequate deterrent penalties on their behalf and offers nothing in the way of equity penalties such as compensation or restitution. Bikers see unfair procedures that protect the citizen from the penalties of justice. A biker who has been victimized easily develops a hostile attitude towards a generalized other, 'assholes who drive cages.' He might attempt to fight the injustices from within the system and join an activist group like BAM (Bikers Against Manslaughter). However, his antagonism towards 'the man' may lead him to drop out of the system and take justice into his own hands. In a five-year period I was deliberately run off the road three times. I managed to catch up with the cars on two occasions. In one instance the perpetrator pulled alongside a police squad car when he realized I was following him; I was searched and warned while he chuckled and drove off. In the other instance the police were not around and I meted out my version of street justice. When frustration leads to vigilante tactics, the 'injustice' of the system makes for another emotionally charged brick in the wall between biker and citizen. 'Now I pack a ten-inch wrench in my back pocket when I ride the highway,' Jim (Rebels MC) said sardonically. 'The next asshole that tries to run me off the road is going to eat it!'

Outlaw bikers do ride hard, and they do take chances. But these kinds of performances are considered as 'class acts' only if the man has the skill to pull it off. The Rebels talked of their hogs with affection; for the veteran riders it was affection that included respect. 'A motorcycle gives you a lot more responsibility. You need better reactions. It demands more of you; it develops your self-discipline. It does a lot of things, and it does what you want it to, provided that you're capable ... You have to respect your motorcycle. You're asking for a quick exit if your attitude is "Aw, it doesn't matter if I go out and ride like I'm in a demolition derby." If you decide to pull that little trip, then you're finished!' (Blues, Rebels MC). Each patch holder knows that he does not have the right to endanger his brothers' lives. If he chooses to play Russian Roulette with the motto 'Ride Hard, Die Fast,' he does it on his own.

Outlaw bikers have a highly romanticized view of themselves as being set apart as risk takers and adventurers who seek excitement and stimulation wherever they can find it. A biker who rides his motorcycle hard and fast creates an ultimate experience that involves both thrilling sensations and a personal challenge. When he cranks open the throttle, his concentration leaves him absolutely alone. He must face himself in an intense internal struggle to synthesize two very basic and opposing human emotions, the fear of death and the compulsion to test his limits. Conflicting impulses of fear and fascination pound away in his mind. The closer he 'rides the edge' the more difficult it is to find that balance. He can master the challenge of his own fear, he can back down, or he can lose it all in a split second. At one hundred miles an hour the pavement is a grey blur of instant oblivion that passes six inches beneath your feet. 'There is absolutely nothing else in the world except you and the five hundred pounds of thunder you're riding. And at a hundred miles an hour you and the thunder both weigh less than ten pounds. If you hit a half-brick on the road you won't stop rolling for two days. You've entered that zone that runs parallel to instant death. It's only a fatal twitch away, and your fate is finally in your own hands! Let me tell you, man, that's better than sex, drugs, anything you can name' (Wild Bill Henderson, Hell's Angels MC, 1968: 12).

The biker who 'reaches for the edge' is not oblivious to the danger, and he is no more driven by a death wish or a compulsive ego defect than is the skydiver or the mountain climber. The specific motivation may vary from youthful liberation and the sheer fun of feeling free to a show of taciturn individualism or an angry striking out after having been pushed too far. What remains constant is that the biker creates a situation that is a challenge to the machine he has built and the skills he has developed. It is a test of courage that requires the biker to act despite fear or doubt. Risking it all returns a sense of self-control, confidence, and personal power. The biker creates his own ultimate experience that puts him in an intense face-to-face encounter with the reality of his own being; it allows him to transcend himself by virtue of having overcome a primal challenge and conquered his own fears.

HASSLES: THE PRICE TAG OF FREEDOM

As a man fine-tunes his outlaw-biker image, he learns first hand that social rebellion does not go unpunished. The price the biker will pay in social condemnation, moral censure, legal harassment, or vigilante tactics may be far from trivial. Youthful outlaw bikers soon lose any naïve notions about the exuberance of liberation and the myth of 'freedom of the road.' After he has gotten into his first bar-room brawl because 'You're a fuckin' tough biker, eh!,' after he's been turned down by insurance companies even though his driving record is clean, after he's been ticketed for doing five miles over the speed limit by a cop who has followed him for three miles, after some KOA (Kampgrounds of America) camp-ground operator has refused him a place to stay and the local RCMP are threatening him with vagrancy charges, after he's been refused service in a bar or restaurant, after his licence plate has been confiscated because the seat of his motorcycle seat is twenty-seven and a half inches below the handlebars instead of twenty-seven inches, after some moronic idiot has tried to run him off the highway, he then begins to feel and show the other side of freedom. Youthful exuberance gives way to a sense of struggle to pursue his own path. He grows contemptuous of a world that hypocritically pays superficial tribute to personal freedom and talks endlessly about a democratic heritage, but tries to destroy any alternative to the conventional way. Even an established club member may find the social liability of being an outlaw biker too hard to take. One patch holder who finally quit his club explained, 'I'm tired of getting hassled. You can only take so much. If you went to pick up a girl at her home, her parents didn't like you from the moment they saw you on a bike. The cops were always stopping you, always giving you tickets. Unless there were four or five of you there was always some car driver who played games with you on the highway' (Ken,

Chosen Few MC). Alternatively, a biker may withdraw further his psychological allegiance from the established social mainstream and seek a sense of community in the outlaw-biker subculture. He may show the darker side of freedom and adopt the taciturn individualism of a philosophy that screams, 'Don't fuck with me!'

BIKER SELF-IMAGE: HEROES OF FREEDOM AND INDEPENDENCE

> The notion of the self-sufficient individual transcending his culture's restrictions, his social class, and the demands for conformity still strikes a solemn and potent chord in the hearts of those who cannot quite escape their culture. The ideal remains and has become an integral part of our value system. If individualism cannot be achieved in reality, it can be achieved in principle through symbolic rituals.
> (Wetherington, 1967: 170)

The novice biker is drawn into a highly romanticized ideology in which outlaw bikers become the good guys: 'bikers are real people with respect and compassion for our fellow man.' What the outsider sees as the transgression of conventional norms – social and criminal deviance – the biker views as the transcendence of restrictions in order to achieve personal freedom. Their prose, poetry, and editorials paint a picture of the contemporary biker on his Harley as the spiritual descendant of the frontiersman on his horse; they see themselves as North America's last heroes of independence and self-reliance. If a biker admits to being an anachronism in contemporary society, he feels it is because he clings to his heritage of freedom while most citizens have abandoned it for the bland predictability that comes with the rigid structure of bureaucratic control. In the process of creating a positive image of himself, the biker reinforces the subcultural boundary by forming a negative stereotype of outsiders. In the outlaw-biker ethos he learns that the citizen is the bad guy, the philistine who has sold his soul to the status quo for security and who operates those regulatory agencies that destroy what they cannot control – the biker.

> Probably the biggest reason most of us have gotten into the lifestyle we live has to do with freedom. The freedom of feeling the wind in your hair, of taking off ... with just a sleeping bag,

the ol' lady and a few bucks ... Then why are so many of us in prison? Image ... The image we project by our love of freedom, and our willingness to fight for our way of life separates us ... They're jealous. They feel bad because they haven't got the *huevos* to live free. They wish they could. That makes them fearful of people who do. The fear manifests itself in a dislike of themselves for their weakness, and that self-doubt then becomes dislike of those who have the strength to do what they can't. So, in order to maintain their whimpering dignity, they 'show us' by passing laws that enable their guardians to harass us. (Bob Bitchin, publisher, *Biker Lifestyle*, October 1986: 3)

In the world-view of the outlaw the biker is seen as one who acquires his individuality in spite of conventional society rather than within it. Ironically, for most bikers this separation is largely symbolic. While the principles of the hedonist biker psychology lead to a search for a free and unconditioned lifestyle, the experiences of a biker do not represent a radical departure from street culture. With little difficulty one can find male examples of hard riding, heavy drinking, risk taking, and sexual exploits in all lower-working-class bars. For the most part the separation does not extend into the workplace. While bikers do indeed like to drink, get stoned, have great parties, and go on adventurous runs, most also have jobs to go to when Monday morning comes.

Outlaw bikers see themselves in a continuous struggle to defend their lifestyle from an unfriendly society. They protest and rebel against regulations, such as mandatory helmet laws, that eliminate their freedom of choice and can be used by law-enforcement agents to legalize harassment. They feel threatened by legislation passed by cities such as New York (1980) banning motorcycles from designated areas of the city during certain hours of the day. They resent government regulations restricting the customizing of their hog. 'Every year there are new rules about what we can ride, how we can ride, and where we can ride.' Interestingly enough, the Harley-Davidson Motorcycle Company shares the outlaw viewpoint on bikers being singled out by government bureaucracy. 'In all, motorcycles account for only 1.2 percent of the total number of vehicle miles driven each year ... This being the case, it seems that the EPA is focussing its attention on a relatively minimal part of the problem, that they are needlessly ... chasing after motorcycles ... It all boils down to a basic dislike of our sport by certain bureaucrats ... It's time to stand up to the ever-deepening infringements upon our freedoms and be heard' (Harley-Davidson Motorcycle Company, in *Easyriders*, November 1979: 69).

Today there are a number of organizations which actively crusade for the rights of bikers. Joining an organization like ABATE (dedicated to the repeal of mandatory helmet legislation) or BRO (Bikers Rights Organization) pits a biker's time, effort, and money against bureaucratic agencies that represent the Establishment. He learns quickly that, as a member of the outlaw-biker collective, he is subject to prejudicial legislation. For example, police forces in Alberta enforce helmet legislation in a province whose then attorney-general, Neil Crawford, refused (1986) to consider mandatory seat-belt legislation for motorists on the grounds that 'such legislation would infringe on the rights of Albertans to make personal decisions.'

The outlaw biker sees the political situation as one in which an individual's right to make decisions is being gradually but continually eroded. Once again, the outlaw biker breaks from 'respectable identity' and distances himself from what he considers to be a populace that is becoming increasingly incapable of decision making. 'They think we're animals because we don't play their stupid middle-class games; we don't parade around in little suits and ties telling each other how respectable we are. Those fucking dudes are so worried about being respectable they've probably never made a decision on their own that didn't have the rules all spelled out for them ... like fucking rubber stamps! ... Always doing what they're told, when they're told. They'd be happy with a government that made it illegal to fart and told them what time of the day they could fuck' (Jim, Rebels MC).

The outlaw-biker community is an enclave of right-wing patriotism. Major biker events, such as those held at Sturgis and Daytona, feature a plethora of stars-and-stripes flag waving. For their part, the Hell's Angels went out of their way to defend returning Vietnam veterans against militant peace marchers at the Los Angeles airport. Outlaw bikers are staunch defenders of *laissez-faire* democracy wherein the individual becomes solely responsible for his own destiny. For them the best government is the government that ensures personal liberty and governs the least. Communism from without, and bureaucratic control from within, are seen as being the major threats to their ideal. While talking about federal gun-control legislation, Tramp of the Rebels saw the two threats as being inseparable:

'People are so used to having government take away their freedom that this country is in danger of going communist.' Outlaw bikers envision themselves as social rebels who defend their personal freedom and who exercise their right to choose and their freedom to associate. The outlaw biker feels that he is different because he has not been completely subdued by social routines, rules, and regulations over which he has no real control. For him a large part of the appeal of being an outlaw is living according to his own law.

THE NEED FOR BROTHERS

An outlaw biker has turned riding in the wind into something to live for. He has made the motorcycle the cornerstone of his identity, the master symbol of his lifestyle, and a metaphor for his personal freedom. He has found a tradition and mystique that romanticize his self-image; he has found something to arouse his interests so that he invests himself in goal-directed behaviour. He has found ordeals and tests that confirm his manhood. He has found ultimate experiences that transcend the earthbound traps of the ordinary. He has found core values around which to focus a lifestyle. What else does he need? Fellowship. He wants to be able to compare, discuss, exchange information, socialize, and share the mystique. The full impact of this identity drama requires a stage, fellow actors, and an appreciative female audience. The motorcycle becomes a catalyst of social interaction that draws him into a society of bikers and may eventually lead him to the doorsteps of an outlaw club. A club offers a social framework of biker activities and a sense of community that provide the biker with positive feedback about his developing identity and support his personal philosophy of biking as an acceptable alternative lifestyle. To the extent that the club enhances the biker's sense of this lifestyle being 'real to me' – that is, expressing his authentic self – it will be able to fuse the biker's dedication to his machine with allegiance to the club. The border separating the club from outside society will be reinforced with a degree of personal commitment that could not be generated by formal group ideology and social bonds alone. The biker may eventually come to view group membership as being inseparable from self-actualization; club ties very much become personal ties. 'The club means everything and is everything to me,' Tramp of the Rebels once commented. 'The club gives me the freedom to be the kind of biker that I want to be.'

MAKING CONTACT WITH AN OUTLAW CLUB

New bikers meet other bikers through chance encounters in motorcycle repair shops, at custom-bike shows, at biker swap meets, ABATE and BRO meetings, and especially in biker bars. Some bars are club bars – public bars or taverns that the patch holders of a club frequent on a regular basis. A club bar is neutral territory, where the club can maintain ties with the larger biker community and check out prospective new recruits. This is where the vast majority of bikers will make their initial contacts with an outlaw club.

A biker who wants to meet club members in the bar is well advised first to observe the members at a distance and to maintain a low profile. No two clubs are exactly alike in their behavioural style and the public image they like to project. Each club will have worked out its own understanding with the bar's management, personnel, and bouncers regarding the club taking responsibility for controlling its members. This is a working arrangement that could be strained by an outsider behaving inappropriately. The Rebels reacted adversely to any outsider whose behaviour was not consistent with their public image. Blues, a veteran biker who has met and partied with clubs from the Hell's Angels in Oakland to the Los Brovos in Winnipeg, once advised me, 'When you come across a club just remember, don't make waves and don't try to impress by putting on a show. Just keep your cool and watch what's coming down. Try to get a feel for what kind of scene they're into and what they're all about. Hey, that's no guarantee that you'll pull it off, but at least you won't be digging your grave' (Blues, Rebels MC).

Blues's comments followed an incident involving a member of the 13th Tribe MC, from Nova Scotia. Usually an outlaw club will respect a patch holder from an out-of-town club and be hospitable and tolerant. However, the 13th Tribe member was boisterous, boastful, and acted as if he had the lead role in a grade-B movie about drug-crazed bikers. Onion of the Rebels commented: 'When a guy is as full of shit as he is, it's just a matter of time till somebody knocks it out of him.' Most of the Rebels treated this biker as a bad joke. The visitor sensed that he was being ignored, and his behaviour got out of hand. He began tossing beer glasses and threatening some of the patrons. The bouncers took notice and expectantly looked at Ken, the club president. It was now a Rebel problem. Steve, the club sergeant at arms, got up and lifted the 13th Tribe member out of his seat and dragged him out of the bar: 'Let's go for a walk!'

An example of successful contact shows the features that the Rebels want to see in a potential recruit. Some of the members were drinking at the Kingsway Motor Inn, the club bar at the time. A French Canadian seated at an adjacent table leaned over, offered me a beer, and struck up a conversation. René was 6 feet and 200 pounds of biker, with a trim beard and shoulder-length hair, wearing a cut-off jean jacket, Levis, and steel-toed boots. The Harley eagle (trademark) tattoo on his forearm confirmed that he was a biker with taste. He began a conversation with the universal subject of motorcycles and biking: 'Hey, that must be one terrific rush when you guys open up on those mountain highways!' René then began asking questions about the Rebels and expressed an interest in meeting the club. His experiences as a biker included previous contacts with outlaw clubs. He had recently ridden his motorcycle from Montreal to Edmonton, coming part of the way (to Winnipeg) with the Montreal and Toronto chapters of the Satan's Choice MC, a club whose colours the Rebels respected. Given René's credentials, and his overall biker appearance and personal demeanour – confident but unobtrusive – I made the decision to invite him to join us at a Rebel table.

The club members sitting nearest to me immediately questioned my invitation and then proceeded to 'case out' the stranger:

Gerry: Who's your friend, Coyote?
Coyote: The man's name is René; he rode his bike out here from Montreal.
Gerry: So what kind of bike do you ride, René?
René: I have a chopped '64 panhead. I redid the power mill and she displaces 80 inches.
Gerry: Sounds pretty righteous; I ride a panhead myself.

Later René showed us his scars from a deep cut in his wrist, the result of an accident three months earlier that severed a number of nerves. As a result he was no longer able to operate the throttle of his bike, which required a twisting action with the right hand. René said that he loved to ride and that he was still determined to ride his panhead home. Although he could no longer twist his wrist he was capable of opposing his fingers to his palm, the action required to operate the clutch, located on the left-hand side of the motorcycle. His plan was to switch the location of the clutch and brake mechanisms. René wanted to make the clutch-brake alteration along with other mechanical improvisations by himself, and he asked where he could locate the necessary parts. In addition to owning a hog, René displayed evidence of his self-reliance, intestinal fortitude, and devotion to biking, all of which are integral elements of the outlaw community's image of the ideal biker. Gerry appeared satisfied – 'That's pretty cool.' – and he handed René a beer. Another Rebel, Danny, ripped the back off a cigarette package and proceeded to write out the address of Brothers Custom Cycles Ltd, a motorcycle shop owned by two Rebel patch holders: 'Go down and see them if you need parts or advice. They'll give you a good deal.' René stuffed the address into his jean jacket and went on to talk about his times with the Satan's Choice: 'They are beautiful people. They don't go out of their way to hurt anybody. When I was with them the president said, "Don't be an asshole and start anything with anybody." But if somebody starts something with them, they finish it. What else are you going to do, eh? You've got to stand up for what you believe. If someone hurts you or your bike you've got to fight. You've got to be a man! And it takes a strong man to have strong beliefs and keep them!'

The code of values and behaviour expressed in René's comments closely reflect the Rebels' image of a righteous biker. It is a collective identity that features an anti-hero image, that of a strong-willed individual participating in an unconventional lifestyle, subjected to both social censure and moral condemnation. Most important, the Rebels saw in René a willingness to maintain that lifestyle with a degree of commitment that leaves no room for compromise despite the inevitable adversity that accompanies it. When the Rebels meet a staunch biker like René, they know that there is a strong possibility that he can develop an additional and equal commitment to an organization that revolves around that activity – their club. Commitment to the club is predicated on a commitment to biking. By the time a man earns the right to be called a brother, the two are inseparable. At this point in the conversation Danny was quite pleased with the hard-nosed René. 'Drop down to the shop to just talk,' said Danny as he slammed another brew down in front of René, 'or if you need a hand with anything at all, just let us know.' Danny's offer of assistance and the biker handshake that followed it were, in effect, an invitation to become a 'friend of the club.'

Part Two

BECOMING AN OUTLAW: THE GROUP-SOCIALIZATION PROCESS

Friend of the Club: Forming Bonds of Brotherhood

If a man successfully impresses club members as a righteous biker, he may be given the opportunity to proceed to the next developmental stage in becoming an outlaw patch holder, 'friend of the club.' Friends of the club are bikers who have no official club affiliation, and who may have no intentions of ever striking for the club, yet have established friendship ties with several members. As friends they are invited to attend club parties, runs, and related club activities. Collectively, these friends of the club become part of the club's extended social network. They constitute an informal but significant component of the outlaw-biker subculture as a whole. By encouraging these friends, the club surrounds itself with a mutual support group whose resources, from the trading of motorcycle parts to physical self-defence, they can readily draw upon. However, as far as the club is concerned, the most vital resource that friends of the club provide is new members.

During this stage of the recruitment process, club members attempt to attract bikers who they think have the potential to become 'solid' patch holders. In this sense we can say that 'the club strikes for the prospect before the prospect strikes for the club' (Saint, Rebels MC). The biker gets a clear idea of what the club is all about while he enjoys many of the benefits of club affiliation. As a biker, he has already committed himself to a number of values and activities that set him apart from the four-wheeled culture. Now he will learn how to take part in activities that generate subcultural values and constitute subcultural boundaries. He will learn where these boundaries are, how they are to be crossed, and how to maintain them through participation.

In the outlaw club subculture bonds of friendship precede formal organization ties. An unknown biker would not be allowed to strike for the club. If an unacquainted biker expresses an interest in becoming a member, he is told to 'hang around for a couple of weeks and first become a friend of the club' (Jim, Rebels MC). With some clubs this expectation is a formal one and is encoded in their constitution: 'Strikers must hang around for two months and then strike for six weeks minimum' (Lobos MC constitution, Windsor, Ontario).

To gain entry into the 'club scene' the biker must first establish a strong friendship bond with an established member. The biker must impress and earn the trust of this patch holder who, in effect, becomes his unofficial sponsor. Requiring that a sponsor act as a screening agent at this early stage of recruitment is necessary because a club like the Rebels MC is a closed paramilitary organization. Each member must accept individual responsibility for defending the integrity of the club's borders. The sponsoring member will be held personally accountable for any indiscretions on the part of the guest he invites. Conversely, if the member recruits a promising prospect he gains status in the club, along with a friend and a potential ally in future club politics should the prospect become a member.

Early participation in the outlaw-biker fraternity is by invitation only. A biker requires an invitation by at least one member, if not a vote of approval by all members. During these initial encounters, when not all the Rebels have gotten to know or accepted the prospect, even the seemingly innocuous act of joining members for a beer in the club bar can fall under the scrutiny of a wary patch holder: 'If someone is sitting at the table that I don't know, and he's sitting beside one of my brothers, I'll go up to my brother and say: "Well, who is this guy? I don't know him!"' (Caveman, Rebels MC). In order for a guest to visit the clubhouse there must be both an invitation and escort by a member. To ride with the club on a run, a biker first has to have his name brought up at the weekly business meeting by a member who considers him righteous enough to sponsor. Success in getting an invitation approved depends on how well the biker is represented by the member who endorses the invitation, the sponsoring member's overall status and reputation for making sound decisions, and how many members the biker has gotten to know on a casual basis. The prospective guest is discussed by the membership as a whole and voted on; two negative votes are sufficient to overrule the invitation (Rebels MC Book of Rules). However, even the fact that a biker has received 100 per cent approval by all twenty-five members does not necessarily ensure that his presence will go unchallenged. During the course of a club event, if a member thinks that a guest is 'fucking things up,' he has the right to ask the member who sponsored the invitation to tell the guest to leave (Rebels Book of Rules).

As members get to know and trust the biker, invitations to participate in club activities become more frequent and more diffuse in terms of both the members who give the invitations and the activities involved. The screening process gradually becomes less stringent and assumes a more casual format. After spending three weeks with the Rebels on a run from Edmonton to the west coast, I received an invitation to come to a clubhouse barbecue. The invitation was given by Whimpy, a member of the executive board, prior to the club meeting at which the barbecue was to be discussed, that is, prior to any official discussion about who would be allowed to attend. When I questioned Wee Albert about this bypass of standard procedures, he said: 'Whimpy should have at least waited till after the meeting; but you've been nothing but good with the club, and I can't see anyone objecting.'

Over time interaction with club members extends beyond the boundaries of formal club events to include non-club activities. For example, at one clubhouse party Jim discovered that the rear tire of his motorcycle had gone flat. Jim, along with everybody else, was too 'wasted' to even consider detaching the back wheel, breaking the bead on the tire, removing the tube, isolating the tear, scrounging around for patches, and so on. As Wee Albert had commented: 'It sure is drunk out tonight!' Luckily, I happened to be 'packing' a can of Flat Proof in my saddle-bags. I was able to seal the leak from the inside by removing the valve stem, squeezing the Flat Proof into the tube, then reinflating the tire using an air pump that I carried. The whole process was completed in a matter of minutes. Jim had an ear-to-ear grin when he saw the repair: 'Hey, look at this! Coyote's a fucking mechanic! Haw! Haw! Haw!' Jim filled a quart container with draft beer from one of the kegs and brought it over to me: 'Tell you what, Coyote. Why don't you and Sandy [my lady] come over Sunday afternoon and my ol' lady [Gail] will cook us this goose that I shot last week?' I accepted the invitation.

After the Sunday dinner the four of us went riding, and I decided to treat everybody to a movie. We were the centre of attention –

stares and gawking from the local citizens – while standing in line for the movie. Amidst all this attention Jim pulled out a plastic bag from his leathers. He very nonchalantly proceeded to roll a couple of joints of marijuana: 'Tell you what, Coyote, I'll roll, you get the popcorn!' Feeling somewhat paranoid and at a loss for words, I replied: 'Yeah, but there's no way I'm buying popcorn if we get busted before the movie.' These types of social encounters act as informal screening processes. A friend of the club gets a good idea as to whether or not he is compatible with members in terms of their personal values and social strategies, such as the risk involved in committing an illegal act in public. The commission of such an act simultaneously reinforces a novitiate's self-identification as a biker and differentiates him from the citizens around him. In effect, Jim was teaching me to say, 'Fuck the world.'

These border-creating activities are not deliberately contrived by members, nor are they necessarily conducted under test conditions. For members this behaviour is part of the standard logic employed in everyday decision making. It is a logic that they presume is shared by those individuals who care or dare to interact with them. These social scenarios are behavioural expressions of underlying biker values, values that may never be verbalized or elevated to an ideological level. Participation in these social scenarios leads the members to assume that the prospect shares their criteria for judgment and evaluation. They are assured that you share their everyday world. The greater the degree of sharing, the greater the ease of interaction, and the greater the chance of solidifying bonds of friendship.

Our foursome returned to Jim's house to 'down a few brews' and smoke some more of Jim's home-grown marijuana. While we were sitting on the porch watching the sun set, Jim mentioned: 'Armand [Rebels MC] was always bragging about how he's got the best weed [marijuana] in town, so I asked him over to try some of my home grown. Haw! You should have seen his face after he toked up [ingested by smoking].' When I asked Jim whether or not Armand conceded that Jim had the better-quality weed, Jim replied: 'Naw! He just took a few more tokes. Then he crawls out the door, crawls down the sidewalk towards his bike yelling back: "Not bad! Not bad at all!" Haw! Haw! Haw!'

Friends of the club become involved in an underground economy, the exchange of non-taxable goods and services. The most common medium of exchange in this underground economy is parts and services related to motorcycle maintenance. For example, during the winter months of 'repairing, rechroming, and rebuilding,' Raunch, a professional welder, offered to repair a crack in the primary chain case of my motorcycle. A few days later I went over to Raunch's residence – an old three-storey wooden house that he shared with Crash, Snake, and Melody (Snake's ol' lady) – to pick up the casing. Raunch brought out some of his beer stock, which we critically tested while discussing the plans he had for his 'sled' (motorcycle), which he was 'tearing down' (disassembling) right there in the living-room. In between 'brews' Raunch brought out the casing, which he had not only welded, but also polished to a mirror-like finish. When I asked how much I owed him, Raunch replied: 'Well, I don't usually do this sort of thing for money.' Realizing my *faux pas* – that money does not belong in this sphere of exchange – I told Raunch that he was welcome to the next-to-new front tire that I was replacing on my bike. Raunch tipped back his Molson's beer, reflected for a moment, then said: 'Yeah, Wee Albert was saying that you change tires about as often as some guys change socks. Sure, it sounds like a good deal to me.' As a result of such instances of interpersonal reciprocity, a friend of the club becomes increasingly involved in the network of mutual assistance that consolidates the brotherhood.

A special form of gift giving that is highly symbolic in nature is the exchange of outlaw-biker paraphernalia. Gifts that I saw exchanged included a .44-calibre bullet key-ring, a 16-oz. beer mug that was a reproduction of the old 1920s Harley-Davidson oil can, a biker wallet with a sewn-on Harley-Davidson eagle patch, a Harley-Davidson ebony eagle belt buckle, a 1950s Marlon Brando–style biker cap, a 'roach clip' for holding a marijuana joint that mounted on a motor-cycle tire as a valve-stem cover, riding goggles and gloves, and a 1940s Harley-Davidson service manual. Especially valued were items of nostalgia that reflected Harley-Davidson's venerated history. The exchange of these gifts represents and reinforces shared biker standards and values.

Bikers in general, and club members in particular, adorn their leathers and colours (jean jacket and club emblem) with pins, badges, and pendants that are emblematic of the biker subculture. These pendants and badges are a personal statement by the indi-vidual that he is a biker. The exchange or giving of a badge or pin symbolizes the mutual sharing of that biker status and conveys a sense of in-group comradeship. While drinking and 'shooting the shit' with Rebels members in the club bar, I traded a silver skull pin to Dale for a Harley-Davidson eagle/logo pin. Inscribed on the logo portion of the pin was the message: 'Harleys the Best, Fuck the Rest.' When two clubs have established a political alliance, as was the case with the Rebels MC of Edmonton and the King's Crew MC of Calgary, some members will customarily exchange pins and tokens to show that the political alliance has been cemented by interpersonal bonds: 'It's an expression of friendship. Like Mick [King's Crew] just brought me one [badge] back from their run down to San Francisco. It says: "Kiss Me, I'm a Rebel." I've never lost a badge that someone else has given me; I'll sew it on, or wire it on, but I'll never lose it. Like this [German] Iron Cross. It's an original given to me by Crow of the [King's] Crew. Two years from now I'll give it back to Crow and say: "Remember that?" And he'll tell me the party he gave it to me at and everything about it. You know that it means something!' (Steve, Rebels MC). When the exchange is between club brothers, the gift becomes a token of interpersonal loyalty and caring that a brother publicly declares by mounting it on his colours: 'If a brother gives me something, I'll put it on my colours because it means something to me ... Like Blues gave met this HD-74 [Harley-Davidson with a 74-cu.-in. engine] emblem. It took him over two weeks to make. He cut it out of brass by hand. He must care for me a lot to take so much time and put in so much effort. I appreciate that, it's something that I'll always carry with me' (Larry, Rebels MC).

Outlaw motorcycle clubs do not have a written history, only an oral one, a mythology made up of intangible recollections and stories that can easily be swept away. The only tangible vestiges of the club's past are the club minutes and photograph albums that are kept in the clubhouse, along with the pins that members wear on their colours. Pins and badges are often kept by members as keepsakes of their personal history as club members: 'There's a large part of my life sewn on that jacket' (Indian, Rebels MC). Like any cultural minority, an outlaw club cannot afford to lack a consciousness of its collective identity.

Another characteristic feature by which the club distinguishes itself is its use of language. A distinct vocabulary and verbal style marks club members as an identifiable group; it implies cohesion and reinforces group solidarity while keeping the public at a respectable distance. In the outlaw-motorcycle-club subculture, group solidarity and boundary maintenance are verbally achieved through the use of jargon, a distinct verbal style, and nicknames. The successful prospect must master biker jargon and the biker verbal style that characterizes the outlaw-biker fraternity.

Jargon is 'the collective term for words, expressing technical terms, etc., which are intelligible to the members of a specific group, social circle or profession but not to the general public.' On a surface level, every profession or specific-interest area develops its own special shorthand in the name of convenience and efficiency. On a more subtle level, individuals may use jargon to make themselves more accepted by their peers, rather than simply understood. Jargon can furthermore be used to signal a person's membership in a group while keeping outsiders at a distance. With outlaw bikers, the use of jargon becomes a matter of efficiency, cunning, humour, and border marking.

The everyday distinctions that are important to the members of a subcultural group are likely to be reflected in their specialized jargon. The conversation of outlaw patch holders is usually conducted against a background of motorcycles and motorcycling. When a biker speaks of his chopped hog, he is referring to his customized Harley-Davidson motorcycle, not his lunch. When he suggests going for a run, he wants to ride his motorcycle, not go jogging. A comment made by Larry in the club bar typifies the highly jargonized exchanges between members of the Rebels, much of which would be quite unintelligible to anyone other than a biker: 'Over the winter I'm going to rake the frame and wrench in a stroker kit to juice up the mills of my shovel.' Larry is talking about improving the looks and performance of his motorcycle, not about his garden tools. The following is a rough translation: '*Over the winter I'm going to rake the frame* [cut a section out of the neck portion of the frame of the motorcycle frame, which will allow for the addition of an extended front end without elevating the machine's centre of gravity] *and wrench in* [install] *a stroker kit* [a customized cylinder head, flywheel, valve, piston, and carburettor system] *to juice up the mills* [a stroker kit will increase the power of a Harley-74 engine by approximately fifteen horsepower] *of my shovel* [shovel or shovelhead refers specifically to the engine head style, and designates an era of Harley-Davidson motorcycle models, circa 1966–84].'

When Voodoo warns you that 'the man is uptight, and you can't fly colours without drawing the heat,' he is telling you that public relations between the club and the local police (the man) are at a low ebb (uptight), and that anyone riding with their club emblem (fly colours) is likely to receive an inordinate amount of attention from the police (draw the heat). The jargon that bikers use is more than just an effective instrument to communicate ideas and feelings – a condensed and efficient shorthand. Language and culture are intimately related; the language of a group defines and reinforces its world-view. Whether one refers to a uniformed constable as a police officer, cop, or pig has some very definite connotations of meaning and implications for action. The point at which language and culture intersect is the human personality. Like the lexicon of any language, bikers' jargon reflects their particular view of the universe and conditions their emotive responses to that reality.

The use of jargon is especially striking when club members talk about their area of specialization: chopping hogs. Outlaw patch holders who chop, or customize, their motorcycles are involved in the mammoth task of virtually redesigning and rebuilding the entire machine. As a topic of conversation these activities provide the Rebels with a mystique of technical know-how. In most social situations biker mechanics gives members something to ponder and argue over; for instance, how does installing a five-speed transmission unit on an older 'shovelhead' compare with a stroker kit as far as speed and engine wear are concerned? It provides for discussions about members' experiments; for example, some of the more mechanically unconventional Rebels installed the then-new Phase 3 belt-drive system in their drive train in order to establish whether or not it would prove to be more efficient and dependable than the once-traditional chain-drive system. The Rebels carried out this innovation four years before Harley-Davidson reintroduced the belt-drive system on the 1979 Sturgis model; actually Harley had used a belt-drive system since day one in 1903 till it was replaced by a chain drive in 1913. This experiment of the seventies worked for both the Rebels and Harley-Davidson; today the belt-drive system is a standard feature on all H-D Big Twins. If you joined them for a brew this evening, you might find those same Rebels speculating on how the Harley-Davidson engineers could design a truly leakproof 80-incher by building an internal oil pump that would completely eliminate the need for any external lubrication lines ... Watch for it to happen!! These brain-storm sessions furnish a subject-matter to philosophize about, as members debate whether the Harley-Davidson 'knuckle-head' of the 1930s was a superior engine to the 'shovelhead' of the seventies, or how it compares to the contemporary V-2 Evolution engine. The discussions are pratical in that they produce helpful hints: 'Say, Coyote, you can get that same Diamond drive chain that Steen Hansen's [Harley-Davidson] sells for forty-nine dollars at Main Line Tool & Bearing for nineteen bucks' (Onion, Rebels MC). The exchange of words of mechanical wisdom often implies a sense of camaraderie: 'Once you start extending that front end more than 14 inches over stock, and raking the frame more than three-quarters of an inch, you begin to get handling problems. Won't bother you much in a straightaway, but watch yourself on those fucking mountain roads' (Ken, Rebels MC). The collective knowledge represented by those seated around the tables in the club bar provides an immediate reference encyclopedia for any member having mechanical problems:

Crash: My bike gets this snaky feeling when I'm going into turns.
Steve: Check out your axles. Make sure they're tight. If that doesn't end it, then you'll probably have to fork out a couple of bucks for new wheel bearings. But before you go fucking around with all that shit, make sure you've got proper air pressure in your tires.

The highly technical and arcane knowledge required to engage in these conversations in an intelligent manner is symbolic in its portrayal of the participants as dedicated bikers. Just as these conversations provide a common medium of verbal exchange among bikers, they also serve a converse function as a border marker by setting the group off as a distinct social unit. The blank expressions on the faces of some non-bikers seated at the bar attests to the fact that the purpose of these conversations is not only to enlighten members, but also to exclude 'straights.' Conversation becomes an exclusionary tool reserved for the already-tenured. Thus, the message of these conversations is not always their content; rather, it may be putting the listener in his place – maintaining non-bikers as mystified outsiders.

Mixed in with tales of motorcycles and motorcycling is dialogue about the club or members themselves. The ties of brotherhood that have formed between members readily facilitate the sharing of personal problems that individuals may be experiencing. These personal problems might include topics such as difficulties at work, a troublesome domestic situation, or a specific source of frustration. What will sometimes appear to outsiders as an abusive exchange is actually a 'bare-knuckled' (candid) verbal style that is acceptable to patch holders by virtue of their intimate comradeship. Excerpts from a conversation carried on by members of the Warlords MC at the Airway Motor Inn provide a case in point:

> *Ron*: Hey, Renegade, loosen up! You've been acting like a genuine prick lately!
> *Renegade*: Look Man, when I'm working on my engine and things aren't going right, I start to burn!
> *Ron*: You've gotta let us know. Curse at the fucking thing! Kick in a wall! But let us know. We don't know what's clicking inside of you when you get like that.
> *Dump*: That guy's like a fucking grenade!
> *Renegade*: Just lighten up and give me a little space! I can work things out.
> *Ron*: What the fuck! That's what we're here for.

Under the social circumstances of friendship, abusive terms and obscenities lose their purely semantic intent, and the careless use of insults actually becomes a show of solidarity. For example, when patch holders couch their bare-knuckled verbal style within the context of a joking relationship, they are able to criticize aspects of a brother's behaviour under amiable circumstances:

> *Dump*: Randy, you ride like a blind man! Looking here, looking there! Jesus! Watch what you're doing!
> *Randy*: I'm watching you guys, I don't trust anybody.
> *Rae*: Yeah, now there's a guy who is really on the ball. He likes to keep his eyes on at least eight bikes at once!
> *Dan*: Take it easy, Randy. What you don't see won't hurt you.

This bantering is one area of verbal participation in which a prospect had best be sure of his ties with members and exercise some discrimination, otherwise he might miss a subtlety and wind up on the wrong end of a boot.

The joking relationships that exist between members serve to dissipate feelings of anger or frustration that inevitably arise in a small close-knit group. The joking relationship acts as a safety valve.

Human emotion is effectively channelled in a socially prescribed manner that is acceptable to all concerned. The joking allows for the expression of negative emotions yet deflects their impact away from the sentiments of brotherhood. The sting of any personal criticism is blunted by the overall style of the joking relationship, which might be best described as a form of light-hearted verbal jousting:

> *Dump*: Hey! You're getting fat. Look at this love roll!
> *Dan*: What do you expect when you drive a truck [Dan's job]?
>   The only exercise you get is farting.

At this point Dan farted. He had switched his strategy from verbal jousting to non-verbal communication, a none-too-subtle form of body language.

> *Dan*: Well! There you go. That oughta be worth twenty push-ups!
> *Barry*: Your voice is changing, Dan, but you've still got problems
>   with bad breath.
> *Ron*: He's the only guy I know that got kicked out of a bar for
>   farting. I don't know how a guy could be so rotten and still walk.
> *Dump*: I'll get you, [Dan] Baxter. I'll drink beer, eat Chinese food,
>   and won't shit for a week. Then I'll dump a load on yah!

Conversation that is spiked with storytelling and joking reinforces solidarity in the club. It enables the members to deal with sensitive issues in a manner that strengthens, rather than threatens, their highly personalized relationships.

The prospect must learn the biker jargon, master the distinctive biker verbal style, and be able to manage a joking relationship in order to truly participate in the outlaw subculture. These communication skills are necessary in order to be able to interpret and generate social behaviour in a natural manner. If he is unable to develop these skills the prospect will remain an awkward and marginal participant – at best, a translator and imitator.

By unifying the members and providing group exclusivity, the whole lexicon of biker talk serves to set bikers apart as an identifiable group. One further example can be seen in the use of pseudonyms. It is a common practice for members of the outlaw-motorcycle subculture to adopt nicknames. While not all the members of a club will have club names, many will be given 'handles' such as Spider,

Crash, Blues, Terrible Tom, and Voodoo. Club names are particularly effective in facilitating the incorporation and maintenance of outlaw roles and identities. A nickname serves to bolster a patch holder's self-esteem by making him feel both important and unique as an individual; it is a declaration of personal identity. Collectively, nicknames enhance solidarity by boosting club morale and cohesiveness. The psychological impact of a club name in part results from the power of words to confirm personal qualities or social status. Every time a patch holder gives the biker handshake and introduces himself using his club name he declares his personal existence as a biker and his social standing as a club member.

A club nickname may refer to a particular biographical incident. For example, Dump, a Warlords patch holder, received his club name after an accident in which he was cut off while riding his motorcycle and run over by a dump truck. Dump had his back broken in the incident, but not only did he survive, he lived to ride and fly the club colours again. Club names may publicize personal traits whose meaning is couched in local knowledge or is specific to the functioning of the club. For instance, most clubs will have a Bear, Tiny, or Caveman who, by virtue of their personal prowess as enforcers, are the most likely candidates to be elected as the club sergeant at arms. A club name may serve to highlight or promote underlying group values. For example, nicknames such as Tramp or Vagabond suggest the biker freedom-of-the-road ethic. A club name can provide a historical shorthand to the mythology of the club. For example, a new member of the Satan's Choice MC of Brampton, Ontario, inherited the name of Gypsy from a member who had acted as his club sponsor, but who was killed shortly thereafter in a highway accident. Giving Gypsy's name to the striker he sponsored was a testament to his memory and the dramatic show of force displayed at his funeral by the thirteen chapters and more than two hundred and sixty members of the Satan's Choice federation.

The social function of the use of pseudonyms by secret organizations lies primarily in their potency to act as social border markers. Some club nicknames are explicitly counter-cultural in nature. However, pejorative names such as Mouldy Marvin (Hell's Angels MC) or Snake (Rebels) do not attest to personal qualities. Nor are nicknames that are suggestive of the transgression of social norms, such as Dale the Butcher (Rebels) or Charley the Child Molester (Hell's Angels), indications of specific behavioural characteristics or disorders. Rather, these nicknames are simply acts of verbal spontaneity that reflect a defiant underworld social order that those members have helped create and sustain. The use of club nicknames is restricted to members or close friends of the club. Given this aspect of privileged use, club names act as verbal declarations of separateness that serve to reflect the club as a counter-hierarchy to the established, but now excluded, outside social order.

A club nickname represents a subcultural value orientation; and as a personal label it assumes a self-fulfilling character. Once a biker is labelled with a special nickname, he will live up to that name in some way. The label will influence a biker's perception of how he relates to a particular social situation and channel his behaviour accordingly. For the outlaw biker a club name acts as a personal metaphor, a reminder that his interpretation and generation of social behaviour are to be consistent with the subcultural ethos that his name represents. The psychological effect of a club nickname is to confer an outlaw identity upon recruits and confirm that identity for established members. The social function of a club nickname lies in its ability to reinforce subcultural separateness and to symbolize that the outlaw bikers are acting in a world that is of their own devising.

As a friend of the club becomes familiar with the borders that separate and define the club, he gradually learns the values of participation that are basic to the outlaw-club subculture. Sharing in club events presupposes a certain degree of mutual trust and involvement. Many of the activities, especially those involving high-risk situations, require implicit acknowledgment of the rules of brotherhood: the right to ask for help and the obligation to provide assistance. An example of this occurred while I was riding with the club on a run through the Rocky Mountains. I dropped out of the club formation in order to remove my leather jacket and ride in my cut-off jean jacket. It would prove to be a costly mistake in judgment, but fortunately one that I would live to regret. I restarted my shovelhead and was making good time pursuing the pack when I reached one of the tight turns in the mountain highway. As I geared down and leaned into the curve, I saw an oncoming Winnebago that had failed to negotiate the turn and was crossing over into my lane. Faced with the possibility of becoming someone's hood ornament, I headed towards the shoulder. I narrowly avoided the steel edges of the Winnebago, but now I was headed to the right while the roadway made a hairpin turn to the left. I tried to hold the bike on the shoulder, but when the front wheel began to wobble I knew that I was on gravel and that the party was over. One moment I was in the ditch with the motorcycle vibrating furiously, the next I was headed up the side of the mountain. The bike flipped over, and I couldn't tell which way the ground was coming. The mechanical clatter and engine roar suddenly ceased. There was silent stillness, then blackness.

A few miles down the road the club was having lunch at a roadside diner, when a patron rushed through the doorway and announced that he had just seen a biker killed on the highway. By the time the Rebels arrived at the scene I had regained consciousness to the point that I could hear their conversation. Ken was asking a park warden, 'Is he really dead?' The warden replied, 'He's alive; he's breathing. I've called for an ambulance. I don't want to touch him because he's not moving and he might have broken his back.' When I heard that I tried to raise my arm, but the muscles wouldn't respond. I was unable to move a finger or blink an eyelid. Growing anxious with fear I tried to feel the pain that I knew must be there, but there was nothing. For a brief moment I contemplated life as a paralysed invalid and concentrated my fear and rage on trying to strike out. A forearm begrudgingly moved and an eyelid opened: 'Hey! He's coming to!'

I had escaped without any disabling or permanent injuries other than a severe case of 'road rash,' which we took care of with some on-the-spot repairs using the warden's first-aid kit. The motorcycle had taken a beating but was still operational. The area that demanded immediate attention was the fork tubes, which serve to hold the front wheel in alignment; they had been badly bent. Ken sent two riders ahead to the next town to scout out a machine shop. When we reached the town of Hope we stripped down the front end of the motorcycle. Ken and Steve took the fork tubes to the machine shop, where they used a dial indicator to locate bends in the tubes and an arbor press to straighten them. While we were reassembling the motorcycle in the parking lot, Wee Albert removed a rear-view mirror ($30) from his bike and gave it to me, since both of mine had been smashed. Raunch replaced the front brake cable ($60), which had been torn off the hand-lever anchor pin, with a spare that he carried: 'You owe me one, Coyote.' A sizable piece of metal had been ripped off the front fender, so it was junked. Onion told me that he had a stock fender ($200) that was 'collecting dust' in his garage, and that I was welcome to it for 'maybe thirty bucks' and 'a bottle of that fine whisky that I've had over at your place.' When we had my shovelhead reassembled Steve took it for a test drive.

> *Steve*: It handles all right as long as you don't do more then eighty [mph]; anything more than that and you'll get a (high-speed) wobble. We did a good job truing [straightening] the forks, but there's always some stretching [metal distortion] when you bend them like that. You've done enough racing for the day anyways.
>
> *Coyote*: That wasn't racing, maybe a little moto-cross and hill climbing though.
>
> *Saint*: If you have to scrap those [fork] tubes, I've still got the stock forks [$250] from when I chopped my [Super] Glide. When we get back to Edmonton you can have them for twenty bucks, or whatever.
>
> *Caveman*: Naw! He doesn't want your [stock] forks. Hell, he's got his bike halfway chopped [removal of stock parts] now.
> Personally, I like to do my [customizing] work in a garage. It's a helluva lot easier than driving into a fucking mountain.

Wee Albert took me aside. He gave me a beer that striker Gerry had picked up from town, and told me the obvious: 'Just about anything can be pulled off when you've got tight brothers in the area. Even putting a bike back together can be done without sweat and a whole lot of bucks. You'll have to take a lot of ribbing and bullshit [about the accident] for the next couple of days; just remember that most of us have been there.' Experiences such as these dramatize the sense of sharing a common fate. The impact of the drama is to break down the barriers of normal hesitancy that mark the borders between friends who are only casual. The long-term effect is to establish the foundation for self-disclosure and mutual acceptance that characterize the relations among biker brothers. The immediate result is a definite and observable switch from a casual to a close friendship.

If the prospect is successful in establishing himself as a friend of the club in general, and he forms at least one very strong personal tie in particular, one of his closer contacts may suggest that he attempt to join the club: 'Hey, Coyote, why don't you strike for the club? Come to Wednesday's meeting and state your case' (Tiny). The member who makes this suggestion will likely serve as the prospect's mentor during the probationary or striking period. With more extreme outlaw clubs, especially those involved in organized crime, the boundaries are drawn even tighter in terms of the screening process, and the prospect will require an official sponsor. The sponsoring member accepts full responsibility for the striker's future actions:

> If a guy is voted on and accepted, then he becomes the respon-
> sibility of the member who brought him to the meeting. Because
> of the responsibility the member takes on he must be careful on
> who he chooses to bring. If a member brings in a bad 'prospec-
> tive' and he fucks up, this reflects back on the member and
> could result in his suspension.
>
> One main thing a striker must learn is that, if he gets busted
> or gets hassled by the cops, he knows nothing and nobody. One
> time the OPP [Ontario Provincial Police] pulled a raid on the
> Toronto chapter [Satan's Choice MC] for bike theft and arrested
> four members and one striker ... The members warned him not
> to say anything. The cops realized that the guy was new to the
> whole thing and decided that if they threw a scare into him he
> might start talking. The poor fucker was so scared that he
> started singing like a stool-pigeon. Apparently the cops fed him
> a bullshit line that he was going to jail for a long time and that
> the rest of the guys in the club would never get near him if he
> cooperated; so he tells the fucking pigs the whole story. After
> he spilled the beans, the pigs put him back in the same cell with
> the other four members. They asked him what happened. He
> said nothing. Maybe the shithead didn't know that the others
> would be questioned also. Anyways, when their turn came, the
> others found out what really happened. The cops had what they
> wanted so they just showed the members dates, times, and
> places and signed statements. When they went back to the cell,
> the striker was all smiles. They beat him up so badly that he
> spent three months in the hospital before he went to trial
> himself. His court case went in his favour, and since he had a
> clean record he received a suspended sentence from the court,
> but not from the Choice. Two weeks later, he was back in the
> hospital, but this time the pigs weren't around so he was in
> much worse shape. He lost complete sight in one eye and
> remained in the hospital for another six weeks.

The members that assaulted him in jail were charged with assault, but the charges were dropped when they agreed to plead guilty on the other charges [plea bargaining]. The sponsoring member was suspended from the club for four weeks and was barred from ever running for any [club] office. (Gypsy, Satan's Choice MC)

If and when a friend of the club decides that he wants to be a Rebel, he comes to the weekly Wednesday meeting and states his reasons for wanting to join the club to the membership. The applicant must be at least eighteen years old (Rebels MC Book of Rules), which is adult status in the province of Alberta. The age of Rebel club members falls within the range of early twenties to late thirties, with the majority of club patch holders being in their late twenties. The friend-of-the-club stage is a time of observation and affiliation, when the prospect demonstrates the qualities of being a biker, the ability to interact socially with the members, and the capacity to participate in club events. He has learned how to cross the subculture's boundaries and, through participation, how to maintain these boundaries. This observation/affiliation period ends with a formal screening/selection process. At the meeting the members will be asked to decide whether or not they feel that the friend of the club has the potential to learn how to be a Rebel. The prospect's performance will be reviewed and he will be queried about an additional number of formal and informal qualifications. Members feel that these personal qualities and attributes are crucial ingredients if the prospect is to be successful in the subsequent learning/testing stage of striking.

For the Rebels, relationships of mutual trust and acceptance required honesty. As Wee Albert explained, 'Honesty. Sincerity. I want to hear it from the heart; any dishonesty, I vote no! Honesty to me and the club. He can be a thief but he must be honest to me.' I recall what one Rebel patch holder said to a fellow member who he thought was 'selling him a line': 'Hey, look! You can bullshit your friends; and I'll bullshit mine. But we're brothers; we don't bullshit each other!' (Clayton).

The candidate is asked if he can afford the time that is involved in being a member, and whether or not he is in a position to make the Rebels MC his primary obligation: 'He's asked if he has the time. If a man is married we ask him what his wife thinks of it. If a man can't handle his wife, then he can't be a good striker or a good member.

Like if it's Saturday night and some member phones up a striker and says, "We need you, striker." If the striker says, "Well, you see I was planning on taking my ol' lady out tonight," they just say, "We need you striker," and that's that!' (Wee Albert). Older members are also wary of any impending elements of personal instability that could undermine the effectiveness of the prospect's transition to the brotherhood:

> *Blues*: I mean, if a guy just got married in the last few months, or is even thinking of getting married, I'd consider him and I'd say 'No, forget it!'
> *Coyote*: You would tell him to get his personal scene together first?
> *Blues*: Yeah, for sure, get established. Get a relationship established with this chick, or whatever else it is before he even considers coming to the club. Because the club is well known for fucking up relationships between a man and a woman.
> *Coyote*: You mean in terms of the time commitment and the emotional commitment?
> *Blues*: That's right.

One of the tenets of social-network analysis is that the number of intense social relationships that any one individual can maintain is restricted owing to limitations of time, energy, and resources. The Rebels give empirical credence to this theoretical proposition; they realize that the intensity of Rebel ties leaves little of these personal commodities to pass around elsewhere. The prospect is questioned as to the nature of his present 'outside' relationships. The expressed understanding is that most of these ties will have to be modified, and many of them terminated as the prospect becomes encapsulated within the Rebel social network: 'We also check this person out to the best of our ability. We find out where he works, what he's been doing for the last little while, who he lives with, who his friends *were*. If everything checks out he's allowed to strike' (Ken, Rebels MC).

The veteran Rebel patch holders are well acquainted with the fact that each prospect brings with him his own unique set of personal values and goals that he hopes to actualize through group participation. What members try to determine is whether or not these individual proclivities can be successfully merged with those of the club, or at least operationalized within the club's range of accepted behaviour. 'He must have a sincere wish to be a Rebel and not just be using the colours for an ego trip. We realize that everyone has their own little power trip and this is usually overlooked as long as the club comes first ... yet any extremes are discouraged and kept to a minimum' (Jim). Jesse was an example of one prospective member who didn't work out. As Steve later explained: 'I didn't want him to strike at all ... He's just an asshole. I've just seen him perform and do stupid things for no reason whatsoever. Like jump up and smack some guy in the bar when the guy said "Excuse me" and tried to step around him. To me that's an asshole stunt with no sense or reason behind it ... it reflects on me and I don't need that.'

Apart from these flagrant extremes, judgments on the suitability of a prospect based on personality characteristics are usually deferred until the striking period itself, during which the prospect will learn how to adapt his individual behaviour and personal inclinations in terms of the group image.

> *Coyote*: Do you consider personal qualities, like how well you get along with him?
>
> *Raunch*: Not so much that, because you can get a bad impression right off the bat. We like to give him a chance, because people change, especially when they're striking.

Contrary to the popular stereotype of the 'drug-crazed biker,' the Rebels MC and most outlaw clubs will flatly refuse the opportunity to strike to any prospect who regularly uses 'heavy' drugs, such as heroin. This rigorously enforced criterion of the selection process reflects an important aspect of the nature of outlaw clubs. The aggressive behaviour style of the biker, the inter-member obligations of the brotherhood, and club responsibilities cannot be fulfilled by an individual whose self-control and sense of loyalty have been jeopardized by the use of heavy drugs: 'He's asked, "Do you do heavy drugs?" We don't want any dope freaks ... We can't afford to have anybody around who is so spun out that they couldn't take care of themselves ... The first thing we tell [those prospects who are accepted as] strikers is to stay away from dope pushers or heavy users. We disapprove of friends that interfere with the functioning of the club' (Wee Albert).

The use of drugs among outlaw bikers is largely confined to the non-addictive variety, including hallucinogens such as 'acid' (LSD-25, lysergic acid diethylamide), amphetamines such as 'speed' or 'meth' (methamphetamine hydrochloride), and, to a lesser extent, 'coke' (cocaine). However, the use of these particular drugs is more the exception than it is the rule. Patch holders use mostly 'grass' (marijuana, cannabis leaves), 'hash' (refined marijuana), 'booze' (alcohol), and 'cigarettes' (nicotine). Outlaw clubs, such as the Rebels and Hell's Angels, enforce strict prohibitions against the use of opiate narcotics (opium and its derivatives codeine, morphine, and heroin) because of their potential to induce physical and psychological dependence.

The members of outlaw clubs are very sensitive to the social and psychological stability of their brothers and do not hesitate to act to ensure that stability. When a member of the Rebels MC began to drink too heavily – to the point where his behaviour displayed some of the ineptitudes characteristic of an alcoholic – he was 'put on the wagon.' During this time his colours were confiscated and he was considered 'under probation' by his brothers. His behaviour and drinking habits came under close surveillance until the members felt that 'he had his act back together again.' An outlaw club is particularly sensitive to having its members expose themselves and the reputation of the club to outside threats – whether they emanate from the police or roadside vigilantes – by being incapacitated in public. Thus, if a member wants to get drunk at a bar, he makes sure brothers are there who aren't; if he wants to get 'stoned,' he is expected to show discretion and enough common sense to find friendly confines such as his own residence or the clubhouse.

I remember one day I decided to go tripping on acid. It was a bright sunny afternoon and that night was our regular meeting. I decided that I was really going to get stoned so I copped [ingested by swallowing] a whole whack of purple micro-dots which is a fantastic stone; but I started popping [swallowing] them one after another. Pretty soon I was fucking wrecked [incapacitated] and I was down at the park by the Brampton Hall. I didn't know who the fuck I was or where I was. I guess I was falling all over my bike by the drugstore when who should walk out but Jack [president, Satan's Choice MC]. At first, he thought I was drunk, but he realized that I was stoned right out of my fucking head. He took me with him to his apartment and made me stay there and listen to records. He phoned Dave to go pick up my bike. All I can remember is taking off my colours and staring into Satan's face [part of the Satan's Choice MC emblem]. I stayed like that for almost four hours, listening to Satan. When I finally came down, Jack gave me a good shit kicking. I knew it was for my own good. (Gypsy, Satan's Choice MC)

For outlaw clubs such as the Rebels or the Hell's Angels, the continued abuse of drugs, in particular heroin, is a 'patch pulling' (loss of membership) offence: 'No hypes. No use of heroin in any form. Anyone using a needle for any reason other than having a doctor use it on you will be considered a hype. FINE: Automatic kick-out from club' (Hell's Angels MC By-laws, Oakland, California). Both Rebels and Angels have had to 'pull the patch' of members who were caught up in excessive drug use.

Another critical consideration of the applicant is the type of motorcycle he rides. The motorcycle serves as the dominant symbol of subcultural commitment, and it acts as the most visible border marker between the club and host society. However, not all motorcycles are created, or re-created (customized), equal. Outlaw clubs will enforce differing standards regarding (1) the make and model of motorcycle required; (2) the required minimal engine size or displacement; and (3) whether or not the motorcycle must necessarily be customized, or chopped. These different standards result in varying demands on their respective members in terms of financial cost, time, effort, mechanical knowledge, and overall ingenuity. It becomes possible to gain a preliminary insight into an outlaw club's internal stability and external relations simply by observing what constitutes an acceptable or 'righteous' machine to the club or its members. The more rigid and demanding the requirements regarding the motorcycle, the more 'solid' the club is in terms of being established with a long-standing committed membership, and the more 'heavy' the club is with respect to how it separates itself from the host community. Outlaw clubs themselves will compare and measure each other based on the premise that 'the more super the scooters, the more righteous the club.'

The ultimate outlaw motorcycle is the HD-80, a Harley-Davidson motorcycle that is propelled by an engine that displaces 80 cu. in. (1340 cc) of brute power. The HD-80 superseded the venerated HD-74 in 1979 when the Harley-Davidson research team further refined their classic V-twin engine. The engine size of the Harley-Davidson makes it the largest stock motorcycle that comes off a production line. For veteran members of the outlaw-biker fraternity, the Harley-Davidson is the only motorcycle: 'Until you've been on a Harley, you haven't been on a motorcycle!' If a biker 'rides to live, and lives to ride,' then it will be a Harley-Davidson, his hog, that he will ride and live for.

The Rebels MC is an 'all-Harley club'; ownership of a Harley-Davidson is a prerequisite to membership. The Rebels' constitution allows a prospect to strike for the club while riding a Harley of lesser engine size than the HD-80, specifically the Sportster XLS or XLH models that displace 1000 cc. The constitutions of most outlaw clubs are less restrictive and only stipulate that a prospective member must have a street machine that has a mid-range engine size:

> A prospective member and all members must have a four stroke motorcycle of not less than 500 cc's. (King's Crew MC constitution, Calgary, Alberta)

> To be a member, one must own a motorcycle of approved size and make. A member in his first year will be allowed to run a bike as small as a 500 cc engine displacement, as long as it is a British or American product. Japanese machinery is not allowed under any circumstances. A Harley-Davidson, or motorcycle of minimal 750 cc, must be owned by the second year of membership. (Satan's Choice MC by-laws, Brampton, Ontario)

The King's Crew and Satan's Choice technically allowed a prospect to strike while riding a British-made motorcycle. British machinery included Norton, Triumph, and BSA, whose larger model bikes have engine capacities in the 750 to 850 cc range. However, striking on a British bike wouldn't enhance a prospect's chances of gaining membership in an all-Harley club.

During its early formative years – when survival requires numbers – an outlaw club will not be afforded the luxury of selecting only Harley owners as prospects or members. For example, the majority of King's Crew MC patch holders rode Nortons in the early seventies, with three of their members holding down jobs as mechanics with a Norton dealership. Over the years the King's Crew evolved into a predominantly Harley club with several members employed as Harley mechanics. The Rebels MC, an older, more established club, is exclusively Harley-Davidson. The Hell's Angels MC of Vancouver goes one step further than the Rebels and requires that its patch holders

(1) chop their hogs, and (2) install stroker kits in order to increase the horsepower of their machines. While a Rebel is not officially required to customize his bike, only four of twenty-five members rode a stock, or unmodified, machine.

After fielding the questions that the Rebels have put to him, the prospect is asked to leave the clubhouse while the members discuss his application. It is significant that an official vote is not taken. There is no room for dissent at this point in the recruitment process; the striking period cannot prove successful if all the members are not amenable to teaching the prospect how to be a Rebel. This screening procedure based on open consensus, as opposed to a secret majority vote, enhances group solidarity. Objections and opinions are openly exchanged, and the club as a whole reviews its purpose and consolidates its ideology. The friend-of-the-club period is a time of observation and affiliation and ends with this screening/ selection procedure. Since the striking period is to be a learning/ testing process, 'the foremost quality becomes honesty and sincerity. We want to see if he is both willing and capable of learning how to be a Rebel' (Wee Albert). After the decision is made, the sergeant at arms escorts the prospect back into the clubhouse. If the prospect's application to strike has been rejected, he is so informed. However, in order to avoid unnecessary hard feelings, he is not told the specific reasons why his application has been turned down. This leaves the individual with the option of reverting back to being a friend of the club. If the Rebels are in favour of the prospect, he begins his probationary period as a striker.

4

Striker:
Earning One's Colours

The purpose of the striking period is to see if a man can get it together enough to be a member. We want to find out whether he'll be a brother, a righteous member that'll give to the club.

(Wee Albert, Rebels MC)

The striking period is a socializing process. It is made up of a series of learning and testing situations that ultimately serve to integrate the prospective member into the club: 'A striker has to learn how to be a Rebel' (Voodoo, Rebels MC). These learning and testing procedures draw the prospect or striker into three discernible dimensions of club participation. First, on a personal level, the prospect adopts a system of core values that are specific to the outlaw-club subculture. Second, on an interpersonal level, the prospect is incorporated into a network of informal social relations. Third, on an institutional level, the prospect is introduced to the formal role regulations and expectations of the club. The prospect finds himself in a position of having to convince the Rebels – through his performance as a striker – that he has a commitment to the club, its members, and motorcycling. From the perspective of the members, 'a striker earns his colours by showing a love for the club, a love for his brothers, and a love of biking' (Blues, Rebels MC).

Each aspect of the striker's participation in the club makes specific demands on the prospect, all of which are critical in maintaining the inter-member strength, operational cohesiveness, and ultimate survival of the group. The prospect must meet stringent entrance requirements that support a social atmosphere of intense interpersonal relations and shared ideological commitment. These requirements will prepare the striker to meet the demanding expectations that will be had of him as a member. In return the club provides the striker with a strong sense of participation and involvement, intrigue and adventure, brotherhood and allegiance, purpose and meaning. The strong emotional appeal of these aspects of group participation makes them particularly effective in drawing the striker into the club mould. If he is successful in his quest, the striker achieves a sense of special identity; it is the sense of social validity that comes with having achieved membership in an élite group through great personal effort and sacrifice.

The length of the striking period depends on the abilities, attitudes, and attributes of the prospect. For the majority of outlaw clubs the length of time involved falls within a range of three months to two years. The Rebels MC has no official minimum or maximum striking period; however, a prospect would have to strike for at least one month before he would be allowed to attend the weekly club meetings. Over three years I observed eight striker periods that varied in length from four and a half months to one year. The striking period necessarily includes the summer riding season. This policy enables the club to evaluate the prospect's ability to handle himself during the course of a long bike run, or tour. On a run a prospect will have to demonstrate prowess in riding his motorcycle and show ingenuity in making on-the-spot repairs. He must be sensible when handling outsiders and display a certain behavioural 'cool' when being hassled by 'the man.' As a rule outlaw motorcycle clubs will limit themselves to one, or possibly two, strikers at any given time. Of the eight different prospects that I observed, five were successful in their attempts to become Rebels.

The prospect formally initiates his striking period by purchasing a striker patch for twenty dollars. For most clubs this emblem of identification consists of a rectangular felt patch with either 'striker' or 'prospect' embossed in red against a white background – the specific colour combination will vary with the club. Alternatively, some clubs will give the striker the club patch (for example, the lion's head of the Warlords MC) but withhold the top rocker with the club name (Warlords) and the bottom rocker with the club's territorial base (Edm.) until the striking period is completed. The club emblem in combination with the top and bottom rockers constitutes a full set of 'club colours.' The striker will sew his striker patch on the back of a sleeveless denim jacket or leather vest that he will wear over his 'leathers' (leather jacket), a T-shirt, or by itself. The striker patch is the prospect's first symbol of official club ties; and just as members do not appear without their colours, so too a prospect does not appear without his striker patch. From this point on, the man is referred to by members as 'Striker Rick' or 'Striker Gerry,' and so on. As far as the prospect is concerned, he is now 'Striker': 'For a while, I thought that "Striker" was going to be my nickname, because all I ever heard for twelve solid weeks was: "Striker, come here!" "Striker, fetch some beer!" "Striker, clean up the clubhouse!" Every time I heard that word I jumped' (Tiny, Rebels MC). The use of the term 'striker' in the outlaw-club subculture is restricted to club members. If an outsider were to address a prospect as 'striker,' the prospect would be expected to 'set the guy straight.' Because of these kinds of misunderstandings, the Rebels in 1985 voted to do away with the striker patch altogether. Now they just give the prospect the bottom rocker bearing the club's chapter location, such as Edmonton, Calgary, or Saskatchewan. 'This is because the prospect is a striker only to the members of the club,' explained Tramp of the Rebels, 'not to the outside world!'

PERSONAL QUALITIES: LEARNING TO BECOME A CLUB BIKER

There are a number of club activities whose performance both demands and symbolizes certain personal qualities in the members, qualities that become part of the outlaw-biker identity. Being a member of an outlaw club includes 'partying,' 'drinking heavy,' and 'riding hard,' while avoiding 'dying fast.' A biker 'lives to ride' and 'rides to live.' A club patch holder goes on adventurous bike tours whose destinations are decided 'when we get there.' These activities symbolize freedom, masculinity, adventure, and when they're done together, they foster brotherhood.

Flying the colours of an outlaw club guarantees you a date with a situation where you will have to act despite your personal fears. While an outlaw-biker identity can be symbolized instantly in terms of dress and demeanour, certain realities of the role can only be learned slowly. Success or failure for the striker depends on whether or not he is capable of 'holding his mud' (displaying intestinal fortitude) in those social circumstances in which his outlaw-biker identity is 'put on the line.' If he hopes to 'keep his bike on the road' and 'his ass out of stir [jail],' a striker must learn how to cope with surveillance and harassment from police officials: 'I'm a member of the Rebels ... we expect a tough time from the police' (Steve, Rebels MC). He learns that a 'solid patch holder' means 'being there' whenever and however his brothers are in need; this is a core responsibility on which the endurance of the club depends. As a member he will be expected to 'show class' (display a minimum of anxiety or concern) and remain cool (unperturbed and controlled) in high-risk situations. Finally, a striker has to accept the risks and responsibilities that come with the fact that outlaw patch holders must handle outside threats to the club and its members by themselves. These qualities become part of the standard of behaviour the Rebels set for themselves and expect of one another. As far as strikers are concerned, 'some guys may join this club as boys, but by the time they leave, they're every inch a man' (Wee Albert).

Members need to find out how sincere a prospect is about becoming a Rebel. The patch holders have to assure themselves that the prospect will be able to take the many hassles that come with being an outlaw biker and not quit when the going gets tough. In many ways the striking period is an artificial creation of hard times; members reason that the harder an individual works for a goal, the greater its value will be to him. The striker exhibits sincerity 'by being willing to do just about anything he's asked to do by a member without bitching' (Danny, Rebels MC). Gypsy, a road captain with one of the Satan's Choice MC chapters in Ontario, recalls: 'When you become a striker you are classified as nothing but dirt. You have no say concerning club activities; and you are always wrong no matter what you are talking about, even if you're 100 per cent right. It's during this period that you have to start proving yourself to the club. Many times the other members will razz you because you're a striker. He will have to take shit from any member in any chapter; he will have to do whatever he is told by any member, and still do whatever his sponsor tells him to do.'

In the past there was some abuse of strikers that resulted in the Rebels placing the following rule in their constitution: 'Strikers do not have to do anything that maims body, bike, or costs him money. Orders are restricted to club duties, club functions, and clubhouse.' In practice, this constitutional ruling served as a guideline to members; however, a striker would never use it as grounds for refusing to perform. The relative non-abuse of Rebel strikers was ensured more by a common understanding that a spirit of fairness would prevail.

'Oh yeah. A striker is required to do whatever the member asks him,' explained Indian, 'but a guy is only going to ask a prospect to do things that he himself would do. Of course there are a lot of things that members will do, eh!'

There are a number of commonplace duties that strikers perform on a regular basis:

- *Clubhouse*: The striker is assigned tasks such as cleaning the premises of dirt, bottles and caps, glass, empty oil cans, and so on. He is responsible for keeping the beer fridge stocked with brew, and for general maintenance, such as refuelling the portable generator that supplies the clubhouse with power and repairing the stove and stereo. He conducts methodical checks of the security system (locks, bars, and firearms) and guards the clubhouse while the weekly business meeting is in progress.
- *Club runs*: On club tours the striker will find himself having to perform a wide range of activities including 'just about anything' that the situation demands. He is customarily delegated to labours such as retrieving and chopping firewood, maintaining the fires, setting up a member's tent, getting a member a quart of oil, a pack of cigarettes, or a beer. The striker may be assigned to driving the 'crash truck' (backup support vehicle); and he will be expected to assist with and learn general motorcycle maintenance and on-the-spot repairs.
- *Club functions*: A striker will make his labours available to the various club committees, such as those that might be in charge of food and entertainment, or ticket sales and hall rental. During the course of these events he will run general errands. For example, at events such as 'boogies' (club-sponsored dances), he will help sell tickets, set up the venues, purchase and distribute the beer, and clean up the rented hall in the aftermath.
- *Club bar*: At the club bar a striker will be expected to take a member's order to the food concession booth, reserve pool tables, find empty chairs for arriving members, and conduct the occasional 'bike check' to guard against vandalism.

The patch holders of an outlaw club will closely watch the striker to see how he handles himself in social situations that occur on a regular basis. They want to assure themselves that the striker is not an individual whose erratic behaviour will eventually endanger either the club or its members. The Rebel patch holders pay particular attention to how the striker acts when he has been drinking heavily. Wee Albert explained that the Rebels are attentive to any self-disclosures on the part of the striker, and that they are specifically evaluating the striker's capacity for self-control. 'In some ways you've got to take that sort of thing with a grain of salt; but in other ways you might also learn what the guy is all about. People react differently; we like to watch to see if he says anything he might not otherwise say about the club. We also like to see how a man handles himself. We have to know if he can keep his cool when he's drunk, or whether he goes off half-cocked.'

One prospect, Striker (Bruce) Russell, was brought up for discussion at the weekly business meeting because of his totally reckless behaviour and unheeding nature after he had been drinking. 'Bruce gets ignorant ... At a Halloween boogie he attacked a girl and the guys had to jump him. Otherwise he's a really nice guy, but he's dangerous when he's drunk' (Saint). After the Wednesday meeting most of the club rode over to the Rex tavern to 'down a few brews.' It wasn't long before Steve, the Rebels' sergeant at arms, had to tell Striker Russell to go outside to 'walk it off and cool down!' I followed Striker Russell out in time to see him kick-start his panhead into action. Russell did an erratic ten-yard catwalk (driving with the front wheel propelled off the ground) out of the parking lot. He failed to negotiate the driveway, fishtailed off the curb, and missed an on-coming car by two feet. After yelling some obscenities at the stunned motorist, the striker rode his bike down the sidewalk back into the parking lot and weaved in and out of parked cars. This was Striker Russell's way of 'walking it off.' That evening Onion and Snake offered to drive Russell and his bike home from the Rex tavern. Russell initially consented, but then he jumped off the back seat of Onion's bike and took his own from Snake, saying, 'Nobody but me drives my hog!' Later that night the Edmonton city police received a call from some irate citizens complaining about a drunken biker who had broken into their house by driving his motorcycle through the basement window. Jim's opinion of Russell succinctly summarized how his Rebel brothers felt about the striker: 'That guy has got to be wearing himself pretty thin. He's out boozing and smoking dope every night. One of these days he's going to fuck up in a big way, and I don't want to be depending on him when it happens!' At the next weekly business meeting, Striker Russell was voted out of the club and his striker patch was confiscated.

The Rebels MC exerted both formal and informal influence on members' personal (non-group) behaviour. Personal accountability in a formal sense was demonstrated when action was taken to deal with a member whose excessive drinking was perceived as a threat to both his health and his reliability as a member. The individual was told to 'go on the wagon till he dried out,' which he did under the scrutiny and with the moral support of his brothers. The Rebel influence on personal behaviour is usually of a more informal nature, being independent of group normative guidelines and external sanction expectations. Caveman provides an interesting example of this informal influence: 'I know that if I wasn't a member of the club I'd be a lot more of an orangutan than I am now. I used to fight a lot. I mean I used to be in a scrap maybe four nights a week. I've settled down a lot. I feel better for it. I'm easier to get along with now.' Caveman's commentary is of particular interest in so far as the group effect on his behaviour style runs counter to the public stereotype of outlaw motorcycle clubs, which is that they only foster sociopathic behaviour.

It is essential that a striker make himself accountable to the club because the club and its members will eventually become accountable to the public for the actions of the striker. A striker must display sensitivity towards the general expectation that no one will do anything to jeopardize the club: 'No, there isn't too much [rules] that would influence personal activities. Some of the rules are, let's say, not to cause trouble in the bar ... Anything that's going to cause trouble for the club you don't do ... but you don't have to read the club rule book to know that' (Ken, president, Rebels MC).

The Rebels Motorcycle Club is a highly visible group with a very negative public stereotype. These two factors make them a highly saleable news item. The stories that result from overenthusiastic journalism result in public indignation which, in turn, pressures the police to respond. This chain of events can be set in motion by the actions of a single member. For example, one summer Armand (Rebels MC) was sold some poor-quality marijuana. Armand was none too pleased at having his 'Mexican Gold' turn out to be Safeway's oregano, and was determined to express his displeasure with the deal. He waited for the two pushers in the parking lot of a bar that they frequented. When the first pusher came out of the car he was caught flush in the chest by Armand's boot and was sent across the hood. Armand turned just in time to avoid most of the looping right aimed at his head by the second pusher. He threw a hard combination to the pusher's head, followed by a well-placed boot to the ribs; the skirmish was over.

The two pushers sought revenge and staked out Armand's apartment with a shotgun and a rifle. As the front door was broken down, Armand dove behind the couch. The pale light of the room was briefly illuminated by two bursts of flame and two ear-ringing explosions from big-bore weapons. Some of the buckshot from the shotgun round entered Armand's upper body and skull. Armand, in a state of shock, ignored the pain and had the presence of mind to grab his shotgun from the wall. He spun around and fired both barrels in the direction of the two figures silhouetted in the doorway. The police arrived and an ambulance was called. Armand, weak-kneed and faint with relief, was hospitalized for several days with his gunshot wounds. The pushers were arrested three weeks later and charged with attempted murder. The entire incident was an individual affair and had nothing to do with the Rebels MC as an organization. However, for the *Edmonton Journal*, it was an opportunity to inform the public of a shoot-out between 'rival gangs':

Man Shot in Gangs Meeting
Police say Armand —— has wounds on his head and shoulders and his condition is not considered serious ... Shortly after 1 a.m., police say, two rival gangs met in the neighborhood; some gang members were armed with shotguns and high powered rifles. (*Edmonton Journal*, 30 Oct. 1975)

The incident led to increased police surveillance directed at controlling the alleged drug trafficking and gang warfare. For the next month Rebel patch holders did not ride the street without expectations of 'drawing the heat.' 'I was pulled over two times just coming from my house to the party tonight,' mentioned Steve. 'All this because Armand wants to know how it feels to be a fucking Mallard duck during hunting season.'

In addition to his being accountable and dependable to the club, a striker is evaluated with respect to his being a 'righteous' biker. The brothers will take note of the number of miles that he puts on his speedometer, the weather conditions under which he will ride, his overall mechanical skills, and the enthusiasm he shows towards maintaining his hog. All of these are considered valid measures of a striker's commitment to biking. The striker has to be capable of taking care of his own motorcycle. If he is uncertain about aspects of motorcycle maintenance, members will be more than willing to teach him. Each of the Rebels tends to specialize in a particular area of motorcycle maintenance or modification: Caveman is an expert with the various carburettor systems; Raunch, a professional welder; Jim, a professional painter and autobody man; Shultz, a genius at designing engine modifications; Ken, an expert in dealing with engine top ends; Blues, the resident adviser on body moulding. The striker is expected to develop the ability to remain independent in the critical area of motorcycle maintenance, repair, and modification. The Rebels would not tolerate a member going outside the club boundaries in this highly symbolic behavioural domain. That would be embarassing. 'We don't want anybody that can't keep up their own bike. We don't want one of our members going down to some shop to have someone replace the points on his bike. That's just something that is out. If you can't take care of your hog, you don't deserve to ride it. You certainly don't have what it takes to fly our colours' (Indian, Rebels MC). The motorcycle is the most obvious border marker between the Rebels MC and the host society, and the striker has to learn to enforce that border.

INTERPERSONAL RELATIONS:
LEARNING THE CODE OF BROTHERHOOD

> Brotherhood is love for members of the club ... You know there's going to be a brother there to give you a hand when you need it. There's going to be a brother there to loan you five bucks for gas when you want to go for a ride. There's going to be a brother there to talk to when you need someone to talk to. Brotherhood is something that grows from being with the members; its something you feel, not something you explain. You never have to worry because there's always going to be someone there to back you, and you know it.
>
> (Onion, Rebels MC)

The prospective member discovers that his involvement in the club is expected to go beyond institutional participation (love of the club) and beyond motorcycling (love of biking) to include the formation of friendship ties – 'love for your brothers.' In a parallel manner, the participation of members as a collective transcends formal organizational tasks to include the generation and maintenance of group solidarity. For outlaw motorcycle clubs such as the Rebels, a group social network – the 'brotherhood' – becomes one of the underlying realities of group association: 'Well, basically it's a riding club. From that stems a brotherhood, people that you can believe in, and count on all of the time. It's good to have people that you can depend on, that's always a good feeling. When you get right down to it, the club has changed my life a lot. I've got somebody to think about besides myself now' (Raunch, Rebels MC). A striker who is successfully integrated into the club has been drawn into an intense social network of contacts and interactions. This network of brotherhood is extended beyond the walls of formal club events as 'being a brother' gradually comes to dominate the striker's social world. These informal but crucial social ties magnify the overall effect that the formal group structure has on members. The meaning of club association is extended beyond the formal group structure and the range of club influence becomes more extensive and diffuse.

The ties of brotherhood are multifaceted and serve a multiplicity of interests. Members assist each other in matters such as the repair and maintenance of their motorcycles, the loaning of money, the sharing of living accommodations, finding employment, and the solving of personal problems. Just as one's brothers come to represent the good times – riding, partying, hunting, and drinking together – the brotherhood also provides assistance in times of duress, be it jail, hospital, or personal threats. The interactions between members are intense: 'You've got to be willing to risk all for your brothers and your club' (Blues). They are frequent: 'As a member I have little time for anything else but the club' (Voodoo). They are exclusive: 'That's what new members find out ... a year after they begin striking they can't remember half the people they knew outside the club. All they know is the people inside the club. That's just the way it works' (Ken). They are durable: 'Rebels Forever, Forever Rebels' (part of the Rebel skull tattoo on the shoulder of several members).

The brotherhood represents simultaneously the integration of the striker into the outlaw subculture's social network and his isolation from outside social ties. The striker becomes encapsulated in a social network that is characterized by a high degree of (1) connectedness or frequency of interpersonal contact, (2) intensity or strength of interpersonal commitment, and (3) scope or range of interpersonal contact situations. Thus, while striking duties are officially restricted to formal club activities, the reality of subcultural

commitment obviously goes well beyond those and, as a consequence, so also do members' expectations of the striker: 'He may not
be obliged as a striker, but you'd like to see what his commitment
was to you as a friend' (Gerry). The premise that underlies the ideology of brotherhood is a principle of cooperation based on a sense of
common purpose and welfare – of common fate – without which an
outlaw motorcycle club could not survive. If one chooses to view the
Rebels Motorcycle Club as a form of social mutiny, then the brotherhood becomes the Rebels' cause.

A number of outlaw clubs institutionalize the 'all for one, one for
all' ethic by incorporating it into their constitution, set of by-laws, or
book of rules. This mutual-support clause stipulates that, regardless
of the circumstances, all members of the club will support a fellow
member when threatened. The rules and regulations of the Satan's
Angels MC of Vancouver provide an example of formal enforcement
of the brotherhood-support ethic.

> Breaking any of the following Rules will be reason for immediate
> dismissal.

> ... If a group or individual attacks any member, the whole club
> shall stand behind and fight if necessary. If, however, the
> member is drunk and aggressive and purposely starts an argu-
> ment, the rest of the members will escort him away, or step
> between before trouble starts ...

> (The above rules will be put forward to applicants. If they feel
> they cannot abide by these rules and are not in favour of them,
> they will be denied membership to the club.)

The mutual-support ethic, especially the general public's awareness
of it, acts as a protective group border marker; it functions effectively to inhibit hostilities between the club and host society. The
knowledge that a violator faces retribution from the whole club serves
to restrain assaults by outsiders. The threat of retribution from the
whole club serves to protect the members in a variety of areas
covering a wide range of circumstances: from the all-too-typical bar-
room scene where a drunk who is in a 'I-can-take-on-the-world' mood
and perceives the patch holder as an ideal target, to the highways –
the bullrings of North American society – where a citizen vigilante

may choose to exercise a little moral entrepreneurship by using his 'cage' (car) to run an outlaw off the road.

The Rebels MC has no formal ruling on the 'one for all, all for one' ethic. The doctrine of mutual support is simply taken for granted – 'to have that feeling for any member, for any brother.' A Rebel striker learns that he can always count on support from his brothers in threatening situations; but he also learns that the club will not tolerate him abusing that support. Any member who unnecessarily draws the club into a conflict situation, such as a bar-room brawl, would be held fully accountable – and face possible retribution – for his actions when the members returned to the confines of the clubhouse.

> *Coyote*: Would I be correct in saying that you would support any member under any circumstances?
> *Steve*: Um hm, right or wrong, I'd be there. If wrong, though, I would take it up with him later about what the hell he was doing. But I wouldn't let him take a licking and then say: 'Well, that's why I didn't help.' I'd help him and then tell him: 'You know, I think you're an asshole! Think about that when we get to court!'

The King's Crew MC of Calgary deliberately set up a test situation to see if the striker has the 'jam' to put himself on the line for a brother. A King's Crew patch holder will invite the prospect to go out drinking. The member then picks a fight with a bar patron and lets the citizen lay a beating on him (the club members draw straws to see who is 'privileged' with this assignment). Then it is observed whether or not the striker will fight for the member. Failure on the part of a striker to live up to the outlaw code of mutual support simply cannot be tolerated by any outlaw club that has realistic aspirations towards survival. Gypsy, a road captain with the Satan's Choice MC in Ontario, recalls how the club reacted when a striker failed to live up to his commitment:

> We were an outlaw club, but that doesn't mean that we went looking for trouble. But when it came, we didn't back down from it. Like myself, Stu, and Mack, we went down to Rochdale, this university complex in Toronto. It was a big drug-dealing centre in Toronto. We went in there and came out with a bit of hash. We were walking down an alley and there were these five

Italians. Complete fucking greaseballs. Like these guys slid down the street, they didn't walk. And they say: 'Well, here are the Satan's Choice, we should beat the fuck out of them!' They came at us, one of them grabbed a two-by-four. Stu took away the two-by-four and we beat them. They could have been dead for all we knew. We didn't have time to find out 'cause the sirens began, and we hit the road. And we had this striker with us. While we were there fighting like fucking cats and dogs this fucker stood back and watched. When we got back to the clubhouse, Stu said: 'You Fucker! Get out of the building. Either get out, or I'll drag you out! If you're in a fight with us it's all for one and one for all. If we're getting the shit kicked out of us, you get in there and get the shit kicked out of you. You're no fucking bloody special!' Stu took that poor fucker outside and he beat the supreme shit out of him. Stu left him lying outside the clubhouse. When we came out the next morning, he was gone.

Brotherhood demands uncompromising commitment from the striker. In return the striker receives unwavering group fellowship and support.

In addition to testing a striker's sense of allegiance and his ability to perform, the club will closely scrutinize the prospect's social network of friends and non-club commitments. The purpose of this monitoring process is to ensure the absence of any outside ties that might eventually interfere – in terms of time, energy, or commitment – with a striker's ability to 'pull his weight as a righteous brother.' Disaffiliation from most outside ties is an expected norm of the striking process. According to Gerry of the Rebels, 'We like to know what kinds of friends he left behind to come to the club.' Why are old friends left behind? From the perspective of the striker, earning his colours becomes so much a focal point of his lifestyle that other commitments begin to pale by comparison and simply atrophy. Furthermore, the positive bonds that he forms in the context of a secret society inevitably are viewed as negative boundaries by former friends who are now 'outsiders.' 'The people that I considered at that time to be friends weren't, because when I joined the club they turned their back on me. So I don't consider them to be friends. They felt I was doing something immoral, something wrong, that I was crazy to do it. Only because they didn't understand what I saw in it' (Caveman, Rebels MC). After riding with the club for three years

I found that I had 'left behind' all personal male acquaintances, with the exception of my best friend, Phil, a policeman who lived in Calgary. Furthermore, being the patch holder of an outlaw club is such an all-encompassing badge of identity that when a Rebel does socialize with former close friends, the topic of conversation inevitably becomes the club. 'I don't have enough in common with them anymore,' related Steve of the Rebels. 'When I go to their places it seems that we always talk about the club anyways because *they* always talk to me about the club. Stuff like "What's the club doing? How's this, and how's that?"' Ironically, when these former close friends attempt to communicate with the Rebel about what matters most to him, it invariably emphasizes the fact that insurmountable barriers do exist. 'I mean, you can only go so far in that category too,' continued Steve. 'There are a lot of things that I don't want people to know about the club, so I just don't talk to them.' As Blues summarized: 'I'll rap with anybody if he's got a good story, but 99 per cent of the time I communicate with my brothers.'

Friendship ties of the past are replaced with brotherhood ties of the future. The striker is expected to get to know and interact with each member on a personal level. To that end, a personality conflict between a striker and a patch holder is never overlooked; but as far as strikers are concerned, the member always prevails. The striker will either change or adapt, or he is eventually asked to leave: 'The club would expect the striker to come around, and this would be watched' (Slim, Rebels MC). Considering the paramilitary cohesiveness of the group, I was surprised at the degree to which they tolerated differences of opinion. The personal exchanges between members were characterized by a no-holds-barred straightforwardness. It was another subtle but effective border marker between the outlaw-club community and the outside world: 'Look, you're going to have to bullshit people out there, and so will I. But we don't bullshit each other' (Clayton). The underlying premise was honesty. When a member was happy, everybody knew it; when a member was angry, everybody felt it. Open lines of communication made for a quality of emotional exchange that was critical to the sense of brotherhood: 'The brotherhood has helped me in numerous ways. Anytime that I've had a personal problem, or a plan, or whatever, I discuss it with a few of my brothers ... I get a few ideas, or maybe they can help me out because they've done that sort of thing before. The brotherhood ... helps you face up to reality. If you screw up, or if you ignore something that's important, you can bet on one of your brothers asking you what the fuck you're doing' (Blues). Most of the brothers would not accept a striker into their extended family until they felt that he was worthy of their honesty and was capable of handling their frankness:

> I feel a striker is ready when I can party with him and say any-thing I want to say to him, about anything at all. That's got to be there. Like with Whimpy, I can say what I mean. Lots of times at the [motorcycle] shop I'll get mad. I've got a wicked temper. He'll say: 'Quit your yelling!' And I'll say: 'You just shut your fucking mouth!' And I know in two minutes later it's all forgot-ten. Whereas if I said that to some striker, he'd go around with a pout on his face for two weeks. You know I just don't have any use for the fucking guy. Who needs him? I don't and the club sure as hell doesn't. (Steve)

The establishment of personal face-to-face ties between all the members ensures the possibility of open communication within the group. This quality of universal communication enables members to create and maintain a working consensus or 'common head space.' 'Each member should take the time to personally go out with the striker, just himself and the striker. He should take the time to get to know the striker personally' (Saint). Radical, moderate, and con-servative factions can be discerned within the Rebel ranks. The interpersonal bonds that exist between all Rebel patch holders serve to counteract the potentially disruptive effects of members forming separate and opposing subgroups within the club. When ideological and personal differences do arise, universal ties of friendship and open communication between the members minimize the tendency towards subgroup polarization. An effective striking period is crucial to constructing a social community whose interpersonal ties have the strength to transcend political issues:

> *Caveman* (Rebels MC): I look back on my striking and it was the best time I ever had: 'Hey striker, get you and me a beer!' 'Hey striker, let's go for a ride!' Everybody was saying 'Let's do this!' 'Let's do that!' When I was striking, I was closer to more members. Well, I shouldn't say that I was closer because I wasn't closer, but there was more ... I wanted to be part of

everything that was coming down. And I feel most members, once they get their colours, they sort of fall into a couple of little factions within the club that are happening.

Coyote: So the members tend to gravitate towards one of the groups after they complete their striking?

Caveman: Right, one or the other groups. Like there's the bandits and then there's the good guys.

The Rebels MC consists of approximately twenty-five individuals, each of whom has a slightly different concept of what the club is all about and what it should be. It is this variation that underlies much of the political rhetoric that takes place at the weekly business meeting. An effective striking period ensures that the divisive forces of intragroup factionalism and polarization are counterbalanced by the integrative forces of a common frame of reference, the brother-hood. What they share as brothers overshadows conflicting opinions or personal disputes. From an organizational perspective, an effective striking period guarantees the club a degree of adaptive flexibility. In effect, an all-encompassing brotherhood enables the Rebels to accommodate ideational and behavioural variation (personal differences) without sacrificing group cohesiveness.

INSTITUTIONAL PARTICIPATION: LEARNING THE POLITICAL PROCESS

After demonstrating that he has both the desire and the ability to fulfil personal expectations as a biker and interpersonal commitments as a 'brother,' the striker is gradually introduced into the institutional level of participation. 'New strikers are to strike one month before being allowed to attend meetings' (Rebels MC constitution).

It is reasonable to assume that an individual's reasons for joining a group initially reflect his own personal wants and desires more than the goals of the organization. The individual must subsequently show that he is willing to modify his personal proclivities in a manner that supports group tasks and complements the group image that members wish to have of themselves. During the striking period a prospect has to demonstrate – as members must continue to display – a willingness to accept some loss of personal autonomy. On one level, a member must acquiesce to the club rules; but more important, a member is obliged to remain sensitive to the opinions of his brothers. While we were working on his motorcycle's carburation system, Wee Albert discussed some of the ground rules for becoming a Rebel patch holder: 'It's an unwritten law that if a brother says you're out of line, you've got to listen. If I saw you laying a beating on someone in the bar, I'd say, "Coyote, you're out of line!" If you kept on doing it, I'd say, "Brother, you're out of line!!" And you'd better straighten out, because for something like that I could have your colours [temporary suspension]; or Steve [sergeant at arms] could lay a beating on you.' A member's compensation for this loss of personal autonomy is his being able to articulate a corporate group identity. He is able to claim the Rebel group identity as his own and fly the Rebel colours.

Striker Jesse failed in his bid to become a Rebel because his perception of what the club was all about – and consequently his behaviour – was too far out of alignment with that of the members. 'Some guys I just take a look at and say: "Fuck, I don't want that creep around!" ... Jesse is a good example ... I didn't want him striking at all ... He's just an asshole. I've seen him perform some very stupid things for no reason whatsoever. Like one time at the bar he jumped up and floored some poor bugger who said, "Excuse me," and tried to step around him ... To me that's an asshole stunt, there's no sense or reason behind it. That kind of bullshit reflects on me [as a Rebel], and I don't need that' (Steve). The Rebel group image serves as a collective referent for a member's personal identity. Jesse's behaviour tarnished the image of the Rebel: 'tough,' but only if and when necessary. Consequently Jesse's performance was tantamount to a personal insult to those members whose sense of self is closely interwined with the Rebel skull patch.

The Rebels will test a striker's willingness to follow orders. These trial situations may involve enacting behaviour that runs contrary both to a striker's personal inclination and to what otherwise would be normal club expectations. For example, a striker may be removed from a fight involving members and outsiders and be told to stand there and watch. 'Caveman's hauled me out of three fights when I was a striker. Once he says: "You stay between those two cigarette machines and you don't move!" I literally had to stay in between the two cigarette machines, and I didn't move' (Wee Albert). Each Rebels striker is given a copy of the constitution and has access to the Book of Rules, which is kept within the confines of the clubhouse. However, learning and adjusting to how the club functions is not merely a matter of rote memorization and adherence to a codified set of formal rules. Rather, it is 'just something that's gained from experience, from being around. There's nobody that can rattle off the rules, rule for rule, except for maybe old Terrible Tom' (Dale). What the striker 'gains from experience' is a knowledge of what anthropologists would call 'cultural themes': ideational and behavioural generalizations that serve to integrate and organize the culture as a whole. The themes that are crucial to a striker's successful integration into the club are love of biking, love for your brothers, and a love for the club. These are the core values that hold the club together. By virtue of their generalized nature, these themes can guide a striker's decisions in novel or unfamiliar situations that have no regulatory directives or personal precedents. In effect, these subcultural themes enable a striker – and later the member – to interpret and generate behaviour in a fashion that is consistent with the collective expectations of the group.

If, after a month of striking, a Rebel prospect is judged to have respected the club's rules and to have remained sensitive to his brothers' opinions, he is admitted to the weekly club business meetings, the arena of formal club politics. The first meetings that a striker attends introduce him to procedural rules and the format that meetings follow.

For many members the club becomes a collective leverage against the conventionalism and restrictions of the host society. But 'freedom' for a Rebel patch holder does not mean unrestricted and random behaviour. The Rebels MC is not an invitation to political anarchy, just as the brotherhood is not an invitation to social apathy. One of the most important lessons a striker learns is that Rebel society does not offer him a flight from social and political responsibility; it offers a route towards meaningful participation. Attending a club meeting will introduce the striker to the ground rules of Rebel political power. He is given a first-hand introduction to the fact that the Rebels' formal decision-making process is based on open discussion and democratic rule. This democratic format allows members to innovate, evaluate, and control group policies. It is this aspect of ideological participation that allows members to say: 'The club gives me the freedom to do what I want.' A striker learns that he is not expected simply to conform to club policy; rather, he is expected to take an active part in deciding that policy. The opinion of the members about whether or not a striker has a genuine concern for the club will be influenced by how aggressively he takes part in the political decision making that affects the club's future. 'What really

impresses me about a striker is when he gets up and voices his opinion ... I don't give a positive vote for a striker until he gets up and
says: "No, I feel that's wrong!" or "Yes, I feel that's good!" Strikers
aren't encouraged, though, they're just watched' (Indian). Once the
striker begins to take an active part in shaping the club, then it truly
becomes 'his club.'

An astute striker will come to realize that in order to find institutional freedom in the Rebels MC, he must first participate in the
formation of its policies and rules.

The weekly business meetings provide the striker with information
about a variety of topics that concern the club, ranging from 'what
the brotherhood means' to strategies for dealing with 'police harassment.' Group discussion will reinforce the importance of these topics
to the striker and, one hopes, elicit his personal and formerly private
inclinations. Active participation in the consolidation of opinions
among like-minded individuals can be expected to lead to greater
personal commitment on the part of the striker. For example, the
open discussion that preceded the Rebels' demonstration run to the
Alberta provincial legislature to protest mandatory helmet use led to
the exchange of new information and the reinforcement of the members' resolve to overturn the existing legislation. Ideally, the striker
will express his personal experiences, concerns, and insights, and he
will continue to shape these in a manner that is consistent with the
viewpoints presented by the patch holders.

The severity of the entrance requirements and the length of the
striking period will vary according to the membership needs of each
club. The size of outlaw motorcycle clubs will range from ten to thirty members. For sound reasons there are few exceptions. Having less
than ten members leaves a club vulnerable to outside threats, such
as the formation of new competitive clubs within their territorial
base. Conversely, having more than thirty members would necessarily dilute the quality of the interpersonal bonding that forms the
community basis of the club. The logistical restraints imposed by
limited time and resources effectively limit the size of group that is
capable of maintaining intense face-to-face personal relationships.
After a club reaches that point, any further gains achieved by a
'strength through numbers' policy will ultimately serve to weaken
the social fabric of the brotherhood. Club members consciously
attempt to avoid either extreme as far as numbers are concerned:
'The voting procedure [number of positive votes required for mem-

bership] never changes. What changes is the attitude of the members. It's sort of a feeling that everybody has. Like nobody stands up and says: "We need more members!" or "We're big and strong, we don't need more members." Everybody knows what the story is and just sizes up the situation' (Wee Albert).

Outlaw motorcycle clubs evolve. Older, more established clubs can generally afford to be more selective in their recruitment process than newer clubs. Conversely, the immediate priority of a newly formed club necessarily becomes one of establishing credibility and enhancing survival through numbers. During the course of my four-year association with the club, the Rebels kept their membership between twenty-two and twenty-five active members. Breaking into the Rebels' line-up in 1991 is a more formidable task than it was in 1980. The club has been in operation for twenty-two years and features a very strong nucleus that can afford to be increasingly selective. Today it may take several years for a Rebel prospect to meet entrance requirements that have become even more stringent. The entrance requirements of established clubs also make infiltration by law-enforcement agents a difficult and dangerous venture: 'Our officers have been largely unsuccessful in their attempts to infiltrate these motorcycle gangs' (W.T.F. Sherman, superintendent, O Division, RCMP).

The immediate impact of having a striker goes beyond providing the club with numerical stability and its members with somebody to perform menial tasks, such as doing all the 'shit jobs' around the clubhouse. The striking process by itself serves to revitalize the group. Striking is a communal activity in that all the club members become involved in the collective socialization of the novitiate, and are expected to become actively involved as instructors. As teachers, the members must be prepared to define what being a Rebel is all about. This problem of definition cannot be left to intuition; there is an explicit set of values and an outlaw-biker philosophy that members are compelled to share and communicate. Through words and action all the club members are involved in communicating the collective social identity of the Rebels MC. Participating in the socialization of a striker means that each member must review his own image of the ideal club biker. More important, each patch holder will in turn be forced to compare his ideal with the reality of his own personal performance. When a patch holder tutors a striker he cannot avoid rethinking what being a Rebel means to him. For his part, the prospect must meet stringent entrance requirements that involve a variety of commitment-building practices. For their part, members must embody and exhibit those community standards that they are asking the striker to commit himself to.

The progress of a Rebel striker is discussed by the membership at large during the course of the weekly club meetings, at informal gatherings in the bar, and at various impromptu congregations of members. The striker himself continually receives feedback from members on a personal basis: 'A striker is told how he's doing. I'll personally tell him if he's fucking up, or if I think he's got his shit together' (Voodoo). Members recognize that bonds of brotherhood and personal commitment take time to mature: 'The strikers, and even some of the younger members, will just go through the motions, but it takes time. It takes time for them to realize what the actual meaning is' (Blues). Each member has to decide whether the striker has shared enough experiences and built enough bonds of trust to warrant becoming a Rebel patch holder. When I asked Wee Albert how he personally decided when a striker was ready for membership, he replied: 'It's got to be a natural thing, you've got to feel that he is your brother ... When I catch myself calling him "brother" instead of striker.'

Members of the Rebels MC executive board – club officers – have the responsibility of monitoring the members' personal opinions and evaluations of the striker. If the executive members decide that there is an informal consensus among the members as to what should be the fate of the prospect, they will call for a formal decision to be made. At the next business meeting the prospect is told to leave the clubhouse and a membership vote is held. The vote takes the form of a secret ballot on which members can exercise one of three options:

✓ = membership
0 = continue striking
X = terminate club association

These choices allow for a number of options to be exercised on the future status of the prospect:
- more than five X's, he's asked to leave the club;
- more than two X's (but less than five), he continues to strike;
- more than two 0's, he continues to strike;
- less than two X's and less than two 0's, he is granted membership.

A ruling in the Rebels MC constitution ensures that this vote will reflect the will of the membership as a whole: 'Quorum for a meeting is sixty percent of membership. Eighty percent for membership votes.'

Given an average membership of twenty-four, less than two X's (terminate club association) and two 0's (continue striking) represents 92 per cent approval of the striker applicant. The high percentage of approval that is required reflects the selectivity and stringent requirements of the recruitment process; furthermore, it ensures that the all-embracing bonds between members – the social fabric of the brotherhood – remain firmly entrenched.

During the course of the 'discussion on striker,' voting, and tabulation, the prospect has been nervously awaiting the results outside the clubhouse. For the prospect these are tense moments. He has invested perhaps a year or more in 'taking every kind of shit imaginable,' one year in hard-core 'jamming' (biking) and partying and learning what it means to be a club biker. His thoughts are suddenly interrupted by the sergeant at arms: 'Come on, Striker! You're wanted inside!' The striker is escorted back into the general meeting and solemnly informed of the club's decision by the president. If the prospect receives the necessary 92 per cent approval for membership, the announcement is greeted with a lot of shouting and laughing as the striker is doused with beer by his new brothers. The first thing the Rebel striker sees when he looks up through eyes stinging with beer is the president standing in front of him with his club colours – the Rebels' skull patch – and preparations are made ready for his upcoming initiation.

5

Initiate:
Becoming a Patch Holder

The night you get your patch, the night you don't get any
'no' votes, that's your night to howl. The club has told you
that they can depend on you, and you can depend on
them. You're 100 per cent a brother ... You worked at it so
hard and a lot of the time you figured you're never going
to be accepted, and then it happens ... I was so proud ...
You just feel like letting loose and getting a little crazy ...
Caveman shoved a beer into my hands and said, 'You
made it, mother fucker! Let's party!'
(Gerry, Rebels MC)

All outlaw clubs mark the formal incorporation of a new member
with some form of initiation ritual. The man is near the end of a
series of transformations in his personal status and identity. He
began as a citizen, a 'wanna-be' who separated himself emotionally
and symbolically from the dominant society when he became a biker.
The transition continued when he affiliated as a friend of the club
who was then allowed to become a striker in order to earn his
colours. The final stage is his accceptance into the club and the lives
of his brothers as a patch holder. The initiation ceremony dramatizes
this change for both the new member and the club.

Outlaw clubs initiate new members in different ways. The Satan's
Choice have an Initiation Night, the King's Crew hold a Colours Party,
and the Rebels ride on an Initiation Run. While clubs have always
differed somewhat in terms of the specific activities they include,
over the past two decades there has been a noticeable change in the

degree of intensity and function of the initiation ceremony for all outlaw clubs. In the 1960s and early 1970s striking periods were relatively short. For example, the average striking period of the Satan's Choice MC in 1973 was only three months. Outlaw clubs of this era compensated for the brief socialization period by having a backup, one final assurance for the club. This took the form of a test-by-fire initiation that would impress upon the novitiate the organizational imperative of club solidarity – 'Act the way we tell you to act or forget it! Fuck off now, if we see you on the road you're dead!' – and the structural necessity of strict border maintenance – 'You've gotta be one of us now! You can't be one of the outsiders' (Jack, president, Satan's Choice MC). The initiation of Gypsy into the Satan's Choice in late November demonstrates this sort of group control:

> They decided that I was going for a swim in the Skeena River. I had no choice in the matter. They tied this rope around me; they said they wanted to be able to pull me back in case I drowned ... When I hit the water it was so cold that I couldn't even breathe! ... Everything turned black and I was scared ... They began to pull on the rope.

It was also a test of personal courage:

> I go back to the clubhouse ... and they said: 'Go outside, Stu wants to see you for a minute' ... He had a fucking brick in one hand and a chain in the other. He says: 'You come at me or I'm gonna kill you!' ... I dove at the fucker. He roughed me up a bit, got up, and shakes my hand and says: 'I wasn't going to hurt you at all. I just wanted to see if you had the guts to stand up to me.'

And it provided a sample of the pleasures that are to be had by those that are accepted by Satan's Choice: 'Mac tells her to get on her hands and knees. He tells her to crawl over and give him a blow job. While she's sucking away, Stu gets some tranny oil and lubricates her asshole. We took turns screwing the ass off her.'

Initiation in the 1980s features less in the way of tests and trials and more in the way of jovial hazing and celebration. The psychological and behavioural manipulation that took place during the course of a sometimes violent initiation ceremony in the sixties and early

seventies is more assuredly accomplished by a longer period of pre-
membership association in the eighties. Anyone who strikes for the
Rebels in the nineties can look forward to two years of being a
prospect, while a biker may have to be a Hell's Angel prospect for up
to three years. There is no need to have an initiation that psychologically shocks the initiate into alignment with the club's expectations. There are no more questions to be asked.

The Rebels MC Initiation Run is a collective celebration, three days
of riding, camping out, and heavy partying. The Rebels recognize
that their initiation run involves more than good times, and they
have made it a mandatory run with compulsory attendance. All
members must participate in this ritual that confers and affirms
membership. As members of a small, tightly knit community that
must maintain rigid boundaries with the outside world, they cannot
afford to have any doubts about the impact the new member will
have on group integrity. There can be no weak links in the chain of
group consensus, real or imagined. Each member has voted his
approval of the prospect, and now each member not only observes
the formal change in status, he takes an active part in confirming it.
That action makes the initiation a collective statement of confidence
in both the new brother and the brotherhood.

Steve and Gerry's joint initiation is a typical example of the Rebels
in action. After the two strikers were voted into the club, the veteran
patch holders began to make preparations for the initiation run.
Destination's end for the run was Amisk Lake, a secluded campsite
located in the forests of northern Alberta. For several days the world
of the two initiates would be that of the outlaw biker. Steve and
Gerry were effectively isolated from all statuses and patterns of
interaction that had anything to do with the straight world. Moreover, the initiation run was closed to outsiders and visitors; it even
excluded the patch holders of other clubs as guests. Only members'
ol' ladies were allowed to come along. Four hours of hard riding
brought the Rebels to a knoll overlooking the scenic lake. Each man
found a comfortable spot and set up his tent alongside his scooter.
Ol' ladies retrieved personal belongings from the crash truck, un-
packed sleeping-bags and cooking utensils, started cookfires, and
began brewing up coffee. Most of the patch holders grabbed a luke-
warm beer and attended to their bikes. Drive chains were tightened
and lubricated, oil levels were topped up, tire pressures were
checked. There was the usual mutual assistance as Whimpy helped

Raunch adjust his carburettor. There was also the usual minor bickering as Danny chided Crash, 'Your bike still leaks like a fuckin' sieve. You should hire out to the government to oil their roads! Whaddaya do, cut your gaskets out of used cigaret cartons?!' What was unusual, however, was that five patch holders were changing their engine oil rather than just topping up. Then I noticed several members had brought out containers from the crash truck and were collecting special offerings. Jim shoved a pail into my mid-section and said 'Hey, Coyote, everybody gets to contribute!' The pungent stench struck me well before I looked down at the contents. Inside the pail was a concoction of engine oil and transmission fluid, grease and urine, STP and shit. 'That's great if you're going to throw up,' laughed Jim as he watched me turn green, 'but do it in the pail. It'd be a shame to waste it on the grass. Haw! Haw! Haw!'

Steve and Gerry sat somewhat apprehensively by the fire, sipping beer and talking about what lay in store for them. In nervous anticipation Steve was using his hand axe to fashion himself a club. He wasn't sure what was going to happen, but 'if those guys think I'm going down easy, they've got a big surprise coming!' There is no set procedure or institutionalized format to an outlaw-club initiation. The initiation is a creative event that allows members to act out personal feelings and affections in group action. Unlike most identity-confirming rituals in industrial society, such as weddings or graduations, no two outlaw-club initiations are ever the same. They are never formalistic or boring. Almost anything goes, and the only limiting factor is the collective imagination of the members. Three large groups of patch holders sat around their collection of pails, mallets, stakes, and rope. There was loud laughter and guffaws as they passed around wine bottles, made suggestions, and deviously plotted. The Rebels' ol' ladies became conspicuous by their absence. What was to follow would be for members only, a final cementing of exclusive brotherhood ties.

Several members suddenly jumped Steve and Gerry. Gerry flailed away at the three Rebels who had him pinned. Steve scrambled to his feet and used his club to ward off his attackers. Voodoo took a running leap and threw himself through the air. Steve felt his legs buckle as he was blind-sided and the ground came up hard and fast; both he and Gerry succumbed to the force of Rebel muscle. The initiates were dragged to a clearing in the bush where they were roughed up, stripped, and then staked spread-eagled to the ground.

They were then marked with ashes and charcoal from the fire – burns were accidental extras. Jim's pails of sludge were brought out and dumped on the unfortunates. A couple of the members took added care to ensure that Gerry's long California-beach-bum-styled blond hair was thoroughly blackened with grease.

The Rebels stood around and drank beer while making unflattering remarks about the initiates' unenviable position: 'Hey, Gerry doesn't look like he belongs on a surfboard anymore!' Some of the members feigned sympathy; they covered their beer bottles with their thumbs, shook them up, and sprayed their victims to clean them. 'Naw, you're wasting good brew doing that,' commented Raunch. 'To make it work you've gotta refine it through your kidneys first. Like this!' And Raunch proceeded to urinate on Steve. Despite Raunch's 'good intentions' that technique didn't work either: 'Boy, the STP sure holds that shit on, no way they're ever going to get it off!' 'Maybe we should just strap them to their bikes and make them ride through a car wash,' suggested Ken. Steve and Gerry eventually were cut loose, herded to the lakeside, and cast in.

The Rebels had just stripped, pummelled, and ridiculed two men they called 'brother.' Why? In effect, the patch holders use this part of the ceremony to strengthen two aspects of the club-member inter-face that underlie their survival as an organization. The first relates to the ability of the club to exercise control over its members; the second concerns the interpersonal bonding between brothers. Both of these elements had been stressed and tested during the striking period. They are now acted out in ritual and symbolically reinforced.

Hazing conveys club regulation and demonstrates club control. The club members made a strong statement about their being a separate entity unto themselves when they symbolically stripped Steve and Gerry of their former striker and citizen status. In sequence, the events follow a transitional theme of ritual death and rebirth within the context of the group. The initiate dies as a member of straight society and is reborn as a Rebel. The physical beating and hazing symbolizes the subjugation of the individual to the dictates of the group, in defiance of the authority of the larger society from which they have emerged.

On a more personal level, hazing promotes emotional bonding among brothers, old and new. Hazing and rough-housing can destroy personal defence mechanisms. By creating situations that cause the initiate to experience the shock of sudden vulnerability and the loss of personal control, the members break down barriers to psychological connectedness. Steve and Gerry were literally stripped of any pretences of personal power. For a few brief moments they were cut off from anything that defined and separated them as individuals. Under these conditions they were both suggestive and receptive. The lowering of defence mechanisms psychologically opens the initiate to communicating with his brothers on a genuine, straightforward, gut level. Open communication leads to a depth of trust in one another. In turn, this trust enables the Rebels to give new members the freedom to act on their own and the responsibility of being a brother.

By itself, the simple act of breaking taboos against physical contact can efface the remnants of any emotional barriers that might still exist between members. For example, prior to the initiation run I had always felt somewhat intimidated by Steve's raw personal force. We tend to turn our emotional inhibitions into bodily inhibitions, and my behavioural style around Steve was unduly reserved. During the course of the initiation run I found myself wrestling with Steve. I knew that I was overmatched. While I could bench press 225 pounds he could do over 300 and was a vicious street fighter. But I had made a point of remaining sober – Steve hadn't – and I pressed my advantage quickly and pinned him. Our grips loosened and we fell back laughing and exhausted. Striker Mike brought us a couple of beers, we drank a little, and poured the remnants on each other. Danny, who was watching the proceedings, commented to Steve that 'he [Coyote] got you down but he's still fucking sober.' To my surprise, Steve supported me. He looked at Danny and said, 'Take a look at Coyote's long-legged woman walking around in those tight jeans and that yellow tank top. Jesus, if I had that fine-tanned flesh waiting for me in my tent I'd stay sober too!' We lay there together in the dust and finished our beers. While there had been only a temporary lapse in Steve's defence mechanisms it had long-lasting implications. That short incident erased much of the inhibition that had marked my dealings with him. Sharing peak emotional experiences under these open circumstances greatly enhances the bonding between members; it erases any lingering feeling of marginality that may be felt by any of the brothers.

After they had gotten dressed Steve and Gerry were led to the Rebel campfires where the ol' ladies had been making preparations for the all-night party. There was a banquet of corn on the cob, weiners, beans, hamburgers, watermelon, and fresh pike caught from

the lake. Striker Mike retrieved thirty lake-chilled cases of beer and a
dozen bottles of wine. Since an outlaw club uses the initiation to
dramatize its own separation from the dominant society, the ceremony invariably features the suspension or inversion of conventional
norms. In this isolated camp the Rebels were able to exercise their
impulses towards freedom and pleasure. Their uninhibited partying
featured a free flowing of emotions, language, and behaviour. Members engaged in friendly rough-housing, consumed large quantities of
food and liquor, smoked marijuana and hash, and enjoyed the
sensual pleasures of their ladies by the bonfire. Members' collective
performance during the initiation reinforces their sense of belonging
and sharing experiences. Lasting until early dawn, the celebration
mobilized emotions that would strengthen their sense of community.
A couple of members brought out guitars from the crash truck and
everyone joined in drunken sing-along revelry. A tire was thrown on
the fire, and there was a roar of approval as Ken held up two worn
striker patches and tossed them into the flames.

Steve and Gerry slipped on the cut-off jean jackets that held their
club colours. The Rebel skull patch now rode on their backs. Club
colours are a physical symbol of membership. But more than that,
the colours are a catalyst for outlaw behaviour. They dramatically
change the social and psychological reality of the patch holder.

COLOURS

Jack took a machete down from the clubhouse wall and
cut the sleeves off my jean jacket. Then they gave me my
colours [crimson devil's head on a white background].
When I got my colours it was the proudest moment of my
life.
(Gypsy, Satan's Choice MC)

'Colours' are the official club insignia that a member wears on his
back. An outlaw club's colours comprise three separate sections or
'rockers.' The top rocker carries the name of the club – Rebels. In
the centre is the club emblem – the Rebel skull patch. The bottom
rocker designates either the location of the club or the territory that
the club lays claim to – Edmonton, along with the MC contraction
that stands for motorcycle club. Patch holders sew their colours on

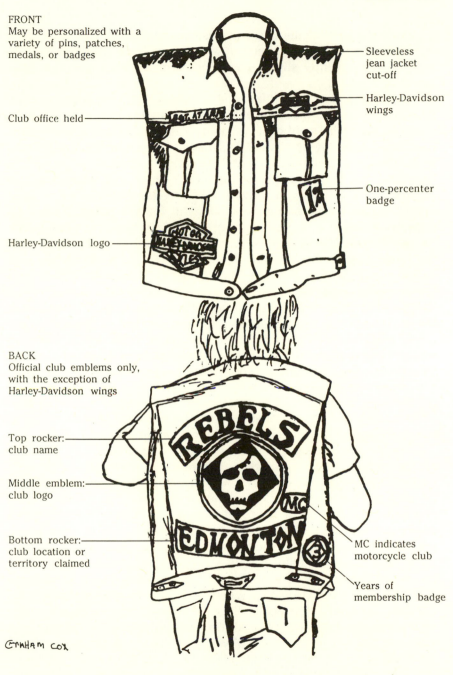

FRONT
May be personalized with a
variety of pins, patches,
medals, or badges

Sleeveless
jean jacket
cut-off

Harley-Davidson
wings

Club office held

One-percenter
badge

Harley-Davidson logo

BACK
Official club emblems only,
with the exception of
Harley-Davidson wings

Top rocker:
club name

Middle emblem:
club logo

Bottom rocker:
club location or
territory claimed

MC indicates
motorcycle club

Years of
membership badge

GRAHAM COX

FIGURE 1
The 'colours' of an outlaw-motorcycle-club member, or 'patch holder,' as
typified by the Rebels Motorcycle Club

the back of a Levi's 'cut-off' (sleeveless denim jacket), or on the back
of a leather vest. The member can wear his colours' jacket or vest by
itself or conveniently slip it over other apparel such as his leather
jacket.

The emblem that an outlaw club chooses for its colours emphasizes its separation from the rest of society as a powerful and élite
macho group. The symbolism is bold. It might feature a skull patch
(Rebels), a laughing devil's head (Satan's Choice), a skeleton holding
a shotgun and handcuffs (Bounty Hunters), a shrouded skull (Grim
Reapers), or a horned and grinning death's-head skull wearing an old
leather flyer's helmet with wings (Hell's Angels). These are images of
death, power, freedom, and rebellion. But for the patch holder the
underlying theme is that of heroism; his colours represent him as the
warrior hero. Regardless of whether the colours depict the skull of
the Rebels or the lion's head of the Warlords, they are symbols of
heroic sentiment that promote feelings of pride. The message is that
the bearer is not afraid of what his symbol stands for and that he has
the 'balls' to make it his ally. To both the cop and the club member
the colours are an unmistakable border marker that locates the
identity of the patch holder outside the social mainstream. In-group
solidarity is reinforced and results in definitions of all others as outsiders. However, from the perspective of the patch holder, equally as
important as the social separation that comes with his colours is the
provision of an aura of élitism: 'The colours separate you from anybody else on the street,' Albert said. 'The purpose of the colours is
to let people know who you are. A Rebel is a cut above.'

Club by-laws stipulate that only the club insignia are to be worn
on the back of the colours jacket, with one exception. Most clubs will
allow their members to sew the Harley-Davidson wings emblem
beneath the bottom rocker. The front of the jacket is highly personalized, with elements of personal meaning and history. It is significant that all these bits and pieces of personal-identity symbolism
are allowed to share a place with the club's emblem on what is
essentially the club uniform. The strength of the club rests on the
members' ability to achieve a balance between their sense of collecti-
vity and their individuality. When a patch holder looks at 'his
colours,' he reads 'his story.' This 'documentary' begins when the
man's colours become soiled during the initiation ceremony. The
stains and scruff marks are a physical reminder of his initiation. In
the sixties, seventies, and early eighties it was an outlaw-club tradition that colours were never washed. The long-standing tradition was

based on the premise that whatever happens to a man's colours becomes part of his personal history. 'The badges and things that are on my colours mean different and individual things that I've done with my brothers ... My colours are a documentary of my life. Even the vibes coming off them that I feel, they tell a story to myself every time I look at [the colours]' (Blues). Faded colours become a testament to the staying power of a man's intestinal fortitude and commitment to the outlaw lifestyle. A veteran rider is a survivor, and he will 'fly' his weather-beaten 'originals' with the greatest of pride. Since the mid-eighties outlaw clubs have undergone a stylistic change that sees members paying more attention to the 'sharpness' of their colours. In the nineties club colours that are judged to be 'too far gone' are to be replaced (Rebels MC Book of Rules). However, a Rebel patch holder may still indicate his seniority in the organization by wearing a small circular club crest that designates his years of membership; for example, '3' or '5.'

Depending on his personal tastes and preferences, any number of pins, badges, or patches may find a temporary or permanent place on the front of a member's jacket. The patch holder who chooses to adorn his colours' jacket in this way can purchase various pins and badges from motorcycle shops or magazine mail-order outlets. Alternatively, he may receive an item from a brother as a token of their valued friendship. Some of these insignia are directly related to the club itself. The most common ones would be a badge indicating that the member is a club officer, for instance, 'Vice President' or 'Sgt. at Arms,' or a sign of his club commitment, such as, 'R.F.F.R.' (Rebels Forever, Forever Rebels).

Bikerdom's most famous emblem is the '1%' (one-percenter) badge, a symbol that represents outlaw motorcycle clubs in general. The 1% badge was created by the Hell's Angels, Gypsy Jokers, Satan's Slaves, and several other clubs in the early sixties to symbolize an alliance they formed in order to counteract a common enemy, police harassment. The American Motorcycle Association had attempted to distance itself from the outlaw phenomenon by referring to its members as the 99 per cent of motorcyclists who are respectable citizens; outlaws were labelled as a 1 per cent deviant fringe element. The Hell's Angels and their allies welcomed the badge of distinction and proceeded to have it tattooed on their arms. Today, use of the 1% emblem is confined to the élite of outlaw bikers and designates members of hard-core outlaw clubs who are 'capable of taking care of business.'

A variety of items reflect the outlaw-biker lifestyle in general, such as a Harley-Davidson wings pin, a 'Coors' beer badge, a '69' sex (felatio/cunnilingus) badge, a '13' drugs (marijuana) badge, a 'FTW' (fuck the world) badge, or a bullet key-chain. Much of the memorabilia amounts to a theatric display of personal power, such as a silver mercenary medallion that features a dagger embedded in a skull. Some of the symbolism is worn strictly for its shock value or its effectiveness as a border marker, perhaps the most infamous of which is the display of Nazi paraphernalia, iron crosses, and swastikas. Bikers who wear these Nazi symbols will give different reasons for doing so, such as 'They were strong and fearless,' 'It just looks good,' or 'White Power.' None of the reasons would be definitive, none would be political. While outlaw bikers indeed are politically right-wing and conservative, they are neither Nazis nor neo-fascists. Outlaw bikers consider themselves to be highly patriotic. For example, numerous Vietnam veterans MCs are listed and get exposure in various outlaw-biker magazines that also contain regular feature columns such as 'Stateside with Sarge' in *SuperCycle*, and 'Nam Notes' in *Outlaw Biker*. A 'White Power' badge, consisting of a white fist on a black background, may also find its way on to a biker's colours. Outlaw motorcycle clubs practise racial separation. While I have never heard of it being formally incorporated into any club's constitution or by-laws, all outlaw clubs operate within a policy that stipulates 'no negroes allowed.' For example, one could go through the thousands of pictures of tens of thousands of bikers featured in the pages of *Easyriders*, *Outlaw Biker*, and *SuperCycle* over the past two decades, and not find a single picture of a single black person.

Colours are forever when they are indelibly fixed beneath the skin. Fifteen of the twenty-four Rebels I knew had the Rebel colours tattooed on their shoulders. Above the skull patch the ink is electronically embedded to spell out 'Rebels'; the date of membership is tattooed beneath the emblem. When the man leaves the club he is required to date the tattoo. Having a club tattoo is optional for the Rebels; for some clubs, such as the Hell's Angels, the practice is mandatory. An interesting variation on this theme is provided by a member of the Outlaws MC in Florida who had the full-sized club colours – featuring a skull with piston crossbones – tattooed across the width and breadth of his back. Twelve of the Rebels had the rhombic-shaped '1%' patch permanently etched into their arms. Caveman profiled the Rebel skull on one shoulder, a large cobra and the one-percenter patch on the other arm, while Harley-Davidson wings spanned his chest. Tattooing is as integral as leathers and bikes for the lifestyle of many patch holders, and it is a relatively common practice among the biker fraternity as a whole. A man uses a tattoo to make a statement about his personal identity. While the skin artistry of bikers is both esoteric and varied, there are some common themes. The biker may be making a statement about being a unique individual who is capable of operating outside of society (a skeleton riding a chopper beneath a large F.T.W.). An eagle entitled 'Ride to Live, Live to Ride' is dedicated to freedom of the road, while a stalking leopard or a Viking with sword drawn conveys personal power and an image of the warrior hero. Tattooing is the most perm- anent, if not the most personal form of artistic self-expression. 'It's always there; every time I look at my shoulder I'm reminded that I'm a Rebel,' said Gerry as he gazed at the skull patch. 'I guess part of me always will be.' The fact that the symbol is made an inseparable part of his self, forever etched in layers of skin, makes the in- corporation of the qualities portrayed by the symbol into the man's psyche all that much more real.

In addition to the colours, outlaw clubs will supply their members with a variety of club paraphernalia. For twenty dollars a member can buy himself a Rebels' T-shirt, a black shirt with a small version of the skull patch on the right side. Outlaw clubs also make courtesy cards available to their members (see figure 2). These cards feature the club emblem and, as long as they are signed in ink, can be given out at the discretion of the member. A classic example was a card that I received from Roach of the Outlaws MC of Chicago. It features the Outlaw skull-and-piston crossbones emblem on the left side of the card. In the middle of the card is the outline of a triangle showing a forearm with a swastika on the back of a fist that has the middle finger raised, a gesture meaning 'Fuck you!' Printed in the three vertices of the triangle are the letters 'O,' 'A,' and 'A,' a contraction for Outlaw Association of America. At the corners of the card are the numbers '69,' '13,' '88,' and the '1%' symbol. On the back of the card is printed 'You Have Just Had the Honor to Meet *Roach* of the Outlaws MC.' A courtesy card may contain a traditional phrase such as 'When We Do Right, No One Remembers. When We Do Wrong, No One Forgets' (Spokesmen MC, North Saskatchewan), or an anecdotal comment such as 'A Brother's a Brother Regardless of His Colours' (Road Rebels MC, Spartanburg, SC) or 'Heaven Don't Want Us; Hell Is Afraid We'll Take Over' (Devil's Saviours MC). Another very popular item among patch holders is 4 by 3 inch club stickers. The Rebels

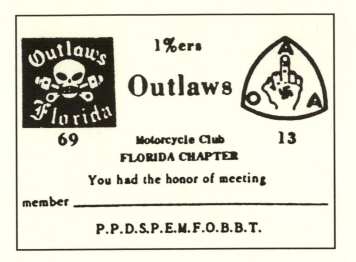

Outlaws MC courtesy card that features 'Charlie' their club emblem, a skull, and crossed pistons

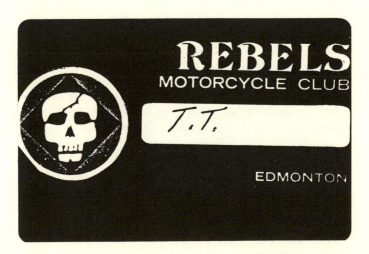

Rebels MC courtesy card (signed by T.T., Terrible Tom)

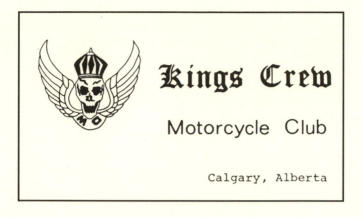

King's Crew MC courtesy card

FIGURE 2

would place these stickers on the oil tanks of their bikes in order to discourage theft and vandalism. In this manner, the member's motorcycle – a foundation-stone of his identity – becomes more than 'my hog'; it is now 'Rebel iron.'

Outlaw colours are a powerful symbol that focus both identity and values. The prospect who earns his colours inevitably views the process as his not only having achieved membership in a club, but also having 'found himself.' 'I was green when I first came into the (Satan's) Choice,' recalled Gypsy. 'You learn a lot ... from growing up and finally getting an idea where your head's at, to knowing what direction you plan on going.' For many of the patch holders whom I knew, the fact that their voyages of self-discovery had taken them outside the realm of polite conventionalism made it all that much more satisfying. If nothing else, the transgression of social norms conveys the impression of personal choice. Their pathway to a 'deviant' identity satisfied feelings of having to transcend the institutionalized and go beyond the ordinary in order to find themselves. Undertaking an identity venture 'on the wild side' of social rebellion imparts a feeling of self-control, the freedom of having chosen one's own destiny.

When I first met the guys I was not going in any particular direction at the time ... With a club you definitely have to make a choice. You have to decide where your head's at, where your commitments are. You have to sit back and organize your life and say: 'This is where I want to go.' A lot of people go through life without really reflecting on what they're all about ... A lot of them do want to change, but they won't because society won't let them. We do what we want to do, when we want to do it ... They [straights are] like sheep. Maybe they're right about some things and we aren't, but that doesn't change the fact that they're like sheep. (Blues)

For young men who share Blues's sentiments, wearing a club patch becomes a personal declaration of independence, of not being compromised, a symbolic leverage against the pressures of a society that has done them no favours.

When a patch holder flies his colours he changes the reality of his social world along with the way he deals with it. He escapes from the everyday into the special world of the outlaw where the bonds that hold him to his duties in everyday life, such as work and family, disappear. He breaks the confines of conventional society, which has failed to provide him with enough in the way of ultimate thrills, meaningful experiences, and a sense of self that sets him apart as a distinct entity. Colours inject his life with intensity and intrigue, and reduce the frustration of ordinary roles by evoking heroic imagery. They bestow upon the patch holder a personal and public image of male independence, power, and adventure. No matter how mundane the activity might be, wearing his colours while doing it allows him to act out these biker traits that might otherwise be repressed in the turmoil of day-to-day frustration and remain unexplored. It doesn't matter whether he is sitting in a McDonald's ordering a hamburger, riding down the street to a car wash, or strutting into a bar, his colours put him on stage. Not only is he conscious of the fact that he is accountable to the club for his personal behaviour while he wears his colours, he is also well aware of being closely watched by outsiders. He knows that he will be admired by some men and condemned by others. He thinks that some men will despise him in order to hide their envy. He will be intriguing to some females and repulsive to others. He believes that some women will loathe him in order to quiet the allure of capturing the love of a 'wild and mysterious' rebel who has the substance to break the chains of conventionality that they fear. During his career as a patch holder he inevitably will run the full gamut of these responses, from being attacked by a 'sidewalk commando' in some smoke-filled bar, to making love to a girl who rode by in a red sports car and then slowed and signalled him to follow. The specifics don't matter. What matters is that when he puts the club patch on his back his every move takes on meaning because his every action gets a reaction.

The outlaw who flies his colours is psychologically transformed. For the rest of his remaining days in the club, the colours will actually magnify the member's ability to perform as a patch holder. On one level, the colours act as a uniform that conceals the limits and inadequacies of the members' concept of self, giving them an aura, a collective power. They aren't just Steve and Gerry any more; they are Rebels. The colours reinforce many features of the outlaw's presentation of self, including the way he carries himself, the sureness of his posture, the energy in his gestures, and the authority in his voice. It would indeed be difficult to put on the colours of an outlaw club without adding a dimension of reserved heavy-duty-cool to one's body image and social performance. 'With those colours on your back you represent the whole club,' stated Larry of the Rebels, 'so everything you do is done with pride.' But while this explanation of the transforming capacity of the colours is a good place to start, it is only part of the psychological story. More important, the reader should not fixate on the metaphor of 'uniformity' that I have used, for by itself it is misleading.

Colours do not so much cloak a member in nondescript uniformity as act as the connecting point between the member's personal identity and the group identity of the club. The colours become the symbolic interface between the individual and the group. As the link between a member's personality and the image he has of himself as a patch holder, the colours act as a psychological catalyst. They stimulate two psychodynamic processes. First, the colours draw out aspects from inside the psyche of the member that otherwise would be repressed. Second, they enable the member to go beyond the boundaries of his self in order to incorporate qualities of the group identity that he might otherwise be unable to achieve. The colours are a member's mask, his licence to perform on the stage of outlaw theatre. On the one hand, he feels less inhibited about expressing hidden parts of his psyche under the guise of the wild-eyed romanticism of the biker image. On the other hand, the patch holder takes on the spirit of the colours, becoming the embodiment of the character of the outlaw patch. When a patch holder puts on his colours he is invigorated by a sense of purpose and direction. The ambiguities and shades of grey that he has to deal with in his daily life are replaced by vivid clarity. 'You know who your friends are, you know who your enemies are,' recalled Tramp of the Rebels, 'and you know how to deal with both.' The influence of colours on a patch holder's sense of self will go beyond club activities. Because aspects of personality are never totally discrete or self-contained, the psycho-behavioural changes that come with the colours, such as an enhanced sense of personal power and prestige, will inevitably spill over into other areas of the member's life. This is another subtle aspect of Tramp's statement that 'the club allows me the freedom to be who I want.'

For many club members the club patch symbolizes the psychological fact that their personal identity has become inseparable from that of the club. The colours become part of who they are, ingrained in the way they think, act, live. There is no distinction between their sense of self-esteem in being righteous patch holders and the 'love' they feel for the club. Club colours blur the boundary between the patch holder and his club; the fabric of the felt patch merges personal identity with group commitment. 'My colours are an embodiment of my feelings for the club, all my love for the club. That patch on my back means that I'm a Rebel. I love the club and the patch is the symbol of the club' (Raunch). Like many of the Rebels, Raunch used the colours to transcend his own feelings of loneliness. Feelings of connectedness and the sense of a shared common fate are necessary for the survival of the club. The colours ground these feelings in a common identity and a shared perspective. When a member faces a threatening situation by himself, the colours act as a physical reminder that he is not alone. Notions of duty and honour stem from the colours. Colours remind the member that every freedom that the patch provides him with comes with a responsibility. When a man rides with his colours he rides with a moral obligation to be willing to take risks and face all odds in order to defend his club and his brothers.

Wearing the colours of an outlaw club means that the power and reputation of the club become part of your personal force. When dealing with outsiders, the psychological edge of the club patch can be as effective as a cocked shotgun. While the club controls its members and comes down hard on those who abuse the power of the patch for personal reasons, brothers will always protect a brother under any circumstances. 'If a citizen hits your brother, you will be on him without asking why' is an outlaw-club rule of survival. 'Your brother isn't always right, but he is always your brother.' The skull patch makes a statement to outsiders that if you start a fight with a Rebel, you lose. The Rebels have a reputation of not losing fights, especially when they involve the club as a whole. But the same distinction sometimes makes the patch holder a marked man. 'Because we value our colours so highly, it's like putting a chip on your shoulder,' related Voodoo. 'You know, knock it off if you dare. You can never totally let your guard down.' Club colours by themselves can trigger hostilities from outsiders and, because both brotherhood and reputation are wrapped up in the patch, a member would be expected to defend them. The situation can become particularly risky if your colours are targeted in a war between two clubs. If the conflict escalates to the point where the clubs are exchanging beatings and bombs, then capturing a rival's colours becomes a top priority. In the early seventies when the Satan's Choice and Vagabonds of Toronto were going after each other, they each put a bounty on the other club's colours, no questions asked.

The multidimensional meaning of club colours often results in their becoming a patch holder's most prized and tenaciously guarded possession: 'Let someone try and take them and I'll show you what they mean to me' (Caveman, Rebels MC). How far does the club expect a member to go in order to defend his colours? The patch holder must be willing to bleed for the club. 'A member has gotta be unconscious before you take them off his back,' Wee Albert stated in a matter-of-fact manner. 'I guess there's always the chance that he might literally die while he's doing that.' Depending on the circumstances, outlaw clubs will discipline the member who loses a club crest with everything from a heavy fine or loss of political office to probation or expulsion. At the bare minimum he will be expected to spare no cost or risk in order to get them back. Have the Rebels ever lost a set of colours? 'No!'

The final piece of the outlaw-biker identity puzzle has been set in place. The man has been initiated, he flies the colours of an outlaw club, his transformation is complete. In his mind he is now a folk hero looking for romance, freedom, and adventure with his brothers.

Part Three

THE DYNAMICS OF
OUTLAW SEX AND GENDER

Women and the Outlaws

The newest and fastest-growing phenomenon on the asphalt high-ways of contemporary North America is the solo female rider. Every year more and more women are turning to motorcycles and motor-cycling, *on their own*. For the purpose of mutual companionship and support these sisters of the highway have begun to organize them-selves in groups that are independent of males. The following is an excerpt from a letter to the editorial section of *V-Twin* magazine: 'Our name is Against All Odds MC and our patches will consist of the Queen of Hearts playing card in the background. In front will be two dice showing three and four circles representing the number seven ... We will hopefully show that women can ride motorcycles and still be ladies and that we actually have brains in our heads, not mashed potatoes' (September 1989: 9).

In addition to the emergence of individual clubs, there is a grow-ing number of national associations for women motorcyclists, such as Women on Wheels, Leather & Lace ('Ladies of the '90s, Leather stands for our inner strength, Lace depicts our femininity'), Women in the Wind, and Ladies of Harley (20,000 members and associates). In 1986 *Harley Women*, published by Asphalt Angels Publications, Inc., emerged as a magazine 'dedicated to all women motorcycle en-thusiasts' (October 1990: 3). An increasing number of women bikers are also taking an active role in the policy-making and lobbying pro-cedures of major bikers' political-rights organizations, such as BRO (Bikers Rights Organization), ABATE (pro-choice helmet legislation), AIM (Aid to Injured Motorcyclists), and NCOM (National Coalition of Motorcyclists). Finally, according to *V-Twin* magazine, as of 1990 over one-third of those individuals taking a motorcycle safety course in the United States are women (October 1990: 26).

Little has changed, however, in the world of outlaw bikerdom. The frontier of the outlaw biker 'riding for freedom in the wind' *remains an ostensibly male domain*. The women's liberation movement that emerged in the sixties and crystallized in the seventies and eighties has not yet made any impression on the outlaw subculture. The very chauvinistic attitudes that have traditionally dominated biker ideology remain intact. Formal membership in an outlaw motorcycle club is restricted to males; women do not become members. Women do not participate in official decision making regarding club activities or policy formation, and they do not attend the weekly business meetings. The regular female associates of members do not wear club emblems, nor are they allowed to appear at the clubhouse without escorts. The pervasiveness of chauvinism in the outlaw-motor-cycle-club subculture is explained in this chapter by relating it to the need to (1) ensure the overall psychological appeal of the group to men as an élite organization; (2) minimize the potentially disruptive effects of the male-female bond on the ties of brotherhood; and (3) reduce the occurrence of confrontations with outsiders by maintaining the stereotype of the feared biker.

A man's relationship to the outlaw subculture is a direct one, achieved by owning a hog (Harley-Davidson motorcycle) and earning his colours (club membership). A woman gains entry into the outlaw subculture in an indirect manner, by virtue of her having established social-sexual ties with one or more members. The reason women do not ride their own motorcycles or become club members in the outlaw subculture does not relate to lack of interest, ability, or desire. Rather it is because the fabrication of male and female gender identity and roles within the subculture requires female participation only in a marginal and supportive manner. A man's image of 'machismo' (dominance and aggression) is achieved in part by contrasting it with a woman's image of 'femininity' (subservience and passivity). From a comparative perspective, gender relations defined by outlaw motorcycle clubs are not a radical subcultural departure from but, rather, an exaggerated statement of the traditional values that have dominated North American society for several centuries.

The exclusion of women from formal participation and the pervasive attitude of chauvinism do not negate the importance of the female presence, nor do they result in the complete absence of a female influence. Women who participate in the outlaw subculture fall into one of three major categories: 'broads,' 'mamas,' and 'ol' ladies.' These categories are fundamentally distinct statuses and represent different ways that women relate to the club and to its members. 'Broads' is a general term used to refer to the wide range of women who drift in and out of the subculture. It is an introductory stage of social interaction with one or more members on a casual and usually temporary basis. 'Mamas' are women who maintain an informal affiliation with the club as a whole. This informal affiliation includes social-sexual interactions with the members and, in some clubs, an economic arrangement. 'Ol' ladies' are women who have established a long-standing personal relationship with an individual member. An ol' lady may be the member's girlfriend, covivant, or wife.

The women in these three categories play subcultural roles that meet distinct male needs and result in different types of male-female relationships: from 'loose broads' and 'mamas' who often become the passive objects of displays of machismo and sexual gratification, to 'ol' ladies' who are respected as long-term personal companions, and loved as the active partners of club members. These categorically different roles are often in conflict by virtue of the one thing that they have in common: social ties with the male members. This chapter describes the content of these women's roles – particularly the dominant ol' lady status – and examines how they are integrated within the outlaw club subculture.

MACHISMO: THE MALE MYSTIQUE AND FEMALE IDENTITY

The masculine principle is better understood as a driving ethos of superiority designed to inspire straightforward, confident success, while the feminine principle is composed of vulnerability, the need for protection, the formalities of compliance and the avoidance of conflict – in short, an appeal of dependence and good will that gives the masculine principle its romantic validity and its admiring applause.

(Brownmiller, 1984: 16)

Some guys may join this club as boys, but by the time they leave, they're every inch a man.

(Wee Albert, Rebels MC)

The psychological appeal of membership in an outlaw motorcycle club rests heavily on the club's ability to provide its male participants with a distinct sense of personal identity. As the membership requirements of an organization become more exclusive, so also does the identity; and the more specific the identity provided, the more compelling membership becomes. The outlaw subculture supplies a rich repertoire of symbols and rituals – values and behaviours – that allow an individual patch holder to both locate and define himself as a valid social entity within a distinct group. A critical part of the outlaw image is the male mystique, a quality of being proudly and unabashedly masculine.

All societies take the biological fact of sex differences and construct sexual identities: status positions, role expectations, and personality traits that are ascribed on the basis of gender. The specific nature of the values and behaviour assigned to an individual by virtue of his or her sexual identity will vary from society to society. However, the social reality of the male/female dichotomy rests on a universal process of differentiation wherein masculinity becomes the antithesis of femininity. Anthropologists Spradley and Mann conclude their study of sexual identity and social interactions with the statement that 'masculinity can only acquire its meaning in contrast to femininity' (1975). In order for the outlaw-motorcycle-club subculture to establish itself as a bastion of masculinity, its male participants must distinguish themselves from anything that resembles a female influence or femininity. Furthermore, this extraordinary emphasis on masculinity results in bikers being more chauvinistic than males in the larger society. That is, the achievement of a masculine biker identity is ensured in part by restricting women to a highly 'feminine' presence: 'Femininity pleases men because it makes them appear more masculine by contrast' (Brownmiller, 1984). While women are integral components of the outlaw subculture as a whole, to allow female participation as club members would necessarily dilute the psychological pay-off for the male members. Female membership and competition would break down the gender contrast and result in a blurring of roles, power, and identity. In effect, the presence of women as club members would change the very idea of what a biker is. It would detract from the authenticity of the outlaw biker identity by robbing it of one of its major reference points: masculine prowess. This has not happened. Within the outlaw-motorcycle-club subculture, the activity of motorcycling and the role of patch holder remain exclusively male enclaves.

In the social philosophy of the outlaw-biker culture, being male means being tough. Outlaw patch holders have to be strong and powerful enough to maintain the freedom and independence that they believe underlie the integrity of one's being. The 'freedom ethic' of an outlaw biker is continually tested in terms of persevering in his commitment to the club despite the social censure and moral condemnation that the biker lifestyle receives from mainstream society. For Blues, being an outlaw is synonymous with having the independence to exercise freedom of choice: 'We're an outlaw club because we do what we want to do, and not what the average citizen expects us to do ... In the club's eyes, an outlaw biker means doing what we believe in, not what everybody expects us to be like. After you've stood up for your patch [club emblem] then it's an outlaw patch.' To earn his colours a striker has to go out of his way to demonstrate a commitment to the Rebels Motorcycle Club and the brotherhood under adverse conditions.

There is in our society a constellation of personality traits that are considered feminine. One of these, dependency, in effect makes women unsuitable candidates to meet the challenges of outlaw-motorcycle-club membership. In our culture, boys and men are expected to demonstrate greater degrees of independence and are socialized accordingly. The forces of socialization encourage the converse effect – higher dependency needs – among females. According to psychologist Judith Bardwick: 'The dependency, passivity, tears and affection-seeking normal to both sexes in younger children are defined as feminine in older children, and girls can remain dependent and infantile longer ... Unless something intervenes, the girls will continue to have throughout womanhood a greater need for approval from others. Her behaviour will be guided by the fear of rejection or loss of love' (1979: 51–2). Some of the most conspicuous aspects of personality are related to social definitions of gender; consequently, some of the most pervasive personality differences between individuals are related to the biological fact of being male or being female. As a result of being more sensitized to seeking approval and affection and to serving the needs of significant others, females are disproportionately less likely than males to develop an independent sense of self.

In the outlaw-motorcycle-club subculture a striker establishes his identity by emotionally and symbolically breaking dependency relations with the host society. Because of their dependency needs and the cultural restrictions on their behaviour, women are less likely to make such a radical departure from social conventions. A woman may view her entry into the biker subculture as an act of rebellion in the name of personal freedom; but she is not the rebel, only the companion. She becomes an important part of the outlaw scene, but she never actively defines or shapes it. 'For me it was like a rebellion, mainly against my father and my lifestyle, all the boring superficial people. It was a way to break away from all the rules and more of an opportunity to be myself. I relate to this [biker] lifestyle because you don't really care what other people think about you. I don't feel like I have to do anything anymore that I don't want to ... No, I have no desire to ride my own bike. That would take away from it. I'm perfectly happy on the back. My trip is to be John's woman riding on the back of his Harley' (Marilyn). Marilyn's rebellion is vicarious. Her independence and power are a reflection of her man's and, as a consequence, her freedom is limited by her man. 'John usually decides what we're going to do and when we're going to do it ... Yeah, in a lot of ways I have to be very careful about who I talk to ... I used to be single and very outspoken. That was hard to change. We had lots of arguments about that. But now people who knew me a year ago wouldn't recognize me. I had to become a lot more passive ... The hardest thing to get used to was being told what to do' (Marilyn).

An outlaw patch holder achieves a sense of personal satisfaction and authenticity by being able to stand up resolutely for club values, remaining true to these ideals under adversity. The fact that a woman could do the same would by itself devalue this sense of accomplishment. In effect, female membership in an outlaw club would blunt a man's experience of being set apart by virtue of his having achieved a special goal. In the outlaw-biker community, rebellion as a road to independence remains a male venture. It is highly unlikely that women will ever gain equality in the social philosophy of the outlaw-motorcycle-club subculture; females as equals would shatter the image of a biker as a rare breed of male independence and courage.

In addition to promoting a positive male image and precluding the participation of women in the club on an equal basis, the machismo ideal extends its influence, not surprisingly, into the arena of male-female relations. Women play a role in members' self-definition in that interaction with women becomes part of the process of defining maleness. Male chauvinism is cultivated as part of the machismo ideal: male dominance and aggressiveness are complemented by female passivity and subservience, especially in the area of sexual gratification. The asymmetrical quality of sexual relations reflects the nature and distribution of power in the outlaw subculture. Certain club events in particular feature sex-oriented role performances that express the machismo theme of male power. These ritual perform-ances both define and communicate what is considered appropri-ately masculine and feminine; participation confirms that identity. 'Women are here to serve, so we make them serve ... the first thing we do when a visitor comes to town is to get him a woman to get his balls off, and give him lots of head. At this one party we had, splashing [passing females around in a group orgy] got to be a little boring; so we started pouring wine up their pussy, and we used cunt for wine glasses' (O.J., Coffin Cheaters MC, Sudbury, Ontario). The above example is both exceptional and extreme; most events of this nature are more restrained, such as wet-T-shirt or no-T-shirt contests for women at inter-club parties. The portrayal of these masculine (dominance) and feminine (submissive) traits is not as deviant as may first appear to outsiders. From a comparative perspective, these dramatizations of the machismo ethic are extreme statements of traditional values in the larger society. It is noteworthy that when these intermittent instances of extreme machismo do occur, they are limited to 'loose broads' and mamas; they do not as a rule involve ol' ladies, the long-standing personal companions of members. The presence of these distinct categories of females allows members to separate dramatizations of the machismo ethic from displays of emotional togetherness and companionship that are reserved for their ol' ladies.

WOMEN: A POTENTIAL THREAT TO THE TIES OF BROTHERHOOD

> We have both seen many Hell's Angels come and go, and most of them have gone because of a woman. We both lost our place as Hell's Angels because of a woman – but we made it back. Most of the men don't never make it back ... Our biggest downfall is women.
>
> (Frank Reynolds, secretary, Hell's Angels MC,
> San Francisco, 1971: 79)

> Only a woman can force a biker's allegiance away from his bike, his buddies, and his lifestyle to her. That is why a woman never gains immediate acceptance by either men or women; they must first determine if she represents a threat or if she is willing to accept the biker as he is.
> (Susan, a Grim Reapers ol' lady)

Surprisingly, the major threat to the social cohesion of an outlaw motorcycle club is an internal one: members' personal ties with women. Unless a member's female companion (ol' lady) is effectively integrated within the outlaw subculture, the strong male-to-female bond will compete with the club as an alternative social commitment. Caveman, a road captain with the Rebels, pointed out that the club doesn't always win these competitions: 'I've seen a lot of members fall because of ol' ladies.' Club members work on the assumption that their brothers will not compromise the priority each gives to club participation: 'The club comes first and that's the way it is! It has to be that way' (Blues). When members were faced with a possible one-or-the-other choice in a conflict situation, the club always received priority over outside commitments such as the member's job, other organizations, parents and siblings (family of orientation), immediate relatives, or outside friends. Members did not hesitate in giving precedence to their club commitment, as is exemplified by Steve's response: 'If it came down to a choice between the two? The job would definitely go by the boards. I'd say: "Shove it up your ass!" I'll be a Rebel' (Steve, Rebels MC).

However, when the issue becomes one of the club taking precedence over a member's wife and children (family of procreation), some very significant differences in members' collective expectations become evident. Representing one extreme are patch holders such as Blues and Caveman who believe that club members should not be married while active in the club. For Caveman it was a matter of membership and marriage being incompatible by virtue of the tremendous time and effort that both required: 'Marriage and biking don't mix. If the time ever comes that I want to get married and settle down, I'll quit the club, because I know that I won't be able to put the proper amount of time into both. Like I'd have to be devoted to one or the other, but not both.' As far as Blues was concerned, the idyllic biker existence was one that was not bound by the obligations of marriage: 'There are no biker weddings, only ex-biker weddings.'

There are a number of Rebels who don't agree with this position in either theory or practice. Larry and Steve, for example, are both active members; and the fact that they have been elected to executive positions – Larry as treasurer, Steve as sergeant at arms – indicates that their performance as club members has been 'righteous' in the eyes of their brothers. Yet both Larry and Steve have ol' ladies to whom they are married and with whom they are raising children. Larry furthermore claimed that he would choose his ol' lady and family over the club if the situation arose: 'Yeah, my ol' lady is ahead of the club. She and my family are number one to me.' Steve differs with Larry on this point, and for him the question isn't an academic one: 'It's already come up several times now. She [ol' lady] threatens to leave me because of the club; but in the end, she never does.' For other members, who fall somewhere between these two polar perspectives, the choice is neither an obvious nor an easy one: 'Well, what kind of question [one-or-the-other choice situation] is that, Coyote? Cut off your balls or cut out your heart? I don't really know. I love 'em both. I think it would depend on who pushed me first' (Ken).

The subcultural value of not compromising club participation for the sake of outside commitments is reinforced by the way it is merged with the outlaw biker freedom ethic. Ideally, having no social entanglements – such as a marriage that entraps – allows a biker to revel in 'the magic-carpet freedom of being able to take off any time, for anywhere, on any whim ... [to be an individual who] doesn't fear the wildness of life, but instead is a part of it and free' (J. Via, 'The Last Frontier,' *Easyriders,* December 1980: 30). According to Wee Albert, a Rebel patch holder who is married: 'It's a single man's club with a single man's freedoms. They [vested members] look down on marriage. They like the members to be in a position where if the chick crosses him up at all, he can say: "The hell with you!" and end it all right there; and then move on to someone else.'

These ideals have far-reaching ramifications for the type of personal relationship that members can establish with women. Striker Loud moved in with a woman who was an 'ex' ol' lady of a member of the Warlords MC. It was an affair that eventually led to his expulsion. 'We didn't approve of his ol' lady. We asked that he just drop her at first. Then we saw that he was reasonably serious about the girl, so we just asked that he spend more time with the club ... He was going overboard on this chick and finally he was asked to leave and his striker patch was picked up. We could see that this chick was no good and taking up too much time. We warned striker about this chick' (Snake, Rebels MC).

If a striker is already married his wife will be casually interrogated and their interaction will be closely scrutinized to ensure that there is no conflict of interest regarding the striker's impending commitment to the club. 'Basically, the members want to find out whether the striker can get his own way when they want him to' (Dianne, Wee Albert's ol' lady). Dianne recalls one afternoon when several Rebels rode their bikes over to down a few brews with her ol' man while he was striking for the club: 'Before they'd consider Albert [as a potential member], they put me through the third degree. They'd come over and sort of harass me to see how much I'd take, and to see if Albert got his way when he wanted it. Finally, I just said: "Look, as long as the club doesn't step on my toes, I'll be the last person to step on theirs." They want the women to be around to pour the coffee, make the meals, keep the house clean, and fuck them when they decide to be around. They look on marriage as something perverse.' Dianne referred to her informal interrogation session as 'my very own striking period.'

In addition to looking for reassurances that she will not be an interfering element, the members will converse with the ol' lady with the expressed purpose of deriving information about the striker's character that otherwise might not surface until a later date. 'A man's old lady is a mirror of himself. They've grown accustomed to each other and they think alike. Although a guy may be very interested in becoming a member, he sometimes camouflages his true personality. He may cover up some trait that he might feel isn't good for the club. His old lady will let something like that slip' (Wee Albert).

Providing that it doesn't interfere with his participation in the club, a Rebel's relationship with his ol' lady is formally considered to be his personal affair. However, the impact of group affiliation on a member's decision-making processes can extend beyond both formally organized and collective activities into the area of what would otherwise be considered personal behaviour. As a result of the intensely emotional commitment that an outlaw has to his club, brothers, and biking, combined with his relative isolation from outside social influences, the outlaw subculture emerges as an effective and often exclusive reference group. As an effective reference group the club can and does (1) apply pressure on members to conform to certain standards (normative influence) and (2) provide information on what is desirable and how to act (exemplary influence). By exerting a combination of persuasion, exhortation, and inspiration, the members are able to influence a brother's personal decision making regarding his ol' lady. During the course of a conversation, Dianne and Wee Albert documented an instance of Rebel club members exercising their persuasive capacity:

Dianne: Clayton has been going out with Donna [Clayton's ol' lady] for three years, and been living with her for another two years. A year ago he announced their engagement; but he received so much pressure [from club members] that he called it off. Donna was saying that Clayton was so irritable after talking with his brothers that he was almost impossible to live with; so she returned the engagement ring. The pressure from the club stopped and everything was fine. He's recently gone out and bought her another engagement ring, though his brothers don't know about it as of yet. This will be interesting.

Wee Albert: But Clayton is a solid member and a lot of members will support him.

Dianne: Yeah, but if he shows the slightest hesitancy they'll have his head spinning and [he'll be] a confirmed bachelor in no time.

Wee Albert: He's got to be firm and know what he's doing, and there's nothing wrong in that. But the fact is that the club does not like anything that ties a member down or interferes with the club.

Wee Albert's prognostication proved correct. Clayton made it clear that there was no doubt in his mind as to what he wanted to do either as a club member or in his relationship with Donna. His performance as a 'solid' (dependable) member was without question, and there was therefore no reason to pressure him not to marry. The Rebels attended as a collective and were the best men at 'bro' (brother) Clayton's wedding.

An outlaw motorcycle club must remain cognizant and wary of the disruptive potential that is introduced when a brother attaches himself to a woman. A woman invariably brings with her a social network of non-club associates, obligations, activities, values, and behaviours. Ideally the woman will become integrated within the outlaw subculture as the member's ol' lady. In reality there is always some degree of tension between the ties of brotherhood, biking, and the club on the one hand, and the male-female bond on the other. The situation can become one of competition for the member's time, effort, affection, and other limited resources. If the elements of competition and conflict outweigh the aspects of integration and sharing, then a one-or-the-other choice situation results. When and if such a social drama unfolds, the club will attempt to protect its interests by exerting normative and exemplary influence while acting as an effective reference group. However, the freedom ethic is not a hollow concept and the Rebels can never lose sight of the fact that they derive their collective psychological strength from self-motivated individual commitment. In order to survive an outlaw club must be viewed by its patch holders as a vehicle that 'allows me the freedom to do my own thing.' Thus, while one's brothers are always there to share, advise, and pressure, they respect the fact that it is the member alone who is ultimately responsible for his own lifestyle.

FEMALES, IMPRESSION MANAGEMENT, AND OUTSIDE THREATS

> A man's presence suggests what he is capable of doing to
> you or for you. By contrast, a woman's presence ... defines
> what can and cannot be done to her.
> (Berger, 1983: 45–6)

Outlaw bikers use their negative public stereotype as a border marker to prevent both unwelcome intrusions and unwarranted hostilities by outsiders. The effectiveness of this border marker is based on fear and intimidation. However, the explicit rules and tacit assumptions that are learned by females in our culture run counter to the use of fear and intimidation as a social tool. Women are for the most part unschooled in the art of territorial defence. The psychological effect of a woman's socialization process in North America is to mould a feminine psyche whose resources are geared towards the primary function of providing support. Women are socialized – more so than males – to provide tenderness and nurture and, equally as important, to be passive in their interactions with males. The social result is that women are far less aggressive than men in the areas of speech, dress, body movement, and overall demeanour. To allow a woman to become a member or official associate of the Rebels MC would make her a gatekeeper of a subculture whose territorial boundaries are maintained and respected by virtue of the assertive aggressiveness of its members. A woman wearing the colours of an outlaw club would almost certainly be challenged by outside males. Such a situation would, in effect, expose both the woman and the club to hostilities that would otherwise not materialize.

The one frequently recurring social situation that finds the Rebels in close physical proximity to the public is drinking in the club bar, which is located in a public tavern. The Rebels' response is to stake out a territorial claim on a section of the bar by joining several tables together and occupying them as a group. An outsider entering the bar is hit by a wall of sound and engulfed by patterns of smoky haze illuminated by dim lights. He is unable to make out individual features, only the silhouettes of some very rugged-looking bikers and the unmistakable white skulls of the Rebel colours draped over their chairs. This aggressive presentation by club members effectively curbs any inclinations on the part of curious citizens to be social. In terms of the types of behaviour and range of activities that are available, the bar-room setting is basically a male domain. Women do not establish or maintain territorial claims. One commonly used tool of impression management in the bar is the use of eye contact. A stare from a male constitutes an unmistakable territorial warning to another male, while the equivalent stare by a female could be interpreted as a social invitation. In North American society women customarily avoid direct eye contact with males unless some type of reciprocal social interaction is sought. The fundamental framework of social passivity leaves the woman of our culture in a position of having to play a subtle, coy role, demurely enticing, not assertively aggressive. Steve noted that the members are themselves aware of the psychological dynamics that underlie the maintenance of the social border and its potency: 'Most of your average citizens are afraid of us and leave us alone. They don't have a clue to what's coming down [happening] except for what they've seen in movies and cheap magazines, and that scares them. It's better that people just avoid us. This way I don't have to tell some guy to: "Fuck off, cunt!" when he comes up and says: "Geez, you're an outlaw biker. How many guys have you got in your gang?"' (Steve, Rebels MC).

At their worst, curious citizens can be a 'royal pain in the ass.' Of greater concern to the Rebels is the 'sidewalk commando,' that genre of bar-room patron who is inclined to look for an opportunity to test his street-fighting techniques. For sidewalk commandos, the Rebels – with their heavy machismo image and reputation – present an obvious challenge. However, the known fact that an act by anyone outside the club against any one of its members is considered to be an act against all its members functions to deter most hostilities of this nature. While it is highly unlikely that women wearing colours or insignia would be singled out as targets by these types of individuals, it is probable that the colours themselves would be sought after as trophies. The situation would be particularly dangerous if the Rebels found themselves in a dispute with another outlaw club. Warring clubs have been known to put a bounty on the rival club's colours and forcibly attempt to remove them if the opportunity arises. Few females would care to risk walking or riding the streets with a bounty hanging over their heads. No outlaw club has ever taken the risk of entrusting their colours to a woman. Since its inception in 1969, the Rebels Motorcycle Club has been involved in fourteen territorial disputes with other clubs that have come and gone. The Rebels have yet to lose a set of their skull colours. It is a club policy that if the Rebels do find themselves in a conflict situation, they will attempt to resolve the situation without involving their women. When a brawl between members of the Rebels MC and the Canadian Airborne Regiment erupted at the Kingsway bar, the ol' ladies stayed inside the bar while the members went outside to face their adversaries in the parking lot. If their women wore club colours, they might not be afforded that choice.

THE ROLES OF WOMEN: BROADS, MAMAS, AND OL' LADIES

Broads

The term 'broad' is often used in reference to unattached single women who are engaging in initial or casual contact with the club. This category of women represents a transitional stage of association that will either terminate after one or several social encounters or, alternatively, result in a woman establishing ties with the club either as a club mama or as a member's ol' lady. The somewhat uncomplimentary label 'broad' is not restricted to this subcultural context, but is commonly used for women in general. Nor is the term universally used by bikers. Depending on their mood or what their intentions are, members might use terms such as chick, fox, pussy, bitch, honey, sweetheart, or lady to refer to the wide variety of would-be 'scooter starlets' who drift in and out of the outlaw-club subculture. The number of broads present at any given time will vary according

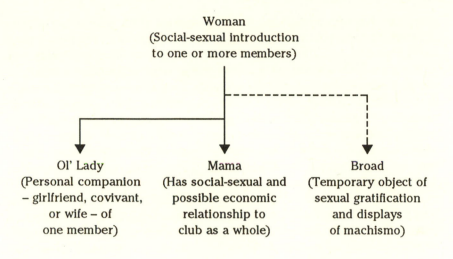

FIGURE 3

The integration of women into the outlaw-motorcycle-club subculture

to the situation, from several women who like to sit with the Rebels at the club bar to any number that members might encounter at a private or clubhouse party.

These women appear to be similar to the bikers in that many of them are young, restless, and bored. One woman who was being 'hustled' by a Rebel patch holder in the club bar offered the following commentary: 'When it comes right down to it, most of these guys are really nice. Some, like Caveman, are pretty awesome; I guess you could say scary. But then that's a big part of it [the attraction]. These guys are action. I get a lot of stares [while riding on the motorcycle] from straight chicks stuck in boring cars; and I just know what their fantasy is. Just being around, being part of the [outlaw club] scene, brings an excitement all its own' (Deborah).

The Rebels present an intriguing alternative, practising their night moves within the shadows of the outlaw mystique. The women themselves are initially attracted to the heavy macho image that the bikers embody, the intrigue of association with an outlaw, the thrill of flaunting social norms, and the partying and excitement of the hedonistic lifestyle.

The majority of broads are transient visitors in the subculture. The full extent of the interaction is usually limited to socializing over drinks at the club bar, 'getting it on' at a club party, and a possible one-night sexual stand. Accepting an invitation to 'go for a ride on my bike' may be extended to a visit to the clubhouse. Providing that the member 'gets lucky,' the visit converts into an overnight stay. As is the case with most outlaw clubs, the Rebels' clubhouse features a 'turnout room' where members who 'get lucky' can complete the sexual liaison in relative privacy. Turnout rooms are generally not very elaborate; typically the contents will include one or two mattresses on the floor, a chair, a nightstand, and possibly carpeting. The Rebels have two such rooms on the second floor of their clubhouse. For a nominal fee members are able to rent one of these rooms as a temporary residence if they so require.

If the girl consents to having sex with the member who brought her, there is the possibility that she – with or without a little 'friendly persuasion' in the form of booze, dope, or covert intimidation – will be shared sexually among several members, a practice known as 'pulling the train.' On one occasion the girl's pink panties were removed and nailed to a ceiling rafter to announce the 'free lunch.' It should immediately be pointed out that, as far as the Rebels were concerned, 'friendly persuasion' was never to include physical coercion. How covert intimidation works is perhaps best explained by one who has experienced it. Cathy, a university coed, was invited by her girlfriend to attend a Rebels' house party:

> I found myself being more passive, more tolerant around the bikers. If it were anywhere else there's no way that I would have behaved like that. I felt intimidated. It was inconceivable that I show any anger. He was a huge guy that they just called 'T'. He physically lifted me up, pulled me to the middle of the floor, and danced with me. I didn't want to dance, but I danced with him. He was a nice enough guy; he tried to be polite; but he was just frightening to look at. I was shocked at how I reacted. It's not like me to be so passive when I'm asked to do something I don't want to. I suppose that I might have freaked out at that moment, but I didn't. I tried to laugh it off ... I just could not say no, all I could do was laugh.

Despite the questionable chauvinistic treatment that they sometimes receive, there never appears to be any shortage of young girls who are willing to risk 'taking a walk on the wild side.'

From the perspective of the club, members try to ensure that the 'sweet young things' that they pick up are at least old enough to be of adult status in a legal sense. One summer twelve Rebels and six members of the King's Crew MC of Calgary made a three-week 'stag run' (males-only motorcycle tour) of the Rockies and west-coast area. One of the clubs that we spent several days visiting and partying with was the Bounty Hunters MC of Victoria, BC. The first night of our stay the Bounty Hunters picked up two girls at a local tavern and brought them over to the clubhouse. The girls enjoyed the attention of the bikers while they drank Cuba Libras. Rum and coke was a Bounty Hunter tradition, as witnessed by the two hundred or so empty Bacardi bottles that lined the clubhouse walls. There was only a mild protest from one of the girls when they were told to strip to the music. The young females swayed to the music of the stereo while they slipped out of their clothes in sensual drunkenness. Their undulating performance was cut short when a Bounty Hunter shouted 'Too slow!' and jumped to the floor to help them out. Two eager patch holders threw the naked women over their shoulders and carried them into a room with mattresses where they were 'turned out,' proclaimed sexually available, to any of the bikers. When the two girls left the clubhouse they were immediately apprehended by the Victoria city police who had been maintaining surveillance of the clubhouse since the arrival of the two Alberta clubs. There was a police cruiser adjacent to the clubhouse itself, another two cruisers at either end of the block, and two plain-clothes officers with binoculars in a hotel room across the street. Inside the clubhouse the Bounty Hunters were using a high-frequency receiver, a scanner capable of picking up short wave, VHF, and UHF transmissions, to monitor the police radio calls. Most Canadian police departments have, as of 1984, made room in their budgets for mobile and portable radios that, when installed and used in cruisers, send out a scrambled signal that only police radios will be able to pick up. According to the radio transmissions that the Bounty Hunters were able to intercept, the two girls were first questioned as to whether they had any complaints and wanted to press charges. When the girls said the visit to the clubhouse was their idea and declined the opportunity to press charges, the police proceeded to check out the girls' identification to confirm that they were indeed of legal age. Had the girls not been of adult status – one was nineteen and the other was twenty – charges of statutory rape and contributing to juvenile delinquency could have been laid against any or all of the patch holders, regardless of whether or not the girls chose to press charges.

Social interactions with broads are usually temporary in nature. They involve the compartmentalization of feelings of emotional warmth in favour of satisfying purely sexual desires. The naïvety of some girls – 'Do you think that he'll still respect me after this?' – is returned with scorn: 'Baby, if you want to be wild, you've got a lot to learn!' There are, however, those patch holders who yearn and search for that 'special lady' who will provide them with the pleasure and security of constant female companionship. A patch holder who is attracted to a particular woman to the extent that he would like to try to establish a steady relationship within the context of sentiments such as caring, affection, and love certainly won't 'turn her out' (share her sexually with his brothers). If the two are successful in this emotional venture and the relationship stabilizes over time, then the woman will be protected and respected by the club as the member's ol' lady. If a woman does not establish herself as an ol' lady, but continues to have social and sexual interactions with a number of club members, there is the possibility that she might be incorporated within the outlaw subculture as a club mama.

Mamas

Mamas are women who have established an informal association with the club as a whole. At the outset it should be stated that the majority of outlaw clubs do not have mamas per se. Among those clubs that do, mamas are the numerically least significant – from one to several – of the three categories of females (broads, mamas, and ol' ladies). The Rebels had one woman, Athena, who could be classified as a mama, over a period of four years. The actual significance of the role that mamas play in the outlaw subculture will vary substantially from club to club.

A mama's interactions with a club are usually limited to those of a social-sexual nature. As distinguished from an ol' lady, who maintains an exclusive relationship with, and 'belongs to' a particular patch holder, a mama has inclusive ties – including sexual availability – with the club as a whole. For example, while the Rebels were partying at the clubhouse of the Bounty Hunters MC in Victoria, two young women visited the clubhouse on an almost daily basis. Brenda, a cocktail waitress, and Helene, a secretarial student, maintained an easygoing relationship with the Bounty Hunters. The two women would clean the clubhouse premises, cook an occasional meal, party, ride, and have 'a good time' with the members. It is part of the outlaw code that the host club will share these females with a visiting club. Brenda and Helene engaged in sexual liaisons with a couple of Rebels whom they found attractive and 'got off on' during the course of our visit.

For a small number of outlaw clubs, the mama role will take on an added economic dimension. The club may require that the mama bring in living expenses. For instance, a mama may donate part of her wage earnings as a waitress, secretary, or dancer to the club coffers. Under certain circumstances the mama may work for the club itself in some money-making venture. For example, several of the twenty-seven chapters of the Outlaw MC that are located primarily in the eastern United States – Chicago, Tennessee, North Carolina, and Florida – operate massage parlours that employ club mamas. A variation on this theme is for any number of members to use mamas to obtain money from the sale of sexual favours. Two members of the Grim Reapers MC in Calgary, Alberta, were recently charged with living off the avails of prostitution (1984). A number of the Hell's Angels MC chapters reportedly utilize mamas to sell narcotics such as methadrine and cocaine. As a rule, however, clubs or members involved in trafficking operations will employ ol' ladies who, by virtue of their close personal ties with members, pose less of a security risk. In return for her various contributions, the club provides the mama with access to drugs, alcohol, and physical protection if required. The element of social support in this arrangement may enable the mama to achieve a sense of belonging in a social community, albeit as a marginal participant.

Once these relations terminate, so too does the mama's affiliation with the club. A woman's role as club mama, especially the aspect of sexual promiscuity, precludes the possibility that a member will consider her as an ol' lady.

Ol' Ladies

Ridin' Free
Forgetting all our problems,
having not a care;
Just enjoying the wind
blowing through our hair ...

> We know there's nothing like it,
> being totally free
> Cruising down the highway
> the bike, the man, and me.
>
> (Bonnie Gaudette, *Easyriders*,
> November 1982: 20–1)

Ol' ladies are the dominant female force in the outlaw-club sub-culture, in terms of both the role that they play and their overall numerical presence. An ol' lady is a woman who has established a personal relationship with a particular member. When a member states that 'this is my ol' lady,' he tells his brothers that the relationship is 'solid' (stable), and that it is to be respected and not to be jeopardized by 'making a run on' (advances towards) the woman. Provided that the relationship is of a permanent nature – or intended to be so – the term 'ol' lady' is used irrespective of whether the woman is the member's girlfriend, covivant, or wife. A woman might be introduced as 'Lorraine, Blues's ol' lady,' or 'Donna, Clayton's ol' lady.' Sixteen of the twenty-four Rebels have ol' ladies: fourteen of these arrangements involve cohabitation, five members are married, and three members have children as part of a nuclear-family situation. The use of the term ol' lady rather than more socially conventional labels, such as wife or girlfriend, has significance other than just creating a convenient linguistic border marker between the club and host society. Within the ethos of the outlaw-biker culture, ol' lady comes to mean much more than a wife and implies some very definite personal values and behavioural orientations.

It is somewhat ironic that while the ol' lady is the most important female element in the outlaw-motorcycle-club subculture, she is also the principal threat to the solidarity of the brotherhood because of the competition she offers. Conversely, the reality that an ol' lady has to face is that her greatest rivals for her ol' man's time and attention are an iron mistress – the motorcycle – and the brotherhood. This rivalry is rarely subtle, and at least once a week it is expressed within the context of formal club activity. Every Thursday night is Boys' Night Out. On this evening the presence of ol' ladies at the club bar or clubhouse is forbidden. The express purpose of Boys' Night Out is to provide an opportunity for members to get together privately – without their ol' ladies – to discuss personal matters and intensify the ties of brotherhood while having a good time partying. During these evenings and similar events such as a stag run, an ol' lady will have to reconcile herself to the fact that her ol' man is out riding, partying, and 'getting it on' without her. During a moment of reflection, Denise, Larry's ol' lady, conveyed the following sentiments to Sandra, my ol' lady: 'Oh, there'll be nights when you'll be lying alone in a big empty bed, and you'll be either swearing sweet somethings at the ceiling or worrying about whether he's dead or alive. But it'll sure feel good when he's home beside you.'

The reactions of ol' ladies to their ol' man's subcultural affiliation will vary along a continuum ranging from resistance and challenge to support and personal identification as a biker's woman. If an ol' lady chooses to resist her ol' man's involvement with the outlaw-biker lifestyle, her own participation in club events such as runs and parties will be minimal. Furthermore, if this resistance becomes too overt and intense – to the point of noticeably interfering with the member fulfilling his obligations – the member will eventually be faced with a one-or-the-other choice between his ol' lady and the club. Alternatively, an ol' lady can accept her ol' man's club affiliation, respect the bond between him and his machine, and become involved in the outlaw-motorcycle-club subculture in the role of supportive companion. This supportive-role position will involve the ol' lady in formal and informal club events and result in her going through changes in personal identity (value and behavioural orientations) that are consistent with those of her ol' man and the collective self-image of the club.

Ideally, the primary concern of an ol' lady is her ol' man. She is expected to accept him as the major decision maker. As a result, ol' ladies assume a secondary position within the extended social network of the club. Within the context of the outlaw-motorcycle-club subculture, women do not act either as initiators or as mediators in social liaisons; all social activities, projects, and ideas are first screened by the man. Most ol' ladies will respond to these restrictions on their social initiative and manoeuvrability within the subculture by maintaining independent (non-club) social ties. In sharp contrast with the members, the more significant personal ties of ol' ladies – measured in terms of whom they would contact for work or leisure activities – tended to fall outside the outlaw subculture. This difference in social network orientation, in particular in the degree to which members become totally encapsulated within the club, can lead to situations of interpersonal discord. The resultant disagreements between a member and his ol' lady are particularly pronounced if the woman feels that the club is becoming involved in what she would like to consider as their personal or family life together. 'We've [member and ol' lady] lived together about five years or more. Call us in love or whatever, but she's definitely the woman for me. But when it comes to the club we clash, we clash very bad. Whenever something [requiring assistance] happens she says: "Oh, I'll go get my dad, I'll go get my brother, I'll go get my aunt." Meanwhile I'll be saying: "I'll go get two or three guys from the club and this'll be all cleared up." Then she'll say: "Why? The club has nothing to do with this!" And I'll say: "What do you mean? The club has everything to do with this!"' (Ken, Rebels MC)

An ol' lady's loyalty to her ol' man extends through him to his brothers. Her home and hospitality are always open to other club patch holders; she may be asked to provide a meal or a 'place to crash' (stay the night), without notice and without question. For example, one Rebel striker, Yesnowski, was provided with room and board by Larry and his ol' lady Denise until the striker was able to find a job and get established in a place of his own. The Rebels will reciprocate the ol' lady's accommodating hospitality with feelings of friendship and respect. They will assist the ol' lady in any way possible and be there as a unit if anything should happen to her ol' man.

The role of a biker's ol' lady will influence her style of dress. The wardrobe is pragmatically selected to suit riding on the back of a Harley-Davidson. The female dress code is very similar to that of a male biker, and includes articles such as blue jeans, T-shirt or tank top, shades, riding boots, jean jacket and/or leather jacket, and gloves as its basic components. A skirt or dress may be worn occasionally, but an ol 'lady must keep in mind that many of her social soirées may still revolve around the club and its 'scooter tramp' members. Choosing such an evening to reveal the latest in vogue fashions would appear somewhat ostentatious. While an ol' lady will never wear club colours, official emblems, or club T-shirt, she will accumulate various other articles of biker paraphernalia. Over time her fundamental biker attire might be supplemented with items such as Harley pins attached to her leathers, a Harley-Davidson eagle wings patch sewn on the back of her jean jacket, biker T-shirts with Harley insignia or sayings such as 'Bikers Have More Fun than People' or 'Genuine Harley Parts' inscribed across the breast, biker pendants, wrist chains, and earrings. There are a number of clubs that do allow the ol' ladies of members to wear a 'property badge' on their jean jackets or leathers. An ol' lady wears a property badge as a matter of choice and prestige. It will usually consist of the club's colour emblem, for example, an Angel's death head, with 'Property of Rogue (member's club name) written beneath the emblem. Like many members who have their club colours tattooed on their shoulders, an exceptional ol' lady may go so far as to have the property badge tattooed on her shoulder or some other area of her anatomy.

An ol' lady must be prepared to adopt the motorcycle as a top priority. This may mean backing up her ol' man's passion for biking in terms of time, sweat, and money. She will have to make certain accommodations; such as when the winter snows silence the Harley engines and her ol' man decides to 'tear down' (disassemble) his 'sled' (motorcycle) and make those repairs and modifications that he has imagined, planned, talked about, and anticipated all summer long. An ol' lady must accept the fact that the motorcycle-mainte-nance role of the male takes precedence over the domestic female role of keeping the house tidy. She should not start to wonder aloud when overly expensive motorcycle parts, greasy tools, and nausea-inducing chemicals leave a trail from the garage, up to the porch, and through the entry hall and end somewhere in the basement (if she's lucky). Raunch was one of three members who solved the problem of spreading his tools around by constructing a ramp over the porch stairway, and then rolling his chopper directly into the living-room: 'It relaxes me if I can work on my tranny [transmission] with the television on. Hah! I guess I do my best work while watching Gunsmoke.' Snake's ol' lady, Melody, who rents the top floor of the house, was none too pleased with Raunch's technical innovation. Melody did admit, however, that Raunch had been considerate enough to place a protective tarp over the hardwood floors. My lady made the following comment on this aspect of learning to live with a biker: 'From talking with some of the members' ol' ladies, I get the impres-sion that one of the first things you have to do is forget about being the best housekeeper on the block. That's not a big deal; and I don't mind you bringing parts of "Harley" to bed and spending some of our time together polishing them. But I don't want to see the decor of our living room changing from early American to late-model Harley-Davidson' (Sandra, Coyote's ol' lady).

Established ol' ladies play an important role in the socialization process involved in integrating novice females into the outlaw-motor-cycle-club subculture. The ol' ladies constitute a loosely defined group that provides both information and psychological support for other women who are attempting to assimilate the ol' lady role. These socialization and support functions become evident during the formal club events and informal get-togethers of the Rebels MC. Outlaw-club activities are similar to those of other organizations and society at large in that, for at least a portion of the time, men and women tend to gravitate into separate gender groups on social occasions. Thus, for example, while the men are locked in the garage having a beer and talking about a bro's bike, the women may be drinking together and playing cards in the kitchen. Overt aspects of socialization would include veteran ol' ladies informing novices of the various subcultural rules of propriety. After a weekend barbecue at the clubhouse, Sandra related: 'Gail [Jim's ol' lady] took me aside and told me that I should never address the [Rebels] club's new prospect as "Striker." She said that I should just refer to him as "Gerry" and that the privilege of calling a prospect "Striker" or "Striker Gerry" was reserved for club members, and club members only.'

Information of this nature familiarizes women with the patterns or themes that characterize the subculture so they can avoid breaching sensitive rules of etiquette. Women can furthermore draw upon the experience of others to formulate tentative behavioural strategies for dealing with as-of-yet unexperienced, or unanticipated, problem situations. While getting a beer out of the clubhouse fridge I overheard one woman advise another on how to exert influence in an unobtrusive manner: 'When (member) chops his motorcycle this winter, make sure that he doesn't get a rigid frame [aesthetically cleaner lines but having no rear suspension]. You'll wind up sitting on one of those little seats [5 by 10 inch pillion pad], and you'll be absolutely miserable. But don't tell him that. Just change his mind by saying how it's such a shame that Randy [Warlords MC] has to wear a kidney belt because he's been riding on a rigid frame for so long.' These sessions also provide a dimension of psychological support by allowing ol' ladies to compare experiences, release anxieties, and share the fulfilments of being the companion of a patch holder.

Informal interactions between ol' ladies may lead to further social encounters in the form of casual visits, getting together for a movie, or going out shopping. Collectively, these contact situations will generate a communications network that will loosely tie together a number of the ol' ladies. However, the ol' ladies do not constitute a tightly knit group. The outlaw-club subculture is controlled by men; men perform the central and important tasks. The female's lack of power leads to role ambiguity; women are defined in terms of the man to whom they belong: 'This is Gail, Jim's ol' lady.' Females are indeed important components of the subculture, but they are restricted to performing supportive tasks as marginal participants. Women in the subculture occupy dependency positions; their presence at club events is permitted only by virtue of male invitation. As in the larger society, the range of behaviours considered acceptable for a woman who finds herself in such a position of dependency and lack of power is limited to an arsenal of 'feminine' weapons. Expressions of sentiment, nagging, crying, displays of helplessness, and other forms of psychological manipulation are used to achieve male compliance or initiative. 'Actually, the women I know who live with bikers have a great deal of power; it's just that the men don't know it. Things like hints and sexual denials and playing on their egos, they all work as long as you don't make it too obvious that you're telling them what to do' (Marilyn, a biker's ol' lady). Interestingly enough, these emotionally dominated patterns of behaviour are thought to be feminine precisely because they fall outside the direct and public route to success and power.

In the outlaw-biker subculture women lack both the solidarity and the power to exercise direct influence as a well-defined integral unit. As a result, relationships among ol' ladies are both derivative and dependent upon the men's club/brotherhood status. The woman becomes dependent on the man for social contact in the subculture; and while most of his friends become hers, her old friends are gradually dropped. 'Most of my old friends are gone,' Marilyn related, 'and all of my new friends that we hang around with I met through John.' In the Rebel community ties between ol' ladies are not independent of club politics. For example, the friendship of Dianne and Gail was close enough that Dianne was the principal architect and organizing agent behind Gail's wedding. Nevertheless, when Dianne's ol' man quit the club, her friendship and interaction with Gail stopped.

There is tension between ol' ladies wanting to protect their steady relationships with members on the one hand, and mamas whom the ol' ladies 'affectionately' refer to as 'sleaze bags,' on the other. The ol' ladies maintain an informal communications network among themselves that provides them with information regarding their ol' man's activities and monitors the behaviour of potential female rivals. If the situation demands action, ol' ladies will make things very uncomfortable for any broads or mamas with indiscreet designs. In one particular instance, Donna, Whitey's ol' lady, was informed by Gail, Jim's ol' lady, that a club mama by the name of Athena was continually offering herself to Donna's ol' man. The following Friday evening, a very infuriated Donna cornered Athena in the clubhouse: 'Well, look what the cat brought in! Gee, I didn't think that they allowed such a little snatch like you here in the clubhouse. Well, tonight you get yours, you little cunt-faced sleaze!'

Donna picked up a pool cue and rushed towards Athena. The male members found this behaviour very amusing and, at this point in the social drama, had lapsed into varying stages of emotional disintegration ... most were on the floor laughing. Steve, the sergeant at arms, managed to recover in time to restrain Donna: 'Hey, Whitey! If your ol' lady wants to kill Athena, that's fine; but tell her to use a broken beer bottle or something. That's an A-1 quality pool cue [stolen from the Kingway bar] that she's got there!' Donna, embroiled in feelings probably best left unexplored, retreated to a corner of the clubhouse with a couple of sympathetic ol' ladies.

The way that a group reacts to internal conflict will reflect the relative sociopolitical power of the parties involved. While conflicts between male patch holders were considered serious business, conflicts among ol' ladies were treated lightly – at least in public. However, although the incident mentioned above was considered amusing on the surface, action was taken to support the ol' lady in that Athena, her rival and source of conflict, was expelled from the group. This came as a concession to the collective pressure of some very indignant ol' ladies. The patch holders persuaded Athena to leave with some members of the King's Crew MC of Calgary who were in Edmonton partying with the Rebels. Thus ended the illustrious career of the Rebels' first and only mama. In a bar-room toast, Steve offered this epithet: 'Here's to Athena! A woman with everything! Except maybe a clean bill of health!' Two weeks later the King's Crew tried to give her back: 'Oh yeah! You guys [Rebels] are a real class bunch of guys. We finally gave the broad to a couple of strikers. I told them that they could use her box as a garage to store their bikes over the winter' (Trock, King's Crew MC). As a further consequence of the clubhouse incident, the Rebels now maintain a book with a listing of the members' ol' ladies. Any ol' lady who violates a club ruling such as spreading gossip – whether the accusation is true or not – or showing up unescorted at the club bar is given a black mark. If an ol' lady accumulates three black marks, she is banned from the clubhouse and excluded from participating in any club functions such as runs or parties.

> *Dianne* (Wee Albert's ol' lady): Al came in and said: 'You'd better watch yourself [spreading gossip], the club is going to give you a black mark.' So I asked him where. He said: 'Just watch it!' It was kind of funny, I had visions of these black marks on my forehead.
> *Donna* (Clayton's ol' lady): I know where I'd get my three black marks from Clayton.
> *Gail* (Jim's ol' lady): Yeah, two black eyes and one fat lip.
> *Coyote*: What did the club do before they started keeping track of these black marks?
> *Dianne*: They would just use their fists.
> *Coyote*: Actually, that sounds like it would be a lot more effective.
> *Dianne*: I hope you understand that gossip is the only defence system that we [ol' ladies] have.

The purpose of the club's black-mark file was to neutralize the information network maintained by the ol' ladies, and thereby protect those members whose indiscreet behaviour might otherwise get them in trouble with their female companions. In effect, the males took direct political action to circumvent the indirect power exercised by the women as a subordinate subgroup.

The outlaw-biker ethos attaches no stigma to members who have extramarital sexual relations or sexual liaisons with females other than their ol' ladies. Such relationships are expected and often joked about. This joking is a vehicle for legitimizing behaviour that is marginally acceptable in the club, but not sanctioned in wider society. It should be noted, however, that not all the Rebel members engaged in promiscuity. 'I've been living with Gail for nine years now. We've got two kids and a great thing going between us. I've never really picked up on any of the offers or come-ons that I get here in the bar. Hey, I've got one sweet honey waiting for me at home' (Jim).

Engaging in promiscuous affairs is strictly a matter of personal discretion; some members participate, some don't, but it certainly isn't discouraged. The male perspective on sexual indiscretions reflects a traditional double standard of the wider society. When a brother tells you that sexual variety is the spice of life, he means for himself and not his ol' lady. If an ol' lady is found out to be 'making it on the sly,' the member would be expected to 'drop the chick.' Conversely, an ol' man is afforded the luxury of being able to compartmentalize his feelings of warmth and affection, which are usually reserved for his ol' lady, from the impetus of sexual gratification, which may extend beyond his ol' lady to include other interested parties: 'Bikers like to party – particularly if the party is female.'

The men of the outlaw-motorcycle-club subculture are in part defined by how their women act. An ol' lady must always be aware of the machismo ideal and her own man's image, especially when interacting in a group context. While a woman will almost certainly be more outspoken and independent when interacting with her man in private, when in public her guiding principle must be one of compliance. An ol' lady who attends a club function must consider that her actions reflect on her ol' man and his 'honour.' The woman must not assert herself to the social detriment of her man; open disagreements that question his authority are to be avoided at all costs. As a rule members will not subject their ol' ladies to extremes of machismo behaviour – aggression, domination, or blatant sexual exploitation – that may befall an occasional broad or mama. The one vehement outburst between a member and his ol' lady that I witnessed at the clubhouse over a three-year period was settled by the member abruptly and with brute force. But a member who uses force on his ol' lady puts himself in a no-win situation. The aggressive assault or beating of a woman – especially one's ol' lady – was not promoted in the club and such behaviour was not a source of prestige. Rather, the use of force by an ol' man suggests that he is not in control of the situation. It is essential to the biker's self-image that he have total control over his bike and his woman: 'A man who has no control over his woman loses status very quickly,' commented an ol' lady named Marilyn, 'almost as fast as a man who can't keep his bike running.' Ideally, a Rebel can maintain the integrity of his position as a man and club patch holder on the basis of a mutual understanding with his woman. Conflict should not be necessary and is considered an indicator of weakness. Both the man and woman are expected to share a definition of masculinity as a positive force that results in personal resolve and a capacity for action that leads to control; but that control is never to be divorced from compassion and mutual respect.

Like other paramilitary and military organizations, outlaw motor-cycle clubs actively promote a strong male ideal that is not to be tarnished with any overtones of female interference or domination. For members of the Rebels MC, this positive male image is another aspect of their collective self-image that separates them from ordinary men. For many ol' ladies who are proud of their ol' men, the quality of masculine independence is a compelling attraction: 'I'd rather be Blue's ol' lady than married to some pussy-whipped sonofa-bitch who doesn't have the guts to stand up for himself or what he believes in. When Blues is with me I know it's because he made the decision, because he wants to be with me, because he loves me' (Lorraine). The women who successfully adapt to the ol' lady role appear to be those who accept masculinity as a positive male quality. Rather than showing envy or attempting to constrain its expression, they affirm, enhance, and ultimately enjoy the masculine power of their man.

An ol' lady is expected to show a degree of maturity and to avoid panicky behaviour when confronted with a crisis situation, especially if it involves law-enforcement officers or a war with another club. An ol' lady of a member of the Highwaymen MC panicked when her ol' man became involved in a possible life-and-death confrontation with a Rebel patch holder. She phoned the Edmonton city police and warned them that her ol' man had gone out looking for the Rebel armed with a shotgun. That evening the police pulled over a number of the Rebels who were riding the street and informed them of the report. The Rebels called an emergency meeting and plans were put into operation to take the Highwaymen MC 'off the road' (terminate the other club's existence). Law-enforcement officers are generally aware of the partnership relationship of a member and his ol' lady, and the subsequent sharing of information between the two. Although ol' ladies are not formally associated with the club and do not attend club business meetings, an ol' lady's intimate relationship with a club member results in her being privy to detailed knowledge of the club, its personnel, and its politics. An ol' lady must remain cognizant of the fact that law-enforcement officers may view and treat (interrogate) her as a valuable source of information. In a national communiqué to police departments regarding tactics for effectively countering the 'motorcycle gang threat,' RCMP intelligence officers viewed ol' ladies as a 'gold mine of information' and stated:

'Sometimes a biker woman caught at the right moment, will reveal more about club structures, and political in-fighting than the most trained biker investigator could ever hope to obtain on his own' (RCMP communiqué to Canadian police departments).

If the situation demands it, an ol' lady may find herself transporting, concealing, or registering weapons for her ol' man in her name. Nearly all the Rebels (twenty of twenty-four) possess firearms. For the most part these weapons are not of the concealable variety, such as handguns, but rather high-powered rifles and shotguns. These weapons are kept for security reasons and because many of the brothers enjoy hunting together in the fall. To display hardware that they are proud of and to ensure ease of accessibility, members often mount these weapons on a gun rack on either their living-room or bedroom wall. Those Rebels who do own guns have also obtained the necessary firearm acquisition certificates, in compliance with Canadian federal statutes. If, however, a member of an outlaw club is unable to procure a firearm certificate, for reason of having a criminal record or being on probation, it is not uncommon for his ol' lady to secure the certificate and legally possess the firearm. Having an ol' lady assume proprietorship over the weapon is a particularly effective strategy in the United States where, under federal jurisdiction, it is illegal for an ex-felon, or anyone under federal indictment, to possess any firearm.

An ol' lady has to learn to balance the good, the bad, and the ugly of motorcycling. The good times are sharing a summertime dream with her ol' man, waking with the sun, riding with the wind, chasing down lonesome stretches of grey after a sun descending behind the blue Rockies, setting up the tent, 'smoking rolled ones' and 'drinking cool ones' around a campfire, and watching the stars come stealing in. Bad times are having to face a flat tire a hundred miles from another sign of life except for ominous black storm clouds that are no longer off in the distance, or the pain and numbness of getting caught in a late spring snowstorm. The ugly times are those when bikers have to deal with incidents that reflect the fact that 50.8 per cent of all motorcycle accidents result from violations of the motorcyclist's right-of-way (U.S. Department of Transportation, National Center for Statistics and Analysis, 1980). During the course of one such event, my lady found herself in the unenviable position of having to watch as a careless 'cage' (car) driver changed into our lane. There is an adrenalin rush of fear and disbelief as you watch hulking steel move in to crush your leg. I noticed what was happening in time to twist the throttle and accelerate sufficiently to prevent the car from hitting Sandra. The motorcycle, at that time an unmodified FLH stock dresser with protective rollbars, glanced off the side of the car and we were headed straight towards the curb. Luckily we hit a driveway, and I found myself slamming on the 'binders' (brakes) in a hotel parking lot. I eased 'Harley' between two parked cars back on to the road and began a pursuit of the car that included running a red light and two stop signs. The car finally stopped outside a southside residence and I pulled up behind him.

The incident and high speed chase left me shaking with anger as I leaned over the bike to allow Sandra to dismount. I told Sandra to stay with the bike, still unsure as to what I was going to do to this guy. Before I could give the matter much thought, however, Sandra had leapt from the bike and run up alongside the car. She began screaming at the driver about the lack of quality of both his driving skills and his questionable ancestry. Sandra, a strong athlete with long legs and a background in karate, then proceeded to use her hiking boots to redesign the side panels of the late-model Chrysler Cordoba with a front snap kick followed by a side thrust kick. The driver, a male in his early thirties, seemed stunned and very unsure as to how to react. When he did manage to roll down his window to protest, Sandra stared at him and said in a matter-of-fact manner: 'Come out of that car and you'll need a vital organ transplant.' All I could do was stare on in disbelief as Sandra calmly walked back to the bike. There was nothing left for me to do; doing anything would have been anticlimactic. As we rode away I pondered the character transformation that had come over Sandra. Later that evening, while having a few drinks with the Rebels at the club bar, she explained: 'When you ran the red light going after that guy, I knew that you were more rage than common sense. I remembered the last time that you laid a heavy on the jerk who almost ran us into that truck [semi-trailer] on the highway ... The [police] squad car came up behind us with his red lights flashing and I thought for sure that you were going to be arrested ... I did what I did tonight so that you wouldn't have to go to jail.' To be a biker's lady a woman must be able to strike a judicious balance between being tough when the situation calls for it and being tender when there is need for a caring touch.

While riding with the Rebels it became evident to me that, in order for an ol' lady to be able to adapt to a potentially wide range of social circumstances, it is necessary for her to develop both flexibility and control in a manner comparable to that of her ol' man. There must be sufficient overlap between her value system and cognitive model of the external world and that of her ol' man to allow her to both interpret and generate behaviour in a manner that is congruent with that of her ol' man and the club. As one Rebels member stated: 'If she doesn't know the rules, then she shouldn't be around' (Danny). In effect, an ol' lady must be capable of displaying many of the same social and psychological skills the member whose companion she is does.

Within the outlaw-motorcycle-club subculture, a 'righteous ol' lady' assumes a supportive-role function; she becomes part of a team with her ol' man. A righteous ol' lady is proud of her ol' man, respects the bonds that he forms between himself and his machine, brothers, and club, and finds room to incorporate them all within her. She will go through personal changes in dress, demeanour, values, and attitudes that in many ways are comparable to, complement, and mirror those of her ol' man. If the woman complies with these expectations, and demonstrates that she can be trusted and depended upon, she is respected as an individual, valued as a companion, and accepted in her role as an ol' lady in the outlaw-biker subculture.

Part Four

LIVING IN AN
OUTLAW BIKER'S WORLD

The Clubhouse:
Patch-Holder Haven

A clubhouse is outlaw headquarters. It is here, ideally in an isolated location behind well-protected walls, that the patch holders conduct their formal business. The patch holders' initial search for a club-house will be a search for a place to do business, party, and crash, all necessary to keeping the members together. While it begins as a staging area for social events, the clubhouse eventually comes to represent a place of refuge for the members. A clubhouse reinforces the outlaw community by providing the members with a sense of permanency and structure. Patch holders come to view the club-house as a physical statement of the club's continued existence. However, this same visibility and presence can result in the club-house becoming the target of hostile groups. The police, upset citizenry, and rival clubs all present the club with a different set of problems, each of which demands its own kind of solution.

Outlaw patch holders will look at their first clubhouse as a sign of having 'made it.' In outlaw bikerdom the acquisition and maintenance of a clubhouse shows that a club is 'solid' or established. A club-house demands financial commitment, time, and physical protection on the part of a cohesive and stable group of members. An outlaw-club that is just beginning to develop will use the home of one or several of its members as a temporary clubhouse. But, if a club has any intentions of ever achieving recognition and acceptance in the political arena of the outlaw-club subculture, it must acquire a clubhouse. From a purely logistical perspective, a club would seri-ously harm its political prestige if it were unable to provide a place of refuge and hospitality for touring patch holders or visiting clubs.

The Rebels considered it 'very righteous' when a new chapter of the Spokesmen MC was able to establish a clubhouse in Saskatoon, Saskatchewan, in only two years' time: 'It shows that they're serious about getting their shit together as a club' (Tramp, Rebels MC). A club's first clubhouse will be a rented house, usually in an industrial or low-rent area of the city. The club will consider buying its own property as the membership stabilizes and the club's financial situation becomes more solvent. 'The richer more established one-percenter clubs can afford more,' according to an RCMP intelligence report in 1980; 'one club plunked down a cool $86,000 in cash in Toronto for theirs.'

When the members of an outlaw club 'case out' their city for a possible clubhouse site, isolation is a major consideration. Isolation means that the bikers will be able to operate with a minimum of police surveillance and be able to party and entertain in their own style without aggravating the local citizenry. The Bounty Hunters of Victoria and the Grim Reapers and King's Crew of Calgary illustrate some of the problems that can occur if a clubhouse lacks the element of seclusion.

The Bounty Hunters' clubhouse was an old, dilapidated wooden structure located near an industrial park. The Bounty Hunters rented the house from the owners of an adjoining lumber yard for a nominal fee; part of the agreement was that the bikers would guard the commercial premises against intruders. Not being in a residential area eliminates the problem of having to maintain public relations with neighbours. However, the clubhouse is still well within the confines of the city, and it is often the subject of police observation. On one summer stag run the Rebels visited the Bounty Hunters and stayed in their clubhouse for several days. Upon our arrival, the Victoria police immediately cordoned off the area by placing a squad car and two motorcycle units at either end of the street. Whenever a Rebel or Bounty Hunter left the clubhouse he was pulled over, searched on probable grounds, and usually given a traffic ticket for a vehicle violation. Two plain-clothes police officers had meanwhile rented a room in the motel across the street from the clubhouse from where they used binoculars – protruding through closed cur-tains – to watch the bikers. One of the Bounty Hunters would occasionally sit on the stairs and stare back with his own set of binoc-ulars, while another Bounty Hunter on the inside of the clubhouse monitored police communications using a short-wave radio.

The two clubs spent the day, night, and most of the morning partying and renewing old acquaintances. The Bounty Hunters' 'house specialty' was rum and coke along with barbecued salmon that some of their ol' ladies had prepared. At 6:00 a.m. the Victoria police staged a raid. However, the Bounty Hunters had monitored the radio transmissions and knew that something was about to come down. The bikers made sure that the clubhouse was 'clean.' Nothing of a legally incriminating nature was to be found, other than the Bounty Hunters' collection of 200-plus empty Bacardi rum bottles that decorated the clubhouse walls. The senior officer who was supervising the raid came in and told us that we were all 'trash' and that Victoria didn't want us there. He stormed back out when one Rebel, just waking up, groggily asked, 'Who the fuck is Victoria?'

An outlaw club that establishes its clubhouse in a residential area faces the additional problem of having to maintain public relations with the local citizens. Some citizens come to view the presence of bikers as a positive stabilizing force in that they act as a deterrent to local crime and mischief. For example, one man who lived adjacent to three Rebels told me that he was able to leave his carpentry tools outside while renovating his house with no fear of theft. 'The bikers are like a neighbourhood police force,' he said. 'No one in their right mind is going to try a break-in on this block!' 'Living in the Los Angeles area of the Hell's Angels, the neighbourhood felt very safe,' claimed Vicki, a University of Calgary engineering student and former Los Angeles resident. 'In fact my mom felt safer leaving me, as a child, with an Angel babysitter than with a teenage babysitter who lived down the block.' However, living next door to club bikers and having a clubhouse in the vicinity are two very different matters. The reaction of citizens to having an outlaw clubhouse located in their neighbourhood will be at best a mixed one. A clubhouse inevitably means heavy bike traffic, occasional loud parties, and visiting clubs whom the host club will go out of its way to entertain in an impressive manner. If the patch holders act in complete disregard of the citizens, the mood of the community can become ugly. In the St Boniface suburb of Winnipeg, the Silent Riders MC subjected the residents to bikers riding on lawns and sidewalks, swearing and screaming, urinating on the lawn, and occasional fighting. Parties were held almost nightly during the summer, accompanied by loud rock music. When the clubhouse was gutted by a bomb the neighbours were delighted: '"It's the best thing that ever happened to this neighbourhood," said one woman while watching police and firemen rake up the remains' (*Alberta Report*, March 1986: 36). Mature clubs, like the Rebels and Hell's Angels, will go out of their way to preserve a low profile. For example, the Hell's Angels maintained their Lennoxville, Quebec, operation with a minimum of public attention. Dubbed 'Les Hells' by French-language newspapers, the Angels remained virtually invisible to the local population.

In Calgary the King's Crew used as a clubhouse their president's house, which was located in an established residential district. Many of the local residents actively opposed the presence of the bikers: 'Neighbours say there has been an ongoing feud since the bikers moved into the clubhouse two years ago. But most of the complaints ... centered around a weekend party attended by the Bounty Hunters from Victoria, the Rebels from Edmonton, and the Spokesmen from Saskatchewan' (*The Albertan*, July 1975: 1). Under these circumstances an outlaw club will usually tell its members to avoid aggravating the neighbours, and to avoid conflict at all costs. One man who had complained, about the King's Crew, admitted that neither he nor his wife was ever subjected to any verbal or physical abuse from the bikers. After the initial shock of their presence wears off most clubs will try to normalize relations with their neighbours.

A married man told *The Albertan* that he felt safer seeing his children talking to the King's Crew than some other members of the community. He added that the bikers often joked and kidded with his wife and children when they walked by the clubhouse, but at no time were they abused in any way.

A waiter at the Shamrock Hotel, a few blocks away, said members of the [visiting] Bounty Hunters showed up in the beverage room ... but their behaviour was beyond reproach. (ibid.)

However, some citizens were apparently still irate enough to 'take the law into their own hands,' and they called a meeting in the community hall to determine what they could do about the King's Crew. The mayor and chief of police received letters of complaint and public accusations about not doing their job. Inspector Don Nelson, information officer for the Calgary city police, said that he sympathized with members of the community, but that 'there isn't much police can do until the bikers break the law' (ibid.). However, this same public pressure may have influenced how the police reacted when the clubhouse of Calgary's Lucifer's Union MC burned down one week later. Several members of the club were badly burned when they attempted to rescue those trapped inside. The police carted members and guests away in paddy wagons, not ambulances, and took them to police holding cells, not hospital emergency wards. Two members of the Lucifer's Union, the owners of the house, were subsequently charged with manslaughter for failing to maintain the furnace properly. The Grim Reapers of Calgary faced a similar problem with indignant citizens when they moved their clubhouse into the Montgomery district. The residents pressured their alderman to eliminate the club's presence, regardless of whether or not the behaviour of the bikers warranted police action. Alderman Dale Hodges found the weapon he needed in a zoning by-law that was invoked to prevent the proposed site – already purchased by the club – from being used as a clubhouse. Realizing that the by-law would not have been used to prevent the Montgomery community ladies aid from opening a clubhouse, two members of the Grim Reapers MC took the alderman out to lunch and asked for an explanation: '"I did tell them that now all this clamor has started it will just never go away," Hodges said' (*Calgary Sun*, 13 March 1987: 24).

An outlaw club can eliminate problems with citizens and greatly enhance its independence by establishing its clubhouse in an isolated area outside the city limits. Seclusion on private property makes police surveillance more difficult and it lowers the public profile of the club, which in turn alleviates pressure on public officials to 'do their job.' The Hell's Angels, formerly the Gypsy Wheelers, of White Rock, BC, had a clubhouse on a remote eight-acre former chinchilla ranch owned by their president, Teo. The chinchilla barns provided Teo with storage space for his antique cars, a bar area for entertaining, and a comfortable hayloft where visiting patch holders could 'crash.' The Rebels' stay at the Gypsy Wheelers' clubhouse was not marked by the police surveillance and hassle that marred their visits to the Bounty Hunters in Victoria and the King's Crew in Calgary.

The president of the now defunct Catwalkers MC of Burnaby, BC, saw physical isolation as a means of easing the heat that was destroying his club: 'There's been so much fucking heat around here it's unreal. We're reorganizing; the man [police] doesn't like that, and we're paying for it. I'm going to buy some land out in the Vernon area. I just missed out on a deal for forty acres; I just couldn't get the cash together on time. Forty acres of private land! Nobody could touch us then!' (Ken Redman). The Minority MC of Calgary developed a unique variation on the clubhouse theme, a houseboat. The 'clubhouseboat' was a joint venture financed by individual members who purchased shares. For Minority patch holders, a scenic run from Calgary to the Okanagan Valley in BC would end with an undisturbed weekend of swimming and partying as they drifted down the Shuswap lakes.

The clubhouse is a territorial marker. In the world of the outlaws, a clubhouse is a fortified concrete-reinforced symbol that proclaims the club's presence. It warns bikers who have thoughts of starting up their own club that the area has been claimed. However, the fact that it is recognized as a territorial marker can result in the clubhouse becoming a visible target. The two major concerns of an outlaw club will be surveillance and raids by the police and life-threatening attacks by rival clubs.

Warring clubs have resorted to bombing their adversary's clubhouse. In Winnipeg, the clubhouse of the Silent Riders MC was blown up in March 1986 – the Silent Riders had been involved in an ongoing war with the Los Brovos MC for a three-year period. In 1983, the King's Crew of Calgary had their clubhouse bombed twice in a three-week period – the King's Crew have been vying with the Grim Reapers MC for the position of dominant club in that city since the late seventies. A club at war will take extra measures to 'harden' the security system of its clubhouse.

Some clubhouses will have a guard on duty 24-hours a day. Others will have a dead-zone perimeter with Dobermans patrolling in between.

Initial defenses often include all the latest electronic surveillance equipment, infra-red heat sensing mechanisms and ultrasound motion detectors on the roof or in other strategic places. Video-cameras, barred windows, and even Vietnam War type, excrement-smeared, sharpened punjee stakes have been found near the base of fences on the inside to deter any would-be fence climber.

Inside, police officers may find scanners tuned to police frequencies, debugging devices, portable radios, weapons, drugs ... A recently stopped biker had in his little book all the listed frequencies for police and law enforcement agencies across Canada including fire and ambulance services for every town and major urban Canadian centre. (RCMP *Gazette*, 1987: 23–4)

At the height of hostilities between the Outlaws MC and the Hell's Angels MC, national Outlaw president 'Stairway' Henderson ordered the Florida chapters to institute additional clubhouse safeguards. These measures included surrounding the clubhouse with a cinder-block perimeter complete with gun-ports, posting a 24-hour guard, and ensuring that there was always an adequate number of weapons within the clubhouse. The Outlaws chapter in west-end Toronto went one step beyond the standard safety code; they further fortified their clubhouse with sandbags and steel metal sheeting, and then secured the rear entrance with a buffer-impact room made from the rear portion of a tractor-trailer.

Police maintain surveillance of clubhouses in order to secure accurate up-to-date information on the club, its membership, network of friends, and activities. If you show up at an outlaw clubhouse, there is a good chance that you will become the focus of a pair of binoculars belonging to someone sitting in an unmarked sedan or an adjacent building. Show up twice and a picture will be taken of you and your vehicle, and your vehicle's licence number recorded. Show up three times and an 'observation file' will be opened up in your honour. 'If you find a one-percenter gang taking up residence in your patrol area, it's definitely a matter of department-wide concern, and one that demands special training' (Ayoob, 1982: 63). Police 'special training' includes techniques of surveillance and surreptitious entry, along with the planting of listening devices and the tapping of telephone lines. The officers who carry out these activities are usually members of élite tactical units, such as the RCMP E-Squad in Vancouver or the City of Calgary Police Strike Force. If a clubhouse is located in the residential area of a city, police are in a better position to closely monitor the movements of the members. Diligent surveillance over an extended period of time will enable officers to tell when the clubhouse is vacated. According to evidence given by one police detective during the Grim Reapers and King's Crew weapons-prohibition hearings (1988), this knowledge made it possible for members of the City of Calgary Police Strike Force to surreptitiously enter the King's Crew clubhouse and plant listening devices. However, according to an RCMP intelligence communiqué (*Gazette*, 1980: 32): 'Police must be cautious when conducting surveillance on clubhouses lest they be taken for rival gang members,' in which case 'shoot first, ask questions later, is the current order of the day.'

Another police strategy is simply to obtain a search warrant to enter the clubhouse. These raids have netted the authorities everything from confidential police radio-frequency lists to a card-index system on policemen and other bikers (including photographs), as were found in the clubhouse of the Vagabonds MC of Toronto. Part of the search team will include members of the intelligence unit. During the 'search,' some of the intelligence personnel take pictures and video of the interior security system – from the types of weapons lying beside the gun-ports of boarded-up windows to the location of security cameras, infrared photorelay sensors, and ultrasonic motion-sensing alarms. Meanwhile, the electronics experts make their 'plants' of high-frequency listening devices. After the police have left the premises, not too much is said by the members until the club president phones up a professional electronics company and has the clubhouse 'swept for bugs.' 'One biker associate in Toronto actually owns an electronics firm that specializes in sweeping clubhouses. His card was found in three different clubhouses on three different raids' (RCMP *Gazette*, 1980: 20). An outlaw club usually cannot hope to match the electronics expertise available to the police in this game of surveillance-countersurveillance. As a result of increased police activity, some outlaw clubs follow a policy of not allowing drugs or contraband, such as a stolen motorcycle, on the premises. Other clubs have moved away from formal clubhouses and reverted to holding meetings and social events at members' private residences. The final alternative is to convert the clubhouse into an unassailable fortress. An example of the extremes that an outlaw club might go to in trying to make their clubhouse impregnable is provided by the Hell's Angels' clubhouse in Lennoxville, 100 miles east of Montreal, Quebec. As the climax to Operation Arrow in April 1985, the Quebec Provincial Police raided the Angels' stronghold. They were confronted by a virtual fortress. When they swooped down on the building in the early dawn, the police found bear traps in the woods, sensor wires under the driveway, closed-circuit television cameras on posts, six guard dogs that had to be tranquillized, and an elaborate system of floodlights and burglar alarms. A construction payloader was used to break down the clubhouse walls, which were reinforced with steel plating. Inside the police found radio scanners, bullet proof vests, baseball bats, a semi-automatic weapon, and several rifles that lay by each window. The clubhouse also contained secret rooms that could be accessed only by electronically controlled panels. Police estimated the value of the Hell's Angels' fortress to be $500,000.

Over the years the Rebels have had quite a number of different clubhouses. While I was riding with the club they followed a policy of rotating clubhouses on a seasonal basis. During the low-key winter months the Rebels would rent a house in an industrial area of Edmonton, or they would find a house that was scheduled for demolition but was still in reasonable condition. In the summer months, when the activities of the club reached full pitch and isolation again became critical, the Rebels shifted their clubhouse to a rented section of farmland along the southeastern outskirts of the city. The acres of trees and farmland provided an ideal location. 'There's nothing out here but land, our clubhouse, our bikes, and us,' said Tiny while we worked on his bike. 'We can be as loud as we want, get as drunk as we want, have as good a time as we want, do what we fucking want, and nobody bothers us!'

For patch holders, the clubhouse is a declaration of independence. The clubhouse is a physical border marker that further defines the points of tangency between the club and host society. It is an enclave where rigid social borders are maintained and subcultural norms predominate: 'Out here it's our society! Our rules!' (Danny, Rebels MC). The trip out to the clubhouse was a four-mile highway ride through pleasant countryside. At the gate of the entrance road to the clubhouse hangs a sign that the Rebels 'borrowed' from a construction company:

PRIVATE PROPERTY
NO CARS ALLOWED
BY ORDER OF SUPT.

The sign nicely symbolizes that one is crossing the borderline between a four-wheeled culture and a two-wheeled culture. Only patch holders are allowed to pass down the entrance road without both an invitation and an escort by a member. The clubhouse guest list is usually restricted to friends of the club, patch holders of visiting clubs, members' ol' ladies, and other women in whom members have an interest. An ex-member in good standing is allowed to phone up the club and ask for an invitation without the necessity of an escort. 'We don't want anyone at the clubhouse unless he's on a motorcycle, or we definitely know as a biker. We don't want any unknown dudes coming out and asking what's going on. They'd be told to take off, gotten rid of, or whatever' (Ken, president, Rebels MC). The entrance road from the highway leads to a thicket of large trees that surrounds two buildings. One is a barn that is used as a storage facility. The other building, a two-storey wooden-frame structure complete with white picket fence, is the clubhouse. The Rebels rented the buildings and use of the land from a farmer who worked the nearby fields.

The quarter-mile entrance road provided the Rebels with a clear view of anyone who was approaching. In order that members not be detracted from either having a good time during parties or taking care of business during meetings, an outlaw club will often use their strikers as security guards. The Rebels posted a striker at the entrance gate, equipped with a CB radio, to act as a sentry during events, such as club meetings, when they definitely didn't want to be disturbed by outsiders. How elaborate the additional security measures were depended on the nature of the political situation. Like many outlaw clubs, the Rebels used police-radio scanners to monitor nearby police-cruiser radio transmissions, and they also purchased a hand-held electronic countersurveillance unit in order to detect police 'bugs' (hidden RF transmitters). Raunch had used his skills as a welder to construct, among other safeguards, a steel doorway that resembled that of a bank vault. The weapons inside the clubhouse, usually shotguns, were legally registered as required by Canadian law. Patch holders realize that no matter how elaborate the security system, their clubhouse is still vulnerable to police raids. As a result, the Rebels enforce rules that prohibit members from storing illegal drugs or 'hot' motorcycle parts on the premises. In 1986 the Calgary chapter of the Rebels failed to follow this policy, and a police raid netted approximately two thousand 'hits' of 'acid' (LSD). All the members present in the clubhouse at the time were charged with possession with the intent of trafficking. The single raid and subsequent charges had the potential of completely shutting down the Calgary operation. Fortunately for the club, a striker took responsibility for the drugs; he was eventually convicted and sentenced on charges of 'possession for the purposes of trafficking.' As far as the club was concerned, he had earned his colours.

The Rebels used their clubhouse to stage formal club functions, such as weekly business meetings, and scheduled social activities, such as parties and barbecues. On an interpersonal level, the clubhouse provided the members with a fixed location where they could seek out social interaction or draw upon the resources of their brothers. In effect, a clubhouse solidifies the group social network by giving it the impression of physical permanency. This function is critical when the sense of community – 'how solid the brotherhood really is' – rests so heavily on members' psychological support and physical presence – simply 'being there': 'With the clubhouse I've always got a place to go and people to be with' (Voodoo).

Most of the five clubhouses that I visited were not weighed down with the excessive paranoia of a seige mentality. Unless a club is involved in a territorial dispute, the clubhouse is primarily a place for letting loose and having a good time. Impunity from moral censure and social control freed the bikers and allowed them to be the architects of their own world. Good times come much easier and mean much more when you control the space and you make the rules. For the individual patch holder, the clubhouse guaranteed an insulated social setting where he could live out those visions that he had of himself as an outlaw biker. The Rebels felt that they had combined the best of both worlds. On a warm summer's night, the clubhouse meant a pleasant 'boogie' into the countryside. Afterwards, if the country spirit stayed with them, the patch holders could wander among the trees and gather firewood for several open fires. The evening might be spent sitting around the warm blazes staring at the stars with your ol' lady or going off and making love in the moonlight and trees. Brothers would exchange exaggerated glory tales while everyone 'downed cool ones' and 'smoked rolled ones.' Raunch would look at the glare of distant city lights and say, 'Fuck 'em! Who needs them!' yet still be only a fifteen-minute ride from Edmonton and all its amenities.

Brother Jim was particularly pleased with the clubhouse arrangement because it enabled him to engage in a personal hobby, gardening. Jim was brought up on a farm in White Rock and plans to eventually settle down in a rural community: 'The city is no place to raise [two] kids.' Jim started a mini-farm alongside the clubhouse barn. 'I asked the farmer if I could use some of his land to start a garden. He said yeah and he gave me a patch. I burned off the thistles and weeds and rototilled it. I planted some cabbages, carrots, potatoes, onions, and some peas. I go out to the clubhouse at least twice a week to weed it. There sure are a lot of weeds!' I failed to fully appreciate Jim's preoccupation with weeding until the following weekend. While sharing a brew with a couple of King's Crew members who were up for a visit, one of their patch holders came around the barn munching on some of Jim's carrots: 'Man, I've never seen "weed" [marijuana] grow that high before! Come look at the stuff. That's fucking awesome!' Jim thoroughly weeded his garden just before the annual Labor Day run to ensure that a good time would be had by all.

A sign beside the clubhouse doorway reads 'Enter At Own Risk.' Inside, some patch holders and the occasional ol' lady would be playing pool on the club's pay-as-you-play table. There were pool cues, ball racks, pool and billiard balls along with a scoreboard. Most of the items had been 'donated' from various bars. The winners of a game would take on new opponents who deposited a quarter in the table for the opportunity to challenge. The losers talked about their bad luck and either took each other on in a game of pinball or went to the fridge for a cold brew. The Rebels had two fridges; one was a beer fridge, while the other was used to store food, wine (affectionately referred to as 'Tangled Spokes'), hard liquor (usually Jack Daniels whisky), and ice. All the alcoholic beverages were sold at slightly higher than retail cost, with profits going to the club treasury. The members would grab the refreshment of their choice from a fridge and then deposit the appropriate 'donation' in an old theatre ticket-stub box. It is illegal to sell beer, wine, or whisky, even in a private club, unless one has a liquor licence; therefore, the system was operated on an honour donation principle. Interestingly enough, when the police raided the clubhouse of the Outlaws MC in Louisville, Kentucky, they laid twenty-two charges, including drug and weapons offences. In court, the judge dropped twenty-one of the charges; only one of the charges resulted in a conviction. The judge fined the club president, Lowell Daugherty, $200 for operating a private club and place of entertainment without a licence. However, the charge of bootlegging is not as insignificant as its trivial fine makes it appear. A person or group convicted of bootlegging may have their residence declared a public place. In effect, the police may then enter the clubhouse at any time without the need for a search warrant.

Other amenities in the Rebel's clubhouse included a stove that was used for everything from cooking meals to preparing hash. Voodoo demonstrated his technique for smoking hash when he took an empty whisky bottle from the 'room of empties' and smashed it against the base of the stove. He then asked a striker, whose duties included clubhouse maintenance, why there was broken glass lying all about and it was promptly cleaned up. Voodoo used the top shaft piece of the whisky bottle as a funnel to draw up smoke from the hashish, which was heated between two hot knives on the stove. Music was provided by a classic old Wurlitzer jukebox and a stereo system; extra speakers were mounted outside the house for outdoor barbecues and parties. The Rebels provided their own power source for the electrical appliances and lighting system by operating a portable gasoline generator. The patch holders had managed to procure an old 1920s wooden telephone booth in which they kept the clubhouse phone. Several of the Rebels were electricians; they used their talents to hook up the phone system independent of the attention and user's costs of Alberta Government Telephones.

The clubhouse is furbished with many trappings and trophies that symbolize both the larger outlaw biker culture and the Rebels in particular. Most obvious were the twisted remains of a Honda motorcycle hanging from the branches of a tree beside the clubhouse.

Steve: Consider it a tribute to Japanese shit!
Caveman: Hah! Hah! Yeah, it used to be a fine sculpture when we had the dork rider strung up there with it, but the buzzards got him.

On one wall of the clubhouse hung the Rebels MC flag, a grimacing white skull on a black and red background. Nearby were a Confederate rebel flag and a Canadian flag that was draped upside down. Beside the flags hung a highway sign that a member had collected as a souvenir during a run; it read 'Stony Plain Indian Reserve.' The walls were decorated with photographs of members posing with their 'scooters.' On tables beneath the photographs were trophies that Rebel patch holders had won by entering their bikes in custom-motorcycle competitions. Between two sofas was a bookcase that held photograph albums with pictures of brothers past and present, along with their motorcycles and ol' ladies. Other albums held the pictorial record of past club runs and parties, newspaper and magazine clippings concerning club events and its public profile, along with courtesy cards from the patch holders of other clubs. While browsing through one of the albums I glanced up and noticed that a patch holder had left a personal trophy on the ceiling to mark his party ventures: a pair of pink panties and a bra had been nailed to one of the rafters.

Evidence of the Rebels 'iron fisted' territorial policy covered two walls of the clubhouse. Since their inception in 1969, the Rebels have taken thirteen clubs 'off the road.' All that remains of these clubs are their colours, draped upside down along the hallway and walls. This trophy-like display of captured colours is a common practice among outlaw clubs. In their Toronto clubhouse, the Satan's Choice mounted colours they had ripped off the backs of members of the Vagabonds MC and the Para Dice Riders MC. The Satan's Choice also had badges and a jacket that they had seized from members of the Ontario Provincial Police, along with photographs of individuals they thought to be undercover agents or police informants. On one clubhouse wall the Rebels have an RCMP plaque that reminds them to 'Maintiens Le Droit.'

The upstairs storey of the clubhouse contained three bedrooms. If a patch holder was experiencing hard times he could rent one of these rooms as a temporary residence for a ten-dollar monthly fee. A member who 'got lucky' with a woman, or who was just too drunk to navigate his scooter back to town, was able to rent a room for the nightly charge of one dollar. 'Those rooms are mainly for fucking, crashing, or getting sick' (Indian). The bedrooms upstairs were the site of some memorable sociological and anthropological digs; and if I may be permitted an archeological dig myself here, the bones of many a good conquestothorus and seductilus were fossilized there. The bedrooms were often the inner sanctum of the inner sanctum; conversations between brothers were held there that were not for the general ears of the rest of the club members. There were confrontations and emotions, a bit of passion and heartbreak. When one of the brotherhood spilled his guts, it wasn't always just his intestinal contents. For patch holders the clubhouse isn't made out of wood and plasterboard or steel and concrete. It is made out of the patch holders' beliefs, the brotherhood of the Harley, and their dreams of power and speed that carry them above the mundane and the pettiness of day-to-day existence.

Aside from their motorcycles, a clubhouse is the closest bikers come to having a permanent spatial embodiment of their culture. In the outlaw-biker community the existence of a clubhouse states for all to see that this club has 'made it' and that its members have a legitimate right to claim and defend their territory. Physical isolation from the host society provides the patch holders with a degree of independence to structure their own world of experience and meaning. For individual members, the clubhouse is a patch-holder haven that 'gives me a place to go and relax with my brothers. You can say "Fuck The World!" because out here it's our world!' (Blues).

8

The Club Bar:
Booze, Borders, and Brawls

> The club bar is more than just a stage for 'downing cool
> ones,' 'smoking rolled ones,' profiling your image and
> 'hustling sweet things.' That's what makes it good times.
> But there's a hidden agenda there; it covers everything
> from recruiting new members to gathering information
> about other clubs. That's what makes the club bar
> indispensable, even though some of the guys would just as
> soon say 'Fuck the bar!'
>
> (Coyote, in interview with Ric Dolphin
> of the *Western Report*)

Outlaw bikers isolate themselves from the citizens of the society that
surrounds them. Their social isolation places contradictory demands
on the group. The club can defend its integrity only by maintaining
clear boundaries between itself and the community, but the club can
perpetuate itself only by crossing those same boundaries in order to
attract new members.

Outlaw clubs deal with this dilemma by establishing a 'club bar.'
This is a public tavern that members use as a regular drinking spot
and rendezvous point. The club bar has become an integral part of
the outlaw-biker tradition. It complements the clubhouse, the location of formal club functions and social activities, by providing an
informal place for group gatherings. While the clubhouse is a private
domain, the club bar is readily accessible to the public. The otherwise closed social network of the outlaws is exposed to non-
members. The club bar becomes a recruiting ground where potential

prospects can exhibit their personal prowess, demonstrate their commitment to the ideals of the biker subculture, and experiment with forming ties with club members. In effect, the club bar functions as a point of interface between the outlaw motorcycle club and host society.

Club patch holders want to attract new members at the bar, which requires them to make their public presence dramatic enough to impress potential strikers. But the club bar is a hazardous stage for this kind of performance. The setting is highly unpredictable, and encounters with citizens are often hostile: 'You never know what kind of shit is about to come down' (Snake, Rebels MC). A successful performance taxes the varied abilities of club members; in fact, some members actively lobby against the club's presence in the bar and question the sanity of trafficking with citizens under any circumstances.

The Rebels in the bar engage in a highly stylized behaviour that repeats itself night after night in a form of bar-room ritual. Together as brothers they share the satisfaction of letting loose in sensual/ sexual pleasure. In addition to this sensual element the bar-room ritual has an ideological component; a Rebel performs in a manner that amounts to a public declaration of himself as an authentic biker – the cultural meaning of being an outlaw is shared and articulated. Yet beneath this stylized surface, the Rebels' behaviour is also highly calculated in order to meet the risks that their mere presence in the bar holds for them. They meet these dangers by drawing upon the strengths of their brotherhood. When danger turns to the drama of an all-out confrontation the Rebels are locked in brotherhood and share a common fate.

PLEASURES OF THE BAR

Rebel patch holders go to the club bar to enjoy the exhilaration of 'getting high' and have a good time with each other. The Rebels affirm their brotherhood by uninhibited drinking, smoking, and eating together; boisterous joking and jostling with one another; 'shooting the shit' about Harleys and their performance; telling glory tales about biking; discussing matters related to the club or members; meeting people who can relate to the outlaw bike scene; playing pool; and hustling young women.

The Rebels park their motorcycles in a group outside the bar.

During the course of the evening members will leave their tables on a regular basis in order to 'check out the hogs.' Most bikers have had their motorcycles tampered with, in one manner or another, while they have been drinking at the bar. This tampering can range from a drunk trying to climb on a chopper and having the machine topple over to vandalism such as the removal of spark-plug wires or the loosening of brake cables. Some bikers resort to putting warning stickers on their motorcycles: 'If you value your life as much as I value this bike, don't fuck with it!' The Rebels attach property stickers (a rectangular decal featuring their skull emblem and 'Property Of The REBELS Motorcycle Club') to the oil tanks of their Harleys in order to discourage both the overly curious and the foolish. In 1985 the Rebels began the practice of posting a striker on permanent guard duty. However, most members still prefer to conduct their own occasional bike check. These checks afford a member an opportunity to escape the bar's sometimes oppressive intense drinking, noise, and smoke. He can grab a breath of fresh air, perhaps have a quiet conversation with another member, compare his own motorcycle with those of other patch holders, and make plans while he draws mental sketches of the work and improvements to his machine that inevitably begin every fall and help him pass the cold winter months.

The members mark off a section of the bar by joining together five or six tables in one corner in a manner that restricts access and provides some members with an overview of the rest of the bar. This territorial isolation is complemented by the Rebels' practice of draping their leathers on the backs of their chairs. Mounted on the leathers are the club colours, a white skull on a black and red background. To the casual outsider who glances through the smoky haze of the bar, the visual effect is a formidable wall of skulls. Members of the outlaw biker subculture and selected outsiders are allowed to cross the club boundary. This peripheral assemblage of individuals includes friends of the club, unaffiliated bikers or 'loners,' ol' ladies, unattached females, members of the Grim Reapers MC, and the patch holders of other clubs passing through the city. The larger outlaw-biker subculture that is allowed to crystallize around the club provides the Rebels with both material and social resources: from the exchange of motorcycle parts to mutual self-defence. The most vital resource that is renewed consists of prospects for membership.

Going to the bar is an informal activity, and the number of

members present on a given evening will vary. However, over time a general pattern emerges, largely as a consequence of formal club activities. On Mondays only a handful of Rebels will show up; the majority of members are recuperating from a weekend of hard partying and riding: 'A weekend can wear you pretty thin. Sometimes we'll ride and party straight through from Friday night to Sunday morning. The only time I get to relax is when Monday morning rolls around and I go to work. By Friday I'm ready to give 'er again' (Dale the Butcher, Rebels MC). Monday evening may also be used as an opportunity to renew acquaintances with ol' ladies or other social commitments that were left behind – either sacrificed or deserted – for the weekend. By Tuesday there is an increase in both the number of patch holders present at the bar and the intensity of activity. The Rebels hold their weekly club meeting on Wednesday evening. The meeting is traditionally followed by the members riding together on an abbreviated run, which always ends at the club bar. Thursday evening is Boys' Night Out: ol' ladies are formally excluded from both the clubhouse and the club bar. Boys' Night Out symbolically re-affirms the club as the patch holder's primary commitment in the face of its most potent competition: the male-female bond. The exclusion of members' ol' ladies provides the brothers with an opportunity to discuss matters of personal importance with one another in private. It also presents some patch holders with the 'space' to introduce themselves to any 'sweet thing' who chooses that evening to take a walk on the wild side. Friday and Saturday nights bring either a full complement of Rebels to the club bar or no one at all. The determining factor is whether the scheduled weekend run is a one-day affair or a full weekend excursion, and whether or not the club is throwing a party at the clubhouse.

For the Rebels, drinking at the bar is no longer a personal pastime. The Rebels MC uses the club bar to solidify its social network. Having a club bar effectively draws another area of members' behaviour into the sphere of club influence. An outlaw motorcycle club places great emphasis on its members 'being around' or 'hanging out.' This aspect of physical presence by itself reinforces the reality of the informal network of expectations and obligations that bind members together in the brotherhood. When the club's focal activity of 'riding in the wind' is temporarily 'put in neutral,' then 'putting down brew' in the club bar becomes a particularly important means of maintaining the ties that bind. In Edmonton from November through March, winter snows silence the Harleys, and drinking at the bar becomes one of the few remaining activities that members can participate in as a collective unit. During the summer riding season the bar serves a parallel function for those members who are unable to ride their bikes because of physical injury or loss of driver's licence.

Clayton (Rebels MC) provides a good example of how the club bar enables a member to 'live his colours' even though he is 'downed' and off the road. One summer Clayton was in a collision with a vehicle that was being driven by a drunk driver who ignored both Clayton and a stop sign. Fortunately, Clayton was thrown clear of his motorcycle and not run over. The crash impact broke Clayton's leg in two places. Hitting the pavement displaced vertebrae in his spinal column. The tools that he was carrying in his pockets tore holes in his leathers as he slid across the pavement. Finally, Clayton's arm was broken when he mercifully slammed to rest against a utility pole.

Three weeks later, Clayton was released from hospital and was able to hobble around on crutches. One of the first places he hobbled to was the Kingsway Motor Inn, the club bar at the time. After arranging his assorted casts and crutches in a half-decently comfortable fashion, Clayton began to make up for lost time. Later on in the evening, Gerry of the Rebels decided to see how well Clayton, a man of finesse with a motorcycle, could handle himself on crutches. Unnoticed, Gerry modified the adjustment on one of the crutches to make it three inches shorter than the other. At about the same time, a couple of members who were playing pool decided that the Kingsway pool cues were of finer quality than those they had back at the clubhouse, and that didn't seem 'very righteous.' Two of the members, pool cues in hand, sauntered down to the tables where the Rebels were seated in order to arrange transportation for what they hoped would be the clubhouse's acquisition. However, the pool-cue heist had not gone unnoticed by the hotel bouncers, and they began to move in. One pool cue was handed to Whimpy, the other to Clayton. Clayton immediately shoved the pool cue down his pants and zipped up his jacket over the top half. Whimpy wasn't quick enough, however, and he turned as the bouncers approached the tables to give them the pool cue along with a big grin:

Bouncer: You don't have any more, do you?
Whimpy: Aw, come on. We're not greedy!
Bouncer: Well, okay then.

While the bouncers were being distracted, Clayton picked up his crutches and was about to leave with the clubhouse's newest prize; however, he failed to notice that Gerry had shortened one of his crutches. The moment he put weight on the crutches, the pool cue shot through his jacket and jabbed him in the neck. There was a roar of laughter and approval as Clayton hobbled along making his getaway, one leg in a cast, one arm in a cast, the other arm negotiating a shortened crutch, a back brace, a pool cue down his pants, and twenty draft beer to act as ballast.

The club bar furthermore provides a place where out-of-town bikers can get in touch with the club. For example, two members of 'les Gitans' (Gypsies) MC from Sherbrooke, Quebec, who were passing through Edmonton, obtained the name of the club bar from a local biker they met in a Harley-Davidson shop. At the bar they were shown biker hospitality: sipping cool ones, smoking rolled ones, an invitation to party, and a place to crash. Members of clubs that have established close relations with the Rebels, such as the Bounty Hunters MC of Victoria, will phone the president of the Rebels and arrange beforehand to meet at the clubhouse. Patch holders of unknown clubs have to follow the indirect route of making contact and forming ties with the Rebels at the club bar. In these types of situations, the club bar allows members to decide upon the appropriate diplomatic strategy. A case in point was Ace, president of the Chosen Few MC of Calgary, who contacted and drank with the Rebels at the club bar, but was never given an invitation to come to the clubhouse. The underlying reason for this restrained hospitality was that the Chosen Few were quiet rivals of the King's Crew of Calgary, political allies of the Rebels.

The club bar becomes an important stage for the member in his public articulation of himself as a Rebel. The people a patch holder associates with, the activities he engages in, and the manner in which those activities are performed will all be in terms of his being a Rebel. In return, the performance of those activities and the identity they symbolize are confirmed by the reactions of the general public present.

In the club bar the Rebels would never drink wine and only rarely indulged themselves in hard liquor. Beer rules! The Rebels have their own style for dispatching large quantities of draft and bottled beer. A patch holder will take it upon himself to call for contributions, and those present will throw a few dollars on the table. The money is collected by a member who then signals to the waiter and orders 'another hundred draft.' Nobody keeps track of how much each member contributes, but then no one takes advantage of the system either. If a member is in dire financial straits, he will make up for his lack of contributions at a later date.

There is a benign relationship between drinking alcohol and the subculture's concern for male prowess. The act of heavy drinking by itself is capable of accentuating the illusion of power. While ethyl alcohol is a sedative depressant drug, it also mobilizes adrenalin in the body which supplies quick energy. For some individuals, the sensation of increased strength arouses positive feelings of increased personal power. For the outlaw biker the positive feelings generated by liquor are likely to be expressed in subcultural themes involving strength and daring, sexual conquests, and high-performance motorcycles. Outlaw clubs' preference for draft beer relates to the uninhibited drinking style of their patch holders. Full glasses of draft are often gulped down one after the other, 'chug-a-lugged' by members in seconds. In the loud and boisterous atmosphere of the club bar, the ability of a member to belt down his liquor becomes another aspect of his public presentation of self. It would be difficult for a patch holder to demonstrate his machismo while slowly sipping on a martini decorated with an olive. Food is purchased intermittently at the lunch counter. Chips, spare-ribs, sausages, and chicken are literally tossed around and shared by the bikers at the tables. The scene as a whole is reminiscent of those consummatory rituals that groups of males have traditionally engaged in after feats of violence, aggression, or adventure.

IN SEARCH OF A BAR

Members look for features that are fortunately characteristic of many hotel taverns: a large seating capacity, live entertainment in the form of a rock band, pool tables, electronic game tables, and a 'young peoples' clientele that includes single females. However, a fact of life that bikers have to deal with is that their public image causes the managers of most bars to be less than enthusiastic about the prospect of having motorcycle outlaws as bar-room patrons. The club must work out an arrangement with the management of the hotel or bar in order to utilize its tavern as the club bar. Management's decision as to whether or not to allow club patch holders on their premises as 'regulars' will depend on the clientele that the hotel wants to attract and the image it is willing to tolerate. Working in favour of the club is the common knowledge that bikers consume large quantities of draft beer and attract a following of their own.

The Rebels may be asked to leave the bar, a negative sign that is often less than subtle. Wee Albert reported on one occasion that 'a couple of us [Rebels] went to check out the Inn on Whyte [a new bar catering to university students]. They told us that we could drink there tonight, but not after that. They said they didn't want their bar to be wrecked.' Conversely, management may not say anything when members come to check the bar out, a silence that is interpreted as a positive sign. The club may even receive an overtly positive reception, as when the management of the Corona Hotel put out the welcome mat and actively patronized the Rebels. In this case the managers were not soliciting business as much as they were manoeuvring to change their clientele, which included a volatile collection of junkies, prostitutes, and heavy-handed patrons whose idea of a good time was a bar-room brawl. The excessive drunkenness, disorderliness, assaults, stabbings, and drug overdoses led the Alberta Liquor Control Board to shut down the hotel's beverage services on a regular basis. Based on their past experiences with the Rebels, the Corona management felt that a Rebel presence would alleviate the situation.

> When we [Rebels] went into the Corona bar, we bought a round of beer and they [management] gave us free beer for the rest of the night. I think they want us to drink there and get rid of the junkies. (Raunch)

> Yeah, they want to get rid of the junkies. Junkies, dope pushers, and a lot of the hippie crowd don't like us. Junkies don't like us because we'll pound the shit out of them. Junkies know what we think of them. We seen a guy shooting up smack and we bust the needle off in his arm. We don't like junk. So when we come around they clear out. (Wee Albert)

The ironic aspect of the Rebels' dislike of junkies is that some of the local dealers or pushers (middlemen of the drug-trafficking trade) would use the Rebels' knowledge of the RCMP undercover narcotics personnel to their own advantage. On two separate occasions I overheard the conversations of drug dealers who were able to conduct their business with relative impunity by sitting discreetly near Rebel tables. The rationale underlying this strategy was that if narcotics officers were in the immediate vicinity, their presence would likely be detected and publicly announced by the Rebels.

In one incident, the Rebels identified some narcotic officers in the Executive House Bar:

> *Armand* (Rebels MC): Hey, Coyote, you see those four guys sitting over there? Well the chubby older guy and the younger dude with the long black hair are narcs. That other dude I'm pretty sure of ... yeah I'm pretty sure the three of them are narcs.
> *Coyote*: What about number four?
> *Armand*: Stick around, there may be something coming down.

Less than five minutes later, the three men that Armand had singled out jumped the fourth person seated at the table. They pinned their suspect to the floor, one holding his legs, one putting a knee on his neck, while the third applied the handcuffs. During the scuffle, Jim (Rebels MC), who was working part-time as a bouncer, rushed into the fracas, grabbed one of the officers by the neck, and was about to drop him with a punch when the guy shouted 'RCMP' and flashed his identification. Armand commented: 'The trick is to deck a narc before he can show you his fuckin' I.D. Jim was just a little slow. He must be getting old, eh? Ha, ha!' The fellow who was being 'busted' panicked. He began frantically kicking out, yelling and screaming. The narcotics officers in this instance were quite efficient; they silenced their captive with a well-placed reverse punch to the solar plexus. This particular martial-arts blow is capable of incapacitating an individual by momentarily collapsing the lungs; and, not unimportantly, it leaves no tell-tale marks or bruises. The officers then grabbed him by the hair and dragged him up the stairs and out of the bar.

> *Armand*: You see! What did I tell you? Fucking narcs! I wish they would try that with us!
> *Saint*: They wouldn't. They know better than that.

Armand later explained that they knew this particular group of narcotics officers from the Kingsway Motor Inn. 'They were drinking with us. There were five of them at tables around us. We started choruses of "1, 2, 3, I smell the stench of the RCMP." Shultz and a couple of the guys started grunting and oinking, you know, "Pig, pig."'

Most outlaw clubs have various strategies they will use if a member finds himself in this type of situation. For example, one narcotics officer who didn't 'know better' attempted to arrest a member of the Satan's Angels MC of Vancouver at a public-bar dance in Penticton during the Peach Bowl Festival. The Angel lit up a joint while he was grooving on the band. The officer presented his identification, confiscated the joint, and made the 'collar' (arrest). However, other Satan's Angels standing nearby had observed what was happening. The Angels reacted by starting a fight among themselves in which they made sure bystanders became involved, especially the narcotics agent. During the fracas, the arrestee made good his escape, and the undercover agent was hospitalized after being thrown out the doors.

In addition to making the bar-room atmosphere uncomfortable for junkies and narcs, an outlaw motorcycle club can effectively curb the amount of violence that the bar management has to deal with. The Rebels exercise stringent self-control and have a ruling that prohibits the initiation of violence in the bar (Book of Rules): 'They [management] don't mind us coming in there at all. We drink a lot of beer, as you know, and that's good for them. We don't go around bothering everybody. That's the last thing we need; because if the fucking heat [police intervention] comes down, it comes down on us, no questions asked! We sit in that one corner by ourselves and drink beer' (Larry). Most bar-room brawlers are intimidated by the Rebels' presence and tend to act with a degree of restraint. At the very least, they conduct their disputes in another area of the bar. In this sense, the Rebels stabilize potentially volatile situations. When members do become involved in a dispute, it is standard policy to try to settle it without violence, and if violence is required, as quickly as possible. Members look for inconspicuous solutions; what they want to avoid is a fight inside the bar that involves the bouncers or lands up in the lap of management.

> *Blues*: With the majority of bars, you know we're welcome back anytime we want.
> *Coyote*: Why do you think they'd do that?
> *Blues*: Because most of them have experienced us. They know what we're all about. We bring them good business as well, and we help keep things in line.
> *Coyote*: Do you ever help in controlling the bar scene?
> *Blues*: We've done that many a time.
> *Coyote*: As official bouncers?

Blues: Yeah, like what you saw last night. Instead of smacking that guy in the head and then waiting for the bouncer to come and throw him out, I just took the whole matter outside. And I've done that on several occasions; and each and every one of my brothers has also.

If the interaction between an outlaw club and bar management continues over a period of time, it is not uncommon for the working arrangement to become predictable to the extent that mutual cooperation occurs with respect to controlling disorderliness in the bar.

Anybody who had any street smarts realized that there was an arrangement between us [bouncers] and the Rebels. It was a highly visible first-name, 'how's it going?' basis. We provided mutual support for each other. They never stood in line, and we always made their favourite tables off limits to other customers. If they ever wanted a guy removed from the bar they'd come up and say: 'Look, there's this asshole over here. Remove him or we'll do it for you.' The guy might have been a flake mouthing off, or he may just have been eyeballin' their woman. It made no difference, either way there were no questions asked, we'd remove the guy. If they ever had to take a guy outside the door [a conflict situation], only the Rebel would return; usually we'd throw both fighters out. For our part we'd use them as our silent partners, and their presence alone would be enough to defuse most situations.' (Samuel, a three-year veteran bouncer at the Kingsway Motor Inn)

In effect, the patch holders will take a personal and active interest in maintaining 'our club bar.' Gypsy of the Satan's Choice MC recalled that 'there used to be a special bar that we would go to. We'd classify it as our bar. We'd act as the bouncers there.' The final stage in solidifying this collaboration between the club and management would be the formal hiring of members as part-time bouncers. For example, the Executive House Inn hired both Jim and Indian in this capacity.

In some instances the relationship between the outlaw-club bikers and the bouncers may eventually include a dimension that is hidden from both management and the police. 'Smoke and beer went together well for the Rebels,' said Samuel, who was selling marijuana to the bikers. Samuel periodically gave free samples of grass to the

Rebels. In return the Rebels invited Samuel to the occasional party where he would be guaranteed some new sales contacts. Across town, one of the bouncers at the Convention Inn Hotel was selling 'chemicals' – MDA that was being produced by a member of the Northern Alberta Institute of Technology chemistry department – on the premises of the bar.

> My profit margin depended on the Highwaymen MC being in the bar. They'd get rid of the competition. All I'd have to say is: 'Sorry, fellas, I just can't afford to give you any more freebees [samples] because that guy over there is cutting into my profit margin.' I'd wind up carrying my competition out of the washroom after they'd finished with him. Once I had a major deal coming down and I was worried about a rip-off. So I invited the Highwaymen over to my house for a party. I told them that I wanted them to try out some new stuff that I'd gotten hold of. When the wholesaler came over to make the deal he saw all the bikers in the living-room. I knew for sure that when he reached into his briefcase I was going to see chemicals and not a gun. We aren't talking 'Miami Vice' here, I was only carrying about $10,000. But people have been ripped off and shot for less, and it only cost me $350 for the grass, booze, and a little chemicals to keep the bikers happy. (Leonard, former bouncer at the Convention Inn Hotel)

Unfortunately for Leonard, the Rebels threw a monkey wrench in his small business entrepeneurship when they took the Highwaymen MC 'off the road.' Leonard eventually decided on a career change and became a psychology major at the University of Alberta.

Part of the working arrangement between the club and management is that the responsibility of keeping the members under control is left up to the club itself, especially the sergeant at arms. When the sergeant is absent, other members will take it upon themselves to exercise both self and mutual restraint. For example, after having to work all day Saturday, Jim was feeling particularly 'raunchy,' and became intimidating while drinking at the Kingsway Motor Inn. He began by taking a beer tray from a waiter and throwing it at a nearby pool table, completely ruining Caveman's next shot. A few minutes later, he smashed a full beer glass against the wall. One of the members remarked that 'when Jimbo starts wasting good brew to wash down the walls, you know something's up.' A couple of the

Rebels tried to get Jim to sit down and relax. Caveman did his part and invited Jim to join him for a game of pool. Unfortunately, Jim noticed a dirty look from a guy playing pool at an adjoining table. Mindful of the club's ruling on violence, Jim waited till the patron had put down his half-empty beer glass. Then, while the fellow was taking his shot, Jim did him a 'favour' and refilled the glass by urinating into it. Jim's only comment was that 'anybody who's got guts enough to give me a look like that when I'm pissed off deserves a full glass.'

Any of the above incidents would have brought a bouncer down on a non-Rebel. But most of the Kingsway's bouncers had gotten to know the Rebels and their style of handling situations. They trusted the discretion of the members. 'They've been drinking here since I started bouncing at the Kingsway, over a year now. And we've got no complaints. Sure, they're rowdy sometimes; they come on pretty heavy and what have you. But I've never seen them go out of their way looking for trouble. Most times they just sit there by the wall and drink their beer. Not like some of the crazies you get in here' (Mike, bouncer, Kingsway Motor Inn). Jim crossed the line, however, when he picked up a chair and was about to throw it. At this point, a couple of the members intervened and suggested that Jim leave the bar, which he did. Jim was subsequently reported to the sergeant at arms by one of the members who had witnessed the performance. Jim appeared before the Rebel executive board, and they exchanged views about the incident. After they agreed on what happened, the board applied an appropriate sanction: Jim was banned from the bar for a period of one month.

It should be kept in mind, however, that as far as the Rebels are concerned, they follow rules that they set, not rules set by management. For instance, Crash was barred from the Executive House Inn by management after he had used his Bowie knife to cut through the band's equipment wires: 'Those guys were much too loud. We had to scream to be heard across the table. We asked them to turn it down, but they wouldn't.' Unnoticed by those concerned, Crash returned the following evening despite his being 'barred for life' by management. Ken, president of the Rebels, commented that 'if we'd barred Crash, he wouldn't be here now. But they look after their rules, and we look after ours.'

Hotel management reciprocates this aspect of bar control by extending special privileges to the club. At any of the club bars, members bypass line-ups waiting to get into the bar with no more effort than perhaps an acknowledging glance at the bouncer controlling the line-up. This courtesy is standard practice in outlaw club–hotel management relations. This deference was extended to me in Calgary at the Highlander Motor Inn when a bouncer who was controlling a Saturday night overflow crowd assumed by my appearance that I was a friend of the King's Crew MC. He abandoned his crowd-control assignment, escorted Sandra and myself past the line-up, and then directed us to where the King's Crew were seated.

Once inside the bar, the Rebels can expect an occasional free round of beer, or even a free night, from management. They are allowed to join together tables and borrow chairs in a manner that allows the biker community to sit together. Certain bars, like the Executive House Inn, require bikers to check their helmets – considered potentially dangerous weapons – at the snack bar. The staff working the lunch counters often give them preferential service. The bouncers frequently wander by the Rebels' tables, duck down behind the members, and chug-a-lug a brew, even though it is illegal for a bouncer to drink while on duty. In return for this 'hidden favour,' the bouncers come by the pay-as-you-play pool tables and use their master key to give members free games. Dominique, the head bouncer at the Executive House Inn, became a good personal friend of the patch holders and eventually hired Jim and Indian to work as part-time bouncers. He even offered the Rebels MC a private parking stall, safe in the executive's supervised underground lot. The Rebels declined on the grounds that they like to have their machines visible, nearby, and accessible. Driving into an underground parking lot seemed like 'a bit of a hassle.' Perhaps the bottom line of this decision was that such a move would have been out of character for the Rebels, a club whose members prefer to face adversaries rather than avoid them.

PERILS OF THE BAR

The mood and demeanour of the Rebels while drinking in the bar is noticeably different from in drinking sessions held at the clubhouse. This change in style is in response to the ever-present threat of conflict. 'Putting down brew' at the bar becomes more calculated in nature. While some members may become totally 'wasted,' others will become more reserved and attentive. They constantly survey the bar for potentially threatening situations into which their inebriated brothers may inadvertently fall. These members personify the image of a bygone western era; outlaws waiting for some 'bounty hunter' to make a foolish move: 'Once you put on colours you draw heat, sometimes fast, sometimes heavy. The cops you can predict; you learn fast where the lines are and where and when you can cross. But with citizens you never know when some guy is going to try and waste you by running you off the road. In the bar you've got to expect everything from drunks who don't know what they're doing, to guys in kung fu who do, and can be tough as nails' (Jim, Rebels MC). The consequence of passing out at the clubhouse might be no more severe than being doused with beer by a member curious to know 'why are you leaving the party so early?' On the other hand, a Rebel who gets drunk at a public bar can become the target of assault: 'I was so stinking drunk that Dale and my ol' lady carried me out of the bar. This guy wanted to get it on with Shultz, and I said "If you want Shultz you'll have to go through me first!" I was really drunk and I didn't know what I was doing; I took a couple of shots to the head. Then someone grabbed me by the hair, had me down, and was choking me. I bit him in the shoulder; and then Shultz, he took over' (Caveman). Two weeks later Larry got Killer out of a similar predicament. Two bar patrons ambushed Killer in the parking lot; one had gotten a tire iron out of his truck and the other had an attack dog. Larry, a man of tremendous speed and coordination, wrestled the tire iron away from one attacker and used it to silence the dog.

If an outlaw club becomes too lax in maintaining a constant vigil over its motorcycles, the results can be disastrous. Such was the case when a number of the Rebels decided to have a drink at the Executive after the regular Wednesday night meeting. That evening I left the bar early, at about 12:15 a.m. Outside the bar I met Onion, who was surveying the Rebel 'iron' (motorcycles). I talked with him for about five minutes about an upcoming run while taking a picture of the line-up of motorcycles. We had no way of knowing that while I had the bikes in the sights of my camera, someone probably had us in the sights of his rifle. Onion went back inside to have a final brew; I fired up my shovelhead and drove off, at perhaps 12:25 a.m. At around 12:30, someone came running into the bar to tell the Rebels that a truck had run over their bikes. What the Rebels found were eight smashed motorcycles, three of which were jammed under the tires of a four-wheel-drive truck: 'Eight motorcycles, each valued at between $5,500 and $6,000 were damaged ... Witnesses to the incident said a truck struck the bikes outside the Executive House ... They said two men fled the scene after the truck got caught up in one of the bikes and couldn't move' (*Edmonton Journal*, 16 July 1976). On top of Jim's motorcycle lay a rifle that one of the men had dropped while abandoning the truck. 'The fire trucks were there right away, even before the cops. They washed down all the gasoline and oil. Some of the bikes were shorting out. If those sparks had ignited the gas, well, that would have been it' (Jim).

What caused this incident? Apparently two bar-room patrons had been beaten up by two bikers. The bikers had no club affiliation, but they happened to be drinking at the same bar as the Rebels. When Caveman asked one of the investigating officers if he could trace the truck – later reported to be stolen – he replied, 'I don't give a fuck!' The Rebels were largely on their own in dealing with settlement or retribution: 'When we catch them we'll lay their legs over a curb and run over them with a bike' (Killer, Rebels MC). Members of the Rebels MC realize that when a man wears the colours of an outlaw club, the police have no use for him, and they expect no help from the police.

Instances of conflict further serve to encapsulate patch holders in the social network of the outlaw subculture. Threatening situations and the constant vigil they require reinforce the bikers' perspective that the outside world constitutes a threat to themselves and their lifestyle. The Rebels are not naive about the potential dangers that come with presenting a heavy macho image and flying outlaw colours. The infamous biker stereotype – 'Don't fuck with me!' – becomes as much a necessity as it is a choice of style. 'The way it is now, people stay away from us because they're scared. They stay clear of us, and that's what we want. Now if we were friendly with everybody, they would try and do their best to take advantage of the situation' (Caveman). The Rebels are not the passive victims of circumstance. Wearing colours into a bar is about as subtle as tossing a hand grenade into a bowl of porridge. Colours in conjunction with a highly macho presentation of self are provocative to many males and a direct challenge to some, especially those whose sense of bravado has been lubricated with alcohol. While 'that's not our fault,' the Rebels are well aware that they can evoke violence by their mere presence. In this sense, although the Rebels may not be the perpetrators, they are often the conscious architects of their dilemma of conflict. An outlaw club cannot afford to have one of its patch holders beaten in a bar. A public beating would damage the club's reputation and make them appear vulnerable; it would serve to encourage further assaults by outsiders. From personal experience I can vouch for the fact that there are already more than enough broken-nose artists waiting in any given bar. The structure of the brotherhood will therefore intervene in a manner that protects the patch holder. The Rebels, like most outlaw clubs, will lend their brother whatever help is necessary to destroy an outsider who starts a fight. If the confrontation was initiated by the club member, the Rebels will mediate and separate the combatants. Citizens will not see the Rebel beaten in the bar. However, they also will not witness the beating that the club will administer to the member for starting the fight when they get him back to the confines of the clubhouse. As a patch holder you use the brotherhood, you do not abuse it.

SOME BROTHERS SAY 'SCREW THE BAR'

Despite the privileges they receive, the good times they have, and the functions the bar serves, not all the Rebels feel that spending time in the bar is a sound idea. As far as Raunch was concerned, 'They give us privileges and what not, but that's bad in a way because our people start spending too much time in the bar.' Some members, such as Blues and Terrible Tom, boycotted the bar. Terrible Tom showed up at the club bar only once in three years, and that was to fight alongside his brothers against soldiers from the Canadian Airborne Regiment. Blues periodically avoided the club while actively lobbying against members drinking there. On one occasion, this lobbying procedure led to a heated argument when Blues suggested that certain members who were 'living in the fucking Corona bar' should change their colours to read: 'Corona MC.' Ken, the president and single most influential Rebel patch holder, found himself in the minority as far as the desirability of frequenting the bar was concerned. While discussing the nature and frequency of contact situations the club had with outsiders, Ken stated: 'The average citizen is mostly the person you see in the bar. And as far as any contact goes, that's where it usually is. Personally, I think the bar is the worst place for a motorcycle club. And I would like to see it end!' The presence of members in the bar had even been an issue of formal debate at club meetings; but the issue remained both contentious and unresolved:

There are a few members that don't care for bars themselves. They don't like going to bars. We don't blame them because you can't talk to nobody in them, the damn music is so loud. Its been brought up at club meetings lots of times, trying to get out of the bar. But you can't do it. Let's face it, you've got thirty guys, and a lot of guys, including myself, want to go! (Larry)

I've got no use at all for the bar; but it's a good place for wanna-be's [prospects] to meet the club. It also helps us collect infomation about what is going on around town. Like if there's a new club that's trying to start up, the bar is where we'll hear about it. There's always debate about going to the bar, but guys keep going there. (Tramp)

The negative sentiments that some Rebels harbour about the bar result from two separate aspects of their group dynamics. The first of these concerns is the preservation of subcultural borders that screen out the infiltration of non-biker values and prevent the formation of non-biker social ties. Some members reason that increased interaction with the public would weaken the club as an integral unit by making it more susceptible to outside influence and diluting the intensity of the bonds of brotherhood. 'I'd just as soon see no contact with them [the public],' said Raunch. 'I don't care what they think of us. The more contact you have with them, the looser you are.' These Rebels want to tighten up the borders between the club and outsiders by eliminating the one point of social interface, the club bar.

A second problem is that of balancing vested group interests and the psychological needs of some individual members. A member may incorporate the group image as part of his personal identity – the psychological pay-off of being able to perform in public as a Rebel – yet he may fail to dedicate himself and his resources to the brotherhood. He may be a patch holder, but not a brother. 'Some of the members mingle with the outside, with the citizens, more than they should. In the sense that they should be with their brothers. They should be learning what their brothers are all about, because they haven't learned that yet' (Blues). The Rebels face the problem of having to maintain group boundaries in order to solidify the brotherhood, yet having to cross those boundaries in order to recruit new members. The necessity of the club bar as a centre of activity becomes evident when the factors underlying the decline of the Warlords MC are considered.

THE WARLORDS: CLUB WITHOUT A BAR

The Warlords emerged in 1968 largely through the organizational efforts of two ex-members of the defunct Coffin Cheaters MC, Edmonton's original outlaw motorcycle club. By the early 1970s, the Warlords had consolidated their position as one of the two established outlaw clubs in the city, with approximately fifteen members. However, the brotherhood ties that developed among the Warlords were so extreme that they precluded the possibility of any non-member breaking into the club's tight-knit social network. During this time, the club had one prospect strike for a period of two years before he was rejected. The Warlords subsequently developed a reputation of being largely unapproachable: 'The Warlords are more a closed clique of guys who stick pretty much to themselves than they are a club. You don't see them around all that much' (biker in a bar). The Warlords furthermore isolated themselves from interaction with other clubs in the province: 'Like they [Warlords] want to be a motorcycle club, but they want to be a motorcycle club strictly on their own, with nothing to do with other clubs. We've never once had the two clubs [Rebels and Warlords] together on a run. Some of their members like Rae and Dump come to our parties and drink with us sometimes, but that's about it' (Voodoo). As part of this isolation from the larger biker community, the Warlords MC did not maintain a club bar. They restricted their drinking and socializing to their clubhouse (a member's residence), or they paid irregular visits to bars like the Airway Motor Inn, which is located on the outskirts of the city. One Warlord commented, 'We're different from the Rebels. We don't go around giving cardiac arrests to little old ladies on the street; and we don't put on a show in bars' (Dump).

However, time, other commitments, and an internal conflict eventually took their cumulative toll. By 1976, Warlord membership was reduced to five. The Warlords MC was in serious danger of dying from internal atrophy and external pressure: 'As far as I'm concerned, the Warlords aren't a club. I've met them three times, once without bikes, once without colours, and another time one of our members received an unsigned card from a supposed Warlord' (Ace, president, Chosen Few MC, Calgary). The Warlords saw the inevitable fate of their policy of isolation when Onion, a well-known biker who visited and had the respect of many western Canadian clubs, turned down the overtures of the Warlords to become a Rebel. The Warlords MC responded to the situation with an overall change in policy. In order to increase their exposure to the biker community, they began socializing at the Rebels' bar and set about establishing their own club bar by drinking regularly at the Capilano Motor Inn. Invitations to outside bikers to attend Warlord runs as guests were more readily given out. As a result of these initiatives, the Warlords MC incorporated two new members and had a third prospect striking for them, all within the space of four summer months. The Warlords furthermore accepted, for the first time, an invitation to join the Rebels and the King's Crew on a joint Labour Day weekend run.

The Warlords had always been a solid enough club in terms of their interpersonal commitment to the ideology of brotherhood. It is ironic that their predicament was largely the result of members becoming overcommitted to that ideology – overcommitted in the sense that they became inflexible with respect to maintaining outside contacts. Because the Warlords failed to establish a club bar, it became difficult for them to form supportive bonds with the larger biker subculture. This isolation decreased the chances of their finding suitable prospects for membership.

Like the Warlords MC, the Rebels MC is neither an economically self-sufficient nor a socially self-perpetuating unit; it cannot survive through self-containment. Like all secret organizations, the Rebels must establish a system of selective subcultural border crossing in order to recruit new members. Unlike the Warlords, the Rebels have always had a club bar, a point of interface between cultures in conflict.

BAR-ROOM BOUNDARIES: BORDER GUARDS AND GATEKEEPERS

The Rebels face a paradox. Social integrity requires the maintenance of club boundaries, while social perpetuity requires that those boundaries be crossed. These contradictory needs are met by members having disparate attitudes towards outsiders and, as a result, enacting opposite roles in their presence. One group might be labelled 'border guards.' The guard comprises those Rebels who actively manipulate (and thereby advance) the harsh biker stereotype imposed by the dominant society; their behavioural style reinforces the boundaries between the club and outsiders. The rules of border maintenance are openly discussed among members: 'Yeah, we'll talk about it. But it's just generally understood that when you're sitting in the bar, you're not supposed to have any straights sitting around the table. If you've got a friend there, and a member doesn't want him there, all he's got to do is say so, and the guy has got to go, no exceptions' (Raunch). The border guards can be less than subtle, even in those instances where their brothers are involved:

> *Killer*: Hey, Snake, what kind of bike does your friend ride?
> *Snake*: He doesn't. He just plays the guitar. He's a close friend of mine.
> *Danny*: We don't give a shit! There's no room for him. Tell him to get lost!

An appropriate label for the other group dealing with outsiders would be the 'gatekeepers.' The gate consists of those Rebels who selectively admit certain outsiders and who make the subcultural image exotic and exploit the popular myth of outlaw-biker prowess, adventure, and brotherhood in an outgoing fashion. These members are actively selling the club: 'You have to remember that before a biker strikes for the club, the club strikes for the biker' (Saint).

The perceptual impact of the guard and the gate is best described by an outsider who encountered them. The outsider in this case is Walter Kowal, a graduate student in archeology who was working his way through university by singing in a rock band. The band, named 'Lover,' occasionally played at the Kingsway Motor Inn, then a Rebel bar.

> *Coyote*: How did you originally make contact with the Rebels?
> *Walter*: Well Tony, the drummer, he's a biker. You know, he has a biker mentality and he thinks they're great guys; it was no problem for him to fit right in. Armand [Rebels MC] bought dope from the bass player ... so I got to know these guys but I was kept on a very removed level. I could get along with guys like Clayton, Tiny, and Terrible Tom, but the rest I really didn't care to, because like I said, they tend to be too volatile; like you never knew what they were up to.
> *Coyote*: How did you differentiate between the two groups? How would you decide which of the Rebels were approachable and which were not?

Walter: Just by their attitude. Most of these guys weren't too bad, but you could feel that you weren't welcome when you sat down at their table; and this was even after we'd [the band] had them over at several of our parties.

Coyote: Were you ever threatened?

Walter: I was never threatened physically by any of them, at any time. But it's just that you could tell. Like a guy, like Tiny, would sit down at the table, break a glass, and eat it. You know, eat the glass! He'd be entertaining and having fun with you all of the time. Whereas the other guys would sit there and remain aloof. They'd stay outside the whole thing. They wouldn't enter into the verbal banter or anything; they'd hang back. You would never know what they were saying, thinking, or anything.

Coyote: Aside from stonewalling you with these non-verbal cues [kinesics and proxemics], did you feel intimidated in any other way?

Walter: It was generally what you called the unapproachable group that got into the scraps. The guys I got along with generally didn't get involved in those things unless it looked like things were getting out of hand. So I didn't feel that they would be sort of explosive and do something weird just because I said something to them. Like Caveman, I saw him drop two guys coming into the doorway of the Kingsway. Those two guys never laid a finger on the sucker. Caveman just decimated them before they even hit the ground. After they hit the ground they didn't move, and that intimidated me. Even though it wasn't his fault. They started hurling abuse at him, and he said something like, 'You'd better leave for your own good,' or something like that. They didn't, and all of a sudden, wham, bam, bam, bam, bam! I never saw anything so fast! I think what stands out most was the force of the blows. I mean I heard those, and they were bone jarring; bummer! That sucker had arms on him that looked like legs. After that I maintained my social distance as it were. Like I said, that's terrifying. Like I figured, 'Wow! Would that ever hurt!' Like 'crunch!' There goes the nose ... another operation.

Outsiders perceive those Rebels who act as border guards as 'bikers who shoot from the hip.' Their street-wise behavioural style ensures that those occasional subcultural border crossings that do take place remain highly selective.

CAMOUFLAGING DIFFERENCES BETWEEN BROTHERS

There are some substantial differences among the Rebels. Members have different perceptions of group goals, are committed to group goals to varying degrees, and have distinct personal goals that they hope to achieve by being a patch holder. The ideological and behavioural diversity that results is actually beneficial in that it allows the Rebels to perform disparate and sometimes conflicting organizational tasks. It is this diversity among members that enables the Rebels to both establish a point of interface between themselves and the larger society (the club bar) and maintain an operational balance between organizational integrity (border maintenance by 'the guard') and organizational perpetuity (border crossing by 'the gate') while conducting activities in the bar.

While inter-member diversity may be an asset to the Rebels MC, the full recognition of that diversity on the part of members and outsiders may not be. The Rebels are not entirely in control of the barroom scene. In the bar they continually face unpredictable and potentially threatening situations. Under these conditions, the expression of variability among members can prove to be an unhealthy luxury. Specifically, the exposure of inter-member differences may (1) be taken as a sign of weakness by hostile outsiders, (2) make the Rebels appear less attractive to potential strikers, and (3) detract from the members' own perceptions of group solidarity. Thus, in the club bar, the Rebels find themselves walking the razor's edge between group impression management and the authentic expression of personal sentiments.

Processes of collective ritual and symbolism, such as flying the colours, tend to hold in abeyance the otherwise disruptive effects of expressing differences in opinion. This symbolic camouflage gives the impression of complete uniformity to outsiders. Even for club members, the effects of internal disagreements are minimized by the sense of mutual empathy – a shared common fate – that bonds individuals who participate in collective risk taking. In the bar one never escapes this constant awareness of the risk of external threat. Furthermore, the Rebels have guidelines that encourage discretion. As a rule internal conflicts are not aired in the bar and the emphasis shifts to mutual participation in brotherhood-affirming activities. When trouble arises, inter-member diversity is transcended by the members' commitment to the club and to one another. Members share *all* risks, and their collective risk taking is an important symbolic indicator of the bonds of brotherhood. On occasion brotherhood has to make more than just a token symbolic appearance in order to clarify to the members the stuff of which these bonds are made. Nowhere was this necessity clearer than in their battle with the Airborne.

BATTLE WITH THE AIRBORNE

When you get right down to it, a good bar-room brawl is good for club morale. These days our club reputation means that fights are few and far between. A few weeks ago we got into a real dogfight. We didn't start it, but the guys were sure as hell in an excellent mood after it.

(Tramp, Rebels MC)

Although the Rebels may not initiate or welcome violence, an occasional violent encounter with outside society is not without its ancillary benefits. It pulls the club together in a way that other group activities cannot. Group coherence is enhanced and group boundaries made more salient by virtue of the presence of hostile outsiders. Cohesion is especially enhanced by violence, which, whether it is constructive or destructive, is for the individual the most intense means of asserting personal identity. When an external threat requires collective violence on the part of the members of a group, individual and group identity are dramatically merged. Just such a social drama was initiated by the Canadian Airborne Regiment.

For nine years the Airborne Regiment was stationed at Canadian Forces Base Namao, Griesbach Barracks, located just north of Edmonton. The specially trained paratroop fighting force, which was then part of Mobile Command, 'was probably the best-known component of the forces stationed in Edmonton with its high profile reputation as Canada's elite fighting force' (McMillan, in *Edmonton Journal,* 15 Sept. 1977: A3). However, part of their 'high profile' included practising their combat techniques in local bars.

The Airborne drank regularly at the Roslyn Hotel, located on the northern outskirts of Edmonton. The Rebels had adopted the Kingsway Motor Inn, located in south Edmonton, as their club bar. The Airborne began showing up at the Kingsway after one of their regiment had been hired as a bouncer. On a Saturday evening in

March 1976 thirty members of the Airborne's 'One Commando' francophone unit came to 'drink.' Three bar-room fights later, the police were called to help a patron press charges, and the Airborne were ushered outside. The Rebels considered the presence of the Airborne a territorial infringement, and they were none too happy or impressed as they watched the proceedings.

I then noticed that no one was moving; both groups had stopped drinking and were watching each other. A confrontation appeared to be crystallizing. Killer made a telephone call to the clubhouse. Whoever took the message immediately sent those present at the clubhouse to the Kingsway. One of the ol' ladies got on the phone to try to contact other patch holders. Back at the bar the Rebels began to prepare themselves mentally and coordinate their plan of action. 'Killer's put in a call to the clubhouse. They'll be here quick enough. Don't go anywhere by yourself, we'll handle this thing together. Just sit tight, and stop drinking. Think about what you're going to do, and run through it over and over again' (Wee Albert). Anyone who has engaged in a bar-room brawl knows that it demands a tremendous amount of energy, usually over a short period of time. Success requires physical prowess, concentration, and intensity, with no hint of hesitation. Wee Albert reminded me of these facts:

> *Coyote*: Well, I suppose what's going to happen is going to happen; but I could have done with a few less beer.
> *Wee Albert*: That's okay, a lot of them look pretty drunk. Try and pick them out, that's who we'll go for first. We'll make them pay no matter what happens. In the meantime sip your beer and play it cool.

'Playing it cool' relates to the basic psychodynamics of portraying a positive self-image. An individual enters a bar-room brawl with the same psychological sensitivities that he uses in the 'real world.' Just as he evaluates his own capacities in terms of the feedback he receives from others, so too will he be keenly aware of the reaction his presence causes an opponent to have in those tense moments prior to a conflict. If you show you fear him, he will feel strong. If you disdain him, he will feel uncertain. During the actual combat one must at all costs remain impervious to the efforts of the foe. If all these seemingly extraneous ploys portray you as cool, deliberate, and confident, you help your opponent fold in the clutch.

Unless there is a decided advantage to one party, a brawl between two groups will require an initial catalytic incident. The arrival of the additional complement of Rebels from the clubhouse balanced the groups numerically and seemed to dampen the Airborne's enthusiasm. For their part, the Rebels were not willing to jeopardize their relationship with hotel management, especially in their favourite 'drinking hole,' by pressing the issue. Personally, I was not disappointed that the fight had been postponed. The night before I had thrown an oi zuki (lunge punch) at my sparring partner and caught my thumb on his karate-gi. My right hand was black and blue, swollen, and useless. I felt lucky. However, both groups had designs on either maintaining or incorporating the Kingsway bar as part of their informal territory. Both Rebels and Airborne waited for the precipitating incident they knew would have to come.

The member of the Airborne who was working as a bouncer at the Kingsway wanted to make room for his friends in the crowded confines of the bar. He picked up a chair that had a leather jacket on it, threw the jacket on the floor, and gave the chair to his friend. The jacket held Larry's (Rebels MC) colours. Larry, shooting pool at the time, came over and took the chair back. When the Airborne bouncer spit on Larry, Larry returned the courtesy and then proceeded to throw his adversary over a beer-laden table. The other bouncers moved in and ushered the Airborne bouncer and Larry to the door. Larry wrestled the bouncer to the ground and then said: 'Fuck you! You're a waste of time. I'm going back and finish my beer!' The Airborne bouncer, insulted, perhaps frightened, phoned the Forces base for assistance.

The Rebels began to notice the gradual swelling in the number of Airborne present. They arrived, two by two, a party of six, and finally a group of nine. At 11:45 p.m., Armand entered the doorway at the same time as three Airborne. One of the Airborne told the bouncer in French to 'Call those asshole Rebels outside!' Armand, a bilingual member of the Rebels, looked down at his club T-shirt, then said: 'Alors! C'est un Rebel!' and then proceeded to deck the startled Airborne. The band stopped playing as both groups scambled to get outside into the fracas, which had moved to the parking lot. Once the brawlers were outside, management immediately locked all the doors in order to protect the bar and its patrons. Although the Rebels were joined by a number of friends of the club, Rae (president of the Warlords MC), and one bouncer, they were still at a numerical disadvantage: 'Police say Saturday night's brawl, outside the Kingsway Avenue, involved about forty paratroopers from the Canadian Airborne Regiment, and twenty-three members of the Rebels Motorcycle Club' (*Edmonton Journal*, 13 March 1976). The Airborne had also brought with them an impressive collection of street hardware, including nunchaku (karate fighting sticks), a steel bar attatched to a chain, a makeshift blackjack (a leather ball inside a sock), steel bars, and a baseball bat. The Rebels that came from the clubhouse brought chains and tire irons; the rest were unarmed.

The Rebels were outnumbered, but a small group that fights as a single unit has a decided advantage over a larger uncoordinated group. The Rebels attacked together, with the viciousness of cornered animals. They had shared too much together to think of deserting any of their brothers. It was now a brotherhood of survival, fighting with a vengeance. In the rush to get outside, the Saint, generally a reserved, soft-spoken, certainly not aggressive individual, found himself trapped with two Airborne in the exit way. With him he had a motorcycle battery that he had intended to trade to a friend of the club. Battery in hand, he swung wildly. The Airborne were caught off guard, and crumpled by the doorway. Ken, leading the way, fell when struck by a ball and chain. Clayton was slashed on the shoulder while trying to help him. Rae, of the Warlords MC, had found an old broken hockey stick in the parking lot and swung at the chain-wielding Airborne breaking both ribs and resolve.

The Airborne began to disperse as they saw a number of their fellows being beaten. These were not raw recruits but soldiers who had completed their training in unarmed combat, weaponry, parachuting, and other special skills ranging from rappelling to riot control. However, they had not yet endured and shared enough to cement those ties of comradeship that result in members presuming, and acting upon, a principle of self-sacrifice. The Airborne may have been the finest in discipline, but they had not yet learned to look out for each other under fire. They fell apart: 'They just wouldn't stick together' (Jim). The bonds of brotherhood do not just happen, nor can they be trained for. Brotherhood must be forged over time through open communication and multifaceted commitment: commitment that is finely honed by experiences of collective risk taking. For the Rebels, these experiences let 'you know you're with guys who really look after you, whom you can trust, and who depend on you!' (Voodoo). This kind of camaraderie precludes any hints of compromise by way of desertion: 'They were out to shut us down and rough us up. For us, it was survival. We were out to maim. We were going out after them with our bare hands and doing something about it. They broke and ran' (Wee Albert). The actual fighting lasted approximately fifteen minutes. The results:

Thirteen Soldiers Hurt in Brawl with Gang
A brawl early Sunday morning between members of a motorcycle gang and soldiers from the Canadian Airborne Regiment at Namao sent thirteen of the soldiers to hospital for treatment of minor injuries. The brawl, on streets near the Kingsway Inn, ... apparently started as a personal argument, then spread to the streets, said an Armed Forces spokesman ... Most of the soldiers were treated for lacerations at the base hospital at Namao. (*Edmonton Journal*, 10 March 1976)

The Edmonton city police showed up and watched the aftermath of the fight, no longer localized on the parking lot, as the Rebels chased off the remaining Airborne. A couple of Airborne got into their cars and tried to run down pursuing Rebels on the east side parking lot. Gerry, who had gotten hold of a gooseneck (a three-pound steel wrecking ball), hit the fender of one car, then threw the bar through the windshield. Crash turned as he heard someone yell, 'Look out behind you!' Crash stepped aside from an oncoming black sedan that he thought was headed for him and laid his steel-toed boot deep into the side panel. The black sedan turned out to be an unmarked police cruiser. Out of the squad car jumped two very upset plain-clothes police officers, who then proceeded to lay the only charges in connection with the entire incident: 'Police say ... [Crash], of ———— St, is to appear in court on a mischief charge' (*Edmonton Journal*, 10 March 1976).

One of the bouncers, Mike, had formed a friendship with the Rebel patch holders, and he fought alongside of them. He was later charged with assault and battery by one of the Airborne casualties. The Airborne in question was actually the victim of the Saint and his motorcycle battery. Unfortunately Mike, as an employee of the Kingsway, lacked the anonymity that often protects the Rebels. The Kingsway Inn would not support Mike in the ensuing legal suit in so far as his duties as a bouncer ceased once he was outside the tavern's premises. A bar-room bouncer generally budgets for one or two torn shirts a week as part of the profession's occupational hazards. However, Mike figuratively lost his shirt in the following legal battle – $4,000 in damages alone. The Airborne bouncer who had initiated the incident never saw fit to come outside, and discreetly left the premises when he saw that it was the Rebels, not the Airborne, who were returning to finish their beer. He was promptly fired by Hank, the bar manager. While hotel management sympathized with the Rebels MC, the incident received such widespread negative publicity that the Best Western hotel chain – the corporate owners – issued a directive to ban all motorcyclists from the Kingsway Inn. From one perspective the ban constituted misguided justice, but from the perspective of the hotel's owners, it prevented the Kingsway from becoming a major battleground: 'One member of the Airborne said they planned to go back with 150 men if they had to. Anything to drink at the Kingsway' (*Alberta Report*, 24 March 1976).

The Rebels were well aware of the personnel resources of the Airborne, and they expected some form of retaliation. An emergency meeting was held on the Sunday. It was decided that members would congregate daily at the clubhouse, which would be continuously guarded by at least three members armed with shotguns. On Monday morning members of the Airborne went shopping at Northgate Shopping Centre. A clerk in a sporting-goods store, who happened to be a sister of one of the Rebels, guessed that they were Airborne by their military haircuts, French accents, and comments about the Rebels. She talked to the store's manager, who phoned up Captain Anderson (assistant regimental adjutant) and asked him if there was any particular reason that the Forces base required seventy-five baseball bats. Captain Anderson ordered the military police to conduct a locker raid and car-truck search, which resulted in MPs confiscating a large quantity of baseball bats, chains, and assorted frying-pans:

Soldiers Warned against Retaliation
Members of the Canadian Airborne Regiment, stationed at Griesbach, have been warned against any retaliatory action after a brawl Saturday night outside a city tavern sent 13 of the soldiers to hospital for treatment of injuries.

Capt. Craig Mills, information officer for the Canadian Forces, said the army has received reports that a group of men, identified as soldiers, purchased baseball bats, frying pans and chains at a city department store Monday.

'We're telling them to restrain themselves and let the matter die,' Capt. Mills said. 'We don't want any further incident of this type.' ... Capt. Mills said the paratroopers have left for manoeuvers in the Wainwright area, and will be there until March 27. (*Edmonton Journal*, 13 March 1976)

The conflict was over. The Kingsway Motor Inn continued to bar from its premises anybody who even remotely looked like a biker, and the Rebels began the search for a new club bar.

The Rebels had reaffirmed their brotherhood. Each member had taken extreme risks and made personal sacrifices for the group: 'I looked at all the hardware those guys were carrying, and I thought, 'Well, this is it! I'm not going to walk for a month!' There must have been at least 55 of them. I don't think they expected us to fight against those odds, but we went at them swinging, kicking, clawing with anything we could find. I got a boot in the head and went down with sore ribs, but that was about it' (Onion). As a result of extensive media coverage and storytelling by members themselves – from joking references to mutual praise – the 'Battle of the Kingsway' became part of Rebel folklore, a historical referent that served to vitalize and confirm a collective identity based upon brotherhood. Loyalty to the club and to one another arises out of the midst of danger, out of the tension and apprehension of possible injury, mutilation, or worse. Whether one considers the process as desperate, heroic, or foolish doesn't really matter. What matters is that the brotherhood stands as a necessary feature of the Rebels' continued existence as individuals and as a group.

9

The Club Run:
Brothers in the Wind

We all have one thing in common – we live to ride and ride
to live.

(Terrible Tom, Rebels MC)

An outlaw biker considers himself a romantic. He carries a strong
mental image of himself: leaning back on his motorcycle, feet up on
highway pegs, his girl tucked in behind him, bedroll and camping
gear strapped to the backrest, mountains in front of him and troubles
far behind, flying down a lonesome stretch of grey highway, riding in
the wind again. The club run adds a key social dimension to this
image. The outlaw patch holder is not a loner; he has his brothers
beside him.

A club run is a motorcycle tour where members ride together as a
group. A run is the outlaw club's fundamental reason for existing,
and it is formally mandated by the club's constitution. On a club run
patch holders take risks, engage in exciting and stimulating behaviour, and indulge in the freedom of mobility. Members use a run to
express and share a wide range of sentiments and emotions, from the
festive atmosphere of an initiation run to the grief of a funeral run.
The sight and sound of thirty Harley-Davidson motorcycles roaring
down the highway make the club run the group activity that most
effectively dramatizes the outlaw-biker identity, that of anti-hero and
social rebel.

An outlaw biker constructs his anti-hero image from themes and
values that are largely hedonistic in nature, from collective risk
taking to the freedom of mobility. For the patch holder, the club run

symbolizes these goals and values, which he considers legitimate, and which he pursues in the name of his freedom ethic. Ironically, the response of the police to a run, 'harassment,' actually strengthens the club's ability to portray the freedom ethic. Harassment heightens the process of group polarization and adds credence and reality to the patch holder's isolation as an outlaw from the mainstream of society. For these outlaw bikers, riding in the wind with their brothers goes beyond being a theatre for episodes of togetherness. It becomes an act of defiance.

THE RIDING SEASON

The late spring, summer, and early fall months are the riding season. It is a time of riding hard, partying long, and 'good times with the brothers.' The patch holder has spent the 'friggin' cold winter months repairing, rechroming, and rebuilding his 'sled,' while 'making a dime' to pay for it all. Now he is ready to ride!

The Rebels inaugurate the riding season with a mandatory run in the spring and terminate it with a mandatory run in the fall. Dedicated bikers ride whenever possible; the Rebels expect their patch holders to have their motorcycles on the road by April 1st and to ride until October 30th or the first permanent snowfall. However, it is during the official riding season (from mid-May to September) that most outlaw motorcycle clubs, in accordance with their constitution or by-laws, will apply formal sanctions against those members who fail to keep their machines operational.

> If a member's bike is not running for a period of thirty days, unless he is in jail or hospital, his colours will be confiscated. A member's bike must be running for at least one week (e.g., not fifteen minutes), to be exempt from the above rule. This period is subject to change at the discretion of the club. (Rebels MC Constitution)

> A member's bike must not be broken down over thirty days at a time, unless the person is in hospital or jail. (Hell's Angels MC by-laws, San Francisco)

The RCMP National Crime Intelligence Branch believes that the purpose of these rules is to make sure that outlaw club members –

whom they think have become wealthy and affluent through criminal activities – don't abandon their motorcycles altogether. According to one RCMP bulletin: 'Even with the arrival of sophistication, bikers must still own their bikes. With the phenomenal profits made in the drug trade, gang members gravitate to Corvettes and other showy or expensive vehicles. Quite a few members would probably prefer to remain members of these criminal organizations without resorting to bikes at all. The trend away from bikes has been so pronounced that the San Diego Chapter of the Hell's Angels passed a by-law levying a $25 fine to anyone not riding their bike at least once a month' (Intelligence communiqué to Canadian police officers, RCMP, 1980). This interpretation is historically wrong. Riding by-laws pre-date the involvement of any outlaw clubs in organized crime. By-laws ensuring riding participation have been a part of the outlaw club scene since the Canadian Lancers MC of Toronto in the 1950s. Furthermore, one would have to question the logic of viewing a $25 monthly fine as a deterrent to someone who is making 'phenomenal profits ... in the drug trade.' During the period of my association with the Rebels a number of the members were indeed told to 'get their shit together' as far as their motorcycles were concerned. But none of these patch holders was well off financially, and none was pre-occupied with Corvettes.

By the time April brings the promise of clearing skies and dry pavement, the Rebels are eager to be riding together again as a group. For five months the Harley iron has been stored in garages and living-rooms. The club has had to endure the tension of petty disputes and minor aggravations that build up during the winter months of non-riding. During this time a member is also deprived of using his club insignia to symbolize his corporate identity; the Rebels MC Book of Rules stipulates that a member will not wear his colours when he is not currently using his motorcycle. A patch holder will lock away his colours with only his ol' lady and a brother knowing their location. The first club run will mediate the tension of disputes and deprivation; it acts as a spring tonic for the social fabric of the group.

Club patch holders always push the season and their luck. This can turn the enthusiasm of 'jamming in the wind' into the dread of 'skidding in the sleet.' I recall one Warlords' Welcome to Spring party that involved riding through mud and snow at −1°C temperatures to attend an outdoor barbecue that featured a club snowball fight. Rae of the Warlords pointed out that one consolation was that 'the snow kept the beer nice and cold.' Two weeks later the Rebels paid a price for being overly optimistic about the Great White North. A weekend run to Pine Lake was planned, a 240-mile round trip from Edmonton. That Saturday morning the Rebels gathered at a roadside café for breakfast. Larry told Denise that she had 'better enjoy that coffee, it'll probably be the last time you'll be warm for the next couple of days.' The Rebels assessed the weather while putting down their bacon and eggs. The sun made a beguiling appearance and, despite the 'bitching' of some very sceptical patch holders, the run began at eleven. After the sun had made its token appearance the clouds came, followed by rain, and finally a dramatic drop in temperature that changed the rain to snow.

> *Danny*: It was pretty weird. You'd be coming into a turn and the
>   wind would catch you and your front wheel would just slide
>   across the wet pavement.
> *Snake*: We had guys going both ways. Tiny tried to turn back but
>   he said he ran into snow so thick he couldn't see more than five
>   yards.

The white-out turned the weekend run into a two-day snow-in as the Rebels took refuge in some rented cabins along the highway. 'The time passed pretty well though,' recalled Raunch. 'After a while the management was buying us free beer and we got stinking drunk.'

TYPES OF RUNS

The Rebels schedule a variety of official club runs. Mandatory runs, stag or holiday runs, and weekend or day runs occur on a regular basis. Other runs mark special events, such as an initiation run, a biker wedding, or a funeral run.

Mandatory runs: Like most outlaws clubs, the Rebels have two mandatory runs. The Victoria Day run in May ushers in the official riding season, while the Labour Day run in September brings it to a close. These two long-weekend runs are of premier importance because of their highly political nature. They become a stage for a club to 'showcase its stuff' for the benefit of its own members, other clubs, and the general public. Attendance by outsiders is highly selective: 'Each person is brought up for a vote ... it only takes two negative votes to exclude them' (Wee Albert). Attendance by members is compulsory. If a member is late or absent, the constitution requires him to pay a twenty-dollar fine. In addition to the automatic fine, a Rebel patch holder will be required to appear before the executive board to explain his absence. If the member's lack of participation is becoming the norm rather than the exception, 'his colours [membership] will be discussed.'

Stag or holiday runs: Once or twice a summer the Rebels hold a stag or holiday run. These runs may last as long as three weeks and cover distances exceeding three thousand miles. The stag run differs from the holiday run in that a member does not bring along his ol' lady. Excluding ol' ladies places a greater emphasis on the comradeship of brotherhood and leads to more adventurous undertakings on the part of the patch holders. 'The stag run is designed to be with your brothers,' explained Wee Albert. 'A lot of the guys tend to be more sedate when their ol' ladies are around.' On the stag run the Rebels traditionally travel south to party with the King's Crew in Calgary, head westward and camp along the lakes and beaches in British Columbia's Okanagan Valley, cross the Rocky Mountains and fraternize with the Hell's Angels in Vancouver, take the ferry across the Strait of Georgia to ride and fish on Vancouver Island as the guests of Victoria's Bounty Hunters, head north to share some good times with the Hell's Angels in Nanaimo, and then give some serious thought to returning home.

Weekend or day runs: Every summer weekend, provided that the club has not scheduled a clubhouse party or barbecue, the Rebels organize either an overnight camp-out or a one-day bike excursion.

Specialty runs commemorate occasional events such as an initiation, wedding, or the death of a member. A specialty run enables the club, as a whole, to adapt to a new social circumstance such as the addition (initiation) or loss (death) of a member. Such a run becomes a collective ceremony that involves an active social response on the part of the members. The adjustment value of a specialty run can be demonstrated by briefly looking at what happens when a brother 'rides hard' and 'dies fast.'

If the death is a result of vigilante activities or careless driving by citizens, the actions of law-enforcement agents, or the biker 'reaching for the edge' while jamming in the wind, then chances are good that he will become a martyr. The biker magazine *Easyriders* has a monthly memoriam column, 'A Tribute to Brothers Lost':

In memory of Youngblood, 8/3/83, a righteous bro who was killed in a fight. He partied hard and was always on the move. We love you and we'll see you in Harley Heaven. Crazy Ray and the bros, Scorpians MC, Bronx, New York.

In memory of Billy Leary, Hell's Angels MC, Salem, Mass. You are missed and loved by your family and brother Angels. Ride forever with Hogman and Hopper.

In memory of John 'Sportster Smitty' Smith, killed by a cage on his favorite south Jersey ocean-view highway. I can still hear your voice singing 'Desperado' when the winds blow from the ocean. Boneshaker and all your bros and sisters.

(*Easyriders*, May 1986: 47)

The outlaw fraternity comes together as a whole when a member dies. Feuding clubs will often put aside differences and declare an informal truce as they prepare for the funeral run. The bereavement and the sense of deep personal loss are shared among the brothers. Patch holders will reflect upon the values that they lived and shared with their deceased brother, values that might lead to a grave-side epitaph: 'He lived and died like a biker.'

The funeral run is laden with outlaw-biker symbolism. The hearse will be escorted by a solemn honour guard of motorcycles in formation, and the casket is draped with the deceased's club colours. Conducting the funeral in this manner prevents the death of a member from demoralizing the group. The funeral run confirms the outlaw lifestyle through joint participation and is an emotive event that is charged with gestures of defiance, such as riding without helmets or the firing of weapons as a final grave-side salute.

We were supposed to meet Paul [secretary, Satan's Choice MC, Toronto] at 9:30 right by the intersection of highways no. 401 and no. 7. When we got to the turn-off we all pulled over and had a smoke and a few bottles of wine. Paul didn't show: so we split from the T.O. [Toronto] chapter and headed home to Brampton. Next morning we got a call from Bernie [Guidion, president, Satan's Choice MC]. He says: 'I've got bad news for you. Paul was killed last night. He was trying to pass a fucking

car and he was ripped out of his mind on speed [methamphe-
tamine]. He went front-end into a fucking grader. It was game
over. You couldn't recognize him or his bike.' You want to see a
fucking funeral, man?! There was close to five hundred motorcycles right through the city of Toronto; and not one of them
was wearing a fucking helmet. I'd like to see the fuckin' cops try
to break that one up! Nothing but a stream of fucking bikes from
Richmond to Oshawa. There was a cop escort at the front, and
a cop escort at the back. Paul had his bike buried with him. I
knew the guy really well; I fucking cried at that. We [Satan's
Choice] wore black armbands for the next few days. We took off
our colours; we never wore our colours for a week in remem-
brance of Paul. (Gypsy, road captain, Satan's Choice MC)

For the club, a last run with a fallen brother becomes a show of both
respect and strength; it helps the patch holders deal with their
individual and collective loss.

Not all jamming in the wind occurs within the scheduled structure
of a club run. Members ride together after regular club activities,
such as club meetings or drinking at the bar. One or more of the
brothers will often combine personal spontaneity with the mobility of
their machines to create some 'two-wheeled freedom' on their own.
The most accurate personification of the outlaw freedom ethic
occurs when a biker mounts his Harley and rides the highway,
whenever and wherever the urge takes him. Late one evening after a
heavy drinking session at the clubhouse, Caveman and Tiny decided
to 'putt' six hundred kilometres to visit the Spokesmen MC in
Saskatoon, Saskatchewan. Caveman was a little short of funds for
gas, but he did remember Raunch saying something about just
getting paid. At four in the morning Caveman and Tiny arrived at the
house where Raunch, Crash, and Snake were living. Caveman didn't
have a key and he didn't want to jeopardize Raunch's public
relations with the neighbours by engaging in a lot of door pounding,
so he simply broke in. Caveman wasn't sure which bedroom to go to,
so he moved through the house quietly calling for Raunch. He walked
into the wrong bedroom and the household was awoken by a scream
from Snake's ol' lady. Snake got up, looked at the intruder, and said:
'It's okay, it's only Caveman. He'll probably go away; maybe he's
lost.' When Caveman finally located Raunch's bedroom he found
himself staring at a twelve-gauge shotgun: 'Holy fuck, Raunch! I only
wanted to borrow a few bucks, not steal your virginity!' Raunch gave

Caveman several bills and said, 'Okay, now go crawl back with the rats. I work for a living, and I'm tired.' Caveman and Tiny found the Yellowhead Highway, laid back on their hogs, and cranked open the throttle.

ORGANIZING A CLUB RUN: STRATEGY AND TACTICS

All runs follow a similar pattern. The description of one Victoria Day run will illustrate the typical problems, logistics, and events that are involved.

The organization of a major run will be set in motion several weeks before the run date. Members will suggest any number of possible run sites or destinations. After members vote on a destination, the road captain and his two assistants draw up an itinerary including highway routes and food and fuel stops. Their decisions are influenced by factors such as highway road conditions, the presence of service stations, and the past history of relations with various law-enforcement agencies along the route. Other tasks are divided among committees and individual patch holders. Some members have the responsibility of ensuring that the crash truck, a support vehicle, is both operational and adequately stocked with repair tools and supplies, such as motor oil, brake cables, and drive chains. Other patch holders are asked to purchase ample foodstuffs and to procure an inexhaustible supply of beer and wine. The president and treasurer draw the necessary funds from the club bank account to pay for these items, while the treasurer collects a predetermined contribution from each member. The members exchange information and opinions about guests who have been nominated to go on the run, and then they vote on their eligibility. The executive committee advises the members about any improvements that they feel are needed in the club's security measures. Finally, the president informs the RCMP of the club's destination. This information will be passed on to the appropriate provincial detachments in order to minimize the number of unpleasant surprises that might otherwise occur.

On the day of the run, club members congregate either at the clubhouse or at a roadside service station with a restaurant, depending on which is closer to the highway. The Rebels want to avoid riding through the city as a unit. The sight and sound of thirty outlaws rolling down city streets to the deep-throated crescendo of 'Harley iron' is as subtle as a military barrage, and 'cops come after loud pipes.' On this particular Victoria Day run, the Rebels were to meet at the Roslyn Hotel at 9:00 a.m., and to leave at 10:00. That morning, at home, each patch holder 'loaded on, strapped down, and moved out.' They had spent the last couple of days checking the mechanics of their machines and applying several coats of wax and chrome polish. Now they used bungee cords to strap sleeping-bags, tents, and assorted camping gear to their bikes.

Sandra and I took part in this run, and we set off to rendezvous with the brothers. Five blocks later I noticed flashing red and blue lights in my rear-view mirror. It was a standard 'shakedown': 'Could I see your licence, registration, and insurance?' 'How long have you owned this motorcycle?' 'Do you have a criminal record?' 'Are you carrying any weapons?' 'Are you carrying any dope?' 'We're going to [radio in and] check you for any outstanding warrants.' The officer very cautiously stepped around the front of my bike while 'casing out' the handlebars, and I wondered whether he had seen an RCMP information film that had been circulated to various police departments. The film warns officers that an outlaw biker may have converted the handlebars of his motorcycle into a shotgun-firing mechanism activated by a hand switch on the bars. In the United States, according to Don Parkhurst of the Federal Law Enforcement Training Center in Glynco, Georgia:

> Most officers by now have been warned about the outlaw biker trick of converting a handlebar to a shotgun barrel ... the outer end of the handlebar was replaced with a threaded tube which held a 12-gauge shotgun shell lightly against a homemade firing pin. A snappy twist of the wrist screwed the tube down on the pin, causing the shell to discharge. Any officer approaching a motorcycle should watch for open ends in the handlebars, and keep an eye out for someone who seems to be aiming a handlebar at the officer, or 'lining him up' with the rearview mirror ... Shotguns have also been built into exhaust pipes, and removable 'sissy bars' sharpened into spears have been used in homicidal stabbings. (Ayoob 1982: 27–8)

Knowing that exhaust pipes get hot to the point where steel and chrome discolour, I would get awfully nervous about riding behind a biker who had converted his pipes into a shotgun. You would also have to hope that the guy who had 'a 12-gauge shotgun shell [held] lightly against a homemade firing pin' never hit a bump on the road that might cause 'a snappy twist of the wrist.' I was tempted to tell the cop that that part of the film was more science fiction than fact, but the best – quickest – approach under these circumstances is to keep one's mouth shut and avoid eye contact.

We arrived at the Roslyn at 10:10 a.m., but the club had departed; all that remained on the parking lot was an empty can of Castrol oil. I was walking across the street to buy a road map when Crash pulled into the lot. Crash had also been stopped by the cops. He had been dragged down to 'the cop shop' to account for an arrest warrant regarding some unpaid traffic tickets. They let Crash go after he signed an affidavit stating that he would pay his debt to society within two weeks. If he failed to comply, then the next time the police checked Crash out he would be thrown in jail. Apparently these officers were familiar with both Crash and his driving habits: 'I would have been all right except that the cops knew me. You know, "Hi, Crash! Paid any of those traffic tickets we've given you?"' Two police squad cars remained in the parking lot, perhaps anticipating stragglers. When Crash and I left the parking lot to pursue the Rebels, one of the squad cars followed us to the city limits. This sort of 'surveillance' is the main reason that the club congregates at least one hour before it is scheduled to leave.

Together, Crash and I 'rode hard' until we caught up with the pack as they were leaving a gas station, and we joined in formation. The visual impression that you get when you first see a club on a run is that of military precision. Riding in formation cannot be done in a haphazard manner; it requires the systematic synchronization of the members and their machines. The operation demands that each patch holder show considerable riding skills and a disciplined professional attitude. Every outlaw club has procedural rules that establish efficient communications and effective plans of action. Otherwise the group would be vulnerable when situations arose that demanded a coordinated response; under these conditions any hesitancy or miscue by one member might spell disaster for all. This necessary merging of individual behaviour into a group phenomenon contributes to the members' sense of interdependence.

The patch holders are on parade; their club is on display; they know it; and each rider will ride at his professional best. The motorcycle pack advances as a column of staggered twos travelling in a single lane (Figure 4). It is the responsibility of each rider to ensure that there are fifteen yards between himself and the bike he is following, and three yards between himself and the bike beside

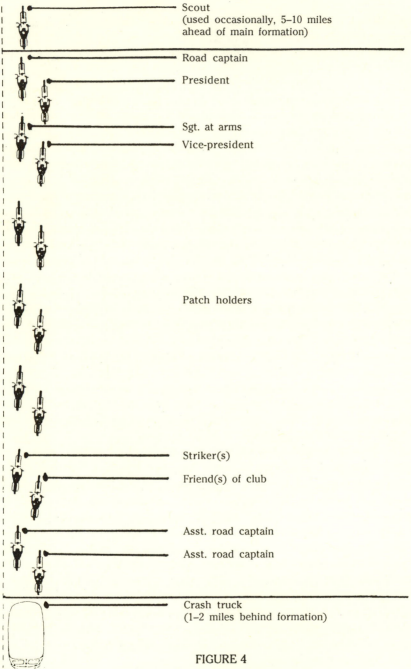

Scout
(used occasionally, 5–10 miles
ahead of main formation)

Road captain

President

Sgt. at arms

Vice-president

Patch holders

Striker(s)

Friend(s) of club

Asst. road captain

Asst. road captain

Crash truck
(1–2 miles behind formation)

FIGURE 4
Typical club riding formation

him. Adjacent bikes constitute units of two, staggered at approximately 45-degree angles, with the motorcycle on the left positioned about one yard ahead of the bike on his right. If the members are properly synchronized, the formation is technically safe and effective, as well as visually impressive.

At the head of the Rebel column is the road captain, who acts as the chief executive while the club is on the road. He sets the speed at which the club travels. The road captain must have a sound knowledge of how the members' hogs will perform under varying road conditions and be able to coordinate long bike formations that may stretch out for a half-mile. He initiates any necessary group action, and his decisions are communicated to the riders through a series of hand signals. Thus, when the road captain decides to pass a slower-moving vehicle, he will make a right-hand-turn signal followed by a 45-degree point signal to the left. The signal is passed on down the column. Motorcycles riding on the left-hand side of the column will increase the distance between themselves to allow the motorcycles on the right to merge and form a single file. Once in a single file, the bikes will pass the obstacle vehicle and re-form the column upon completing the manoeuvre. In some clubs, such as the Pagans MC and Banditos MC, the road captain will assume the added (presidential) responsibility of being the club spokesman while on the road: 'The road captain ... has been carefully selected for, among other things, a clean record and an ability to diplomatically handle policemen. He often carries the club's bail money, never carries contraband, and makes it a point to be immune to arrest. On a run, he is often the key man to talk to' (Ayoob, 1982: 30).

The president rides adjacent to, and to the right side of, the road captain. The 'prez' and 'captain' are followed by the other members of the executive. Next in the column ride the rest of the patch holders, followed by the strikers, friends of the club, and assorted guests. At the rear of the column ride the two assistant road captains. One of the assistants will occasionally pass the formation on the inside shoulder while he conducts a visual mechanical inspection of the members' machines. Both assistants will survey the column watching for 'whiplash,' large gaps between the bikes caused by members not maintaining tight formation while making turns, and they will pick out which riders are responsible. Should heavy traffic conditions make it necessary to split the column into more manageable units, each of the splinter groups will be led by one of the assistant road captains. If a patch holder 'drops out' of formation for mechanical reasons, one of the assistants will fall back to assist the member, while the other assistant road captain will expedite the re-formation of the column.

The last unit in the Rebels entourage is the crash truck, a support vehicle. It follows the main column at a distance of one and a half to two miles. A 'solid' or established club will have such a transport vehicle that it uses on long trips. For example, the Hell's Angels of Vancouver employ a van; the Bounty Hunters of Victoria use a converted school bus; and the Iron Cross of California have a house-trailer. In the late seventies the Rebels used a 'club trailer,' a white 1969 Plymouth sedan pulling an open trailer that had the Rebel insignia painted on either side. Today the Rebels use a converted bus that they painted jet black. The crash truck carries essential supplies that would be difficult or impossible to transport by motor-cycle: (1) liquor, consisting of wine and cases and/or kegs of beer; (2) foodstuffs, such as wieners, buns, beans, corn on the cob, and watermelon; (3) maintenance equipment, including tools, spare parts, and lubricants that enable the Rebels to make all but the most sophisticated on-the-spot repairs; and (4) personal items, parapher-nalia that the members would rather not pack on their bikes, such as tents and sleeping-bags. The crash truck has sufficient room to accommodate any motorcycle that is crippled beyond immediate repair and has to be carried to the run site for 'major wrench work.'

Communications between the column and crash truck are maintained by the president using a CB radio. If the club is suspicious about entering a certain town or area, they will send a scout ahead with a walkie-talkie radio to check for surprises such as a police roadblock. Another security measure that outlaw clubs often use is to equip their crash truck with a short-wave radio to monitor police radio transmissions. Police forces have countered this tactic by using walkie-talkie systems. Since 1984 police departments have been installing new radios in their squad cars, sending out a scrambled signal that only police radios are able to pick up. The RCMP advises other police forces about additional counteractive tactics that they can adopt to neutralize the bikers' security systems.

Bikes cannot transport cases of beer, sleeping bags, illicit weapons or drugs, and the bikes themselves must appear to be 'clean' if stopped on the highway by police ... A crash truck ...

will be equipped with a CB radio sometimes in touch with one of the bikers on the run.

When stopping bikes, policemen should be aware that a warning signal may well be sent to the accompanying truck, possibly by CB radio. If possible, both the bikes and truck should be stopped simultaneously. (RCMP *Gazette*, 1980: 30)

As a further precaution against having the crash truck stopped and the police seizing its contents – whether they be legal, such as booze and registered weapons, or contraband, such as illicit drugs – a club may load these items on a separate vehicle. This vehicle, such as a house-trailer, will have no visible club markings; it will be driven by clean-cut, straight-looking males or females, and may travel ahead of the formation, equipped with a CB radio, acting as an additional scout vehicle. To counteract this strategy, Parkhurst of the Federal Law Enforcement Training Center recommends 'good intelligence.' Specifically, police officers should 'be in touch with other agencies along the route, since the night before [the vehicle] will usually have stopped with the rest of the run, and will have been identified by local investigators if they've been alerted' (Ayoob, 1982: 30).

Another factor on a run is the performance of bike-rider teams. To ride successfully as a club, each member must know not only his own machine and riding skills, but also those of his brothers. Members are aware of the changes in performance that result from customizing their machines. Modifications that will affect performance may include wheel size, tire size, weight of the bike, degree of rake and length of fork extension, the presence ('juice frame') or absence ('hard tail') of a rear shock-absorbing system, and the installation of a 'stroker kit.' A patch holder must remain aware of how he and his riding partner have combined these facts of design with principles of performance. For example, a longer front-end extension will enhance ease and comfort of handling on a straight stretch of highway. However, there is a commensurate loss of manoeuvrability when negotiating low-speed tight turns. If the biker is following a member who is carrying a passenger, he must take into account that the extra weight will drastically affect the braking capacity of even a large motorcycle. For example, a stock Harley-Davidson Electraglide 'dresser' that weighs in at 722 pounds has braking ability that outperforms most cars. However, add 150 pounds of passenger and luggage to that bike at a highway speed of 60 miles per hour, and the required stopping distance increases by 35 per cent. An unwritten rule of thumb is that members will team up with brothers whose riding styles and motorcycles are similar to their own. Similarity of machines facilitates performance synchronization. In addition, familiarity with his brothers' machines allows the patch holder to visually check his riding partner's motorcycle while on the road. Each Rebel eventually gets to know the riding style and idiosyncrasies of ever other member along with the capacities of their machines. It is vital that a patch holder have a good idea of what to expect from his riding partner under any given situation.

> Tiny is a very cautious rider. We always ride near the back of the pack. When in formation, we sometimes leave nearly double the usual space between us and the bikes in front of us. That way, he doesn't have to alter his speed as much when the whiplash of the column comes around when we go into turns. He just lays back when they speed up, and catches up when they slow down as the whiplash takes effect. He's a very good rider. He realizes that with his weight on a bike he can't stop as fast. Like Tiny weighs near 285 pounds. (Wee Albert)

Every patch holder on the run rides a fine balance between fear and fascination. A motorcycle offers no illusion of physical protection; nothing stands between unforgiving asphalt and steel except leather and flesh. A failure in performance can result in a painful death. It is this constant and underlying reality that makes riding a challenge; skilful riding is a defiance of danger. This aspect of collective risk taking further cements the bonds of brotherhood and differentiates the Rebels as an adventurous élite from the citizen, who rides within the controlled and air-conditioned confinement of a 'cage.'

On this Victoria Day run there was one 'gut-wrenching' incident. Dale the Butcher experienced a biker's nightmare, a blow-out of his front tire. Dale would have felt the front end of his bike lift slightly the same moment he heard the loud bang. There is an immediate loss of stability as the wheel rim moves back and forth relative to the tire's tread. After the initial shudder, extreme vibrations shake the bike, causing it to wobble unpredictably. Steering control vanishes as vibrations are relayed from the wheel struts to the steel handlebars. Only the strongest of riders will be able to maintain his grip. If the biker is unfortunate enough to be turning at the time, then it all becomes very simple: 'game over.' In a turning situation, he will not have enough control to even afford himself the luxury of 'laying the bike down' and 'sliding out' in a gracious manner. Voodoo, who was riding beside Dale at the time, heard the explosion and pointed to Dale's tire. The members who were following the crippled bike moved as a unit to the left; while the Rebels were powerless to help their brother, they could at least give him the chance to 'ride it out' on the highway shoulder. Dale was in fact a butcher by occupation; he handled a meat cleaver eight hours a day and had developed perhaps the strongest set of forearms in the club. Dale didn't panic, and with patient determination he managed to slow down gradually. He eventually wound up in a roadside ditch, but he didn't 'drop his bike.' Later that evening Dale's brothers would toast and praise him for a 'class' performance.

In order to minimize the risks, the patch holders conduct 'scooter checks' during the periodic gas stops. Otherwise, any loose nut or bolt always seems to remove itself at the least opportune moment. For example, Raunch used one gas stop to reset his carburettor with Indian's assistance. Meanwhile, the members and their ol' ladies visit the washrooms, eat snack foods, smoke cigarettes, drink coffee and sodas, and engage in good-humoured bull sessions.

The noise of forty hogs coming back to life is overwhelming. I recall not being able to hear the sound of my own engine or even sense its vibrations. All was engulfed in a collective thunder. It was on this Victoria Day run that I concluded that a club run is the single group event that has the greatest psychological impact on the members: 'The run is really what it's all about. That's where it all comes together' (Saint). A run is rich with symbolism and charged with excitement and emotion. It provides meaning within a context of danger, power, and mystique. The run confirms a patch holder's claim to personal and social validity as an outlaw biker. Members are able to validate their identity as outlaw bikers by acting out their freedom ethic:

> I dislike to use the word, but we power trip on each other. It's a time when you can let your hair down and be the kind of biker that you want. If you happen to be on the hell-raising side ... a mandatory run is the time to do it. On a mandatory run we don't take any shit from anybody! (Wee Albert)

They act out their identity as brothers by sharing in mutually enjoyable activities:

> There's a social aspect to it. We become one; we're brothers. It's getting closer to your brother. Riding our bikes together makes us more in tune with each other. (Slim)

They act out their identity as social rebels by brandishing their motorcycles as subcultural border markers:

> That was beautifully heavy! Like I was riding sixth in line; and you'd look back and there would be nothing but fucking bikes! They were stretched out for about a mile. We must have made a few citizens shit their pants. You can imagine the looks on their faces when we passed them by. (Blues)

There are no welcome mats laid out for bikers at private camp-grounds. Their aggressive appearance and raucous style intimidate most campers, especially the proprietors. When the club reached Long Beach, a provincial camp-ground, the rangers said that the camp-site was full. Two of the Rebels rode past the barricades to see for themselves, and the RCMP were called by the nervous park rangers. The scouting party found the camp-ground to be 'packed like sardines, man!' Snake suggested that 'One of us should get one site and invite the rest in as guests; we'd have the camp-site all to ourselves in two hours!' When the RCMP arrived they handled the situation very professionally and advised the road captain and president that suitable accommodations were available at Amisk Lake. When we arrived at Amisk Lake the accommodations were indeed found to be suitable, but they were also occupied. The Rebels decided to take over a field that was adjacent to, but relatively isolated from the main camp-ground. It was the best arrangement for 'both worlds'; the Rebels would be left alone to enjoy the weekend in their own fashion without bothering any of the citizens.

The tents were set up and the members had begun some serious wine tasting, when I decided to unpack my Spalding J5V football.

> *Snake*: When I was riding beside you and I saw that football, I said: 'Jesus, he wants to get us all killed!' A football on a run is a dangerous weapon.

Caveman: He was sent here by the Warlords with a football so that
we'd commit suicide with it.

Steve: Naw, he just wants to see what a bunch of fucking primi-
tives will do when you give them a toy.

A wild game of team keep-away began with members taking occasional breaks from the action to guzzle some wine.

Larry: Killerball, that's what it was. Boy, I'll tell you, I picked up
some pretty wild bruises. You and that football have gotta go.
It's funny, as long as I've been with the club, nobody ever
thought of it before ... we had a lot of fun. It gets everybody off
that drinking scene. Sure, everyone had to be drunk to even go
out there, but two hours later you've sobered right up ... but
then someone put a bunch of acid in the wine and nobody knew
about it.

Coyote: I think that it was Voodoo.

Larry: Yeah, that stupid Voodoo, and all of a sudden everybody
was wrecked and I couldn't figure out what I was doing at first.
It felt like a kill-or-be-killed situation.

The team that was getting the worst of it grabbed the football, some
cans of beer and bottles of wine, along with a hash pipe, and
retreated up a tree. Those members on the ground felt that those in
the tree were being 'elitist assholes' and decided to bring them
down. When throwing branches didn't work, they got hold of some
axes and started to chop down the tree. The men in the tree
defended their position by throwing empties at the axemen. The
members on the ground then went to the club trailer, got out the
emergency flares, and started shooting them into the tree. While the
tree members were able to dodge the flares themselves, the flares
started a grass fire under the tree. The treed patch holders sur-
rendered the football, and some strikers were told to put out the fire
before it ruined their camp-site. And so the weekend went.

Over the three-day period, some Rebels rented row-boats and
motor boats and went fishing. Jim, who only brought 'a can of beans
and my fishing rod,' caught nine on one outing and feasted on
jackfish for the rest of the weekend. Tiny and Shultz were not so
lucky. Shultz was towing Tiny's row-boat, but the weight and drag
was too much, and Tiny's boat sank.

Shultz: Tiny went down with the fucking ship. When the water
  started coming in, he just sat there.
Caveman: Tiny is just too fucking lazy to move.
Steve: They could leave him out there in the lake as a spare
  boat. Just turn him on his belly, paint two numbers on his
  side, and get him to hang on to the oars.

A lot of the members caught fish, which they fried and shared with
their 'bros' over evening fires. There were hopes for roast pig. On
previous mandatory runs, the off-the-farm trio of Raunch, Crash, and
Caveman had raided a farmyard and brought back a pig. But on this
trip, one member of the rustling team, Caveman, had a cast from heel
to crotch as the result of an oil-rig mishap. While he still managed to
ride his hog, he was unable to run down pigs. Crash did try to steal
some chickens from a farm, but 'that farmer must have five dogs for
every chicken he has.'

As with most other Rebel social functions, runs emphasize
partying hard, long, and wild. Members expect that 'everyone will get
wasted.' A patch holder has to take his ability to party seriously, or,
as Wee Albert advised, 'If you leave the party early, someone's liable
to piss in your boots or pull out the pegs from your tent, if someone
hasn't already fallen on top of it.' However, it had been a long day of
riding, football, fishing, wrestling, and initiation ceremonies. Furthermore, members had brought ol' ladies along and were eager to enjoy
their company. The brothers began to crawl back to their tents and
sleeping-bags around 4:00 a.m. However, Terrible Tom was excep-
tionally keen on partying and was not to be denied. At 5:00 a.m., after
the last of his bros has passed out by the fire, Tom started yelling,
'Get up! Get up ! Let's party!' When he didn't get the response he
wanted, Tom began singing his version of Indian war chants while
pounding a rock on a garbage can. The next morning Steve jumped
Tom and handcuffed him to a barbed-wire fence. Steve then proceeded to urinate on him: 'Tom, you're going to smell as sweet as
you sing!'

These hedonistic practices are very much a part of the freedom
ethic. Partying is an expression of the outlaw biker's principle of laid-
back freedom and pleasure. Such impulses run counter to the
Establishment's social tenet of maintaining structure through rigid
control, and the middle-class morality of restraint leading to respectable moderation. In contrast to moderation and restraint, many

Rebel activities are geared towards spontaneity and the generation of intensity: 'it all feels best when we can hang loose and wild.' These characteristics of spontaneity and intensity leave members with the feeling that the ties between them are genuine, that nothing between them is contrived or artificially regulated. The interaction and bonding that result have a substantial psychological impact. Specifically, the feeling that their lifestyle is truly genuine forms a cornerstone of the biker's identity and acts as a concrete reference point of meaning when he asks himself, 'What makes my world worthwhile?' When a patch holder would talk to me of the difference between his world and that of the straight citizen, the pivotal points of dissimilarity inevitably included the dimensions of intensity and emotionality. Bikers often perceive straight society as a theatre of deception, a back-stabbing scenario that is hypocritically disguised by a thin veil of respectability; it is polite, but it is also superficial. Straight society is seen as lacking anything in the way of meaningful commitment or emotional depth. When the patch holders are on a run, they create a world of risk taking and thrill chasing. Collective indulgence in this kind of adventure leads to the formation of bonds of brotherhood that are 'blood true.'

POLICE SURVEILLANCE: RELENTLESS HEAT

The cops are always going to be there, and we're always going to be hassled. It comes with the territory, like rain on a run.

(Terry, Rebels MC)

When they deal with bikers, law-enforcement agencies find themselves in the very difficult position of having to separate legitimate attempts at creating cultural alternatives from criminal deviance. For their part, outlaw clubs come to expect and bitterly accept the fact that they are subject to selective law enforcement. 'Harassment' occurs when bikers are singled out for differential treatment for extra-legal reasons. Under these circumstances, the interaction between the police and bikers goes beyond the parameters of upholding the law; it takes on the added dimension of enforcing social norms and values. The direction and vigour of the 'arm of the law' becomes prejudiced by social concerns as well as legal ones. In effect, the policeman uses criminal law to enforce social norms by treating the bikers – who are perceived as social deviants – as criminals, which they may or may not be.

The biker wants to avoid a confrontation with the police officer, an individual whose power and resources far outweigh his own. A patch holder quickly learns what tactics he can employ and under what situations those tactics can be used, when he is 'pulled over by a cop.'

In the spring, when you first get on the road, for about a month everybody is on your ass, hot and heavy. We need a sensible delegate like you to go down and talk to them. But like you say, it all starts in the [police] locker room. Like I got picked up, and this one cop [in a different squad car] says on the radio to the cop that pulled me over: 'What are you trying to do, keep those Rebels broke this summer?' And this cop says, 'Yeah, I'm going to do my best.' And I just told him straight, I said: 'There's no doubt in my mind that you're a prick!' And he couldn't say nothing to me because it was just him and I; and if he wanted to get smart, I could get just as smart as him. He said 'Well, why do you say that?' I said: 'Because you're hassling me about pick-ass bullshit stuff that you don't really give a fuck about; but you just want to be a prick!' I was riding baffle drag pipes, and my bike was quiet. I got a thirty-dollar ticket for loud mufflers, and I told him: 'You're a prick!' But you know, what can he do if it's just you and him? He can't prove sweet fuck-all. When there's two cops, I don't say nothing, I just take my ticket and go straight home. But if there's only one cop and he's a prick, I'll tell him so. But I told that guy: 'I hope you have lots of time for holidays!' and he said: 'Why?' And I said: 'Because I'm going to be an asshole, plead not guilty, and take you to court and delay the proceedings till I'm sure the date comes on your holidays.' I talked with the crown prosecutor, and the charge was dropped. Same as I was charged twice for driving while under suspension [loss of licence due to accumulated demerit points]. I got out of it both times ... inadequate attempts to contact me in regards to my licence being suspended ... I never sign for or accept a registered letter ...

Yeah, that's maybe what the club should do, use a fucking club lawyer all the time. But the trouble is most of the guys in the club don't have the phenomenal fees that a lawyer wants to handle cases to fight helmet tickets and muffler tickets and speeding tickets that are all of the bullshit variety. And that's also a heads-you-win, tails-I-lose scene. If I want someone in court with me to fight a fucking charge, it's going to cost me $450 to fight a $50 speeding ticket. You beat it and you're out $400. (Caveman)

The 'can't-win/can't-break-even' situation is part of the price that a patch holder has to pay. I had two Edmonton cops follow me for five miles in the city. Eventually, I was pulled over, my bike was searched, and I was given a ticket for doing 35 mph in a 30-mph zone. The police constable said: 'You were breaking the law! That's why you were searched!' When the Rebels' Wee Albert and I were travelling through the city of Calgary, we noticed that we were being tailed. We made a conscious effort to stay under the speed limit. But we were pulled over, and I was given a ticket for having an inadequate helmet. The officer apparently did not like the appearance of my old Bell 'lid.' He tried to force me either to abandon my bike or to walk it, but Wee Albert lent me a spare helmet that he was carrying. After consulting a lawyer, I returned to Calgary to contest the ticket in court. The officer dropped the charge one hour before court proceedings. 'That's the way it goes,' commented Caveman. 'You travel 200 miles for the trial, and they drop the charges. Like, it's no skin off his nose.' My old friend Gypsy of the Satan's Choice recalled an interesting variation on the theme of harassment: 'I was being tailed by the OPP [Ontario Provincial Police] on Highway 401. No way that my insurance company would stand for another ticket. So I slowed down so much that most of the cars were passing me. I got a ticket for going too slow. The fucker says I was impeding traffic.'

A hostile reception from both citizens and police may greet an outlaw club that rides into a community while on a run. The police feel that the annual westward migration of Alberta clubs 'poses a security problem in British Columbia':

Motorcycle Gangs from Alta. to Face Surveillance in BC
[Cpl. Don] Brown said in an interview the outside clubs will combine with local gangs on weekend rides. 'Clubs realize one hundred bikers look more impressive than twenty,' he said. 'When they ride into a town which is hostile to bikers they can put up more resistance.' Clubs which police will observe closely this summer include the Rebels and Warlords of Edmonton and

the King's Crew, Grim Reapers, and Minority from Calgary ...
Brown said some bikers with hunting permits will legally carry
shotguns. 'We are aware of the potential but there is nothing we
can do. And we don't care as long as they keep the peace.'
Members of Brown's team will travel in cars behind the clubs
on weekend rides and step in to prevent local residents from
starting a fight. (*Edmonton Journal*, 28 April 1977: 3)

In Vancouver, BC, the citizenry are particularly sensitive to the presence of outlaw clubs. Public visibility is the key factor here; the
Vancouver city police had told the Satan's Angels not to wear their
colours within the city limits. Public indignation in 1966 over the
activities of the Satan's Angels MC prompted provincial Attorney-
General Robert Bonner to demand that pressure on bikers continue:

Nobody Waved Goodbye
Police don't often bother to welcome tourists to the city, but
made an exception Tuesday with five members of the Rebels
motorcycle club from Edmonton. Since arriving in BC a week
ago, they have been subject to police checks twelve times. (*The
Province*, 12 August 1975: 1)

From the public-relations perspective of the police, either outlaw
clubs should not be seen or the police should be seen to be controlling them.
    When the five Rebels got to Vancouver, they were pulled over by
five police cruisers and one motorcycle unit, a total of eleven
constables. They were checked a second time within a hour. The
Vancouver city police were hard-pressed to find any new faults, but
they did issue three additional tickets for mechanical problems. The
second 'check-stop' was a tribute to the creativity of the officers
involved: Whimpy got a ticket because his spare helmet had loosened from his pack and was covering part of his licence plate. Gerry
gave one of the constables his licence, registration, and insurance
cards as requested. The constable took a quick look at Gerry's
licence, handed it back to him and said: 'I can't read this!' and wrote
out a ticket for not having a driver's licence. The same card had
been accepted by another constable one hour earlier. Danny
received a summons for driving an unsafe vehicle: a balding tire. The
total cost in fines for tickets received during the two Vancouver
shakedowns was three hundred dollars. The Vancouver police were

enforcing a claim they had made earlier to the Rebels: 'There's only one club in this town! That's us!'

Underlying this selective law enforcement is a more subtle aspect of police strategy. None of the tickets was for a moving violation that could be cleared by a voluntary payment of fines by mail. These citations all required a court appearance. The police assume that outlaw bikers will not be willing or able to travel 3000 miles to appear in court. If the bikers do choose to contest what they feel are trumped-up charges, the officers can exercise their option of dropping the charges up to a half-hour before the scheduled court proceeding. However, if the bikers do not appear, a warrant will be issued for their arrest. Outstanding warrants are an effective deterrent against a club's return. If club members risk re-entering the province, they will do so as fugitives from the law. In effect, by not responding to a traffic citation, the patch holder turns himself into a bona fide outlaw: 'I left this BC town and I held her at 60 [mph], because this squad car was following me. He followed me for about ten miles. It turns out the speed limit is 55, and he gives me a ticket for doing 85 ... No, I'm not paying it. Fuck 'em! I'll take the [arrest] warrant' (Onion, Rebels MC).

Police try to discourage outlaw clubs from visiting their areas by subjecting them to continuous check-stops. This strategy is most effective when adjacent detachments coordinate their efforts.

Don Stevenson, president of the King's Crew, out of Calgary, says that throughout the 300,000 or so miles the club logs every year, it is subject to increasing hassles from the RCMP's 'E-squad' and local police. Riding hours are eaten up while officials check for drugs, stolen bikes, illegal weapons and I.D.'s; the search policy only intensifies ill will between riders and police. He claims that although his club members have made a practice for years of phoning ahead to RCMP units to advise them of their routes, local officials duplicate the check-stops impeding riding even more. That could be avoided if the RCMP would radio ahead to local law enforcement units advising that the group has already been checked over, but Corporal Brown explains he can do nothing if local police want to check for themselves. (*Alberta Report*, 2 May 1979)

However, the RCMP do indeed radio ahead to local law-enforcement units. While I was in RCMP headquarters in Penticton, BC, the follow-

ing message came over the radio dispatch at 1:00 p.m.: 'Car 7760 ...
we have the Tribesmen motorcycle gang ... approximately 30 bikers
... now approximately ten miles out of Princeton ... heading east,
Highway 97 ... Estimated Penticton arrival at 14:00 hours ... Will
advise.' The Princeton officer was advising the Penticton detachment, so that they could take appropriate action. The Penticton RCMP
decided to set up their own roadblock. The frustrated Tribesmen
tried to run the blockade but were pulled over. According to Spider,
the Tribesmen's road captain, the opening conversation went something like the following:

> *Constable* (RCMP): Why the hell did you run the blockade?!
> *Spider*: You just finished checking us out two hours ago. What the
>   fuck do you want?
> *Constable*: We're going to give you so much fucking heat, you'll
>   never come back here again!

In the search that followed, thirty-eight cases of beer were confiscated, the charge being suspicion of bootlegging. Four arrests were
made; two were for possession of unopened beer and two for
obstructing an officer. Apparently one member became very upset at
the prospect of the club's beer being confiscated. He hung on to the
door of the Volkswagen van (crash truck) until two officers managed
to break his grip by using their clubs on his hands.

The RCMP are well aware that applying this kind of repetitive
surveillance may result in violence. When they advise police departments on the proper strategy for 'Stopping and Checking a 'Run'
(1980), they warn officers of the possible confrontational and legal
ramifications.

> Bikers may have been checked several times during the course
> of their run and this may be only one of several times that they
> have been checked. Normally they will attempt to maintain a
> low profile, however, one cannot underestimate the potential
> for any sudden action on their part. Be ready for any violent
> explosion but don't overreact.
>   A bike gang on a 100 mile run may have been stopped 11
> times. Confronted by police the eleventh time, language may be-
> come abusive on both sides. Bikers have been known to record
> such conversations, then take them to their lawyers. So watch
> what you say and how you say it. (RCMP *Gazette*, 1980: 31)

Once the bikers have reached their destination and are off the road, the 'heat' will not necessarily stop. When the Tribesmen finally arrived in Penticton, police officials told them to stay out of town. The Tribesmen begrudgingly complied and set up camp in a remote area outside of the town-site. However, the RCMP continued to monitor the club's movements; that night the RCMP raided the Tribesmens' camp-site.

THE REBELS 'INVADE' CORONATION

For seven years the Rebels ended their riding season with a Labour Day run to the town of Coronation, Alberta. A five-man detachment of RCMP managed to police the rally site with no major incidents or complaints from the local citizens. But in 1981 the annual Labour Day run resulted in what the RCMP called 'the largest such police action to have ever occurred in Canada' (Corporal Brant Murdock, public-relations spokesman, RCMP). This exceptional incident provides insight into some of the political considerations that underlie the manoeuvres of both police and bikers on a club run.

North American outlaw clubs have traditionally adopted the Labour Day long weekend as a date for a mandatory run. The Labour Day run not only marks the end of the official riding season, for many clubs it becomes a major political event as well. Existing political ties among clubs are strengthened, and the possibility of establishing new ones is explored as 'the booze flows' and the members 'let the good times roll.' Over the years the Rebels established themselves as power brokers in Alberta and Saskatchewan. The Rebels became active in this role in 1975 when they issued invitations to the King's Crew MC of Calgary and the two Spokesmen MC chapters of Saskatchewan to attend the Labour Day run and celebrate the informal alliance that they had fostered among the three clubs. With the approval of the Rebels, the King's Crew in turn invited the Lucifer's Union MC of Calgary. The King's Crew hoped that an alliance with Lucifer's Union would help them survive a power struggle with the Grim Reapers of Calgary. The highly sensitive Labour Day run is a 'colours only' event. Only club members, strikers, and their female companions are allowed to attend.

A provincial camp-ground north of the town of Coronation (pop. 1500) was originally chosen (1973) as the regular Labour Day run site because of its central location. Situated 120 miles east of the city of Red Deer, Coronation was relatively equidistant for the Rebels chapters and their guest clubs. The success of the initial and subsequent runs resulted in the annual event being nicknamed the Coronation Run. Several factors contributed to the success of the run. These included the availability of provincial camp-ground facilities, an adjacent rodeo racetrack where members could race their bikes, and a nearby town-site that allowed the patch holders to buy meals, refuel their motorcycles, and restock their beer supply at the Longhorn Saloon. However, the most critical factors were that the rally site was isolated and the local RCMP were very accommodating. The mandate of the RCMP was to protect the citizens and their property; the main concerns of the Rebels were to strengthen inter-club ties and to have a 'righteous good time' while doing it. Both the RCMP and the Rebels realized that their mutual interests could best be served by avoiding citizen/biker contact. There was only one access road into the camp-site, and the RCMP would park a patrol car at the entrance. For their part, the outlaw clubs placed a sentry at the gate whose job it was gently but firmly to send on his way anyone who wasn't dressed in the familiar uniform of dusty jeans, leather jacket, and denim-jacket cut-off with club patch. '"They're a good bunch," said one constable, "They just go up there and have a good time. The thing we worry about is that some of the locals might go in and stir things up." For the most part, the locals respect the bikers' wish to hoot and holler in privacy' (*Calgary Herald*, 5 Sept. 1977: 1). The joint strategy of controlled isolation on the part of the RCMP and the Rebels proved effective. After the third annual Coronation Run, an article appeared in the *Calgary Herald* newspaper entitled 'Bikers invade Coronation but nobody's worried':

> The first bikers' convention two years ago caught the farmers and 1,200 townspeople offguard. Some feared for their children and property ... they doubted that the RCMP could do much if things got out of control. Now it seems, folks look forward to the annual Labour Day 'run' of the hairy young men on their noisy machines. Coronation mayor Bud Carl said the first time the bikers came to town, 'we were quite concerned. There were about one hundred of them and we didn't know what they were going to do. There are some pretty wild characters in that outfit ... but they have been coming here for three years and to my knowledge, they have caused no trouble whatsoever. I have had no complaints from the police or civilians; in fact, they bring quite a bit of business to town.' 'We're not looking for any

trouble,' said one biker from the Rebels Motorcycle Club of
Edmonton, 'we just want to have a good time.' (*Calgary Herald*, 5
Sept. 1977: 1)

The unofficial policy of cooperation between the Rebels MC and
the RCMP resulted in a good time for the bikers and an uneventful
weekend for the police. According to the Rebels, the formula for
success was one of mutual 'trust': 'We had a trust deal with the
RCMP. We [the club president] would phone them up and let them
know where we were going, how many guys would be there, along
with dates and times. The idea was that there would be no surprises
for either them or the club' (Tramp). The Edmonton RCMP would
then forewarn those police detachments that could expect the Rebels
in their area. It was this 'trust deal' that enabled a local five-man
RCMP detachment at Coronation to handle an outlaw-club convention
that involved more than 120 bikers without incident. However, all
this would change in 1981.

Instead of the local five-man detachment, the Rebels ran into a
small army of over two hundred police officers who stifled the biker
bash with relentless 'heat.' In addition to over one hundred regular
Mounties, the force included a heavily armed and camouflaged RCMP
tactical squad from the city of Red Deer, a forty-man contingent from
the City of Edmonton police force, the E-squad special biker task
force from the city of Vancouver, numerous plain-clothes officers,
special police photographers, a videotaping unit, and police-dog
units drawn from various central Alberta RCMP detachments. The
equipment used in the military-styled operation featured a mobile
police command centre, a telecommunications truck, a helicopter,
two fixed-wing observation aircraft, two chartered buses, a vehicle
for storing evidence, forty police cruisers, and an arsenal of high-
powered scoped rifles, shotguns, automatic weapons, flak jackets,
bulletproof vests, and tear gas. This small army was quartered in the
local school gymnasium, which was converted into a barracks; a
hotel banquet room served as a mess hall.

The 1981 Coronation Run was an important political event to the
Rebels. They were hosting the Grim Reapers and King's Crew of
Calgary, Vancouver's Satan's Angels, Hell's Angels from Quebec and
Massachusetts, Les Gitans (Gypsies) from Sherbrooke, Quebec, and a
representative of the Vagabonds from Toronto – approximately 155
bikers in total. The Rebels were determined to show their guests a
good time and had arranged for unlimited free beer and steaks for

all. A successful run would enhance the national prestige of the Rebels and affect their future relations with these powerful clubs.

Chilly winds and ominous grey skys foreshadowed the extraordinary events that began to unfold on Friday evening. The Rebel entourage included thirty-five bikers from the Edmonton chapter, along with several motor homes and pick-ups that carried the extra supplies. The Rebels had been on the road all day, the weather had been poor, and they were cold, wet, and tired. Bob, the road captain, was a ten-year veteran of the club; but he decided against sending scouts ahead to check out the situation on Highway 12. The Rebels had already informed the RCMP of their route, destination, and intentions. As far as the club was concerned, the 'trust deal' was still on. It would prove to be a costly mistake. The Rebels had no idea of the 'shit that was about to come down':

> There were about thirty bikes riding with us. We were maybe a half-mile from the camp-site when they hit us. Just as we came over a rise in the road we saw the roadblock. There were twenty or thirty cruisers lined up on either side of the road, with two cars in the middle of the road. There were buses and vans parked all along the highway. A couple of the guys tried to turn around and scramble out of there; but they were surrounded by cruisers and a helicopter that closed in from the rear. I wasn't counting, but it looked like there were four cops for every bike. When we pulled up six guys surrounded me. Before I even had a chance to shut off my bike, one cop puts a numbered card on my chest while another cop takes my picture. They were armed to the teeth. They had handguns, shotguns, and there were four or five sergeants with automatic weapons, all nice and shiny, primed and drawn. There were a couple of cops patrolling around with German shepherds and Dobermans. Then I noticed that they had this plane circling over us. I was surprised, really stunned by what was going on. While I was getting out my licence and registration, Gerry yells out: 'Look over there! They've got a fucking SWAT team in the fields!' Sure enough, there were cops dressed in camouflage, their faces painted in camouflage. These guys were crawling through the fields and hiding behind bushes, drawing a bead on us with their scoped rifles. It was unreal, like an ambush scene

out of Vietnam. From then on it was the usual hassle and shakedown. It seemed like a lot of trouble to give me a ticket for running loud pipes [having inadequate baffles in the muffler system]. (Terry, Rebels MC)

The police handlers of the canine corps attempted to have their dogs sniff out any caches of illegal drugs that they thought the Rebels had hidden on their bikes or stashed away on any of the support vehicles. No drugs were discovered, but the RCMP did confiscate all the beer and wine that the club had in the bus on the grounds of liquor violations. The Rebels and their ol' ladies were then computer checked for any outstanding warrants. Corporal Murdoch of the RCMP stated that strip-searches were done only when police had 'reasonable and probable grounds to conduct such searches' (*Calgary Herald*, 9 Sept. 1981: B1). One ol' lady, a 30-year old nurse, who was pregnant at the time, was strip-searched by three female officers after a computer indicated that she had failed to pay a ten-dollar parking ticket. The woman spent the evening recovering in a Stettler hospital. She was charged with failing to submit a change of address form to the Department of Transport. The charge was later withdrawn by a provincial court judge, Ken Cush, in December. The police proceeded to inspect the motorcycles and issued twenty tickets for minor traffic violations. One bike was inspected three times for equipment violations. On the third check the police decided that the lowest point of the seat was twenty-five inches above the ground instead of the required twenty-seven. The licence plate was seized and the member had to ship his motorcycle home on a trailer. One particularly zealous officer confiscated Tramp's new Sturgis model Harley-Davidson; apparently it had a crack in the licence plate. The police seized six motorcycles for suspected serial number alteration. The motorcycles were loaded on to a hay trailer that the RCMP had requisitioned from a local farmer and transported to the police mobile command headquarters in Coronation. All the suspect motorcycles were returned by the end of the weekend.

The RCMP planned to apply the same 'check-stop' procedures to the other clubs when they approached the camp-ground. However, a scout bike evaded the roadblock and returned, cross-country, to Coronation in time to warn a contingent of eighty King's Crew,

Satan's Angels, and Hell's Angels patch holders. The bikers at all costs wanted to avoid having their motorcycles confiscated, and 'there was no way we would submit to any skin frisk' (Ron, Satan's Angels MC). They decided to 'hole up' in the Coronation Hotel bar. The police task force responded by swooping down and sealing off the town. Time began working against the bikers; they realized that as the hours passed and sunset neared, they faced imminent charges of vagrancy. The bikers outmanoeuvred the RCMP by accepting an invitation from the proprietor of the local drive-in establishment to attend a marathon midnight-to-dusk movie showing. After last call at the Coronation bar, the patch holders bought fifty cases of off-sales beer and retired with their ol' ladies to the drive-in. They paid off the proprietor, spread out their sleeping-bags, and settled in to enjoy *Superman II*, *The Dogs of War*, and *Clash of the Titans*. The RCMP ended the stand-off the next day when they ordered the town's gasoline stations not to sell fuel to bikers. The patch holders were stranded and submitted to the check-stop, but still managed to negotiate for a 'pat-search' (outside the clothes) instead of a 'skin frisk' (strip-search). They wheeled their motorcycles, rented trucks, and Lincoln Continental into the police lines, where they were checked for identification, photographed, and searched. In the meantime, the camouflaged tactical squad had deployed itself in the bushes of the Rebels' camp-site and continued its round-the-clock surveillance after the outlaw clubs gathered together for steaks and beer. 'They were out there all the time. At night you'd go to the trees to take a piss, and you'd hear the branches and twigs breaking. During the day they'd be flying over our camp-site with their planes and helicopter. They forced us to change; the trust deal was over. In the future we'll be a lot more prepared for them' (Raunch). By Sunday afternoon the party spirit had dampened and the bikers began to roll out of town with police cruisers and planes following them.

The joint RCMP and Edmonton city police action resulted in the confiscation of five rifles and a handgun, but as the weapons were registered, no charges were laid. Five motorcycles were seized on suspicion of altered serial numbers, all were returned on the weekend. There were four charges for restricted and offensive weapons (one unregistered handgun and martial-arts implements), one charge for possession of stolen property, fourteen liquor offences, seven charges of possession of marijuana and one of cocaine, ten arrests for outstanding warrants (unpaid traffic tickets), and one hundred and twelve Highway Traffic Act charges, mostly for minor equipment violations.

The Rebels MC of Edmonton decided to take collective legal action to contest the charges. The club organized 'boogies' (public dances) to help defray the costs. Both the members and friends of the club contributed to a collective fund. Approximately $5000 was raised and used to hire George Parker to act as a club lawyer. Parker appeared in provincial court on 27 October of that year. His actions resulted in fifty-one of the fifty-five tickets issued to the Rebels being quashed on technicalities. For example, a number of the summonses failed to indicate that the accused had the option of making a voluntary payment instead of appearing in court. Six of the other assorted charges were also dismissed by provincial judge J.A. Murray.

The RCMP and city-police action was sanctioned by the Alberta solicitor-general's department and the Edmonton police commission. The exercise cost the federal and provincial governments more than $150,000. But the police forces claimed that it was worth the money because it showed the bikers that they could not get away with antisocial and criminal behaviour, such as terrorizing people in a small town. Public-relations officer Corporal Brant Murdoch stated that past biker gatherings in Coronation had resulted in a gang rape, assaults, break-ins, and thefts. However, none of these alleged occurrences was ever substantiated by official complaints registered with the RCMP. Coronation mayor Muriel Heidecker said that the bikers had not caused any problems in the past and that the town council had not asked the RCMP to crack down on the bikers. However, she did have reservations about her town being chosen as a convention centre for outlaw motorcycle clubs: "'They have never done any damage to the town but they fight among themselves and the people don't like them coming'" (*Edmonton Journal*, 3 Sept. 1981: E8).

Colleen Richardson, 19, who lives on her family's farm 300 yards from where the Rebels camped, says there were no problems, nor had there been during the two previous years the bikers had been at the camp-site. In fact, Miss Richardson said, her family let the bikers use the phone several times and her grandmother, who lives in a nearby trailer, invited several bikers in for hot chocolate. Another lady, who lives about five miles from the camp-site and helps maintain the grounds says, 'They never cause any problems; they don't do anything wrong.' And she observes that the bikers leave the camp-site cleaner when they leave than many other campers do. (*Alberta Report*, 18 Sept. 1981: 32)

However, the town of Coronation's reaction to the outlaw bikers was not altogether positive. Some of the prairie town's businesses advertised that they would be closed for the long weekend, apparently in apprehension about the biker rally: '"The last time they were in here [Tasty Mill Restaurant] they took over my restaurant like they owned it and then left without paying"' (ibid.). In the final analysis, there were no violent confrontations between the bikers and police, no fights between the bikers and the townspeople, no public rowdiness, and no complaints from any citizens about abuse from the bikers. All charges that were laid against the bikers stemmed from the check-stop. '"We go a thousand miles out of our way to be in the middle of nowhere, where we won't bother anyone, and they're all here waiting for us"' (member, Satan's Angels MC; ibid.). According to the publisher of the Coronation weekly newspaper, the townspeople were not happy with the actions of the police: 'I look at it as a form of harassment' (*Edmonton Sun*, 9 Sept. 1981: 5).

There was 'no reason at all' for the operation, according to RCMP spokesman Murdoch, 'other than the fact that it's about time. They've ridden into town for six or seven years pretty well unchecked.' Plans for a large-scale police mobilization had been under way for two years; the purpose was to test police capacity to move large numbers of men and equipment on short notice. The operation was not 'specifically targeted' at the bikers; 'having the outlaw gangs here just added to the rationale for having this operation now ... we just seized the opportunity' (Murdoch, RCMP). However, the reason that the Coronation Run became the specific target was probably influenced in part by the clubs that the Rebels had on their guest list, particularly the Hell's Angels. One can speculate that the RCMP were concerned about potential coalitions and mergers. The Rebels themselves were laying the groundwork for another chapter in Calgary. 'The club was growing,' stated Terry of the Rebels; 'the RCMP wanted to show us some power.' The RCMP were likely also worried about the possibility of the Hell's Angels extending their influence into western Canada through a process of either incorporating or affiliating with clubs such as the Rebels, Grim Reapers, and Satan's Angels, a club that did indeed become a Hell's Angel chapter two years later in 1983. The RCMP would view an increased Hell's Angels' presence as having the potential of destabilizing the 'biker problem' in western Canada. In eastern Canada, these kinds of political developments indeed had led to a direct increase in inter-club territorial warfare, homicides, and illicit drug trafficking.

Edmonton Police Chief Robert Lunney would later tell the Edmonton police commission that police intelligence had established 'without a doubt that the gangs are primarily large scale criminal syndicates' (*Edmonton Journal*, 11 Sept. 1981: B1). The check-stop operation provided the police with both identification and photographs of 'gang' members. The police viewed the weekend gathering of clubs as a major threat to peace in central Alberta: 'Intimidation through appearance and overt threats has been a trademark of the gangs. We have been exceedingly fortunate in Alberta that we have not been subjected to the violence and fear that has overcome some communities resulting from large assemblies of bikers' (ibid.) According to Chief Lunney, the RCMP feared that the gathering would result in more crime in the province.

What is lost in these public-relations statements is any explanation as to why it was deemed necessary to use such an unprecedented and disproportionate show of force. For the past five years, the job had been handled by a local five-man detachment, with an accommodating attitude. There were no registered complaints from the citizens, nor did town officials request increased policing. The whole task-force operation was the brainchild of the RCMP, and it is possible that they may have had a hidden agenda: to demonstrate their usefulness and effectiveness. The future of the RCMP in Alberta was uncertain. Their high costs and lack of accountability to provincial complaint boards had caused eight provincial governments to consider replacing the federal RCMP with provincial police forces.

Contract Hassles Jeopardize Mounties' Future in Alberta
Rumours and talks at strategy sessions in provincial offices have shifted to talk of creating police forces to replace the RCMP ... Eastern Canadian police administrators (Ontario and Quebec) have urged their western counterparts to take the big step – to unload the expensive and unaccountable RCMP. (*Edmonton Journal*, 8 Sept. 1981: A2)

The concern senior RCMP officers would have over these 'contract hassles' would stem from the fact that only half of Canada's twenty thousand mounted-police officers work on federal matters; the other half provide police services for the provinces, which reimburse the federal government for costs. If the provinces chose to replace the RCMP with provincial forces, the RCMP would be dealt a devastating blow to their policing presence and political prestige. The number of RCMP officers would be drastically reduced, their training costs per officer would increase, the opportunity for graduate officers to get grass-roots provincial experience would be lost, and the force's ability to integrate and influence both federal and provincial policing would be severely curtailed.

Despite their high cost and lack of accountability, the provinces felt that there was a national aspect to the RCMP that was worth retaining. In addition, the RCMP back their men with an extensive array of support services, special investigative units, laboratories, and an impressive inventory of armaments, dogs, all-terrain vehicles, snowmobiles, boats, and aircraft. One can speculate that the RCMP wanted to show themselves to be indispensable by profiling their sophisticated personnel and arsenal. The check-stop operation featured several unique components of the RCMP, including Project Focus – part of their national database and intelligence centre – and E-squad, a special investigative corps; both of these units are equipped to deal with 'the biker-gang problem' on a national basis. Outlaw motorcycle clubs have a highly negative public image and easily grab front-page media attention. Picking the bikers as targets – traditional symbols of antisocial and criminal behaviour – would ensure that the RCMP's *tour de force* would not go unnoticed. Ironically, coverage of both the 'crackdown on biker gangs' and the RCMP contract dispute appeared side by side in the *Edmonton Journal* (8 Sept. 1981: B2). Shortly thereafter, the Alberta solicitor-general chose to retain the services of the RCMP.

RCMP public-relations spokesman Murdoch stated that the check-stop operation would deter the bikers from returning to Coronation: '"They're not coming back ... No matter where they go in Alberta, we'll be around"' (*Edmonton Sun*, 9 Sept. 1981: 5). But next year the Rebels did indeed return to Coronation. 'We were just hoping that we could have our party without any trouble,' said Gerry, the club president. When the Rebels pulled into town, the sign on the Longhorn Saloon said; 'Welcome Bikers.'

Part Five

MAKING IT ALL WORK: ECONOMIC AND POLITICAL REALITIES

Outlaw Economics:
Financing a Subculture

The more money the club has, the happier the members
are.

(Voodoo, Rebels MC)

THE REBELS' NEED FOR CASH

It costs money to run an outlaw club, more money than the average
citizen might think. The Rebels need cash continually to meet expenditures that are characteristic of all outlaw motorcycle clubs.

The most expensive item is the clubhouse, since members have to
rent or buy and furnish a building. When the Rebels first began in
1969, they didn't have a large bankroll. The neophyte club rotated its
first meetings among members' houses and garages. The Rebels
stabilized their financial position in the early seventies. During the
winter, they would rent inexpensive houses in industrial areas and
houses scheduled for demolition. In the summer, they leased an
isolated farmhouse. Today all three Rebels chapters own their clubhouses. Private ownership allows the club to invest more money in
the construction of increasingly elaborate and permanent security
measures. These fortress-like modifications include renovations such
as concrete-reinforced walls, security cameras, electronically operated locks, radio scanners tuned to police frequencies, and an iron
door – Raunch's welding pride and joy. The bite of the Rebels'
clubhouse security system comes in the form of Remington 12-gauge
semi-automatic shotguns and high-powered rifles. All these measures

cost money. But a clubhouse is more than a fortified refuge, it is primarily a social centre for good times. Clubhouse acquisitions of a more casual nature included a pool table, a movie camera, a screen and projector, video equipment for recording and showing the runs of summer, a stove, a beer fridge (the Rebels had two), a portable power generator, and couches and beds for members and overnight guests. 'Most of the stuff we got dirt cheap,' according to Jim. 'Guys just keep their eyes open for stuff that'll make the cluhouse more comfortable, like that [used apartment] rug you let us know about.'

'Jammin' in the wind' is the core activity of the Rebels MC, and to that end they purchase equipment that makes it easier for their patch holders to keep their scooters 'on the road.' This includes the basic tools of motorcycle maintenance and repair, along with more elaborate items such as a lathe and wheel balancer. Another major expenditure was the acquisition of a used touring bus and its conversion into and maintenance as a crash truck, or support vehicle. The Rebels provide their runs with additional backup material in the way of walkie-talkies that they use to coordinate their movement on the road, and a short-wave scanner that enables them to pick up police transmissions. Furthermore, when runs and parties are planned there have to be enough funds on hand to buy booze and foodstuffs.

Part of a club's mandate is to look after those members who face the prospect of doing 'down time' with the law. The Rebels always maintain enough money in their savings account in the event that one of their members requires bail or the services of a lawyer. These financial reserves, along with working arrangements with competent lawyers, ensure that members will not be unnecessarily incarcerated. In the past some clubs, such as the Satan's Choice in Toronto, would circumvent the necessity of having large sums of money available in the club treasury for bond money by employing a bail bondsman. A bondsman will provide the necessary bail money and charge a certain percentage (generally 10 per cent) for his fee. For example, if a member's bail were set at three thousand dollars, the club would provide the bail bondsman with three hundred dollars and furnish security for the remaining amount. The Rebels rejected this strategy. 'It's pretty rare to have one of our guys in jail who needs bail,' said Blues, the Rebel treasurer, 'but [using] a bondsman is like throwing money away for nothing.' While some clubs in the United States still employ bondsmen, the practice is now illegal under the Canadian Criminal Code.

Outlaw clubs are well aware that the police are usually more reasonable in their surveillance procedures if they know that a club has the money to employ a sound legal defence and does not hesitate to bring up charges of police harassment. Since the mid-1980s, the patch holders of some clubs have adopted a tactic of tape-recording the conversations that they have with law-enforcement officers when they are 'pulled over and shaken down.' Interestingly enough, while the biker looks at the situation as one of 'being harassed,' the police officer looks at the situation as one of 'being baited': 'Abusive language on both sides may be recorded with the police officer losing the argument in court ... So watch what you say and how you say it ... Police and law enforcement authorities everywhere have begun to notice the increasing use of tape recorders each time a biker has been stopped for one reason or another ... Gang members attempt to bait officers into slips of the lip, making compromising or prejudicial statements which subsequently render police officer court statements useless' (RCMP *Gazette*, 1987: 23).

The Rebel reserve fund is also available to patch holders who simply find themselves short of cash. A patch holder who takes the summer off work to enjoy the good life of laid-back riding and roving is prone to unexpected expenses. His 'trusty' shovelhead may decide it needs a lot of attention two weeks before a scheduled holiday run to Sturgis, or a supporting ol' lady who also hasn't received enough attention may suddenly decide that a change in lifestyle and mates is in order. Under these circumstances a Rebel can draw upon the club for a loan at a minimal carrying charge. 'It all depends on how much I need. Like, say it was ten or twenty bucks, well I'd just ask one of my brothers. But if it was a substantial loan, like say six hundred dollars, I would borrow it from the club rather than borrow it from a brother ... I borrowed money [$600 at 5 per cent interest] to go on holidays this year' (Caveman). Apart from borrowing from the club treasury, most club members manage to cope with unforeseen expenses by resorting directly to their brothers. For example, with twenty-four members there is always a surplus of various motorcycle parts to be shared, and a member in dire financial straits can always work out some sort of arrangement with a brother, whether it be the renting of an inexpensive suite in a member's house, or the provision of a temporary bunk and breakfast. When a Rebel is going through lean times, his brothers will 'keep their eyes open' for anything that might be of use to him. This aspect of gift giving might include everything from free beer and invitations to dinner to items such as the 'brand new' (almost) work boots that Blues and Dale got for Raunch.

MAKING A BUCK FOR THE CLUB

The Rebels replenish their club treasury with money from five major sources: membership dues and club fines, the sale of various commodities to members, the brokerage of club shares, sponsoring 'boogies,' and holding 'field days.'

Membership dues are two hundred dollars annually, and are payable every six months (Rebels MC constitution). In order to minimize the administrative duties of the treasurer, members are encouraged to pay their dues in total at the first meeting of the year in January. 'There's no heavy pressure or anything like that,' said Blues, the club treasurer. 'I just tell them that I'll break their leg if they make me mess up my [accounting] sheets.' Fines are a relatively minor but continual source of income. Infractions, such as being late for a mandatory run or disorderly conduct during a club meeting, will result in fines of ten to twenty-five dollars.

The Rebels MC sells a wide variety of goods and services to its members on a regular basis. The hard-drinking lifestyle of the members makes the sale of alcoholic beverages, mostly beer and wine, particularly profitable. Booze is sold at higher-than-retail but lower-than-tavern prices year-round in the clubhouse. On club runs everybody contributes to the booze fund. 'Hard riding' by the members also brings a dollar to the club treasury. Acting through Ken and Steve's Brothers Custom Cycles, the club buys motorcycle parts, accessories, and lubricants in bulk from wholesale outlets and sells them at both a savings to members and a profit to the club. Additional money comes from entertainment facilities within the clubhouse itself. Money is collected for use of the pay-as-you-play pool table, and from the renting of spare rooms to members as a temporary place to 'crash,' or as a convenient place to enjoy a woman after a club party. Patch holders also purchase an assortment of Rebel paraphernalia from the club, such as club colours (back patches), club cards, T-shirts, year-of-membership badges, and club identity stickers for their motorcycles.

One money-making venture that caught me completely off guard was the sale of club shares. The Rebels MC marketed ten-dollar shares to its members on which both the club and the members earned interest. Needless to say, the Rebels were not registered as a company, which makes the sale of capital debentures a contravention of the Province of Alberta Companies Act. But they remained inconspicuous, and worrying about being prosecuted by the Alberta Securities Commission was next to last on their list of priorities. However, I couldn't resist the opportunity of kidding guys like Wee Albert about going public and listing the Rebels MC on the Toronto Stock Exchange. 'Hey, that way I could keep track of you guys just by reading the business section of the *Globe and Mail*: "Rebels MC stock was up 2¾ points after a strong day of raping and pillaging," or "King's Crew Ltd. fell 5 points after rumours circulated about a hostile takeover bid by the Grim Reapers Corp."'

The sponsorship of a boogie, a commercial public dance, is one instance where the Rebels go beyond the boundaries of the outlaw subculture in order to accumulate capital. An entertainment committee is responsible for having tickets printed up. These are then sold by members to select individuals, bikers and non-bikers alike, whom they meet in motorcycle shops or bars. For most outsiders the boogie is an opportunity to dance, mingle, and rub shoulders with the élite of outlaw bikers. However, as far as the club is concerned, a boogie is not an exercise in public relations: 'Strictly money, that's the one and only purpose ... strictly to have money coming into the club, but not out of my pocket or any of the other members' pockets ... We have to exercise a lot of tolerance because a lot of straight dudes come out with some really funny questions, things that aren't their business' (Wee Albert). Traditionally, the Rebels hold two such boogies a year, the dates of which roughly coincide with the beginning and end of the riding season, such as the Harleyween Ball held on October 31st. A public boogie is held outside Rebel territory – usually in a rented community hall – and features live entertainment in the form of a local rock band. Along with the sale of admission tickets, additional money is made from the sale of bottled beer and wine.

Members just do their own thing and ignore the crowd, and that seems to get the crowd warmed up. We get to feeling pretty good, although everybody has their job; everybody is a bouncer. Last time we just had one minor incident. Some dude got drunk and said something stupid to Dump [Warlords MC] when they were in the can. Dump ploughed him one and picked him up and threw him on to the sink. It broke and we had to repair all the plumbing. But usually we drink and have a good time puttin' down brews and dancing, and there just seems to be no hassles. (Wee Albert)

While a boogie has the immediate advantage of producing club revenue without drawing upon the finances of its members, it carries some automatic disadvantages. Aside from the potential for mis-understandings between citizen and biker, these public profile situations inevitably draw the attention of the local police.

Bikers' Weapons Seized by Police
City police seized M-1 rifles and knives from out-of-town biker gangs [Satan's Angels MC] bound for a Rebels' sponsored party Saturday. Eight people were charged with offences ranging from possession of an offensive weapon to traffic violations ... and one was charged with possession of a restricted drug. 'When you get that kind of people involved, you have the potential for a violent situation,' Constable Bruce McMorrin said Sunday. (*Edmonton Journal*, 22 Sept. 1980: A3)

It is difficult to imagine any major gathering of outlaw bikers that would not have the potential for the police to 'collar' a misde-meanour or issue citations for several traffic or vehicle violations. For most members, the carrying of 'prohibitive weapons' such as knives or chains is a taken-for-granted aspect of the dress code of their lifestyle; and the presence of 'offensive weapons' such as high-powered rifles is not uncommon. Yet while chain belts and Buck knives are as commonplace as empty beer bottles, their use is strictly controlled by club rules and any indiscriminate use is highly unlikely. As a testimony to the effectiveness of their tight internal discipline, Rebel boogies have been free of any major incidents of violence: 'Though the street outside the hall was lined with one hundred bikes, police said the bikers attending the six-hour party caused no trouble. "I've seen wedding receptions that were noisier than that," said one neighbour, who said it wasn't the first time the bikers had rented the hall [St Edmund's Hall] for a party' (ibid.). Aside from club boogies, the Rebels follow a policy of physical isolation that avoids the annoyance of police surveillance and the necessity for uncharacteristic restraint.

A 'field day' is an inter-club meet that sees clubs get together for some friendly motorcycle-riding competition and some serious partying. Holding a field-day is a common tradition among clubs in North America, Europe, and Australia. It is certainly the most enjoyable way for outlaw patch holders to make a buck for the club while having a good time with their brothers. A field-day that the Rebels sponsored one Canada Day (July 1) long weekend illustrates the key elements that determine the success of these kinds of collective profit ventures.

A successful field-day depends on weeks of preparation and effort. It is a collective enterprise that demonstrates the strength of the brotherhood as a resource base of diverse skills and a wide network of both business and streetwise contacts. Each member makes a personal contribution, through either his labour or a unique talent. For example, one problem that faced the Rebels' entertainment committee was obtaining live rock entertainment. It seemed that local musicians looked upon playing at a three-day 'biker stompin' bash' with about the same enthusiasm as they would going into a war zone. However, Armand, the Rebel social convenor, had a contact in the illicit drug trade who was a musician. The contact was the bass guitarist in a rock band called Lover, and he owed Armand a favour. The guitarist was able to convince other members of his own band plus three additional groups to play for the bikers – provided they were given some assurances. The Rebels solemnly guaranteed the musicians their personal safety, the safety of their instruments, and future booking considerations.

In order to minimize public contact and police surveillance, the Rebels' entertainment committee rented a ranch located north of Edmonton towards the town of Gibbons. The ranch was an isolated rural private property. This meant that the RCMP had no need to be concerned about the sights and sounds of sex, suds, and scooters offending the public. However, the solution to one problem often contains the roots of another. Lover's manager informed the Rebels that since the festival was being held on open rangeland the bands would need a stage. Crash, an off-the-farm country-and-western Rebel, felt that the heavy metal rockers 'just want to be above the ground when their music starts a cattle stampede.' It was up to Voodoo, a veteran 'rig driver' of fifteen years, to solve this problem. Voodoo used his connections to get hold of two flatbed trailers; and, with a truly remarkable demonstration of driving skill, he parked one flatbed and then backed in the other trailer alongside, leaving only a three-inch gap between the two 65-foot vehicles. The musicians also made it known that they would be unable to perform in the rain. In response, Gerry, a housing construction foreman, supervised the building of an elaborate canopy to cover the flatbed stage, along with some concession shelters to store and dispense the food and booze. Danny, who was an electrician by trade, transported the portable generators from the clubhouse and set up the electrical connections necessary to provide power for the bands' equipment and the floodlights. Dale helped increase the Rebels' profit margin when he was able to obtain weiners at a significant discount in price from the meat-packing plant where he worked as a butcher.

As part of the field-day project several of the Rebels combined their professional talents and resources for an additional money-making venture – a raffle. Ken and Steve donated the facilities and tools of Brothers Custom Cycles; 'wrenching ace' Whimpy supplied most of the mechanical expertise, Jim furnished a paint job from his autobody shop, and other members contributed labour and spare parts. The end product was a restored badass-looking hog, dressed in glimmering chrome and midnight-black steel. The bike caused an instant outbreak of 'panhead fever' among the drooling brothers, who were more than willing to put down some bucks for raffle tickets. The entertainment committee undertook the production and distribution of admission and raffle tickets, and looked after the purchase and transportation of foodstuffs and alcoholic beverages. Members' ol' ladies prepared and vended the various edibles, such as hot dogs, pork and beans, corn, watermelon, and beer and wine. The night before the field-day, Crash and Raunch, who have rural backgrounds and know how to handle animals, teamed up with Caveman to go on a search-and-kidnap mission. They returned with a large pig that they had abducted from a nearby farm. The pig was later skewered and roasted over an open fire. Over the three days Rebel strikers collected and disposed of garbage. In the aftermath a number of the members replaced posts and restrung barbed wire – a natural talent for Albertans – that was part of fencing damaged during the course of the party. What becomes evident is that the success of the field-day depended on a lot of planning, cooperation, and group effort. For patch holders, this kind of joint economic venture differentiates the 'brotherhood' essence of their club life from the impersonal self-oriented society that surrounds them. Furthermore, the significance of the fact that the patch holders have the skills and do it all themselves is not lost: 'There's a feeling of togetherness that comes from making your own world,' according to Saint, 'even if it's only for three days.'

The heavy-duty Los Brovos came out west from Winnipeg and the King's Crew and Lucifer's Union rode up from Calgary for what turned out to be three days of non-stop biker festival. In addition to the three visiting clubs – each of which paid a flat entrance fee – numerous tickets were sold to non-club bikers and especially to single females. The biker bash began on Friday afternoon and continued to Sunday evening, with upwards of four hundred people attending the forty-four-hour-long party.

Some of the field-day competitions were a test of riding skills or endurance, while others were just simple amusement. The drag races were held on a hundred-yard stretch of the entrance road and pitted two riders against each other in a test of speed. In the bicycle-tire toss, the passenger carries bicycle tires and attempts to ring toss them on poles as he or she is driven by. Ol' ladies team up with their favourite scooter tramp in the weiner biting – 'deep throat' – contest, where a woman sees how much she can bite from a weiner that is suspended from a clothes-line while her ol' man pilots the scooter underneath the wire. Endurance and strength are tested in the tire-drag contest. In this event a car tire is attached by a rope to a motorcycle and a biker lays down on the tire and hangs on to the rope for dear life while the rider sees how fast he can drag his partner around a pylon over two hundred yards of rangeland. There are as many different field competitions as there are bike clubs, and each club has its favourites.

The jousting match was my favourite. It was downright dangerous. The idea was to pull the passenger off of the other bike. The bikes will come at each other from different directions and the passenger will have his back to the driver of the scooter. There is only one rule, the bikes are not allowed to go any faster than 15 mph. But guys always fuckin' gunned her [speeded up] when the passengers grabbed hold. It got to the point where we voted to have the St John's Ambulance attend our field-days ... One of the events the chicks used to do ... The chicks would take off their bras and the guys would put them in a pile. The guys would race [ride] their chick to the bra pile and the chicks would scramble for their bras and then have to

run back to the finish line while putting their bras back on.
Once when we had an open [to the public] meet the cops were
there with their cameras, and they told us to fucking can the
contest because it was too obscene for the spectators. (Gypsy,
Satan's Choice MC)

The Satan's Choice were into field-day competitions in a big way and
at the end of the summer they awarded a trophy to the chapter that
won the most events. In addition to trophies that had been donated
by the local Harley-Davidson dealers, the Rebels offered free beer
and food for the winners of individual events, and a keg of draft beer
for the winning club. The Rebels won, but some of the rival clubs felt
that they had been sandbagged: 'They [Rebels] never let us know
what the events were going to be,' said Trock of the King's Crew.
'They've probably been practising all summer long.'

After the field competitions the bands started up and some bikers
danced to the amplified rock music while others were content to just
mingle with their brothers while they compared scooters and tattoos
and eyed the biker women. A lot of the bikers pulled their scooters
into a secluded treed area and set up camp. Most of them had tents,
some just an air mattress and a sleeping-bag. I approached one of the
Los Brovos who had spent most of the day tracing an electrical
problem – a short in the generator – in his scooter. 'This is what it's
all about, man,' he said as he kicked back a brew and tried to forget
the grief his bike had caused him. 'This is freedom, going where you
want, relaxing and being with your people.' I guess his message was
that even a bad day of riding beats a good day at the office.

The isolated setting allowed the Rebels and their guests to indulge
in a number of pleasant diversions, ranging from eating, drinking,
dancing, and making love in the woods and in the hayloft of the barn,
to a wet T-shirt contest that saw the contestants get a bit carried
away in the heat of competition. The contest – an outlaw-biker field-
day tradition – was initiated by Walter, the lead guitarist of the rock
group Lover, whose wit earned him the job of master of ceremonies
for the whole affair. Six of the more endowed ladies were brought up
on the stage. Tramp passed a helmet to collect some prize money,
but the girls were having so much fun that they readily responded to
the cries of 'Take it Off!' and 'Show your tits!' There was no problem
in getting one member from each of the four clubs to volunteer as a
judge. They surveyed the young ladies present, then asked, 'Well,

what are the rules?' Walter replied, 'Taste and touch!' 'This was no problem for those guys; and the girls didn't seem to mind either. I saw nipples redden and harden as some guys nibbled away. I had fun keeping up my running commentary as they went from girl to girl, punning right through: "This is a titillating experience!" It was nice and spontaneous, and a lot of fun. "Obviously he's keeping abreast of things!"' (Walter). Despite the large number of people in attendance and the vast quantities of liquor consumed, the weekend activities were marred by only one minor disturbance. The incident occurred when a lone biker 'insulted' Armand of the Rebels who was on crutches at the time. Armand let his crutches drop and laced his adversary, who sagged at the knees and then fell motionless to the ground. Armand then called for a striker to come and pick up his crutches: 'Give a cripple a helping hand, eh!'

The field-day was both a financial and entertainment success. The sale of the motorcycle raffle tickets ($20), admission tickets ($10), and money from the vending of foodstuffs and alcoholic beverages resulted in the Rebels realizing a profit of approximately $6000.

HOW REBEL PATCH HOLDERS MAKE A LIVING

One of the questions that outsiders most frequently asked me was 'How do those guys make a living?' It was not hard to tell that they expected tales of illicit drug dealing, prostitution, and theft. Most were quite surprised to learn that the majority of Rebel patch holders were either blue collar workers or tradespeople. The Rebels held the following jobs at the time I rode with them:

Ken	Part owner of motorcycle shop	Full-time
Caveman	Truck driver	Seasonal
Steve	Part owner of motorcycle shop	Full-time
Blues	Machinist (plastics/metal)	Seasonal
Larry	Labourer, autobody shop	Full-time
Raunch	Welder	Seasonal
Gerry	Foreman in house construction	Full-time
Mike	Truck driver	Seasonal
Whimpy	Motorcycle mechanic	Seasonal
Clayton	Carpenter	Seasonal
Snake	Labourer, oil rigs	Seasonal
Dale	Butcher	Full-time

Jim	Autobody repairman/bouncer	Full-time
Onion	Labourer, oil rigs	Seasonal
Saint	Mechanic/technological student	Seasonal
Danny	Electrician	Seasonal
Yesnoski	Machinist	Seasonal
Voodoo	Truck driver	Seasonal
Armand	Labourer, oil refinery	Seasonal
Killer	Labourer, construction	Seasonal
Crash	Labourer, oil rigs	Seasonal
Tiny	Labourer, oil rigs	Seasonal
Terrible Tom	Heavy-equipment operator	Seasonal
Wee Albert	Pipe-fitter	Full-time
Ed	IBM technician/bouncer	Full-time
Indian	Truck driver/bouncer	Full-time

The Rebels segregate themselves socially, but they cannot do so economically. Because they are not economically self-sufficient, 'earning a living' means they have to cross club boundaries. Thus, while none of the Rebels belongs to any other type of voluntary social, political, community, or recreational group, sixteen (60 per cent) of the patch holders are members of job-related or economic groups, such as the Alberta Small Businessmen's Association (two members), and various trade unions, such as the Teamsters and the Carpenters Union.

The fact that the Rebels MC does not maintain strict economic barriers is reflected in the relative absence of club controls over how its members make a living. Essentially, individual members are free to make their own job choices. Job choice was neither a matter of official club jurisdiction nor a matter of major concern to other members: 'There's rarely any talk about work,' said Caveman. 'It's not really that important.' 'What a guy does for work? Well, that's up to the individual, eh?' according to Larry. 'They don't talk about jobs that much; that's personal.'

Under most circumstances the Rebels consider work a legitimate reason for not attending group functions. 'Like work is a valid excuse for not coming around' (Caveman). In fact, the Satan's Angels MC of Vancouver went so far as to make specific allowances in their Rules and Regulations for job commitments: 'If the club calls a ride all members will attend. If a member is working, sick, bike not running, he will be excused.' However, if a Rebel repeatedly uses work as an excuse for not 'being there,' he will be 'talked to.'

If you're working all these hours and you're putting time into the club, that's just fine. But if you stopped putting time into the club, then I'm going to talk to you about something like that. (Larry)

If a guy is working three different jobs and you never see him, well he only needs two of those jobs. There are no rules about it. You just have to tell a guy, 'How come I never see yah?' And if he says, 'Well, I've been working hard all the time.' You say 'Well, Forget it!!' (Steve)

Applying pressure to members who are 'no shows' because of work is not exceptional. The club takes action on *any* commitment that hinders a member's performance, whether it be his job or his ol' lady. 'If a guy doesn't come around we want to know why,' stated Raunch. 'It doesn't matter what the reason might be.' Simpson and Hoop of the Warlords used their trailer homes as collateral and borrowed $150,000 to purchase a gravel-hauling truck to do personal contracting in Grande Cache, northern Alberta. Simpson then borrowed an additional $10,000 to purchase a new motorcycle. A couple of the Warlords expressed reservations about their brothers' economic enterprise after a short 'brew run' out to the Airways bar: 'I suppose borrowing another $10,000 doesn't matter a helluva lot after what they've borrowed ... Sure, they're making lots [$500/day] and they're working for themselves [independent]. But how can a guy ever relax or just putt around on his scooter with those kinds of payments to meet?' (Dump, Warlords MC). A few beers later, Dump was telling Simpson, 'You know what'll happen if you don't get that bike running [more often], don't you? It'll be "Hey, *striker* Simpson!"' For most outlaw clubs the bottom line is that the club has to be the centre-piece of a patch holder's lifestyle. After that, anything goes and is ostensibly a matter of personal choice. 'The club has nothing to do with your job whatsoever. Your personal life, well the [Satan's] Choice is my whole life, let's put it that way. But if I want to go out and get a straight job, as long as I'm on time for meetings, runs, and stuff like that, that's my bag. The thing we look at is that the club is the most important thing' (Gypsy, Satan's Choice MC).

While the club per se does not determine a member's job choice, it is not surprising that the brothers will sometimes combine their talents in order to supplement their income: 'Everybody has different ideas, buy things, repair things. Repair and sell them at a profit, mainly motorcycles' (Raunch). 'It's talk that's always about fixing up a motorcycle. Fix up this motorcycle and sell it for that amount of money, and stuff like that' (Blues). In an adventurous approach towards making a buck, three of the Warlords went up north to Dawson Creek in the Yukon Territories to earn their fortune, panning for gold. They bought the rights to rework a section of river that had been previously panned, using better equipment. While the Warlords never found the 'motherlode,' they were ecstatic about their frontier-man's challenge and returned with enough 'colour' to finance a summer's riding.

If a club member learns of a full- or part-time job opening at the place where he works, he will 'put the word out.' When I asked Blues whether or not members talked about good or bad jobs, he replied: 'Like in the sense of "What the hell are you working there for, because it's no good"? Yeah, all the time. And that's where you wind up working for or with your brother.' One afternoon, Terrible Tom, a heavy-equipment operator, came into the back of Brothers Custom Cycle shop and said: 'Hey, I've got jobs for three guys to crew work in St Albert for a couple of weeks. Any takers?' Four other Rebels worked together on oil rigs, three pooled their resources as part owners and mechanics in Brothers Custom Cycles, two laboured together as foreman and electrician in house construction, and three of the brothers freelanced their skills as bar-room bouncers.

The Rebels' economic network goes beyond job search, joint money-making ventures, sharing accommodations, and dealing in bike parts to include a system of barter exchange. Members will often trade off their areas of expertise or swap labour. 'If you've got a job that has to be done, you don't go out and phone up some firm you've never heard of,' said Steve. 'You get your brothers to help yah!' For example, Wee Albert, who is a pipe-fitter by trade, 'straightened out' the plumbing in Clayton's house. Shortly thereafter, Clayton, an electrician, helped Wee Albert install the wiring in his garage. 'The worst part of that little number,' according to Clayton, 'was that Wee Albert made me promise to stop calling him a "turd herder" [nickname for a pipe-fitter].' In another instance, Ken and Caveman bought a side of beef from Ken's uncle, a rancher. They then got Dale, 'the Butcher,' to cut it up for them. Dale received a portion for his labour, while Ken and Caveman got Alberta prime beef for $0.65 per pound.

Although Rebel patch holders are free to choose their occupations, the fact that they *are* Rebels by itself impinges on their choices. Members attempt to make their job choice consistent with their self-image as an outlaw biker. Formal interviews indicated that cultural themes that dominate the Rebels MC ethos influence members' perceived range of job choice. For example, members shared an explicit understanding that being a mechanic would be a valued economic activity, while being a store clerk would not be; attending university was considered a waste of time, while attending a technological institute was endorsed as a credible option; the prospect of being a truck driver was evaluated positively – 'that's cool' – while being a transit bus driver was evaluated negatively – 'that sucks.' Members gave similar reasons for their reactions to certain jobs, reasons that reflected the biker ideal of masculine pride and independence. For example, the prospect of working in a retail store was rejected because 'A man can't take pride in his work. It's a demeaning job' (Raunch); 'It's nine to five. There's no challenge' (Caveman); and 'Too much of an ass-kissing job' (Steve).

Most of the Rebels replace the Protestant work ethic with the biker work ethic: 'Work the winter; ride the summer.' Approximately 60 per cent of the Rebels work seasonally. They work at relatively high-paying jobs – such as those in the oil patch – during the winter and collect unemployment insurance during the summer months. While most of the Rebels worked this strategy rather effectively, a few were prone to budgeting errors: 'I didn't want to work over the summer, but I'm going to have to go back to work pretty soon. I blew my wad and the money is low and I got bills' (Killer). Sometimes the plan of working-the-winter and riding-the-summer can backfire altogether. For example, Tiny, a 'roughneck' on the oil rigs during the winter, was forced to take a month off active club participation in the middle of the summer in order to work in Edson, two hundred miles east of Edmonton. Danny, the club's road captain, attempted to set Tiny straight.

> *Danny*: You don't know how to spend your money. If you spent more carefully you wouldn't have to spend so much time working. Last summer I lived on $4700 and a $1000 income-tax return. What you need is a private accountant.
> *Tiny*: Look, Danny, I haven't wasted it and I don't like working any more than you do. I don't own much. I have a bike, a [half-ton] truck, a few clothes, maybe three pairs of jeans and a few

T-shirts, and I live in Jim's [Rebels MC] attic. The rest of the money I spend on my brothers and having a good time with them.

One way of getting by the financial pitfalls of not working during the summer was finding an ol' lady who was willing to 'take up the slack' during lean times. Blues and Lorraine rented an inexpensive one-bedroom house in the inner city. They shared the house with 'Barney the cat' and 'Brooks the dog' – an abandoned puppy they adopted and carried away inside Lorraine's leather jacket on a club run that passed through the town of Brooks. Lorraine kept the house neat and tidy, and the used furniture was unremarkable except that Blues had carved 'Harley-Davidson' into the wooden arms of the couch and attached a wooden 'HD-74' plaque to the television set: 'I like to carve if we're stuck here watching the idiot box [television].' Blues had three high-powered rifles mounted on the wall and a bayonet rested on top of the doorway ledge. In the backyard was an old Ford pick-up that Blues was restoring. Blues had been married twice before and found the common-law relationship with Lorraine more to his liking: 'Marriage fucks things up, too many obligations, you start putting chains on each other.' Lorraine loved Blues and tolerated his live-and-ride-for-the-day lifestyle. 'Right now we've got no big plans,' she once told my ol' lady, 'but maybe that'll change someday.' While Blues only worked seasonally as a machinist, Lorraine always worked the year round as a waitress. One particularly 'tight' summer Blues took out a club loan to rebuild and sell a bike in order to help pay the rent. For a small commission, Ken and Steve would sell the motorcycle through Brothers Custom Cycles. However, Blues already owed Ken and Steve four hundred dollars for bike parts. Moreover, anyone who shared Blues's radical taste in choppers would be building his own, not buying it 'off the rack.' Lorraine offered to get another job on a part-time basis; Blues vetoed the idea. 'When I haven't got enough money to put spark-plugs in the bike, then she can get a part-time job. She's a real sweet little girl. She works in a restaurant and earns a lot in tips. By the time I come around at noon she's earned enough in tips to buy me lunch. By the time I come around at night, she's got enough in tips to buy us supper and gas money so we can go off riding' (Blues). For a couple of the Rebels, their relationship with an ol' lady involved less romanticism and more financial exploitation: 'You should see my ol' lady. Jesus, mean! If I had my choice between fucking her and a mad polar bear I'd probably have bear cubs as grandchildren. The only reason I live with her is that garage she has ... shelves for tools, work benches, thermostat heat control, fluorescent lighting, wash basins ... She walks in and says, "What do you care more about, me or your bike?" I told her: "How much have I spent on you the last month?" She says, "Maybe five bucks." And I say, "Well I've spent over a thousand on my bike. Does that tell you anything?"' (Caveman).

The outlaw biker also reverses that tenet of the traditional Protestant work ethic that holds leisure to be a means of recuperating from and preparing oneself for further work. For most patch holders the leisure activity of biking is not only a means of isolating oneself from work, it takes priority over work. All the Rebels I talked to gave priority to their commitment to the club over their job:

> For the majority of them [non-club bikers] their bike wouldn't be as important as other things happening around them, because each and every one of them have a definite straight life. Whereas with our club, the club and riding come first. (Blues)

> If it came down to a choice between the club and my job? The job would go by the boards, no doubt about it. (Dale)

To the extent that being a righteous patch holder becomes an end in itself, it affects both job choice and work performance. 'I was making a lot of money [$900 per week] putting in that much overtime at the plant. But I felt that I didn't have enough time to spend with the club. I didn't feel good about that, so I quit [and found a job working fewer hours for less money]' (Wee Albert). Consistent with the biker freedom ethic that advocates a minimizing of ties that bind, only six of the Rebels viewed their present mode of employment as permanent. Most considered their lifestyle to be one of freedom and transition; permanent commitments were a thing of the future. 'Sure! One of these days I'll get married and settle down,' commented Caveman, who drove a truck as a teamster. 'I'm going to save enough money to buy my own rig, maybe start my own company. But you can't do both. It's got to be one [being a Rebel] or the other [domestic and job security]. And it isn't "one of those days" yet.'

Other Rebels already had domestic responsibilities that demanded a more stable economic orientation. Seven of the Rebels were married; four of these couples had children. Two Rebels in common-law relationships also had children. These Rebels were more future-oriented and practised deferred gratification in the name of future plans. All of them engaged in full-time, year-round employment, and four men were making mortgage payments on their own homes. Ken, part owner of Brothers Custom Cycles, was a successful small businessman who would discuss ways of making money in real estate with Ed, an IBM technician who also had a home, wife, and family.

Jim provides an example of integrating the economics of domestic responsibility with club life. He was raised on a farm near White Rock, BC, and began work in the city of Edmonton as a labourer for Double 5 Autobody. Along the way Jim met and married Gail and they had two children together. Jim bought an older two-storey house in the river-valley district; his first home-improvement project was to build an addition in the backyard, a chicken coop: 'Not so much for the eggs as for eating young fryers. I like nothing better than fresh meat. Me and Indian and Blues are going duck hunting next week; you should come along. I needed some sort of coop anyways; I got my kids two little pet ducks. I like large dogs, but they always get stole in the city. I had a prize Labrador. I was training him and Gail was spoiling him. Someone stole him right off the leash when we left the yard. I'll eventually settle down and do mixed farming, either go back to BC or go up north [Alberta]. The city is no place to raise kids' (Jim). Jim was not happy as a labourer; he wanted independence: 'I want to be my own boss. That way it's *my* life!' Jim began by renting Double 5's facilities to do personal contract jobs. He earned the reputation of being one of Edmonton's top custom paint specialists; when a local Harley dealer entered a classic old Indian motorcycle into a bike show, Jim did the paint job that won the first-prize trophy. One morning I dropped into the shop to bring Jim a front fender I wanted him to paint. 'Jim? No, he isn't around yet,' said the foreman. 'He usually doesn't come in till around 10:00. He comes and goes when he wants ... Yeah, Jim's what I'd call a five-dollar-an-hour-a-few-hours-a-day-any-day-of-the-week man.' When I returned several days later to pick up the fender a co-worker told me that 'Jim dropped in a while ago to look at some of the bike parts [he'd painted], then he took off. He told the boss that he had "a bad case of the 26-oz. flu."' Jim eventually established the independence he wanted by starting up his own autobody shop.

Not all the Rebels were as inclined towards or capable of integrating domestic and economic responsibilities with their life as a biker as Jim was. Melody issued the following warning to Snake while she made him breakfast one morning while on a club run:

Melody: You've got good tastes when you're sober, but when you're drunk I can't stand you. If you take off for two weeks like that again, then forget about seeing me or your kid. Just go ahead, go and enjoy yourself!

Snake: Yeah, but it's when I'm drunk that I enjoy you most!

On the surface, Jim's family and economic orientation did not reflect the biker ideal of freedom and adventure unmitigated by domestic responsibility. However, while enjoying a Sunday fresh-killed wild-goose dinner at Jim's place, I realized that these domestic situations serve to reinforce the notion of social community. The fact that some of the brothers have 'real' families enhances the legitimacy of their outlaw society, a recognition that 'we are real people with real emotions.' Conjugal couples with permanent residences further add an element of stability that the free-and-wild young buck Rebels can fall back upon. This was most evident in the area of housing. For example, Tiny lived in the attic of Jim's house; across the street Onion rented the upstairs suite of the house owned by Indian and his ol' lady; Raunch shared accommodations in a house rented by Crash and his ol' lady; newly wed Clayton and Donna moved into the basement of a house rented by the established Wee Albert family, and for a time Yesnowski lived with Larry's household.

THE POTENTIAL FOR CRIME

Bike gangs are like a cancerous growth, you have to keep right on top of them.
(Detective Sgt. Terry Hall, Ontario Provincial Police Intelligence Unit)

In many ways all outlaw clubs are pre-adapted as vehicles of organized crime. Paramilitary organization lies at the core of their tight-knit secret society. It is a society capable of enforcing internal discipline, including an iron-clad code of silence which ensures that information about club operations never goes beyond the walls of the clubhouse. Uncompromising commitments of brotherhood generate cohesion, mutual dependence, and a sense of a shared common fate. The lengthy socialization required to become a legitimate 'biker' and the two years of proving oneself as a striker in order to become a member make the infiltration of a club by a police officer a virtual impossibility. The political structure of the club, the anti-Establishment attitudes and high-risk nature of the individuals involved, and the marginal social environment in which they operate have the potential to produce a clubhouse of crime.

Canadian police officials certainly believe that motorcycle 'gangs' are the biggest organized-crime threat in Canada. In a report delivered to the Canadian Association of Chiefs of Police in 1985, the Criminal Intelligence Service of Canada stated that bike gangs specialize in manufacturing and distributing drugs, prostitution, break and enter, and motorcycle vehicle theft, and also sideline as hit men, extortionists, and bootleggers. 'Hailed as MAFIA II, the bikers are illegally connected with everything out on the street. Wheeler-dealers in drugs, the prostitute/white slavery runners, muscle, hit men for hire, most likely have a biker connection somewhere along the line. Your local neighborhood friendly gang has the right connections to wreck a bar, restaurant, club, disco or to set up the quiet bomb that goes off conveniently at 2 a.m. with the end result, an insurance rip-off; explosives and arson for fun and profit' (RCMP *Gazette*, 1987: 2).

The outlaw-biker reputation for brawn and unbridled violence lends support to this belief. They *are* able to crush their foes with force and suppress witnesses with fear and intimidation. This reputation is a marketable commodity. The sale of their image might include 'policing' public gatherings, such as rock concerts. For example, the Los Brovos were hired as security for the Eagles rock band in Winnipeg, the Hell's Angels protected the Rolling Stones at Altamont, the Vagabonds acted as bodyguards for the Village People in Toronto, and the Rebels have been hired as security personnel for car races at Edmonton's International Speedway. The manager of the Speedway had previously hired various private security agencies, but with little success. His comments after hiring the Rebels were: 'That's the best crowd control I've ever had. If a spectator would try and crawl over the fence a Rebel would politely ask them to get back to their seats, and that was that, no problems.' Underworld figures, such as loan sharks who have run out of patience with an overdue client, may also see the bikers as a potent mercenary force. 'Two weeks ago a guy comes up to me and offers me five hundred bucks to break some guy's arm who owed him money,' said Caveman. 'I told him to go fuck himself!' Streetwise 'businessmen' who want to take over or intimidate a rival, but who don't have the funds to hire 'heavies' on a permanent basis, may learn from bouncers and rounders in the bar which bikers are willing to contract out for extortion that may involve either beatings or bombings.

In the bar a patch holder may link up with a woman who is willing to give up her job as a waitress to work as a prostitute with a biker as her pimp. These connections may develop to the point where clubs are supplying girls to massage parlours and dancers to strip bars. Drug dealers in the bar – often the bouncers – will initially approach the bikers to make sales. The bikers may enter a pact with the dealer whereby they protect the dealer or his territory in return for discount rates on the drugs – 'freebies' – or a piece of the action. The bikers might eventually decide to bypass the dealer and establish direct links with a distributor and market the drugs themselves. The final stage in this process would be for the bikers to hire a chemist to make the drugs – usually methamphetamines – in a 'kitchen' (underground laboratory). As of the mid-1980s the drug of preference for 'clubs who deal, and bikers who use' had shifted from methamphetamines to cocaine. If we move our focus from preference to measurements of accessibility and actual use, then alcohol and nicotine, drugs that have been legalized and taxed by the system, remain the bikers' most popular means of inducing an altered state of consciousness. These legal drugs are followed by the illegal substances cannabis and its deratives (marijuana and hashish), and lastly by methamphetamines and cocaine. A new highly addictive and absurdly dangerous drug, called 'crack,' does not require elaborate laboratory equipment to manufacture – baking soda, a simple hotplate, a heat-resistant glass coffee pot, and a set of scales – had become popular by 1987 on the streets in general, but not among any of the major clubs as a saleable commodity.

In a similar fashion, motorcycle theft *may* evolve from being a matter of occasional individual entrepreneurship on the part of one or two members to being organized crime conducted on a club level. Thus, local bikers may engage in occasional motorcycle theft only to provide themselves with replacement parts or bikes. Alternatively, they may get involved in the theft, 'restamping,' and interprovincial or interstate transportation of stolen bikes between different clubs. Those clubs that are part of a larger alliance or federation have the obvious potential of using their national and international network for the distribution of drugs or stolen property. These international contacts between outlaw-club federations, such as the agreement that was cemented between the Outlaws MC of the United States and the Satan's Choice MC of Canada, can furthermore be used to change the identities of and hide those club members who are fugitives from the law in each other's country.

Outlaw motorcycle clubs vary in the extent to which they may engage in criminal activities for profit. Some clubs hold aloof from what could be classified as recurring organized crime. Clubs such as the Satan's Choice, Outlaws, Pagans, Banditos, and Hell's Angels, who have run the full gamut of crime, remain a distinct minority. Yet, even among these outlaw federations, the amount and nature of criminal activity vary from chapter to chapter and from year to year. Furthermore, even among those outlaw clubs involved in organized crime one will find a diversity of members, not all of whom are criminally active. For example, in the mid-1970s, members of the Toronto chapter of the Satan's Choice were involved in motorcycle theft and prostitution, and operated a drug lab in a cabin in northern Ontario that manufactured methamphetamines, 'Canadian Blue,' for export to the US-based Outlaws MC. Yet, mixed in with the narcotics dealers and break-and-enter artists were labourers and tradesmen, such as an electrician, a plumber, and a truck driver, along with a stock-market office executive. Conversely, a Choice member who worked as a truck driver could always supplement his income by helping a couple of members steal a motorcycle.

The Rebels are outlaws, but they are not professional criminals. When I rode with them, laws were sidestepped, bent, and broken, but rarely for profit. Criminal acts were usually confined to minor misdemeanours, such as the possession of soft drugs, weapons offences, occasional assaults, mischief, and drunk-driving charges, along with a plethora of vehicle violations and traffic tickets. In the late 1970s the Rebels had one club rule regarding good or bad ways of making money: 'If you're selling dope you don't do it as a club member, you don't wear your colours, you don't wear your club T-shirt' (Steve, sergeant at arms, quoting the Rebels' Book of Rules). This rule was adopted in order to protect club members from the increased police surveillance that would ensue as a result of a club member being arrested for selling narcotics. 'We have a ruling that you don't sell drugs at all, if at all possible ... We had one member get busted for just sellling hash [hashish], for which he went to jail. For about two months after that it seemed like everybody and his dog was being picked up and checked for dope. Because if one member had it everybody else had to. Something like that is what brings up a ruling such as don't sell any drugs' (Ken, president, Rebels MC). While the Rebels did not deal in drugs as a means of making money for the club, a couple of the members dealt in drugs on an individual basis. During the time that I rode with the club two members actively supplemented their income by dealing with soft drugs, such as marijuana and hashish. Similarly, while the Rebels were not actively involved in motorcycle theft as a club, one member was. Inspector Doug Egan, the RCMP's senior criminal intelligence officer in 1981, felt that, with a few exceptions, the Rebels were not criminally active. But exceptions do occur. In 1983 four members of the Edmonton Rebels, a member of the Hell's Angels, and two Rebel ol' ladies were arrested on drug charges. All but one of the Rebels were eventually convicted of trafficking and conspiracy to traffic in cocaine. While the 'ongoing conspiracy' only involved six ounces of cocaine – which sold for $3400 an ounce – it did show that some Rebels were willing to use their contacts with the Hell's Angels in Quebec to obtain cocaine for their personal use and possibly to make some 'easy money.' All four Rebels held jobs at the time of their arrest. Three years later, in 1986, a striker from the Rebels' Calgary chapter was arrested and convicted of possession of LSD for the purposes of trafficking. However, excluding the drug busts of 1983 and 1986, the Rebels have not been arrested for or convicted of any charges that involve 'organized crime' in the 1980s.

Crime could give the Rebels true self-sufficiency – for as long as it lasted. The Rebels are aware of the dangers involved and have chosen not to follow that route. While the Rebels are not economically self-sufficient, neither are they totally dependent on the market economy of the larger host society. In fact, their economic system encompasses all the major forms of exchange. Generalized reciprocity – the giving of goods with no obligation to reciprocate – is evident when patch holders receive gifts from their brothers. Balanced reciprocity – mutual exchange of roughly equal value – takes place when the patch holders trade goods, such as bike parts, and barter their various trades skills. Redistribution – obligatory payments to a central agency – occurs when the patch holders pay their dues to the club treasury, which in turn uses the money to provide services for the membership as a whole, such as bike-repair facilities and the clubhouse. Market exchange – commercial transactions – operates in the form of marketing 'club shares,' renting out living accommodations, and hiring other patch holders as employees. In that these exchanges satisfy mutual needs, they represent rational economic decisions. However, the purely entrepreneurial aspects of these interactions are overshadowed by the social variables of solidarity and intimacy within which they are embedded. The more spheres of economic exchange that operate within the club, the greater the members' sense that their club constitutes an independent community with a strong corporate identity.

Political Organization: The Structure and Distribution of Power

The club gives me freedom. It gives me the freedom to do
and be what I want.

(Tramp, Rebels MC)

Although on the outside a biker club may offer the prospective member freedom from society's constraints, the
real truth is starkly different. Biker clubs are more structured and hierarchical than any other organization except
perhaps the military. Biker organizations are tightly knit,
difficult to infiltrate and absolute in their 'execution of justice' from within.

(RCMP communiqué to Canadian police departments)

All outlaw patch holders confront the paradox of how to reconcile
the biker freedom ethic with the necessity of group conformity. Joining an outlaw motorcycle club is a voluntary act, and the member
believes that club life gives him the kind of personal and social
freedom he wants. His image of the outlaw biker is one of a folk hero,
a symbol of individual freedom, especially from the routine of financial and family responsibilities: 'They're [non-bikers] just jealous of
the freedom we have,' said Clayton of the Rebels.'We don't get into
this "society trip" where you get tied down with a house, two cars,
and bank payments.' However, freedom from social conventions does
not mean unbridled self-interest within the club. Outlaw clubs have
discovered that they can survive only if they are able to operate with
the precision and control of a paramilitary organization. It is

precisely because the outlaw clubs are perceived as deviant that group survival requires internal discipline and self-sacrifice on the part of the members. If an outlaw club is to beat the odds and survive, club members must accept some loss of personal autonomy. Ironically, deviance from social norms on a group level requires conformity on a personal level.

The contradiction between personal freedom and group conformity is more apparent to outsiders than to club members. The necessary loss of personal autonomy that comes with receiving one's colours is mediated by organizational features which ensure that, under non-crisis situations, the individual rights and viewpoints of members are not sacrificed. The political structure of an outlaw motorcycle club is based on a constitution and a book of rules. It features a formal system of centralized leadership consisting of 'officers of the club.' This executive body is chosen through a democratic electoral process. Any judicial, political, or administrative decision making has to be approved by a majority of club members as determined by a balloting process. Elections and participatory democracy disperse power throughout the club. In the day-to-day operation of the club, members must react to a wide variety of social and political circumstances that cannot always be anticipated by formal rulings. Given this lack of formal guidelines, members make a lot of their decisions through informal discussions, or consensual politics. In total, a decision-making structure based on democracy and consensus ensures that each member actively shapes the social activities and political direction of the club.

Before joining the club, a biker will have formulated his own provisional image of the club, which will include not only its structure and function, but also its obligations and benefits. While his initial club image is certain to be modified by realities he has not yet experienced, once he is a member he will continue to attempt to make the group correspond to what he considers to be an ideal club. His vision may differ from that of his brothers. The inter-member variation that results underlies much of the conflict and political rhetoric that takes place within the club. The patch holders themselves recognize that within the framework of the club there exists a radical faction – 'the heavies' or 'one percenters' – and a conservative element – 'the good guys' or 'dudes who are pretty laid back and low-key.' Much of the discord that does occur among members centres on one fundamental issue: the extent to which commitment to the club requires differentiation from the host society.

> I don't think it [Rebels MC] is an outlaw club in that we are not outlaws. Mind you, we do wear an outlaw patch; and the Rebels is a well-respected name. But I think it's only an outlaw club because that's what the citizens on the street class you as. (Ken, president)

> When you put on the Rebel patch nobody bothers you. No one hassles you or gets in your way. Fuck them! We have our own society. We care about our brothers, and that's it. If some asshole fucks with your brother, you rip his face off and put it in his shoe! (Danny, road captain)

Rebels vary in terms of how tightly they wish to draw the boundaries of their subculture and how radically they want to depart from conventional society. The question that arises is to what extent and under what circumstances an outlaw club can tolerate variation.

Diversity within the club is positive in that it provides a repertoire of differing talents, ideas, and attitudes that enable the Rebels to assess and deal with different situations. While diversity among members is an asset, it does have destructive potential if not kept within certain limits. These limits are created by a constant awareness by club members that the outside world is hostile to their existence. Their survival is dependent upon the maintenance of common values that are expressed by club members when they talk about 'love of biking,' 'love for one's brothers,' and 'love for the club.' A member's capacity and inclination to adhere to these under-lying values was selected for, learned, and tested during the striking period. It is this common commitment, especially in the face of threat from the larger society, that allows internal diversity to exist without disrupting the quality of interpersonal relations or sacrificing organizational cohesion.

This chapter initially details the political structure that is characteristic of outlaw motorcycle clubs and describes the political processes involved. It then explains how a club deals with the problems of inter-member differences and conflicts. Finally, the chapter explores the paradox that arises when the club's mandate to promote the biker freedom ethic collides with its need to maintain paramilitary discipline. The picture that emerges is one of a dynamic situation in which the tug-of-war between variation/individual freedom and uniformity/group cohesion is contained by a complex process by which club members, as individuals and as a group, attempt to define a meaningful lifestyle.

FORMAL STRUCTURE: THE ORGANIZATIONAL CORNERSTONES

The existence of a community of outlaw bikers is not predicated on a formal organization, such as a club; nor is the formation of a club the inevitable outcome of an enduring biker community. It is significant, then, that the Rebels do choose to operate within the framework of a formal structure. Formal organization adds an institutional dimension to their participation in the outlaw subculture and contributes to the formation of a corporate biker identity. Typically, outlaw motorcycle clubs feature (1) a club name, which becomes a shorthand statement of corporate identity, (2) a written mandate stating the purpose of association, (3) written statutes outlining the criteria of membership and membership obligations, along with (4) formal regulatory mechanisms for enforcing those statutes; all of which result in (5) a degree of autonomy and sense of exclusivity regarding outlaw club activity. These elements establish a corporate entity that is separate from the proclivities of individual members and whose existence transcends individual members. Club organization allows outlaw bikers to draw firm boundaries between themselves and the surrounding society.

The Rebels MC possesses a flexible formal organization defined by (1) a club charter in the form of a written constitution, (2) a 'Book of Rules' that prescribes the formal regulatory and official mechanisms of control, and (3) an executive body made up of 'officers of the club.'

Club charter

An outlaw club's charter can take the form of a written constitution, such as those used by the King's Crew MC and the Outlaws MC. Alternatively, the charter may be in the form of a set of by-laws, as followed by the Satan's Choice MC. The Rebels MC has a constitution supplemented by a book of rules. Table 2 contains an item analysis

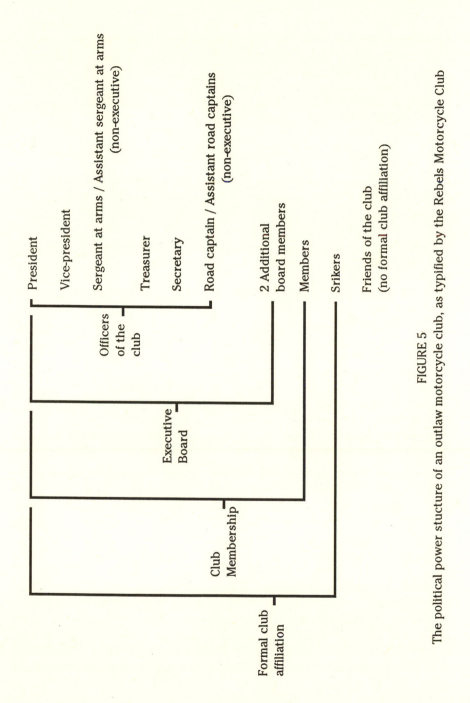

FIGURE 5

The political power stucture of an outlaw motorcycle club, as typified by the Rebels Motorcycle Club

TABLE 2
Typical contents of outlaw-motorcycle-club charters

1. *Political structure*
   Executive positions
     (Officers of the club)
   Executive duties
   Executive powers
   Executive qualifications
   Election of executive

2. *Membership qualifications*
   Age minimum
   Ownership and
     type of motorcycle
   Initiate (prospect/striker) period
   Initiate duties
   Voting on initiate

3. *Minimum participation*
   Mandatory runs
     (motorcycle tours)
   Minimal operation of motorcycle
   Minimal riding season
   Payment of club dues
   Attendance at meetings

4. *Available sanctions*
   Fines
   Probation
   Dismissal

5. *Decision making*
   Scheduling of meetings
   Quorum requirements
   Rules of conduct
   Voting procedures

6. *Change of membership status*
   Honorary membership
   Membership resignation
   Membership challenge
   Membership expulsion
   Leave of absence

7. *Miscellaneous*
   Club emblems (colours)
   Special committees
   Conduct of members
     during conflict situations

of the constitutions and by-laws of five outlaw clubs: the Rebels MC of Edmonton, King's Crew MC of Calgary, Satan's Choice MC of Brampton, Hell's Angels MC of Oakland, and the Satan's Angels MC of Vancouver (see appendix A for a copy of the by-laws of the Hell's Angels MC and the rules and regulations of the Satan's Angels MC).

It is not surprising that the institutionalized frameworks of these five outlaw clubs are alike in terms of basic content. What surprises, however, is that this similarity extends to those motorcycle clubs that are 'officially chartered' (non-outlaw) by the Canadian Motorcycle Association (CMA) and the American Motorcycle Association (AMA). The outlaw constitutions and by-laws closely resemble the 'sample constitution' that the CMA and the AMA (1980) recommend for their affiliated clubs. This structural similarity stems from the fact that both outlaw and officially chartered clubs are all riding clubs, and their formal structure must facilitate that one basic function.

Obviously, outlaw and citizen clubs build quite different social realities from similar organizational structures. The CMA and AMA clubs organize activities that align the club and its members with the larger society: 'Basically you should remember that you and your friends as a motorcycle club are a part of the community ... Get involved and by all means avoid any tendency toward isolation or cliquishness. Staying aloof from your neighbors can only reinforce the sorry misconceptions which many of them already harbor about motorcycling' (CMA Guide to Community Relations and Club Activity, 1980: 9).

Clubs that are not registered with the CMA or AMA are labelled 'outlaw' and considered to be the 'one per cent' deviant fringe that continues to tarnish the public image of both motorcycling and motorcyclists. The AMA's one percenter label is readily accepted by the outlaw community with many outlaw bikers either adopting '1%' badges or having the '1%' logo tattooed on their shoulders as an uncompromising statement of their distinction and self-imposed alienation: 'A 1%er is the one of a hundred of us who have given up on society. And the politicians' One Way Law. This is why we look repulsive. We are saying we don't want to be like you or look like you. So stay out of our face!' – OFFO (Outlaws Forever, Forever Outlaws).

Officers of the club

Outlaw motorcycle clubs are participatory democracies, similar in their formal political structure and distribution of power. Officers of the club are elected and include a president, vice-president, treasurer, secretary, sergeant at arms, and road captain (see table 3). Like most clubs, the Rebels issue badges to their club officers, to be worn on their colours, that designate their executive position. In addition to their specific executive duties these officers of the club constitute a separate decision-making body referred to as an 'executive board.'

Officers of the club serve a twelve-month term of office, and annual elections are held at the last regular meeting of the year, in

TABLE 3
Rebels Motorcycle Club executive structure

President
Vice-president
Sergeant at arms / assistant sergeant at arms (non-executive)
Treasurer
Secretary
Road Captain / 2 assistant road captains (non-executives)
2 additional board members

December. In order to be eligible for office, a patch holder has to have been an active member in good standing for a minimum of one year (Book of Rules). Patch holders who aspire towards particular positions will campaign informally for one month prior to the elections. Electioneering is conducted on an interpersonal face-to-face basis. A hopeful candidate will approach a member, inform the member that he is willing to stand for office if nominated, ask for the member's opinion of his qualifications, and solicit the member's support. Variations on this lobbying theme reflect the personalities involved:

Jim: Hey Albert! I'm going to run for vice-prez this year. Besides being such an all-round nice guy, if I'm elected everyone can have all the home-grown [marijuana] they can smoke!
Wee Albert: Since when have you decided that you can buy a biker?!
Jim: Naw! I'm not trying to buy you; just stone you into submission! Haw! Haw! Haw!

At the year's-end election meeting, nominations are taken for the various executive positions. If there are more than three candidates for any one position, a preliminary run-off vote is held. The three top candidates are then asked to leave the meeting and grab a brew from the beer fridge while the membership as a whole discusses and compares their qualifications for office. After the members have voiced their support for the candidates of their choice, a secret ballot is held. The votes are tallied, the candidates invited back into the meeting room, and the name of the winning candidate is announced.

Runners-up to the position of road captain and sergeant at arms become assistants. When elections are over, the members join their ol' ladies and invited guests for their annual New Year's party. 'It's a good idea to have the party at that time; we celebrate the new club exec's, and the losers usually get a chance to chuck them in the nearest snowbank. It's a helluva party, and that sort of smooths over any hard feelings that anybody might have [about the election results]. Mind you, if the party lasts for more than two days [strikers are sent out for supplies] nobody remembers who got elected in the first place' (Saint).

The executive board, including assistants, includes nearly half (eleven) the members of the club. The high percentage of members involved in executive positions dispels any feelings on the part of patch holders that the club is controlled by a ruling élite. As well as minimizing any feelings of alienation from power, the large number of members with positions of increased responsibility enhances the sense of collective commitment to the club.

The executive positions are listed in the Rebels Motorcycle Club Book of Rules; however, the specific responsibilities and powers associated with each position are not detailed. How an officer performs his duties depends not only on the substance of formal rules, but also on the style that a patch holder brings to a position. Personalities are crucial in the informal politics of reputation (capabilities) and status (respect). The executive, more so than the other members, becomes responsible for articulating the personality of the club. How the club operates is influenced by the personal performance of the members involved, and changes as the members themselves come and go. In order to make sense of collective behaviour and the dynamics underlying the political process, it is necessary to consider individual motives and strategies. Formal ideologies and rules are interrelated with informal personal strategies; their point of intersection is the personalities of the members involved.

PRESIDENT

The executive duties of the president are as follows:
1 To preside over meetings of both the executive board and the club as a whole.
2 To judge items not covered in the Rebels MC constitution or Book of Rules.

3 To act as the personal representative of the club in the area of public relations; as a liaison between the Rebels MC and local-law enforcement agencies; and as a connecting link between the Rebels MC and other outlaw motorcycle clubs.
4 To represent the club in any business contacts and to supervise major economic transactions.
5 To assist Rebel officers in the interpretation of their club responsibilities, and to promote club life among members in general.

The primary role of the president is *not* to run the club. Rather, he should lead the club by integrating the members' varying goals and strategies into a collective plan of action. Autocratic rule divorced from member consent and input would weaken an individual patch holder's sense of commitment to the club, and ultimately destroy the group. The Rebels' president, Ken, therefore did not exercise his presidential-power mandate when the issue of contention was a major one. When a situation did arise that threatened to disrupt the orderliness of a meeting, Ken would try to orchestrate the discussion in such a manner that each individual had an opportunity to participate in the decision-making process. He would first ask the sergeant at arms to restrain any unruly members who might be speaking out of order or trying to monopolize the floor. After order had been restored, Ken would solicit each patch holder's opinion on the matter at hand. Finally, he would summarize the different viewpoints and call for a vote to be taken. Thus, the presidency does not primarily involve the enactment of a supreme mandate; rather, the emphasis is on the coordination of diverse opinions to facilitate the emergence of a consensus.

Occasionally, the president makes judgments on his own concerning minor matters. For example, during a meeting at which preparations were being made for an upcoming run, the question arose as to whether sixty or seventy cases of beer were to be taken along. Ken effectively resolved the issue: 'We'll take seventy! End of discussion!' This sort of autocratic decision-making maximizes the efficiency with which meetings are run and minimizes unnecessary negative feedback between members. That is, minor points of contention are not allowed to create major waves of controversy.

The presidential-power mandate has its greatest implication for decision making outside the context of club meetings and the isolated confines of the clubhouse. In those situations where the club is not in complete control or is faced by a threat, it is vital that the expression of differences of opinion be controlled, if not curtailed altogether. When the club is on display in the public arena, members must portray solidarity and act as a cohesive unit. On one occasion three Rebels – Blues, Gerry, and Jim – had entered bikes (two customized Harley-Davidsons and a restored 1953 Indian Chief) into a competition motorcycle show in the Edmonton Agricom. While the Rebels were admiring the display of righteous scooters, they noticed four bikers who appeared to be wearing club colours beneath their leathers. These bikers were members of the Highwaymen MC, a club whose existence threatened the Rebels' territorial monopoly. The Rebels were undecided as to what course of action to take. A couple of the Rebels wanted to confront the Highwaymen the moment they left the building and confiscate their colours. Ken sided with those Rebels who felt that since the Highwaymen weren't openly flying their colours, there was no justification for a confrontation at that time. When Voodoo objected the decision, Ken told him, 'Back off! We'll discuss this later [in the clubhouse]!'

Ken was a good president. He was adept at making sound decisions very quickly, often under pressure situations. As an eight-year charter member he understood clearly wherein group consensus lay. Most important, he was capable of converting consensus into action. Ken's political impartiality – he did not lean towards either the conservative or radical factions within the club – made it easier for members to accept his autocratic decisions when they were called for. 'He [Ken] is certainly not the most popular guy in the club; but all of the members have a lot of respect for his opinion' (Onion). Ken's aptitude for making delicate judgments under a variety of circumstances led to his being elected president for six consecutive years.

The president represents the Rebels MC in the area of public relations. He acts as a gatekeeper by monitoring and restricting the nature and extent of communication between the Rebels MC and the host society. Controlled communication ensures the integrity of group borders; other than the president, members are expected to maintain a code of silence. 'Ken has everything to do with club public relations. Like he makes a decision as to whether we make a public announcement on something or not. He makes the decision; he does the announcing. We don't want any foul-ups; we want it to come from the top. Different newspapers or magazines come around trying to get stories. The radio stations have been trying to get him to come on talk shows like CJCA; and the [*Edmonton*] *Journal* and *Alberta Report* want to do a story on us. Ken usually refuses them all. That's the way it is' (Wee Albert). As spokesman, Ken would communicate club policies to the host community under those circumstances when contact would serve to avoid or terminate unnecessary conflict. After the highly publicized bar-room brawl between the Rebels and members of the Canadian Airborne Regiment, it was Ken who communicated with a military spokesman at Canadian Forces Base Namao to put an end to hostilities.

The president supervises major economic transactions, such as renting a hall for a club boogie, renting a clubhouse, and negotiating the purchase of land for the club. Ken countersigned any cheques written on the Rebels MC bank account and signed any contracts involving the club. As part owner of Brothers Custom Cycles, Ken was an experienced small businessman, quite capable of handling such transactions. One of his business contacts included a skilled lawyer whose services were used by the Rebels MC as a whole, as when the club filed grievances against the Edmonton city police for harassment, and by members on a personal basis, as when Crash needed a lawyer after being arrested on a weapons charge.

The president acts as a liaison between the Rebels MC and the local law-enforcement agencies, including the Edmonton city police and a local detachment of RCMP. The code of silence is particularly important when it comes to the police. Like other outlaw clubs, the Rebels tell their members to say as little as possible. Misunderstandings and unintentional information leaks are avoided by having either the president or another executive member speak for the club whenever possible: 'It is particularly important for the (police) officer to understand this relative (political) positioning, since the day may come when he is responsible for stopping and checking a group of outlaw bikers ... To speak to anyone in a low position of authority within the club is a waste of time; the officer will probably receive a blank stare or noncommittal answer. The policeman must approach those who speak for the club' (Ayoob, 1982: 29) Ken negotiated a special arrangement with Corporal Ritchie of the RCMP GIS (General Investigations Service) detail. The arrangement alleviated a major concern of the Rebel patch holders: the confiscation of their motorcycles on suspicion of theft by law-enforcement agencies when riding outside the Edmonton area. When bikers chop their motorcycles the serial numbers on the frame may be covered over with moulding, or the serial numbers on the engine casing may not correspond with those on the frame because of the continual exchange and substitution of high-performance parts. Law-enforcement agents are well aware of these practices, and they use them to discourage outlaw bikers from visiting a locality that is under their jurisdiction. This is particularly true of areas whose regional economies are heavily dependent on tourist dollars, such as the Okanagan Valley in British Columbia. Towns such as Vernon, Kelowna, and Penticton want to attract the 'right kind' of tourists. Their law-enforcement agencies, primarily the RCMP, are expected to be 'sensitive' to any 'undesirable elements.'

The King's Crew MC of Calgary found this out the hard way while touring through British Columbia. The 'Crew' were stopped by the RCMP in Kelowna, and six of their bikes were confiscated because of 'suspect registrations.' It took the RCMP three weeks to confirm that the registrations were indeed valid. Under these circumstances the police have the right to disassemble suspected stolen vehicles in order to establish identification; this procedure may result in an outlaw biker carrying his scooter home in a basket. The threat of vehicle confiscation is an effective technique employed by the RCMP in the Okanagan Valley to discourage 'illegitimate bikers.' 'Last year we confiscated six or seven bikes from a Calgary group [King's Crew MC]. It looked like their serial numbers had been altered. We get less bikers now ... Being located [in Kelowna] between Vernon and Penticton, we get radio reports from those centres. When what is left of a gang passes through, we're waiting for them. We give them a police escort from one end of town through to the other' (Ken Attry, staff sergeant, Kelowna RCMP). When I questioned Sergeant Attry as to whether or not any of the motorcycles had actually turned out to be stolen, he replied: 'No, but there's always the possibility.'

Ken dealt with this problem by arranging that every spring the Rebel patch holders would ride their bikes over to RCMP K-Division headquarters and allow the police photographer to take individual pictures of themselves and their motorcycles. For Corporal Ritchie, it was a great way to impress his superiors with his impeccable surveillance of the Rebel outlaws. In return, the Rebels received individual copies of these photographs that included the member's name on the back along with an RCMP certification-of-ownership stamp. Showing professional discreteness and dispatch the RCMP sent me my photographs, along with a thank-you note, in a plain brown envelope.

These photographs were invaluable proofs of ownership and gave the Rebels some immunity from unjustified bike seizures.

It saved my hog for me once. I was in Vancouver doing a little fishing around the bay area when this striker from the [Gypsy] Wheelers comes along and says: 'Hey, Blues, they're taking away your bike!' So I dropped my rod and went running like hell to where my scooter was parked. And there was this tow-truck there and this dink was about to strap my bike on to the truck, and this Vancouver cop was standing there writing something down. I told the tow-truck driver to fuck off. Then I walked up to the cop and said: 'Hey man, that's my bike and you're not about to tow it away.' He says: 'It looks like it was stolen, and you've got no serial numbers.' You see, my bike was chopped and it didn't have any boss [serial] numbers, so I told him I had them written down. But he starts getting heavy and says: 'Don't give me that shit!' and he goes on. So I take out my [RCMP verified] pictures and his whole attitude changes, eh. His face gets really red, but he doesn't say a word. He just waves off the tow truck, hops into his cruiser, and drives off. It must have ruined his whole fucking day. (Blues)

The Edmonton city police will contact the club president if they have any complaints about the action of Rebel patch holders, or the club in general. Ken adopted the policy of informing the RCMP about the destination for any major motorcycle tours such as the mandatory runs. The local RCMP reciprocated by not initiating any 'unnecessary hassles,' such as a bike-to-bike drug check, and, depending on the club's destination, might provide a police escort. These aspects of cooperation and mutual respect resulted in members evaluating the local RCMP as a very 'professional' police force that did little to aggravate a potentially tense situation.

A club's president will also act as the major connecting link between it and another outlaw motorcycle club. The president is usually one of the more sedentary members of the club, with a long-standing place of residence. In that respect, Ken was one of three Rebels who owned their houses. This contrasts sharply with a large number of the other members, such as Caveman, for whom I had to record four address/telephone number changes during the course of one year. Given this relative domestic stability, the president's home address – or a postal-box number – is used for written correspondence between affiliated clubs. When Caveman, Crash, and Tiny were travelling through Saskatoon, they phoned up Smokey Rae, president of the Spokesmen MC, who set about looking after his guests' needs.

The president is expected to assist other Rebel officers in the performance of their club tasks and to promote club life among the members in general. Ken was consulted by members on the interpretation of certain rulings and on options available to members concerning club matters. For example, Saint asked Ken what steps were necessary to obtain a six-month leave of absence so he could spend the winter working in Victoria, BC, instead of Edmonton.

The role of the president goes beyond the relatively simple interpretation of formal rules to include acting as a mediator in disputes between members. These conflicts are often the result of the members having somewhat different interpretations of 'what the club is all about.' Of particular interest are the disagreements between the radical and conservative elements of the club. For example, two members got into an argument over an invitation that had been extended to two outsiders to attend a party at the clubhouse. Earlier, Ken had mentioned to me that there were a number of rules (Book of Rules) and expectations governing clubhouse visitors. 'Yeah, we don't allow anyone out at the clubhouse unless he's on a motorcycle, or we definitely know is a biker, with an invitation and an escort by a member. We definitely don't want a straight coming out and asking what's going on. If anyone came out there without an invitation or escort, they'd be told to take off, or whatever we found necessary' (Ken).

The member who had issued the invitation, Wee Albert – a member of the conservative faction – felt that the two outsiders were eligible as guests because they both rode bikes, had been friendly enough in the club bar, and were stopping over in Edmonton as part of a 'righteous' 6000-mile cross-country tour. As Wee Albert pointed out: 'I'd like to see hospitality to bikers as our [the club's] first name.' The member who challenged the invitation, Blues – an extreme one percenter – was angry that one of the guests was riding a Kawasaki, a Japanese motorcycle. For Blues the presence of the 'rice-burner' was an ideological affront that was not to be taken lightly or causally overlooked: 'I'm not going to have that piece of shit here! That's a racer's bike. You drive a Harley because you know where it's at as far as bikes go. I don't want that thing parked by my clubhouse. I drove out here to get away from that sort of crap!' Wee Albert and Blues both agreed that riding a Harley-Davidson was necessary in order to be a member of the club, a friend of the club, or even to ride with the club. Blues, however, had drawn the club's social boundaries tighter than Wee Albert by limiting guest privileges to those individuals who rode hogs. The majority of members seemed willing to ignore the presence of the Kawasaki, and were more intent on 'getting down to some serious partying.' Blues and Terrible Tom, however, set about looking for the proper metric tool with which to disassemble the Kawasaki: a sledgehammer.

Because of the small, close-knit nature of Rebel society, disputes and tensions are often handled on an interpersonal level through discussion if possible, fights if necessary. Members in dispute will initially try to find a compromise position. If they fail, and the situation threatens to become volatile, another member – usually an executive – will enter the dispute as a third party. If necessary, he will impose an arbitrary decision, ideally one that does not create a losing party. In this instance, Ken exercised the judgment of King Solomon: the guest could stay, but the bike couldn't. The compromise solution involved the guest parking the Japanese motorcycle in a ditch by the highway, two hundred and fifty yards away from the clubhouse and beyond the view of members.

VICE-PRESIDENT

The executive duty of the vice-president is to assume the responsibilities of the presidency when the president is unable to do so. He has no other specific duties other than being an active member of the executive board. However, Terrible Tom – a former Golden Gloves boxing champion – brought a certain style to the position that served to emphasize the brotherhood and counterbalance many of the disruptive effects of participatory democracy. While the president would orchestrate the group process so as to allow for individual participation, Terrible Tom would provide a high-profile (executive) example of uncompromised commitment to the members as a whole. Tom's continual promotion of the brotherhood blunted the cutting edge of any ill feelings that arose as members pursued conflicting personal interests or incompatible group policies. 'His [Tom's] love for the club. That's what got him the position [of vice-president]. His constant concern for the club. Tom was the one who really pushed brotherhood in the club until it became a real thing ...

He'd say: "This isn't the way a brother would act toward another brother." But it's just pointing it out, what is brotherhood and what is not brotherhood. A lot of guys have seen that what Tom has to say is correct; so we founded a brotherhood, a way to act' (Wee Albert). Tom was not one of the more creative or articulate members, but he was re-elected to the office of vice-president with a degree of regularity that attested to his unquestioned and exemplary love for the club.

SERGEANT AT ARMS

The executive duties of the sergeant at arms are as follows:
1 To maintain order at club meetings in particular, and club activities in general.
2 To ensure that members adhere to club rulings, policies, and expected modes of conduct when dealing with other members or outsiders.
3 To defend club members, property, or territory from outside threats.

The sergeant at arms is the club policeman. He is given his authority by the club members, and they will support him in any of his decisions. However, as an officer he remains accountable to the members, and his rulings and tactics, especially the unwarranted use of excessive force, can be officially questioned and reprimanded at club meetings. The sergeant is the only officer who is entitled to use physical force on a member to enforce club policies. When strong-arm tactics are deemed necessary to 'straighten somebody out,' the other members will fully support the sergeant.

This office is second only to that of the president in terms of overall importance to the club and the personal qualifications required to fill the position. If a situation arises that justifies intervention, the sergeant must be an individual who has the capacity to enforce his decision. The most obvious attributes of an enforcer would at first appear to be physical strength and pugilistic prowess. Steve, who was elected the Rebel sergeant at arms for three consecutive years, appeared custom-made for the job: he was built like a small tank that came with blond hair and steel blue eyes as optional extras. However, the key to being a successful sergeant at arms in an outlaw motorcycle club is to be able to enforce group policy *without* having to resort to violence.

Coercion can produce short-term beneficial results for an organization, but only if it is used carefully and sparingly. This cautious approach towards the use of force is particularly apt for an egalitarian society such as the Rebels MC. Rebel patch holders are willing to sacrifice some personal freedom for a collective cause, but only on the premise that they are equal partners in both policy formation and enforcement. Blatant opposition on the part of members is destabilizing and the use of coercion to overcome that opposition is unreliable. If not used judiciously, rule by force would effectively destroy club morale. The use of force in a voluntary organization is the least effective means of achieving social responsibility. In this respect the sergeant must possess a powerful, if not overpowering sense of self; he must be confident and strong-willed enough to be able to enforce club policy without question. In short, the sergeant must be a master at the art of intimidation: 'Everybody knows Steve's [physical] capabilities; but he never hits anybody. It's more his attitude. He can be a mean sonovabitch. Like he does more damage with his voice than anything else. He has the voice of authority. When Steve shouts, people jump' (Voodoo). Commenting on his qualifications, Steve himself said, 'The sergeant at arms has a lot more power now that I'm it!'

A story that became part of Rebel folklore attests to Steve's strong will and his tenacious capacity for independent judgment and action. It began one hot August night when Steve was out 'riding in the wind.' He was cut off and carelessly run over by a car making a left-hand lane change. The last thing Steve recalled was his leg being crushed between the bike and pavement. When he regained consciousness in the Royal Alexandria Hospital, a doctor informed him that he had amputated his right leg below the knee. However, Steve's problems were far from over. While still in the hospital he developed necrosis, a rotting of the skin tissue, and the amputation had to be repeated. This time the amputation was closer to the knee joint. Two days later he was advised that a third operation would be required. Apparently the Royal Alexandria staff had used pillows to elevate the lower part of the leg in order to decrease the swelling, but they failed to ensure that the leg was straight, with full extension of the knee joint. The combination of having his leg elevated and flexed at the knee resulted in decreased circulation. Decreased circulation inhibits tissue regeneration and causes a state of contracture wherein the musculature shrinks and locks the joint in place. Further necrosis occurred, which in turn required further amputation.

I wasn't quite sure what was happening, but somehow I felt sure that they were fucking things up. What I did know was that if they cut off my knee joint, that would be it! With the knee I could get an artificial leg and be able to walk half decently, and maybe be able to ride again. ... Anyway there was no way that I was going to stick around and have those guys screw me up completely! I crawled out of there and down the stairs to a phone booth and called a cab; and he takes me to the University [of Alberta] Hospital. At first they wouldn't let me in there. But I started yelling that if they didn't take me, I'd stay there and bleed to death on their fucking doorstep! (Steve)

The University of Alberta Hospital staff would have been reluctant to admit Steve, who was technically still a patient of the Royal Alexandria Hospital, because of the negative political feedback that it could create between the hospitals. Furthermore, since Steve had in effect discharged himself against medical advice, Alberta Health Care would not pay the attending UAH physician until a period of forty-eight hours had elapsed. However, given the circumstances – Steve's determination to stay – he was admitted. Steve was informed by the attending physician that it was possible to reverse an impending contracture before it solidifies: 'They told me that if I could get the knee to move in twenty-four hours, they might be able to save it.' With the help of some physiotherapists, some morphine, and a lot of pain and effort on the part of Steve, the orthopedic team was able to re-establish a range of motion, restore circulation, and ultimately save the knee joint.

Once Steve was fitted with a prosthesis, he limped back to Brothers Custom Cycles. Steve was full of ideas about rebuilding the motorcycle that had been badly mangled with him in the accident. He found his panhead in the back of the shop, but it wasn't in a basket. His 'old grey elephant' was looking sleek and polished, gleaming in all its Harley-Davidson glory. Steve's brothers had rebuilt it for him.

An interesting addendum to this story is that the following spring the Rebels MC suffered another casualty. Clayton was hit by a drunk driver who ignored a stop sign. Steve was at the scene just as the ambulance arrived, and he asked the attendants where they were going to take Clayton. When they told him, 'The Royal Alex,' Steve said, 'No you're not!' The Smith Ambulance attendants stated that it was procedure to take the victim to the nearest hospital, in this case the Royal Alexandria. Steve walked over to one of the attendants, looked him in the eye, and said in a very calm, but coldly matter-of-fact manner: 'The only way you're taking him to the Royal Alex is over someone's dead body; and I'd lay odds that it won't be mine!' Steve followed the ambulance to the University Hospital.

The patch holder whom the club chooses to be sergeant must be able to exercise extremely good judgment, especially when making on-the-spot decisions. Often these decisions will be in sensitive areas that require the sergeant to both interpret and enforce what he feels are the prevailing club standards. The situation is complicated by the fact the Rebels are an action-oriented group that have to adapt to a wide variety of circumstances. For the sergeant this means that many of his decisions will have no historic or traditional precedent, and even fewer will have any guidelines in the way of formal rules.

The role that the sergeant plays in the formal context of club meetings involves the relatively straightforward proposition of ensuring that the whole exercise proceeds smoothly. For the most part this requires that the sergeant make sure that none of the members drinks during the course of the meeting, speaks out of turn, monopolizes the floor, or becomes too rowdy while expressing or contesting a point. Under these controlled conditions, few members question Steve's authority, which is not perceived as a threat to their personal freedom. Many of the Rebels present initiated the rules of conduct that are outlined in the Book of Rules; all the members present have at least agreed to abide by them. Therefore, no freedom that any patch holder felt he had in the first place has been curtailed. Furthermore, the behavioural options that have been temporarily withdrawn from the members – drinking or being disorderly – are insignificant. As a result, there is little personal motivation to react against the application of sanctions.

Ensuring that club regulations and conventions are followed outside the confines of the clubhouse is a more delicate matter. Aside from the fact that there will be few formal guidelines, there is an increased likelihood that intervention on the part of the sergeant will be interpreted as an infringement on the patch holder's individual freedom. Under these circumstances the sergeant's strategy ideally is one of negotiation, not coercion. This translates into sensitive manipulation by the sergeant that combines creativity and discipline; most important, he avoids a total loss of freedom on the part of the member.

An example of the sergeant applying sanctions in an informal area of club activity occurred while the Rebels were drinking in the Kingsway Inn, the club bar at the time. Larry had become annoyed with a bar patron, seated with three friends at a nearby table, who was making derogatory remarks about bikers. Larry took one look at the guy, then turned to Steve and myself and said: 'Watch my beer. I'm going to take that green garbage bag and smash it over that asshole's head!' The Rebels MC, however, had over a period of time established an understanding with the Kingsway bouncers and management staff that their members would not initiate any disturbances. As sergeant at arms, it was Steve's responsibility to prevent any unwarranted hostilities between Rebels and citizens. Steve felt that the comments being made by the drunken patron did not warrant Larry's jeopardizing the non-aggression pact. Nevertheless, we all knew that it was just a matter of time before somebody 'shut the jerk up.' Steve was faced with a dilemma. It was his mandate to protect the Rebel-management agreement. Yet taking away a member's right to defend himself against an insult would have been interpreted as an infringement on a personal freedom. Considering the tenacity with which Larry and those around him clung to a positive masculine image, the loss of the option of retaliating would have caused a strong negative reaction. The perception of freedom lost would not have been confined to Larry alone. All the Rebels seated at our table – being interchangeable with Larry in terms of status and position – would have experienced the same threat to their freedom and felt the same motivation to react against the loss of freedom.

Steve's approach to the predicament was to veto Larry's garbage-bag solution and to tell Larry to look for an acceptable option: 'No you won't! Look, you can get away with a fuck of a lot as long as you're fucking civilized! The guy is an asshole, but he's also drunk. Use your head!' (Steve). Larry got up and set about achieving his end through 'civilized' means. He went over to the guy's table, lifted him out of his chair, planted a big sloppy kiss on his lips, set him down, and told him: 'Now you be a good boy, or Larry's going to have to take you outside and give you a spanking!' The incident left the customer stunned amidst the roar of bar-room laughter. The man was totally devastated; he had no adequate social responses – including his fists – that could have possibly saved him from total embarrassment. To the satisfaction of everyone present, Larry was able to do what he set out to do, and Steve was able to ensure that it was done without sacrificing the agreement that the Rebels MC had with the Kingsway management. By showing Larry that alternatives were available, Steve was able to take away one of the undesirable options (causing a disturbance) without taking away Larry's freedom to choose and act.

TREASURER

The executive duties of the treasurer are as follows:
1 To monitor and record the club's income and expenditures.
2 To collect the dues and fines owing by members.

The treasurer is the club accountant. The specific tasks associated with the office of treasurer are paying the monthly clubhouse rental fees; collecting the semi-annual membership dues; depositing club funds into the bank and writing the cheques for withdrawals; keeping track of club loans to members; collecting fines owed to the club by members; recording the purchase of supplies, such as motor oil or foodstuffs; paying lawyer's fees or bond money for members; handling the beer fund; and selling club shares to members.

The treasurer is involved in the relatively innocuous activity of recording the club's income and expenditures, and then attempting to balance the two sets of figures. However, even the treasurer cannot afford to lose sight of the fact that officers of the club are ultimately accountable to the members. Like those of the other officers, the decisions of the treasurer – innocuous or otherwise – must remain sensitive to members' opinions and, ultimately, reflect group consensus. Blues once ran afoul of this basic tenet, even though at the time he was making an effort to act out his role as club treasurer in a very conscientious manner. The situation unfolded during the course of a mandatory run on the long weekend in May. The Rebels had gotten a late start and were experiencing difficulties finding a spot to set up camp. When they came across a private camp-ground, Blues took it upon himself as treasurer to give the owner some money for the use of some vacant land adjacent to the main camp-ground. However, some of the members felt that they were being 'shafted' by the camp-ground owner; and they were upset with Blues for failing to consult with them before taking action.

Jim: Did you ask the membership if they wanted to pay?

Blues: No. I did it for the club. The way things are going there won't be a place left in this province where we'll be able to stay.

Jim: Look, we leave less of a mess behind than the average camper. We always clean up, yet people always try to do us in. This dude [owner] tried at first to charge us $5.75 per tent for a hunk of field with nothing but weeds on it. No, one thing we never do is suckhole; and you put us on the spot because you gave him a hundred dollars. Now we have to repay you.

Blues: I didn't suckhole. I just gave him a hundred dollars for all of us for two days. That's a pretty good deal anyway you look at it. I did it to make things easier for the club.

Jim: You've got to remember that the club is made up of members. Right or wrong, we act together as members. If I was buying some land for the club and the price went up and I went ahead and bought the land anyway because it was a good deal, and then I came back to the members and told them they each owed me another eight hundred dollars, what do you think they'd say? They'd say: 'Piss on you, Jim!' You've got to find out how your brothers feel before you do anything like that. The members and what they feel is what makes the club.

In fact, Blues had made a very pragmatic decision, one that the other officers found to be quite reasonable. However, as far as the Rebels are concerned, they are an egalitarian society. Divorcing executive power from group consensus would run contrary to that basic underlying principle.

SECRETARY

The executive duties of the secretary are as follows:

1 To record and safeguard the minutes of the club meetings.
2 To maintain the Book of Rules, recording any additions, deletions, or modifications.
3 To handle any club correspondence.

The main task of the secretary is to keep a record of the meetings of the club in the minutes book, which is safeguarded in the confines of the clubhouse. Meetings of the Rebels MC are technically run according to Robert's Rules of Order. However, the Rebel patch holders introduce a degree of informality that includes joking, verbal jousting, 'bullshitting,' and using vocabulary that 'Robert' would probably consider somewhat less than gentlemanly. Under these circumstances, interpreting 'what was said' is challenging, and getting everybody to agree on 'what was said' is virtually impossible. 'Interpreting what is said and getting it down accurately so that everybody agrees. That's a problem in itself. He's gotta separate the bullshit from what was said. I wouldn't take the job' (Caveman).

ROAD CAPTAIN

The executive duties of the road captain are as follows:
1 To plan the travel route and organize the basic itinerary of the club prior to going on a 'run' (tour).
2 To lead the club in formation while riding on tour.
3 To enforce club rules and procedures for group riding.

The road captain becomes the chief executive officer during the course of a Rebel run. According to Wee Albert, 'When it comes to being on the road, he's sergeant, president, everything!' Once the patch holders have decided on a destination at the weekly club meeting, the road captain consults with his two assistants. Together they plan the specific travel route and itinerary, including food, beer, and gas stops. The road captain must have a sound knowledge of how the members' hogs will perform under varying road conditions. He must be capable of good judgment regarding how to handle long bike formations that may stretch out for half a mile.

When the Rebels are jamming in the wind as a club, the road captain rides lead bike. He sets the speed at which the club travels and makes other on-the-road decisions such as when to pass an obstructing vehicle. In order that all the members in formation are aware of what is about to happen, these decisions are communicated to the pack through a series of hand signals. Should it become necessary to split up the club, each of the splinter groups will be led by one of the assistant road captains. When the club is riding as a single unit the two assistant road captains ride at the tail end of the formation. One of the assistants will occasionally pass the formation on the inside shoulder while he conducts a visual mechanical inspection of the members' machines. The other assistant will pass on the outside and check as to how well the long formation is being held. Both assistants will survey the column watching for 'whiplash,' large gaps between the bikes usually caused by members not maintaining tight formation in turns, and they will pick out which riders are responsible. If a member's motorcycle suffers a mechanical breakdown, one of the assistants will drop off, along with the crash truck that carries maintenance equipment and spare parts, and help conduct on-the-spot repairs.

Most patch holders are accomplished riders, and they tend to be highly critical of any misjudgments by the road captain. Mistakes such as choosing a 'bum road,' moving too slowly and being late, or speeding and getting ticketed leave the road captain open to ridicule. Conversely, a road captain such as Danny, who is able to silence the critics with his superb riding skills, gains a great deal of respect for his judgment and abilities every time he orchestrates a 'righteous putt.'

Executive board

The executive board consists of those members who were elected as officers of the club along with two additional elected members who are not club officers. The board holds scheduled meetings every two weeks. Emergency meetings can be called if a situation arises that demands immediate attention. The executive board is responsible for

1 The monitoring of conflicts within the club.
2 The application of disciplinary procedures.
3 The evaluation of strikers and their progress.
4 The presentation of a summarized assessment of the overall club situation to the membership.

The board presents organizational advantages for the operation and cohesiveness of the club. It centralizes administrative and judiciary responsibilities; yet the large number of board members ensures that the full spectrum of members' opinions will be represented in executive decision making. Having a structured administrative body safeguards the club from becoming overly dependent on the personal abilities of any one individual, such as the president. 'More heat would come down on him [president] if the club got into trouble. The heat [police] would go right to the top ... They'd go after him for a couple of reasons. One would be for information; if anybody knows more than anybody else, he's the one. The other is that he is the key to the club. They consider him the kingpin; knock him over and the rest will fall. This is what they think, but it's not the way it is' (Tiny). Tiny's view that the police operate in terms of a 'kingpin' theory received some credence during an informal conversation with an RCMP constable. It concerned the actions of the RCMP E-squad, a special task force established in the mid-seventies for the surveillance and control of outlaw-motorcycle-club activities.

> We have no more trouble with the Catwalkers [MC of Burnaby, BC] than anybody else. A couple of days ago they invited one of our officers inside [their clubhouse] for a beer. The officer said, 'I just might do that!', and in walk forty RCMP officers and special-service men. We had warrants for three Catwalkers related to assault charges occurring in the Vancouver area. Their president, Frank K——, is what holds that club together. If it wasn't for K—— the Catwalkers would fold. He keeps them out of trouble, he's a great organizer, he's a good businessman, and he knows which side his bread is buttered on. (RCMP constable, who requested anonymity)

In effect, the sharing of administrative responsibilities among several patch holders makes outlaw motorcycle clubs less vulnerable to outside threats.

The executive board constitutes a formal judicial and sanctioning authority within the club. While the board is responsible for its decisions to the club as a whole, it is in a position to apply sanctions or resolve conflicts between members without dramatizing either the infraction or conflict by publicizing the details in front of the entire club.

The eruption of heated disputes between members is not a common occurrence. When a conflict does materialize, the primary concern is to re-establish social equilibrium through informal means. The disputants are expected to attempt first to resolve the issue by themselves. If this endeavour fails, an executive member will be called upon to intercede in the quarrel. However, disputes are not always easily settled; sometimes it becomes necessary to try and end tensions on a more formal level. Under these circumstances the antagonists will be brought before the executive board, which will recommend a resolution without necessarily involving the club as a whole.

Similarly, gossip and ridicule are common means by which members withdraw group support and bring pressure to bear on patch holders whose club or personal performance is found to be less than adequate. A biker earns his colours as a striker; as a member he must continue to 'live his colours.' The reality of an outlaw motorcycle club depends on continued expression and validation in terms of being with one's brothers. A member who neglects this vital aspect of 'being there' will find himself the topic of gossip. The conversation that follows took place among members around a campfire on a club run.

> *Gerry*: How many runs has the Saint been on this month?
> *Steve*: Just the one.
> *Indian*: He's been out working on his cabin on Lac La Biche.
> *Steve*: Well, that's kind of dumb to build a cabin 135 miles from Edmonton.
> *Gerry*: It's time that I brought that up with the board.

A member who learns that his club participation is being called into question may himself talk with other members to either solicit support or help him assess his situation and determine how to deal with it. One week after the above conversation took place, Saint dropped in for a brew while I was visiting with Blues:

> *Saint*: I know for sure some of the guys don't like it, like Danny. Maybe they're right to a certain extent; but I'm around at least four days a week even though I've missed a few weekends. And as far as miles on my bike goes, I've put less miles on this summer than last, but it's still more than a lot of the other members.
> *Blues*: Yeah, I know how you feel. A couple of years ago when I was married I spent a whole month working on this house me and my ol' lady were going to move into. I only made four appearances all month, and I was called up before the board to defend myself. I found that pretty depressing, being brought up before the board after I'd been a solid member for four years. Like, we had to fix up the house or we'd have nowhere to go.

Blues advised Saint to frequent the club bar and attend the upcoming club runs, and 'the whole thing will just blow over.'

If and when these informal mechanisms of control – gossip and persuasion – are not effective in bringing a patch holder's performance up to standard, the objecting member can make a formal 'membership challenge.' The plaintiff and defendant will state their cases before the executive board, which in turn will decide whether or not the situation warrants disciplinary action.

This procedure, whereby members settle disputes through the executive board, reaffirms their unity within the Rebel social system. The resolution of conflict within the moral order of the club underlines the ties of brotherhood that bind members together, rather than the issues of contention that separate them. If sanctions are deemed necessary, the negative implications for the brotherhood are minimized if they are applied by an executive board, as opposed to a single officer of the club. The rulings of the executive board are one formal step removed from personal decision making, which minimizes the likelihood that a member will interpret a club sanction as a personal vendetta. The executive board has several gradients of sanctioning measures at its disposal to enforce club discipline. Depending on the seriousness of the infraction, the board may impose a fine, black mark, temporary suspension, suspension with a required striking period before reinstatement, or permanent expulsion from the club.

Fines are levied for a minor infraction, such as disrupting a meeting or being late for a club meeting or run. Black marks are given to members, in addition to fines, for misdemeanours such as causing a disturbance at the club bar or missing a meeting without having a legitimate excuse, such as being in the hospital, in jail, or at work. If a member accumulates five black marks over a three-year period, there is a mandatory 'vote on his colours' (membership status) by the club as a whole (Rebels MC Book of Rules).

Temporary suspensions are applied most often when a member is negligent in meeting club standards of minimum participation, such as failing to have his motorcycle running for a thirty-day period during the riding season (Rebels MC Constitution). Suspension of membership with the additional requirement that the suspended member endure a mandatory two-month striking period is reserved for serious offences that fall short of membership dismissal. Although the suspended member does not have to wear a striker patch, his colours are taken and kept in a safe within the clubhouse. Members who lose their colours also lose their voting privileges and their control over strikers. In one instance a member was found to have committed a theft from another member. Normally this offence would result in immediate expulsion from the club, and likely a severe beating by the offended member. However, there were mitigating circumstances in that the accused member had developed a drinking problem. With the help of his brothers, the suspended member made restitution, solved his drinking problem, and earned his colours back.

Permanent expulsion from the club is reserved for offences such a stealing from the club or club members, 'bringing the heat down on [causing the police to take action against] the club,' or engaging in behaviour that endangers either the club or its members. During a four-year period there were two 'patch pulling' offences. One expulsion involved Jack, a member whose unwarranted aggressive acts against citizens brought a lot of unnecessary attention from the police. 'Jack had two assault charges laid against him in a week. He broke one guy's arm in the Corona, and another guy's leg. Someone would hassle him a bit in the bar and he'd try to tear them apart ... He used the club. He jeopardized the club; he'd lay threats on people and use the club as his heavy card. It just went on and on. One thing you don't do is bring heat down on the club' (Steve). Another member was ejected from the club when it became known that he was 'into smack' (using heroin). A member whose judgment is distorted by physical and psychological dependence on a narcotic is both vulnerable and unreliable, and he constitutes a security risk to the club and its members. His brothers attempted to persuade the imperilled member to quit cold turkey, but their efforts were of no avail. Expulsion involves the confiscation of the member's club colours, by force if necessary, and the dating of any club (Rebel skull) tattoos.

The executive board also continually evaluates the progress of any prospect who is striking for the club. The evaluation will be based on their own opinions and the feedback they have received from the other members concerning the prospect. If there appears to be a consensus of opinion one way or the other, then the executive board will vote on the striker's eligibility for membership. In the event that the prospect does not receive any negative votes, his eligibility for membership will be voted on by all the members at the next general meeting. The practice of having a preliminary test vote has the advantage of making the general meeting more efficient by virtue of eliminating any unnecessary 'striker votes.' Considering that two negative votes are sufficient to deny the prospect membership, conducting a vote by general membership would be counter-productive without first ensuring total executive approval.

Finally, the executive board reviews aspects of the club's functioning, such as its financial situation or the presence of outside threats. Recent developments in these areas of the Rebels MC operation are discussed and summarized. The board then presents its assessment and recommendations to the membership as a whole at the weekly club meeting. The Rebels will then formulate appropriate plans of action to deal with various situations. For example, if there is a shortage of capital in the club's operating budget, a boogie may be planned. If the club faces the possibility of another club attempting to establish itself in Edmonton, plans will be made to improve the security system of the clubhouse, update the club arsenal, and formulate contingency plans and strategies for dealing with the impending threat.

The executive board acts as the Rebels MC 'brain trust' in summarizing issues and preparing collective solutions for the club's problems. However, the board is not an independent body in that any of its decisions – administrative or judiciary – first have to be approved by the membership as a whole at the weekly club meeting.

CONSENSUAL POLITICS: MAINTAINING A 'COMMON HEAD SPACE'

The success of the Rebels MC political system rests upon the fact that it operates within a larger framework of consensual politics: reaching an accord through informal discussion. Prior to the weekly club meeting members will inevitably exchange information concerning matters of club business and possible solutions to problems at hand. These discussions take place in settings such as the club bar or at Brothers Custom Cycles shop. The informal social context – conditioned by the frank biker verbal style – emphasizes the sociability of 'brother rapping with brother.' Under amiable circumstances that include 'sipping cool ones' or just 'shooting the shit,' there is minimal emotional hostility or aggression. Differences in opinion come to be viewed as logical alternatives rather than aberrations. These brainstorm sessions promote an undisciplined, sometimes humorous, but always creative exploration of raw ideas. Furthermore, they result in the maximum exchange of opinions among members by using a discussion format that is incompatible with the more structured procedures of club meetings.

Casual conversation thus becomes part of the group's decision-making process. The establishment and maintenance of this 'common head space' – unity of purpose – is vitally important to an action-oriented group such as an outlaw motorcycle club. It affords the club a necessary degree of adaptive flexibility by allowing it to operate through consensual politics. Reaching a consensus on key issues in the informal atmosphere of the club bar reduces the possibility of disagreements, bad feelings, or possibly worse when these issues are dealt with formally at club meetings. The emphasis on rapping with your brothers minimizes the need for formal debate and ensures a cohesive relationship between formal and informal decision-making processes. By keeping decision making within the framework of brotherhood, consensual politics reduces the possibility of the members focusing on a we-versus-they, as opposed to a we-versus-the-problem, orientation. Ideally, formal decision-making processes, such as standardized voting procedures, formal rules, and executive decrees, serve to ratify decisions already agreed upon through consensual politics.

Consensual politics firmly entrenches the system of personal relations – brotherhood – into the groundwork of the political structure. It thereby helps Rebel patch holders accept the fact of variation and the inevitability of change as a natural part of the political process.

> *Blues*: They're [new members] not living up to my [personal] expectations, but they're living up to my [club] ideals. We [older members] pretty well built the club; and like they live up to the constitution and things like that, that we've laid down. But I'm not saying that they follow us a hundred per cent; because then we'd never change, and we're always changing.
>
> *Coyote*: Why do you feel that there would be no change?
>
> *Blues*: Because the idea of the club would get so monopolized that it wouldn't work. You wouldn't get any change and we would always be staying with the same horse. It just wouldn't work without new ideas and change.
>
> *Coyote*: In that case, what, or who, decides what the purpose of the club is?
>
> *Blues*: It's something that is going on in the mind of each and every member.

Club meetings: Participatory democracy

Issues that hold implications for the club as a whole, whether they be administrative, judiciary, or political in nature, are eventually dealt with at club meetings. Meetings are held in the Rebels' clubhouse every Wednesday during the riding season (April 1 to October 30), and every second week during the winter months. Robert's Rules of Order govern the proceedings. The standardized order of business is (1) roll-call, (2) reading of minutes of the previous meeting, (3) unfinished business, (4) report of the executive board, (5) beer break, and (6) new business.

Behind the guarded walls of the clubhouse, members are freed from the constraint of having to convey an impression of solidarity and strength to outsiders. They can air their differences, negotiate an ongoing identity, and engage in controlled self-expression. There is a tacit understanding among members that these processes are healthy and that a variety of viewpoints contributes to a more informed decision-making process.

Meetings held in the clubhouse are characterized by a number of features that generate genuine and equal participation by members in an orderly fashion. The president chairs the meeting, providing each patch holder with an opportunity to speak and preventing the domination of the floor by any one person or faction. The sergeant at arms enforces formal rules of etiquette – backed by the threat of fines or eviction – that ensure the orderly handling of any dispute that threatens to get out of hand. Finally, members vote.

This formal structure and process for decision making does not preclude a group style that is characterized by openness, candour, and general 'bullshitting' that produces a relaxed, non-stressful environment. Each club and its members will add its own particular flair and style to the procedures. For example, at one meeting Indian attempted to take centre stage under the pretext that he had gotten drunk during the course of the mid-session beer break. Steve was the sergeant at arms at the time.

> *Steve*: Are you drunk?
> *Indian*: [Jokingly responds] Yeah, sure, why not!?
> *Steve*: Good! That's a ten-dollar fine. Pay up after the meeting!
> *Indian*: Hey, wait a minute! I'm not drunk!
> *Steve*: Glad to see that you've sobered up. You can stay
>   for the meeting, but you still have a ten-dollar fine
>   to pay.

Sometimes the secretary will record these events for posterity: 'George farted and cleared the room. The pig!' (Minutes of meeting, Satan's Angels MC).

Club meetings involve mechanisms for the expression of varying individual opinions, the elicitation of conflict through debate, and the reaching of consensus through formal votes. Internal diversity is channelled in formal clubhouse meetings by procedures for conducting business. There are rules to facilitate the negotiation of and compromise over contentious issues, and rules for overcoming an impasse (via the vote), should compromise fail.

Rebel patch holders accept both the procedures involved in the parliamentary strategy and the possibility that a partial agreement, a compromise solution with which none of the members is in complete accord, may have to serve as the basis of club action: 'No one person can stand there and say: "Well this is what the club is all about, and that's that." Everything that happens to the club or that the club does is put to a vote. Everybody knows what is expected of them, but then everybody also has their say. You don't always get your way, but you always get your say. It's put to a vote; majority rules' (Raunch).

For example, during the time that I rode with the Rebels, a situation arose that saw members take incompatible positions regarding a fundamental issue affecting the club's future. The issue was whether or not the Rebels MC should form a chapter in the city of Red Deer. Members promoting expansion wanted to see the Rebels become a larger organization. They argued that a Rebel chapter located in Red Deer, halfway between Edmonton and Calgary, would deter the northward movement of the Grim Reapers MC, another outlaw club based in Calgary. 'Bloody warfare threatens to explode over an attempt by a Calgary motorcycle gang to move into the city [of Edmonton] ... Edmonton's Rebels Motorcycle Club has warned the interlopers their attempt to move into the city will be resisted ... The Grim Reapers have already been involved in violence here ... shots have been fired say police ... The gangs are normally kept under surveillance by the RCMP and members of the city's elite task force' (*Edmonton Sun*, 31 Jan. 1979). The defensive strategy of establishing a chapter of the Rebels in Red Deer was opposed by those members who wished to promote the Rebels Motorcycle Club as a tightly knit unit. They were concerned that expansion would result in the depletion of both personnel and material resources, and that forming new chapters – 'becoming an organization,' as they explained it – would detract from the strong sense of brotherhood. When the two opposing groups failed to reach a consensus through informal discussions, the matter was raised at a meeting, debated, and resolved through a formal voting procedure. Expansion was rejected. The Rebels resorted to other means to prevent the Grim Reapers MC from starting a local chapter in what they saw as 'their territory.'

As members come and go, the consensus of opinion will change, leading to a change in political strategy that will itself create a new political reality. Often that new political reality is in sharp contrast to the doctrines and policies of previous times. For example, four years after the above non-expansionist decision was made, the Rebels MC had taken over the Warlords MC, incorporated the Spokesmen MC, and formed four chapters in two provinces; and, as impossible as it seemed in 1979, the Rebels had forsaken their allegiance with the King's Crew in favour of a pact with their old nemesis, the Grim Reapers.

Diversity among members becomes evident in the form of ideational and behavioural variation. While variation can be a social liability if it is not handled properly, it is also a potential social asset because it provides a degree of operational flexibility. In fact, intra-cultural diversity is a vital resource, like variations in a gene pool, that lies at the core of social-system adaptability and change. It was this variation that allowed the Rebels to reverse their decision not to expand and form chapters. The fact that a significant number of members earlier had favoured the formation of Rebel MC chapters in other cities meant that the social system contained the seeds of its own transformation to a system of greater complexity. When the political situation changed in the early eighties, the Rebels responded by forming chapters (see next chapter).

In conclusion, the Rebels mediate the contradiction between group conformity and individual freedom by aligning group policy with individual wants and desires. This alignment is facilitated by a political process that emphasizes consensual politics within a structure of participatory democracy. To the extent that the political process is successful in this respect, group affiliation becomes a means for members to achieve their personal ends. Members recognize that while some club policies may lack total consensus, the club's survival in an often hostile environment depends on a total commitment in carrying out those plans of action: 'In many ways the club is like a safe. There may be a lot of loose change on the inside; but when the tumblers fall in place and the door opens, look out! Because the Rebels come out as one!' (Wee Albert). Participatory democracy gives members of the Rebels MC the opportunity to fashion the sociopolitical reality of the club. Members take part in a decision-making strategy that allows them to innovate, evaluate, and ultimately control club policy. This aspect of political participation induces a degree of personal identity with group decisions on the part of the patch holder; it also generates the degree of commitment that is necessary to ensure that Rebel club policy is successfully carried out.

There is enough flexibility within the political process to allow the Rebels to accommodate considerable diversity and not merely demand uniformity from the members. There is enough ambiguity in the Rebels' social system to allow members to manoeuvre and express their varying perspectives concerning group goals and strategies. Much of the group tension and organizational dynamics that occurs within the club is focused on the process of negotiation as members – each with his own unique concept of the ideal club – attempt to bring the club into alignment with what they feel it ought to be. To date, the collective decision-making strategy of the Rebels, including their accommodation of variation, has enabled them simultaneously to produce change and reproduce stability. More important, it is the aspect of active participation in shaping the club that substantiates a patch holder's claim that the Rebels' organization is 'my club.'

12

Territoriality: Alliance, Invasion, Warfare

The two Rebels stood in the shadows of the parking lot outside the Bonaventure Motor Inn. Steve and Clayton were waiting for a man to come out from the bar. This man rode a Harley; he was a biker and a patch holder who shared their lifestyle. These Rebels had more in common with him than with anyone else in the bar. But there would be no biker handshake of brotherhood. Steve was the club sergeant at arms, and he knew that it was his responsibility to break this man. The reason? The man wore the wrong patch. As the member of the Highway Kings MC walked towards his bike the two Rebels blocked his path. 'Nothing personal,' said Steve, 'but I'm going to have to take that patch.' 'Fuck yourself!' said the Highway King. 'You know I can't do that!' Steve slammed his fist into the man's stomach, then brought his knee into the man's face as he doubled over. The Highway King was still flailing away on the ground when the parking lot was suddenly lit up by flashing red and blue lights. A siren wailed and a loudspeaker voice said 'Police! Hold it right there!' 'What's going on here?!' one of the officers asked as he rolled down his window. 'We're taking a patch,' replied Clayton. The cop looked at the Highway King on the ground and said, 'Yeah? Well, keep up the good work!' And they drove off. 'We maintain control over the clubs in this town. The police know that we're doing it and they give us their cooperation ... Of course they don't help us. But if they see us ripping some guy's colours off most of these guys will just look the other way ... You see, neither the cops nor us want the scene to become fucked up with too many clubs' (Steve).

Outlaw clubs are self-regulating. The major force that prevents the emergence of even more outlaw motorcycle clubs than exist today is not a lack of interest or a shortage of prospective recruits. Nor is it the controlling actions of law-enforcement agencies. It is other outlaw clubs. If the situation calls for it, inter-club rivalry and warfare can completely override any considerations of the common bonds of biking. It is a paradox of the world of bikerdom that a patch holder's greatest fear may be of another biker, who, under slightly different circumstances, he would call 'brother.' The imperative that compels one outlaw club to destroy another can be understood only when it is viewed within the context of territoriality.

From the day a club is founded it is involved in the politics and intrigue of territoriality. The Rebels MC emerged in Edmonton in 1969 as part of an attempted expansion by a Rebels club located in Red Deer. The Rebels were allowed to start up in Edmonton only because the Warlords MC 'allowed' them! The Warlords themselves had been established a year earlier from the remnants of two clubs, the Coffin Cheaters MC and the Sinners MC. The apparent generosity of the Warlords had more to do with their own long-term survival. They were aware of the fact that a club attempting to carve out a niche for itself will often do so by displacing the weakest of the clubs already operating in the area. By allowing the Rebels MC to establish itself, the Warlords created a buffer zone between themselves and the invasion or formation of other new clubs. Ironically, the Red Deer Rebels folded within the year. The Edmonton Rebels and Warlords would coexist in informal alliance for the next fourteen years. During that time they would prevent any other outlaw clubs from gaining a foothold in the city of Edmonton, remaining 'the only clubs in town.'

Less than a year would pass before the young Rebels faced their first territorial challenge. In the winter of 1970 members of the Fearless Albinos MC moved from Montreal to Edmonton. According to club president Mick Grimaldie, the move was an economic one, based on the availability of jobs in the Edmonton area (Alberta was experiencing an economic boom). The Fearless Albinos were unique in their use of attack dogs. Each club member owned and trained at least one guard dog. The dogs travelled with the members on their motorcycles in specially built trailers. The *Edmonton Journal* announced their arrival. The Rebels were treated to a picture of the Fearless Albino clubhouse, with the six executive members and six

Doberman pinschers and German shepherds. In the background was the club emblem – a large outline of a Doberman pinscher head – which was flanked by semi-automatic rifles with fixed bayonets. 'Here's One Motorcycle Club That Fights Shy of Violence,' read the caption. 'We go out of our way to avoid trouble of any kind,' the Fearless Albino president was quoted as saying, 'but if there is trouble we protect ourselves' (*Edmonton Journal*, 30 March 1970: 46). The Fearless Albinos had made a serious tactical error by allowing their territorial invasion to be publicized before being able to defend it. While the Albinos claimed a total membership of one hundred members, 'most of the members are still back there [in Montreal].' The Rebels began their territorial defence by isolating members of the Fearless Albinos in street encounters and forcibly confiscating their cut-off denim jackets with the Albino colours. By the end of the summer, all that remained of the Fearless Albinos MC was one set of colours that hung upside down on the Rebels' clubhouse walls.

The foresight of the Warlords' decision to create an informal alliance with the Rebels became evident three years later when the Skull Riders MC tried to start up in Edmonton. The Skull Riders were more astute than the Fearless Albinos and followed a sound strategy of maintaining a low profile during their formative period. They rode with their colours beneath their jackets while they steadily recruited more members. The Skull Riders were 'buying time.' They faced the same problem as any new club trying to invade an established club's territory: they lacked both numbers and commitment. In the formative stages of a club there is always an initial period of high membership turnover until a solid core of members crystallizes. In order to be able to withstand brutalization by established clubs, a new club requires bikers who have more than just a passing fancy in wearing a back patch. A new club is also vulnerable because it lacks a sound economic base and legal-network ties. While police tactics will never be feared as much as those applied by a dominant club, money and lawyers will still be required for the defence of members, posting bond, contesting questionable traffic violations, and filing charges of harassment against the police in order to reduce the pressure. The odds are stacked against a neophyte club being able to emerge and survive in a city that already has a dominance hierarchy of established clubs. If it is to have any chance at all, the club requires time in order to increase and stabilize its membership and build up its financial resources.

For the Skull Riders, confidence and daring came with growing numbers. They finally announced their presence when they cornered and severely beat up two Warlords who were drinking in the Klondiker bar. The Warlords called the Rebels to an emergency war council. Both clubs were concerned with the fact that the Skull Riders now had more than twenty-five members, too large a club to handle on a random street-fighting basis. Conducting a protracted campaign of skirmishes against a large club like the Skull Riders comes with no guarantees other than having continually to look over your shoulder and try to make sure that you don't come out on the short end of a long hot summer of escalating beatings and retaliation. The Skull Riders had to be shut down immediately as a group. That evening the Rebel and Warlord club officers devised a plan that would settle the issue with dramatic finality. They planned to trap the Skull Riders in their clubhouse and finish them there.

In times of war an established club holds the advantage of having an invaluable information network that enables the members to monitor the presence, activities, and whereabouts of enemies. Rebel patch holders would pool the information provided by their contacts – from friends of the club and motorcycle mechanics to bar patrons and bouncers – in order to establish a file on the opposing club that would include names, addresses, types of bike and/or car, and personal and club habits. Basically, the club that has the superior intelligence is able to strike first. The Rebels used their contacts in the outlaw-biker community to find out which bar the Skull Riders frequented on a regular basis. They also learned that the Skull Riders rotated the location of their club meetings as a security precaution. To carry out their plan it would be necessary to infiltrate the Skull Riders' organization. The Warlords and Rebels had no idea as to how closely they themselves had been scrutinized. Consequently, a regular member would be running too high a risk of being recognized as an infiltrator. The unenviable task fell to a relatively new Rebel striker. The Rebel striker approached a group of Skull Riders in their bar and stated a desire to strike for them. In their haste to augment their numbers in anticipation of the hostilities they knew would follow, the Skull Riders were cutting corners on their security checks of prospects. It was a gamble that an experienced club would not take and one they would regret. The Skull Riders invited the new 'prospect' to come to their clubhouse and be introduced to the club. The Rebel agent phoned in the address, date, and time of the Skull Riders' meeting to the Rebels' sergeant at arms.

The Skull Riders' secretary was reading the minutes of their last meeting when the garage door splintered, then crashed open from the impact of axes and monkey wrenches. The Rebels and Warlords stormed in. The Skull Riders were lined up and told that if they could run a gauntlet of Rebels on one side and Warlords on the other, they could keep their colours. All the Skull Riders would have to try; none would succeed. Any Skull Rider who even came remotely close to making it through was held up and passed along to the end of the line where Terrible Tom of the Rebels, an ex-Golden Gloves boxer, expertly finished the job.

The overwhelmed Skull Riders stood by and watched as their colours were seized and burned, with one exception. The final set of Skull Rider colours was taken to the Rebels' clubhouse, where it was draped upside down on a wall alongside colours from the Fearless Albinos MC. Over the next ten years the Rebels would add club patches taken from the Shadows MC, Highway Knights Car Club, Satan's Soul MC, Jokers MC, Devil's Own MC, Renegades MC, Highway Kings MC, Loners MC, and the Sundance MC. The Rebels' 'graveyard of colours,' all seized from clubs that they had 'taken off the road,' covers two walls of their clubhouse. The trophy-like display of captured colours is a common practice among outlaw clubs. For example, the Satan's Choice of Toronto exhibit colours they have torn from the backs of the Vagabonds MC, Para Dice Riders MC, and Red Devils MC. Displaying captured colours enhances the reputation of the club as one that can handle territorial incursions. The colours graveyard is something a visitor to the clubhouse cannot fail to notice. It is a ritualized threat display that dampens the enthusiasm that any visitors to the clubhouse might have for starting a club of their own.

COLOURS AS A TERRITORIAL MARKER

A biker values his colours more than anything else ... His colours represent his club. If you can take his colours away from him, that's total defeat. When you've taken a club's colours you've beaten them to the point of insulting them.

(Wee Albert, Rebels MC)

A club is 'shut down' by the highly symbolic gesture of capturing its colours. Patch holders feel that seizing a rival club's colours when they take a club off the road is both necessary and sufficient. In the outlaw community, an unwritten law is that a club that cannot defend its colours will not fly those colours. Of course, the effectiveness of this law ultimately depends on the strength and resources of the club enforcing it. In actuality, a club could simply continue to replace its lost colours. However, not only would the club lose credibility in the eyes of the outlaw-biker community, such a 'classless' move would also increase the tenacity with which the replacement colours would be ripped from their backs.

Because colours are a club's primary territorial marker, I expected them to play a significant role in territorial maintenance, as would the flag of a nation or the colours of a military unit. Yet I was still surprised at the larger-than-life importance that these symbols assumed, often to the point where the symbol defined a reality that was contrary to the facts of the matter. In particular, the outlaw-biker viewpoint that a club did not exist unless its members openly wore colours, and that its existence was automatically terminated when they lost those colours, interfered with what I considered to be sound decision making regarding the basics of survival. For example, I questioned Steve, the Rebels' sergeant at arms and master strategist, as to why the Rebels were not taking action against members of the Highway Kings, a new club that was making its presence known in the outlaw-biker community.

Coyote: What I don't understand is how come you've let the Highway Kings wear their colours underneath their leathers in the Executive [bar].
Steve: They can sew their colours on their fucking shorts and I wouldn't give a shit. I'm not going to go around pulling their pants down to see if they are wearing colours. If they wear them under their jackets I don't care. But as soon as they uncover and fly those colours, then I'll take them any way I have to.
Coyote: Yeah, but we know that they show their colours just as soon as they're outside the city limits. Is it going to be matter of catching them with their colours on outside the city?
Steve: No. If I see them outside the city with their colours on I couldn't care less. But not in this town!
Coyote: You realize that they're just laying low till there's enough of them to show themselves. In the meantime, shit is

going to come down like that cop pulling us over and telling
us some asshole from the Highway Kings is out gunning for
us with a shotgun.

Steve: Sure, I hope that they make a move [public show of
colours]. I just hope they try something. If forty-five [Canadian]
Airborne couldn't whip us [see chapter 8], I'm sure that those
cocksuckers can't.

The Highway Kings had the structure, organization, and membership
of a club, and indeed they functioned as a club. Furthermore, the
Rebels were fully aware of the growing and imminent threat to their
territorial control and individual safety. However, the Rebels would
not take countermeasures until the insurgent group publicly flew
their colours within the city of Edmonton. It was a very macho and
self-assured approach to the question of survival. If there was a
public message from the Rebels to the Highway Kings, it was 'If they
don't have the balls to fly their colours, then they don't exist!'

A clash between the Hell's Angels and the Memphis, Tennessee,
city police demonstrates an interesting situation in which the local
officers used this inordinate importance of the colours to prevent the
Angels from expanding into their city. A contingent of Hell's Angels
had arrived in Memphis with the intention of establishing a local
Angels chapter. The group was subsequently raided by club-wielding
Memphis policemen. During the course of the shakedown the Angels
had many of their civil rights blatantly violated. The Hell's Angels are
an international organization with tremendous financial and legal resources at their disposal. They threatened and subsequently proceeded to press charges in a civil suit against the City of Memphis
and its police force. However, the police force held a trump card.
They had confiscated the Angels' colours. Without their colours the
Angels could not return to their home base in Cleveland, Ohio. Loss
of colours could mean either probation or a loss of membership. An
out-of-court settlement between the two parties was arranged
whereby the Hell's Angels MC would drop the civil suit and agree
never to return to Memphis in exchange for the return of their
coveted colours.

Colours are such a sensitive issue that club bikers may react to
a perceived symbolic threat where no real threat exists. In Calgary,
a city approximately the size of Edmonton, seven outlaw clubs
jockeyed for position during the mid-seventies. The political situation
was so volatile that members of the King's Crew MC would confiscate

the denim vests of loners who posed no actual territorial or personal threat, but who had gone so far as to put a symbol on the back of their vests. Similarly, the San Diego Hell's Angels intimidated the Spirits MC into changing their name and club insignia. Why? The Angels had objected to the Spirits' club patch because it contained the colours red and white, the same as did the Angels' colours.

None of the Rebels that I knew enjoyed breaking bones with their fists or using chains to tear flesh. Club warfare places tremendous pressure on the members. You are continually looking over your shoulder. You return from a midnight run, just you and your ol' lady chasing the moon and stars in a cool summer evening breeze. You park your bike and begin to chain it up to the steel railing as your ol' lady starts up the apartment stairs. Then it hits you. 'What if they sabotage the bike?' 'Your ol' lady is walking up the stairs alone. ... What if?!' 'Maybe they're in those shadows?!' You yell at your lady to turn on the porch light; you grab a wrench; and then you just stand there and listen to the sweat trickle down your arms. As a patch holder you will feel pressure being applied from three different sources: first, demands placed on you by your own club to 'be there' and 'hold your mud'; second, harassment and surveillance by police anxious to demonstrate that they have the situation under control; and third, the continual threat of violence to you, possibly your ol' lady, or your motorcycle from an unpredictable enemy. The enemy is unpredictable except for one rule that all clubs and all members must abide by: 'no cops.' Patch holders may be beaten unconscious, pistol whipped, stabbed, or shot, and clubhouses may be bombed, but 'the cops are never called.' If the police do arrive on the scene, then no cooperation is to be given in the subsequent investigation; a patch holder who is a victim must never identify his assailant to the police. For example, when King's Crew member Wayne Jordan came out of a convenience store in April 1984, he was confronted by two Grim Reapers pointing a shotgun at him. Jordan panicked, three King's Crew had been murdered in a four-year period. He retreated into the store and summoned the police, who arrested the Grim Reapers as they fled in a car. While Jordan refused to provide testimony in the resulting court case, he was nevertheless expelled from the King's Crew for calling the police in the first place. Cooperation with the police leads to further investigation by the police. Therefore, the cardinal rule is that clubs must 'take care of business' by themselves. A patch holder of a club who wakes up in a hospital recovering from multiple stab wounds has nowhere to turn except his club. If his club is unable to take care of business, then he may feel trapped and the pressure mount as the screws of the three-way vice turn.

TERRITORIAL IMPERATIVES

Outlaw clubs, like other forms of government, see territoriality as being both necessary and inescapable. After assessing the situation, unfortunately I had to agree. Territoriality is not simply a matter of blind instinct compelling the defence of a given geographical space. It is a conscious decision taken to protect vested interests. Specifically, territoriality is a system of behaviours used by an individual or group to define and defend a set of beneficial relationships with its environment. In order to understand what motivates a biker to territoriality and why it is indispensable to outlaw clubs, one has to understand these relationships. I concluded that potentially there are four distinct sets of relationships, each of which can lead to inter-club rivalry and provide its own unique motivation or 'imperative,' for territorial maintenance: personal pride, group power, public relations, and, for some clubs, criminal profit.

The psychological imperative of personal pride

On a personal level there is a positive relationship between territorial behaviour and self-esteem. Claiming the city of Edmonton as their own enhances the Rebels' sense of legitimacy. When the Rebels defend 'their town' against invasion by others their proprietary sense, the notion that they somehow represent, if not own, that geographical area, is reinforced. 'This town belongs to us,' declared Tramp of the Rebels, 'and that's the way it's going to stay.' Their city is the stage on which they perform; and the Rebels incorporate the nature of the city as part of their character and substance. According to Saint, 'The larger and tougher the city, the more respect for the patch that covers it.'

A patch holder's identity is so closely tied to his colours that personal space and club territory become inseparable. I noticed that Rebel club members would take the invasion of their territory and its defence very personally. 'We used to party with some of those guys, like Magoo. Now they stab us in the back,' Blues said of the upstart Highwaymen MC. 'Nobody does that to us. Nobody does that to me!' Additional personal motivation to enforce territoriality comes from a patch holder's desire to protect his self-image and public profile as an outlaw. One of the psychological cornerstones of being a patch holder is seeing oneself as a member of a powerful, exclusive and élite group: 'The last thing I need is some dipshit on a Honda pulling up beside me wearing a back patch. Fucking embarrassing!' (Steve). Invariably, a new club will not be able to meet the standards – from bikes to behaviour – of an established club. If the Rebel patch holders want the right to define who and what is *the* outlaw biker, then they must 'keep their city clean' and not allow it to be polluted by what they would refer to as a 'Mickey Mouse' club. An example of a club that tarnished the outlaw image was the Rumplestiltskin Raiders MC in Calgary. The Rumplestiltskin Raiders had club cards printed up that carried the exclusive one-percenter symbol. Yet, they were in actuality a very conservative bunch with very little in the way of being a solid club to back up their claim to outlaw fame: 'We are very idealistic white knights' (member, Rumplestiltskin Raiders MC). I couldn't help but laugh when a 'candy-assed' Rumplestiltskin Raider gave me his club card with its '1%' logo. The hard-core Grim Reapers, who take pride in being legitimate one-percenters, failed to see any humour in the situation, and simply proceeded to 'knock the shit out of them.'

The sociological imperative of club power

Outlaw clubs in the same territory, usually a city, inevitably compete with each other. At stake will be power – measured in terms of status, influence, and access to scarce resources, such as new members. How antagonistic inter-club competition becomes depends on the extent to which the needs of the clubs overlap, leading to competition for the same resources. For example, the strong identity function of outlaw club membership results in a desire to be seen as the best; all patch holders want to be seen as the élite of their breed. But, since there can only be one 'best' club, club bikers sometimes indulge in a little selective perception. 'There's only one club in Calgary,' Ace, the president of the Chosen Few MC, once told me in a bar. 'That's the Chosen Few!' In fact, there were seven outlaw clubs in Calgary at the time, and, two years later, the Grim Reapers had taken Ace and his Chosen Few off the road. The importance of overlapping needs becomes most conspicuous when it motivates outlaw patch holders to enforce territoriality on organizations that are not motorcycle clubs. For example, patch holders who use their motorcycles as projections of personal power may find themselves in competition with car clubbers who do the same thing with supercharged automobiles. The Rebels in Edmonton took a car club called the Highway Knights off the road after a number of personal disputes, while the Hell's Angels of Vallejo were involved in a feud with a car club called the Slicks. Similarly, an outlaw motorcycle club that prides itself on being an enclave of hard-core machismo may find itself in competition with a military unit whose self-image is based on the same premise. The Rebels have been involved in two major bar-room brawls with members of the Canadian Airborne Regiment. 'Those assholes [Airborne] knew the Kingsway [tavern] was our territory' (Wee Albert). Conversely, the absence of overlapping needs will result in patch holders feeling no need to enforce territoriality on organizations that are indeed motorcycle clubs. For example, 'legitimate' Canadian Motorcycle Association (CMA) chartered clubs construct a totally different world than do outlaw clubs. This dissimilarity precludes their being considered either a threat or competition. Thus, a CMA road-riding club, such as the Greater Vancouver Motorcycle Club, or a CMA competition club like the Edmonton Motorcycle Club, is simply ignored by outlaw clubs in those cities.

Uncompromising territoriality enables the Rebels to maintain their position of power by giving them the edge in the competition for scarce resources. For example, when it comes to the critical question of recruiting new members, the club that has the greater territorial status will have the advantage of being able to attract and choose from the pick of the outlaw biker community. Clubs are very conscious of the fact that the strongest reputation attracts the best prospect and will go out of their way to enhance their image. For his part, a prospect is aware that 'the heavier the patch' of the club he joins, the greater the weight of his personal prestige. Earning the patch of the city's dominant club means greater personal status and power in areas as diverse as receiving looks of admiration from bikers when buying parts in a motorcycle shop and deference from bouncers when drinking in bars to having access to women whose fantasy is to be a hardened outlaw princess.

In today's highly political world of interrelated outlaw clubs, territory means power. A high-status club will command more respect and effort when they are being entertained by clubs whose territory they may be riding through. More important, higher-ranked clubs will be sought out and given preference by clubs in other territories when it comes to the politics of alliance formation. The bottom rocker of a club's colours acts as an area patch and states the club's territorial location or its territorial claim. The larger the geographical area claimed on that rocker, the higher the position of dominance and the status accorded to a club. Today (1990) there are only three clubs in the province of Alberta. The Grim Reapers, with chapters in Calgary, Red Deer, and Edmonton, are the 'top dog' club and fly a bottom rocker that reads 'Alberta.' The Rebels, with chapters in Edmonton and Calgary, are next in line and have bottom rockers of 'Northern Alberta' and 'Southern Alberta' respectively. The King's Crew, with one chapter, display a bottom rocker with the name of the city of 'Calgary.' In the province of Saskatchewan it is the Rebels who dominate with chapters in the cities of Moose Jaw and Saskatoon; the Rebels in this province fly a bottom rocker that reads 'Saskatchewan.' A club will defend its monopoly over the use of an area patch as a matter of club prestige and personal honour. The Grim Reapers have warned the Edmonton and Calgary Rebels not to fly an 'Alberta' bottom rocker. When the Mongols MC of San Diego began to fly 'California' as their bottom rocker in 1977, they in effect challenged the Hell's Angels' position of dominance in that state. One Mongol was shotgunned off his bike while wearing the disputed patch; two Mongols and their ol' ladies were machine-gunned while cruising down an interstate highway; and another was blown to shreds by a sophisticated explosive device hidden in a motorcycle tire that he was given to repair. In all, five Mongols were slaughtered for challenging the Hell's Angels' monopoly of the state patch.

The community imperative of public relations

> When there's other clubs around there's always somebody that is doing something wrong, eh. And to a citizen, guys on motorcycles wearing colours on their back are all the same thing. He doesn't have to be from the same club, he's still guilty. So you have to answer for everybody else's shit too.
>
> (Raunch, Rebels MC)

The short-term violence of taking a club off the road serves the long-term function of stabilizing the dominant club's relationship with the host community, especially its police force. The Edmonton city police know that the Rebels are a long-standing established club, and that as a result the club has rigid control over its members. Thus, at least according to one police spokesman, police policy towards the Rebels was one of begrudging acceptance. 'We leave them alone as a rule, but they know if they get out of hand we'll come down on them hard. Every now and then an individual member will get a little crazy, but they're fairly well controlled from within the gang' (Edmonton city police task-force spokesman, *Edmonton Sun*, 31 Jan. 1979: 2) Moreover, as the Rebels are an older club with a more mature membership, they can achieve a better balance with the community. The patch holders of an established club have no need to pull off 'little asshole trips' in order to justify their existence to themselves or anybody else. In their assessment of the potential for violence of smaller novice clubs, the RCMP concluded: 'The sub-culture at this level is more tawdry and perhaps more prone to violence than in those clubs that have achieved a big name in the biker order. The smaller clubs are still "trying" and thus must emulate and carry out their business perhaps with a little more ferocity, as they have not really made it to the big time biker world' (RCMP inter-police force communiqué).

Police reports indicate that community residents rarely distinguish the back patches of different clubs. To the average citizen, patch holders are simply 'bikers' or 'gang members.' Therefore, in order to minimize conflict and avoid police harassment, the Rebels – in their role as dominant club – must become responsible for any individual wearing a back patch in their city. They exercise this responsibility by acting as a pre-emptory regulating force, while maintaining as low a profile as possible. In this role the Rebels must control the number of outlaw clubs on the street and preserve the peace, even if it means using violence on other bikers to do so. 'If we want a hassle, we'll go look for it ourselves,' said Wee Albert. 'The best thing is to do them [new clubs] in with violence in order to preserve the peace.' As a result, the Rebels' rationale for territorial maintenance complements the RCMP and Edmonton city police statements:

> We take colours because new clubs are all power trippers; they get off on their colours in the wrong way. They tend to lay bullshit on the citizens and this causes us a lot of hassles ... Like the Devil's Own [a club eventually shut down by the Rebels]. They wanted to prove themselves and they went about proving themselves in the wrong way. First, they want to prove

they're tough; so they go out and hassle the public. The man [police] comes down and says: 'All right, you bikers have been assholes!' And we spend the next couple of months taking heat from the man. When our club was new we were assholes too, like when we got into that brawl at the Rosslyn [Motor Inn]. You could say we started that. But we survived it; and we grew up. (Larry)

It is both unnecessary and highly unlikely that the relationship between the Rebels and the local police force will ever be an amiable one. However, over time the Rebels have come to realize that their long-term survival depends on maintaining a low profile and some degree of predictability in their activities and the reactions (media and legal) of the host community. 'They know who we are and sort of know what we're all about,' Blues commented about police policy. 'There's no love lost, but they know enough to leave us alone.' An interesting paradox arises. On the one hand, the Rebels represent the élite of outlaw bikers. On the other hand, they inevitably become part of the established order, a new conservatism of sorts.

For their part, the Edmonton city police are aware that the Rebels control both the number and visibility of outlaw motorcycle clubs. They share the Rebels' viewpoint on the prospect of new clubs forming in the city. Edmonton police spokesman Lance Beswick alluded to this overlapping perspective when the Grim Reapers first became evident in Edmonton in 1979.

Gang Warfare Feared
Bloody warfare threatens to explode over an attempt by a Calgary [based] motorcycle gang [Grim Reapers MC] to move into the city. Edmonton's Rebels Motorcycle Club has warned the interlopers their attempt to move into the city will be resisted. Individual members of the Grim Reapers have already been involved in violence here in recent weeks, and on several occasions shots have been fired, say police ... Both gangs are known by police to carry guns at times – particularly shotguns. Police are so worried of an all-out battle that all departments have been told to keep an eye out for known leaders of the Grim Reapers. A police spokesman said: 'The Reapers were booted out of Calgary ... The Rebels don't want them here either.' The gangs are normally kept under surveillance both by

the RCMP and members of the city's élite task force. Both forces are remaining tight-lipped about the situation, a task force spokesman said yesterday: 'This is too delicate for comment.' (*Edmonton Sun*, 31 Jan. 1979: 3)

Ironically enough, the police often find themselves working towards the same goal as the Rebels when it comes to the issue of territorial defence. This overlapping perspective – the elimination of outlaw patch holders – can at times lead to an unofficial policy of tolerance on the part of some police officers towards the Rebels' not-quite-legal techniques of territorial maintenance, such as the patch-pulling incident described at the beginning of this chapter. According to Cecil Kirby, former vice-president of the Toronto Satan's Choice, police officers on patrol in other cities also have looked the other way when they've come across an assault that pits outlaw against outlaw. 'He [member of the Henchmen MC] saw me with the wrench, and he started to take off his colours. Then he stopped. That's when I let him have it with the wrench. I took off his colours and left him lying in the street. The cops were at the motorcycle shop a good part of the time. They saw the fight, but they didn't do anything. They just walked into the shop and waited until it was all over. They watched as the biker got up off the street, staggered to his car, and drove off with blood streaming down his face' (Kirby and Renner, 1986: 54). The decision by the two officers not to intervene does not represent official police policy. It is a judgment call on their part, knowing that they will receive no cooperation from either of the two bikers involved either in breaking up the fight or in laying subsequent charges. At most it represents police locker-room policy making: 'If they want to crack each other's skull, then good!'

The profit imperative of crime

For some clubs territoriality is a matter of profit. What is at stake is money from criminal activities that may include, in order of importance and frequency, the illicit drug trade, prostitution, and extortion. The clubs that most often are implicated and convicted of these types of criminal activities are chapters of the four club federations that dominate the United States and Canada: the Hell's Angels, Outlaws, Pagans, and Bandidos. These large clubs are national and international in scope, and the number of people involved warrants the label 'organized crime.' Profits can be in the hundreds of thousands of dollars. In the mid-seventies, for example, the Satan's Choice had their own laboratories in isolated cabins in northern Ontario manufacturing methamphetamines, nicknamed Canadian Blue. The Satan's Choice, along with the Vagabonds MC and the Para Dice Riders MC, divided the Toronto market for narcotics into three areas. The three clubs controlled and protected their respective zones from any kind of competitors, both bikers and non-bikers alike. Criminal profit not only provides an imperative for territorial maintenance, it can also provide the necessary motivation for political expansion or affiliation. For example, Satan's Choice crime intensified when they aligned themselves politically with the Outlaws (see later section on expansion).

WHEN TERRITORIALITY FAILS: INSTABILITY AND VIOLENCE

Ironically, there is more violence when territorial control disinte-grates than when it is enforced. If the dominant club or clubs of a city fail to enact a policy of rigid territorial control, or if they them-selves are terminated, a certain sequence of developments is historically inevitable. First, a plethora of new clubs will form in the political vacuum that is created. There are always more would-be patch holders than there are actual club members in any city. Second, the political situation will be volatile. New clubs will have to carve themselves a niche by 'proving themselves' in a hostile environment. Third, these clubs eventually will have to compete with each other in a highly conspicuous manner for territorial domination. Fourth, the accelerating hostilities will garner the attention of the media. Fifth, the public and local city government will pressure the police force to control the situation. Finally, the public demonstration of control by the police will take the form of unrelenting harassment, such as very aggressive traffic-violation enforcement, questioning and warning club officers, increased surveillance, and eventual raids on clubhouses and the private residences of club members leading to the seizure of weapons and revoking of FACs (Firearm Acquisition Certificates). The public pressure and subsequent police crack-down will be directed against all clubs, not just the neophytes being intro-duced to the realities of surviving as an outlaw motorcycle club. If they were to allow this sequence of events to unfold, the established clubs would lose the power to define the relationship they have with both the community at large and the police in particular. To a large extent they would lose control over their own destiny, a situation totally unacceptable to a group like the Rebels. While the Rebels and Warlords maintained a tight grip on the city of Edmonton, they watched the above chain of events unfold as the Grim Reapers lost control of Calgary.

The Grim Reapers (est. 1958) had totally dominated the outlaw-club scene in Calgary until the Outcasts MC came along in 1970. The Outcasts were an amalgam of the remnants of three clubs that the Reapers had earlier taken off the road. The Grim Reapers invited the Outcasts to a party at their clubhouse in an effort to convince them to drop their new club. However, Ronald Hartley, president of the Outcasts, became quite drunk at the party and claimed that the Outcasts were going to run the Reapers off the road. One of the Reapers took Hartley aside and beat him up severely while other Reapers restrained members of the Outcasts from coming to the aid of their president. Several were roughed up, but none seriously. After the beating everybody returned to the party. Amazingly, and in the best of outlaw tradition, Hartley joined in and started drinking again, even though his wife Bonnie felt that he needed medical attention. When Hartley's condition worsened he was driven by his club members to the Calgary General Hospital; he was pronounced dead on arrival.

In accordance with their code of silence, none of the Outcasts or Grim Reapers would identify the member who laid the beating on Hartley. As a consequence, all thirteen members of the Grim Reapers who were present at the party were held in police custody. The Grim Reapers had achieved public notoriety by virtue of their tactics used to control the outlaw-biker scene, and the murder put them on the front pages: 'Man beaten on road 13 charged in death' (*The Albertan*, 10 March 1970). In the political climate of public indignation, all thirteen Grim Reapers were charged with non-capital murder, and all thirteen would be convicted. It was the largest joint murder charge ever laid in Canada. By April 1973, the Alberta Court of Appeals reversed the murder convictions of twelve of the thirteen members. But the damage to the biker dominance hierarchy in Calgary had been done.

The Grim Reapers had been thrown into disarray, and the other established club, the King's Crew, was not powerful enough to replace them as a controlling force. Jumping in to fill the void were the Lucifer's Union MC in northeast Calgary, the Chosen Few MC in southwest Calgary, and the Barbarians MC in southeast Calgary. Thus these three clubs, along with the Minority MC, Outcasts MC, King's Crew MC, and the decimated Grim Reapers MC, constituted seven clubs competing with each other in a city no larger than Edmonton. Inter-club territorial rivalry and hostilities led to police harassment of outlaw clubs and loners who remotely looked like outlaw bikers. 'Well, I'll tell you, just between you and me. The way it is now, I'd like to run them [outlaw clubs] all off the road' (Staff Sergeant [anonymous by request], Calgary police force). 'Calgary is just a friggin' mess. It's a total disaster! These new clubs ... are establishing themselves, and are becoming powerful enough that the other [established] clubs can't shut them down. Because if the [Grim] Reapers and the [Kings] Crew said; "Fuck this! We're going to shut down clubs!" they couldn't do it. They can't do it because all of these five other clubs immediately come together and form a block. No, they can't do it anymore. What they have now is a pact amongst all the clubs saying no more clubs, and that once a club is defunct it shall no longer return to the road' (Wee Albert, Rebels MC). The Grim Reapers gradually re-established themselves and regained their position of dominance. During the seventies, territorial battles and take-overs took their toll on the weaker club brotherhoods until there remained only the Grim Reapers and King's Crew in the early eighties. However, the Rebels have established a chapter in Calgary and, as far as the Grim Reapers are concerned, the King's Crew are destined to be the odd club out!

In order to be effective territoriality must be enacted both quickly and decisively. A prolonged war serves no purpose other than unnecessary pain, fear, and suffering. The issue may be decided unequivocally with the elimination of one of the two competing clubs or an agreement may be hammered out. Alternatively, hostilities may ebb and flow, then stop in an undeclared truce as both clubs tire of the beatings, shootings, bombings, and subsequent police arrests. Both clubs will simply try to avoid each other in an attempt to return a degree of normalcy and predictability to their lives. For example, while there was no formal agreement between the two clubs, the King's Crew restricted their activities to the southeastern parts of Calgary while the Grim Reapers ranged over the northwestern sections. But the war continues. Formal declarations of war and peace are rare in biker disputes and, if the dispute has not been settled, hostilities may resurface at any time, at any place, perhaps on the basis of a chance encounter that leads to a rumble. If a war is allowed to drag out for a long period of time, club issues become secondary to a history of personal grudges and vendettas that wrap the members in hate and entangle them in a never-ending cycle of revenge.

Detective Brendan A. Kapuscinski and his partner Detective Jeffrey Massicotte are members of the City of Calgary's special Strike Force Unit, formed to monitor the activities of outlaw bikers in that city. In 1987 the two detectives decided to stake out the clubhouse of the King's Crew MC after one of the Crew members was reported missing by his wife. Three of the Crew came out and approached the two detectives. According to Detective Kapuscinski the conversation was something like the following:

Moyse (King's Crew MC): You're at the wrong clubhouse!

Det. Kapuscinski: You think the Grim Reapers had anything to do with it?

Moyse: You know that!

Det. Kapuscinski: What do you think they'll do to him?

Moyse: They'll probably torture him to get information, and then kill him.

Det. Kapuscinski: How do you think you'll get him back?

Moyse: In a box, or crawling on his hands and knees with his head caved in!

Det. Kapuscinski: Well, in that case we'll stick around just in case someone throws something over the fence of your clubhouse.

Moyse: It would be nice to see you guys around. But you'd be better off watching the field around the clubhouse. Watch for the red streak in the sky ['red streak' refers to a PAW rocket].

Det. Kapuscinski: I can't stop one of those with my badge.

Moyse: Well, at least there'll be someone around as witness.

The missing King's Crew member, Louis Aaron Blatt, never did show up. However, several days later a King's Crew ring was found in a burned-out van east of the city of Red Deer. The inscription on the ring read: Aaron 1980.

The following fourteen incidents are part of a collection of over sixty cited by Detective Brendan A. Kapuscinski in an 'Application for Warrant to Search and Seize' (1987) the said 'firearm(s), offensive weapon(s), ammunition, or explosive substance(s)' of the King's Crew and Grim Reapers motorcycle clubs.

In February, 1983, five sets of King's Crew 'colours' are stolen by members of the Grim Reapers at gun point. These 'colours' were ultimately burned and left at the offices of the Calgary Sun Newspaper ... In March, 1983, several rifle shots were fired into the Calgary clubhouse of the Grim Reapers ... On April 13th, 1983, the King's Crew Motorcycle Gang's clubhouse is bombed again, this time destroying the building ... On April 27th, 1983, the home of Melvin Jordan then president of the King's Crew Motorcycle Gang was bombed and later riddled by fifteen rifle shots ... On May 16th, 1983, Grim Reapers Motorcycle Gang member, Dennis Bullen's truck was bombed causing extensive damage ... On June 8th, 1983 King's Crew Motorcycle Gang member, Larry Graham and his wife are the targets of an attempted kidnapping in which Graham is pistol whipped ... On June 10th, 1983, King's Crew Motorcycle Gang member Ronald 'Wrongway' Moore was killed when his 'booby trapped' jeep exploded after he started it outside his home ... On July 30th, 1983, Southside Harley And Speed Motorcycle shop, located in Edmonton, Alberta and owned by members of the Grim Reapers Motorcycle Gang is bombed. On December 18th, 1983, James St Pierre a member of the King's Crew Motorcycle Gang is admitted to the General Hospital with numerous stab wounds ...

On January 22nd, 1984, King's Crew Motorcycle Gang member, Steven Albert Joell is gunned down at his residence and dies shortly after of the wounds ... On August 13th, 1984, Grim Reapers Motorcycle Gang 'striker,' David Worshek is severely beaten by members of the King's Crew Motorcycle Gang ... On July 26th, 1987, King's Crew Motorcycle Gang member Richard Moyes, was beaten unconscious in a downtown restaurant by Michael Doll, Kerry Eastman and Derek Smith of the Grim Reapers Motorcycle Gang and his gang 'colours' stolen ... On October 1st, 1987, Valerie Blatt, wife of King's Crew Motorcycle Gang member Louis Aaron Blatt, reported her husband missing after he failed to return home after work ... it is suspected that Blatt was in fact kidnapped by members of the Grim Reapers and murdered with his body being disposed of in such a way as to prevent its being found. This is a suspicion which is shared by executive members of the King's Crew Motorcycle Gang. It is felt the reason for disposing of the body in this fashion was to prevent the King's Crew from collecting on the $50,000.00 life insurance policy [as collected on the homicide death of an earlier member] ... On September 14th, 1987 the King's Crew Motorcycle Gang were offered five PAW [Personal Assault Weapon] rockets by a weapons dealer from Edmonton. The King's Crew declined the offer; however, these five PAW rockets were subsequently offered to and purchased by member(s) of the Grim Reapers. These rockets are military in origin and have no purpose other than as a offensive type weapon. These rockets are capable of penetrating 27.4 cm (10.8 in.) of steel and 76.2 cm (30 in.) of concrete, and are normally utilized as an anti-tank weapon. (Kapuscinski, Calgary city police, 1987: 14–23)

Today (1991) the Grim Reapers and King's Crew are locked in a sixteen-year-old struggle that has at times become a matter of life and death. According to William 'Crow' Stevenson of the King's Crew, 'The war has never ended.'

TERRITORIAL EXPANSION: MERGERS AND ALLIANCES

The inter-club aggressiveness that is displayed when clubs defend their territory is opposed by the force of mutual attraction that comes with sharing a lifestyle. Territoriality determines which of the two opposing forces, competition or affiliation, will predominate. The same similarity of clubs that leads to overlapping needs and competition – 'at each others' throats' – when the clubs occupy the same territory leads to mutual attraction – 'the brotherhood of outlaws' – when the clubs occupy different territories.

Like all outlaw motorcycle clubs, the Rebels want to expand their range of operations beyond the boundaries of their home territory. Because the Rebels and their members are highly mobile during the 'riding months,' it is advantageous, even necessary, to establish a network of friendly ties with clubs who live in distant areas, such as the Hell's Angels in Vancouver. Linked clubs provide each other with accommodation and entertainment when they go on extended runs, and they invite each other to major parties and events. Some of the ties that the Rebels established with other clubs remain strictly social in nature; others have evolved into more formal political connections. Not all clubs go beyond the process of inter-club social networking. From 1969 to 1975 the Rebels avoided political expansion as a matter of principle and choice. The Rebels were a solid club with a 'respected reputation.' They continually refused the overtures of other clubs to affiliate politically, even when some of their own members favoured the idea in the name of 'making the club more powerful.' The majority of Rebel patch holders felt that their close-knit independence was the source of their strength. According to Ken, the influential president of the Rebels for five years, expansion was a sign of weakness; it was a quick-fix measure that substituted numbers for true strength. But as the members of a club change, so too does its political policy. After Ken's departure from the Rebels as an active member, the club amalgamated with the Warlords in Edmonton, formed two chapters in the province of Saskatchewan, and then created a fourth chapter in the Grim Reapers' backyard of Calgary.

In the world of outlaw clubs there are two major forms of political affiliation: alliances and federations. An alliance is a coalition of different clubs that enter a pact but maintain their essential independence. Clubs involved in an alliance may design a small affiliation patch that their members wear on the front of their colour's jacket or vest; however, they will retain the distinct back patches of their respective clubs. A federation is a union of 'chapters,' or charter-member clubs, that a single club has incorporated. Incorporation is accomplished by either creating new clubs, 'start-ups,' or merging clubs that are already established, 'take-overs.' Bikers will not use the term federation, but instead simply refer to an organization of charter clubs as members of 'the same club.' For their part, police officers and law-enforcement publications simply will refer to charter clubs as members of 'the same gang,' such as when they refer to the four federations that 'dominate North America': 'Basically, four main one-percenter gangs dominate the North American scene: The Hell's Angels, the Outlaws, the Pagans and the Bandidos with a combined strength of about 2,000 members ... 900 other outlaw motorcycle gangs exist in Canada and the United States that operate mostly locally and with perhaps provincial/state status' (RCMP *Gazette*, 1987: 9). What avenues for expansion or options for affiliation a club can pursue will be determined by some very basic parameters of territoriality. The particular strategy that a club chooses first will be conditioned by its specific territorial needs; for example, do the members

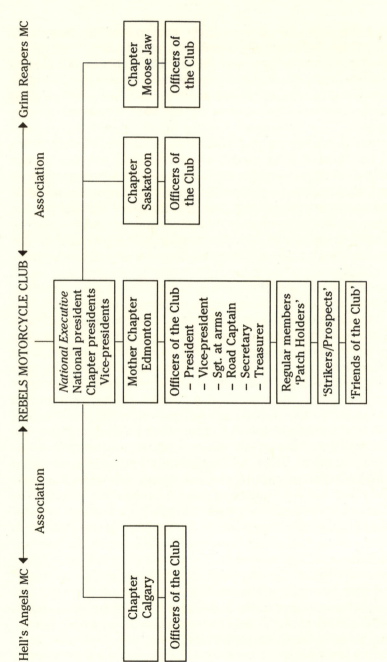

FIGURE 6

The political power structure of an outlaw-motorcycle-club federation,
as typified by the Rebels Motorcycle Club

wish to retain their independence or do they require an ally to help fend off a rival club? Furthermore, that strategy will have to be operationalized within a larger political framework of pre-existing alliances and federations; for instance, it would be foolish for a club such as the Tribesmen MC of Squamish to join the Outlaws federation since they live in British Columbia, a province controlled by the Hell's Angels.

Alliances and federations begin with 'good times.' If two or more clubs feel that it is to their mutual advantage, they will use parties and joint club runs as the medium for establishing some form of association. During the early seventies bonds of trust and friendship were born out of the face-to-face talk, partying, and riding that the Rebels shared with the Spokesmen MC of Saskatchewan (chapters in Saskatoon and Swift Current) and the King's Crew MC of Calgary. The advantage of creating an alliance as opposed to merging into a federation is that the aligned clubs can assume mutual obligations yet maintain their independence. The disadvantage is that the clubs might hold very different views on the degree of allegiance that is involved. The Spokesmen wanted the three clubs to exchange 'mini patches,' small versions of each others' colours, indicating a binding formal commitment to each other's welfare. The King's Crew were more reticent and designed an alliance patch that incorporated part of the colours from all three clubs. However, the Rebels continued to emphasize the element of independence and altogether vetoed the idea of exchanging any kind of subpatch. 'Most of us [Rebels] just didn't like the idea of some guy in Calgary [King's Crew] wearing any kind of patch that had anything to do with us unless we voted on the guy first,' according to Tramp. 'Like if they let some guy we didn't like into their club, he's wearing our patch and we can't do fuck all about it.' For the most part, the interaction between the three clubs remained social in nature. However, there was an understanding that one club could count on the others for backup should the need arise.

A pact has been made between ... the King's Crew and the Spokesmen to eliminate the Apollos MC from Regina ... The King's Crew want them off the road because they tried to do in a couple of the Crew [invited as guests] at a party ... The Spokesmen want to do it because these guys [Apollos] have been assholes ... When they go riding they ride with rifles on their backs, and this is garbage. We don't need rifles when we ride. If you're going to take a piece, you're going to take a piece

to use it ... There's going to be a run just to eliminate them ...
They'll [King's Crew and Spokesmen] catch them [Apollos] at
their clubhouse. They give all clubs a bad name, so the best
thing is to do them in. (Wee Albert, Rebels MC)

I mentioned that 'taking a club off the road is a pretty heavy trip' and
asked Wee Albert, 'Is there more to this?' Wee Albert replied, 'Well,
the Spokesmen are thinking of setting up another chapter in Regina.'
Eliminating the Apollos from Regina would make the Spokesmen the
only motorcycle club in Saskatchewan. However, the logistics of
providing support for a club that is more than three hundred miles
away are prohibitive. The Spokesmen/King's Crew expedition never
materialized, and the Apollos eventually terminated the nearby Swift
Current chapter of the Spokesmen.

A federation differs from an alliance in one very important respect; the incorporated club gives up its independence. A new chapter adopts both the colours and the constitution and/or by-laws of
the larger federation. Initially, the newly created or incorporated
chapter must accept unquestionably the dictates of the central or
head club, often referred to as the 'mother chapter.' After a probation period, usually of one year, the new chapter is formally incorporated. For example, the 13th Tribe MC of Halifax, Nova Scotia, was a
prospect club for the year of 1984 before being accepted as a chapter of the Hell's Angels MC. If incorporation involves the merger of a
formerly independent club, the incorporated members will either re-
tire their former colours or engage in a patch-for-patch swap. Once
incorporated, the new club is allowed to take part in political decision making by sending its officers to represent them at the federation's joint executive meetings. The president of the mother chapter
is referred to as the 'national president' or 'national chairman'; he
automatically becomes the federation's chief executive and organizing officer.

If the patch holders of an outlaw club decide to create a new chapter, it has to be outside their present locality. The psychological and
sociological underpinnings of territoriality preclude a club from having two chapters in the same city. The Hell's Angels, for example,
found that even having chapters as close as the cities of San Francisco and Oakland led to friction and personal disputes between
brother Angels. Starting a new chapter involves at least one or two
members moving to the new city on a permanent basis. In 1982 a

couple of Rebels moved to Calgary to work in the 'oil patch.' Both were solid members and former club officers; they knew what to look for in new members and would uphold Rebel standards. Given these credentials, the Edmonton executive granted them permission to start recruiting for a Calgary chapter of the Rebels in 1984. During its formative period the neophyte chapter was dealt with as a protectorate of the mother chapter. The Calgary chapter retained this dependent status until the officers of the full-fledged Rebels clubs considered it established enough to be voted in as an equal. The advantage of forming a new chapter is that using its own patch holders as founding members ensures both the quality of the members accepted and their allegiance to the mother chapter. The obvious disadvantage of starting a new club is its vulnerability. The fledgling Rebel chapter in Calgary had the King's Crew as allies, but the Grim Reapers still held the upper hand. However, prior to the Rebel incursion into Calgary, a Grim Reaper had moved to Edmonton in 1979 and opened up a motorcycle shop called South Side Harley Speed Specialties. The Grim Reapers activated an Edmonton chapter in 1981. Both the Rebels and the Grim Reapers had started up a neophyte chapter in each other's stronghold. In an interesting political trade-off, the clubs agreed to allow each other's new chapter to settle in 'their city.' The losers in this non-aggression pact between the Rebels and Reapers were the King's Crew. The 'Crew' had hoped that a Rebel chapter in Calgary would help them turn the tide against their rivals and blood enemies, the Grim Reapers. Today the Rebels and Grim Reapers hold joint runs and parties together in conjunction with their mutual compatriots, the Hell's Angels of Vancouver. The balance of power between the Rebels and the Reapers was becoming more complex, but at the same time it was more stable and province-wide in scope.

The advantages of merging with or taking over a club, as opposed to starting one up, are expediency and enhanced survival chances. A federation immediately gains a new chapter that is fully established. In 1980, the Rebels expanded into the province of Saskatchewan when they incorporated the remaining Spokesmen MC chapter in Saskatoon. The long-standing social and political alliance between the two clubs laid the foundation for a federation. The Spokesmen, former allies of the Rebels, saw merging with the Rebels as the only viable option for survival, as they were losing their territorial dispute with the Apollos MC. The Apollos of Regina were determined to be the only club in Saskatchewan, but they wouldn't risk challenging the

Rebels' colours. Today, the Rebels dominate that province and their two chapters fly a bottom rocker that reads 'Saskatchewan.' In a similar restructuring of the balance of power in Edmonton, the Rebels strengthened their position when they incorporated the Warlords MC in 1983. The Warlords had reached a low ebb as far as club intensity and numbers were concerned. At the same time the Grim Reapers had been 'solidifying their position in Edmonton since they made their initial move in 1979. Ironically, the Warlords found themselves in the position of being a buffer-zone club, the role that they had created for the Rebels back in 1969. The Warlords were caught in a squeeze play between the Rebels and the Grim Reapers. Rather than be targeted by the Grim Reapers as the odd club out, the Warlords merged with the Rebels. Warlord patch holders retired their lion's-head colours and donned the Rebels' skull patch. A fourteen-year tradition ended. There would still be only two clubs in Edmonton, but now it would be the Rebels and the Reapers.

Holding together a federation of outlaw clubs, each with its own particular priorities, behavioural styles, political needs, and headstrong personalities who certainly don't always see eye-to-eye on what constitutes either a problem or a solution, can present a formidable challenge. The Rebels' expansion to four chapters – Edmonton, Calgary, Moose Jaw, and Saskatoon – located in two provinces was relatively easy and smooth. The small number of clubs has not presented any insurmountable problems of inter-club communication or cooperation. Larger federations, such as the Hell's Angels (46 chapters in North America and 21 worldwide – approximately 900 members as of 1989), Outlaws (30 chapters in the United States and Canada – approximately 500 members as of 1987), Pagans (40 chapters in the United States – approximately 600 members as of 1987), Bandidos (30 chapters – approximately 400 members as of 1987), and Satan's Choice (13 chapters and approximately 200 members in 1977), have all faced the inevitable problems of controlling diverse chapters spread over a wide geographical area. The larger the organization the greater the need for centralized control. A large federation requires a strong-willed and forceful national president who has tremendous organizational skills and who is capable of astute decision making and balanced compromise. One cannot overestimate the importance of the roles played by individuals, such as Bernie Guindon, past national chairman of the Satan's Choice MC, Johnny Davis and Harry (Stairway) Henderson, past national presidents of the Outlaws MC, and Ralph 'Sonny' Barger, international president of the Hell's Angels MC, in holding those organizations together.

For example, in 1970 the Toronto chapter of the Satan's Choice MC – then a federation of thirteen Canadian clubs – 'got themselves into a war' with the Vagabonds MC and the Black Diamond Riders MC. Gypsy, road captain of the Satan's Choice Brampton chapter, recalls: 'The Toronto chapter did most of the shit disturbing. Now they start a small war with two of the heaviest clubs going and they're asking us to come in and bail them out. This caused a lot of friction between the other chapters. The Vags were a solid club, I knew Edjo their president; and the BDRs [originally the Canadian Lancers MC, Canada's first outlaw club, formed in 1950] had been around forever. The Oshawa, Kingston, Ottawa, Kitchener chapters and us [Brampton] wanted nothing to do with Toronto's mess. Montreal and Hamilton and Brantford were all for it. The other guys [St Catharines, Niagara Falls, Peterborough, and Richmond Hill chapters] didn't know whether they were coming or going.' Bernie Guindon, national chairman of the Satan's Choice MC, realized that the issue of whether or not to declare all-out war with the Vagabonds and Black Diamond Riders was seriously dividing and weakening his organization. In an unprecedented move he called an emergency officers' meeting without informing the Toronto chapter. 'It was a fucking heavy meeting,' recalled Gypsy. 'Some of the officers were called cowards, others were called fight crazy idiots.' Guindon suggested a peaceful resolution. The more militant officers vehemently objected. But when Guindon put his leadership on the line they backed off on their demand that the thirteen Satan's Choice chapters converge on Toronto and 'destroy the Vags and BDR's.' When Guindon asked for solutions to the 'Toronto problem' some officers from Brampton and Ottawa suggested dumping the whole chapter. But Guindon said that it was just a couple of 'fight crazy shitheads' that were causing all the problems and he suggested that those members be brought in line. The resolution was voted on and passed; the war was broken off; the internal dissension ended; and Gypsy shared a brew or two with Edjo of the Vagabonds. As a final note on Bernie Guindon's importance to the organization, the Satan's Choice lost their position as the dominant force in Canadian outlaw-biker politics when he was jailed on narcotics charges in 1976 and four of their chapters voted to merge with the Outlaws federation in 1977.

Expanding into a new territory always comes with political implications and risks. The stakes are highest and the game is deadliest when expansion somehow involves one or both of the two largest federations that dominate the United States and Canada: the Hell's Angels MC based in Oakland, California, and the Outlaws MC originally based in Chicago, Illinois, and now headquartered in Detroit, Michigan. The Angels formed in 1948 in southern California, and took their name from a Second World War army-air-corps bomber group. Today the Hell's Angels MC is the world's largest outlaw motorcycle club. It is an international organization with over sixty-seven charter clubs in eleven countries across four continents (United States of America, Canada, England, Netherlands, France, Australia, New Zealand, West Germany, Switzerland, Austria, and Brazil). However, the Angels are not unique, nor are they unchallenged. In the early fifties, several bikers who rode together on a casual basis formed the Outlaws Motorcycle Club in a bar on the Chicago west side. The Outlaws now have over thirty charters, mostly in the United States Mid-west and east coast, five chapters in Canada, and one in Australia. It was inevitable that the expansionist policies of these two powerful organizations would lead them into conflict. In the early seventies the conflict was sporadic and limited to hostilities that took place whenever their paths happened to cross. In 1978 the presidents of all the American Hell's Angels chapters held a board meeting in Rochester, NY. The ruling council passed a resolution that would cause blood to flow. They formally declared war on the Outlaws MC. Today, the political entanglements of these two mutually opposed giant federations leave few outlaw clubs untouched in both Canada and the United States. Affiliation with the Hell's Angels or Outlaws increases the opportunity for an outlaw club to become actively involved in organized crime, such as the illicit drug trade. In 1977 the RCMP estimated that outlaw clubs controlled 75 per cent of the illegal 'speed' (methamphetamine) market in Ontario, while the San Francisco Police Department speculated that the Hell's Angels controlled 90 per cent of the methamphetamine trade in northern California. Inter-club territorial warfare raises its most gruesome spectre when rival clubs battle for dollars and markets.

In order to establish a monopoly over an entire state or province the Angels and Outlaws try to win over the local club, alliance, or federation that dominates that region. For example, in the mid-1970s the Satan's Angels MC of Vancouver formed the hub of a west-coast alliance of one-percenter clubs in league with the Gypsy Wheelers MC of White Rock and the 101 Road Knights of Nanaimo. In 1977 the

Gypsy Wheelers and Road Knights exchanged their colours for those of the Satan's Angels. As part of lowering the profile of outlaw clubs on the west coast – that aspect of territoriality referred to as public relations – the Satan's Angels took the Bounty Hunters of Victoria off the road in 1980. After this demonstration of territorial control, the Satan's Angels of Vancouver came to act as a liaison between their three-club federation and the Hell's Angels mother chapter in Oakland. On 23 July 1983 the three Canadian clubs buried their colours and donned the winged death skull of the Hell's Angels. In a grand gesture, the three new Angel chapters claimed the province as their own; the bottom rocker of their Angel colours reads 'British Columbia.' Later that same year a fourth Angels chapter was formed in east-end Vancouver. This was a major international coup for the Hell's Angels MC conglomerate. It virtually locked up the Canadian west coast and made the Hell's Angels' position in British Columbia unassailable. Neither of the two remaining outlaw clubs in BC, the Tribesmen of Squamish or the Highwaymen in Cranbrook, would seriously consider forming an alternative alliance, let alone confront the Angels by merging with the Bandidos in nearby Washington or the Outlaws MC. Both of the smaller (fifteen-member) clubs decided to align themselves on an associate basis with the new Hell's Angels.

While the Angels took over the province of British Columbia by incorporating a federation, the Outlaws MC laid claim to the province of Ontario by aligning themselves with the largest outlaw-club federation in Canada, the Satan's Choice Motorcycle Club. In 1975 representatives from the Chicago-based Outlaws MC were invited by Garnet 'Mother' McKuen, national president of the Satan's Choice, to meet with national chairman Bernie Guindon and other Satan's Choice officers in Oshawa. To symbolize the alliance that they forged, members of the two federations exchanged 'mini patches.' In the centre of the patch was a piston from the Outlaws' colours overlapped by a devil's trident from the Choice colours beneath a 1% symbol and the word 'Brotherhood.' The Satan's Choice/Outlaws alliance prevented the Hell's Angels from gaining a foothold in Ontario, while the Montreal chapter of the Satan's Choice gave the Outlaws a point of entry into Hell's Angels–dominated Quebec. Two years later (1977) that same alliance would break up as the Windsor, St Catharines, Ottawa, and Montreal Satan's Choice chapters defected outright to the Outlaws. The members of those four chapters dated (terminated) their Satan's Choice shoulder tattoos with the inscription 'R.I.P. Satan's Choice MC.'

Merger has meant violence when the Outlaws and Hell's Angels federations meet head on. For example, in Montreal the Outlaws-backed Satan's Choice found themselves in conflict with the Angels-backed Popeyes MC. The club warfare that ensued resulted in the murder of one Popeye patch holder, while two Satan's Choice were killed and two others seriously injured in a series of brawls over a four-month period in 1978. Prior to their respective affiliation with the Outlaws and Hell's Angels, there had been no history of conflict between the Satan's Choice and the Popeyes. There is minimal risk of this expansionist warfare spreading to Alberta. None of the three Alberta clubs – Rebels, Grim Reapers, and King's Crew – has any formal political ties to any of the major federations. The King's Crew are politically isolated, while the Rebels and Reapers have long-standing informal social ties with the British Columbia Hell's Angels and, more recently, with 'Les Hells' (Hell's Angels) in Quebec.

Merger has meant violence even when it involves only one of the two competing outlaw federations. The territorial bottom line is that alliances or mergers with larger federations are thrashed out to the political detriment or advantage of local clubs. Fuel is added to the flames of regional wars when clubs compete with each other to be the local representative of either the Outlaws or the Hell's Angels. For example, in Winnipeg the Silent Riders and the Los Brovos engaged in a five-year power struggle to gain control over the province of Manitoba and be recognized as the dominant club by the Hell's Angels. The war dates back to 1983 when an internal argument caused a faction of the Los Brovos to separate and form the Silent Riders MC. The Silent Riders began to recruit members actively and quickly formed three chapters in their attempt to gain the upper hand and usurp the previously unchallenged Los Brovos. In July 1984, Ronald Gagnon, a Silent Rider, was found outside his home, shot through the head. That year six homes and business premises of the members of the two clubs were dynamited. In May 1985, a Los Brovos was shot. The Los Brovos patch holder lived, and though he could have identified his assailant, he remained true to the 'code of silence' and refused to file a complaint. However, the Winnipeg police and the RCMP did not wait for an invitation. They raided the clubhouses of both clubs and seized large numbers of both legal (registered with Firearms Acquisition Certificates, or FACs) and illegal (restricted) weapons. In a landmark court case in 1986, the provincial magistrate revoked the FACs of all members of both clubs. To date, 1990, the war is over. With several members in jail or on restrictive parole, the Silent Riders have been silenced. In Alberta there is no Angels-related motivation for the Rebels and Grim Reapers to go to war in order to gain exclusive domination of the province. Neither the Rebels nor the Reapers have any desire or need to affiliate formally with the Angels or to be incorporated as Angels' chapters. At this time the majority of patch holders in both clubs value their colours and their independence too highly. For their part, the Hell's Angels are satisfied with having strong social ties. They know that the Rebels and Reapers are powerful clubs with the resources to terminate quickly any Outlaws-sponsored incursion, and so far they see no need to upset the status quo with talk of political affiliation with one of the two clubs.

Territoriality is an inescapable part of outlaw-motorcycle club reality. Always dynamic and often violent, it is interwoven with the fabric of personal identity; it is a medium for expanding and expressing political power; it is a fundamental aspect of relating to the host community; and, for some clubs, it is a means of protecting criminal profits. Like all outlaw clubs, the Rebels define, claim, and defend a given area as their own. This does not mean that the Rebels are constantly involved in territorial flare-ups. A strong policy of territoriality enforced by a stable dominance hierarchy of established clubs actually reduces the overall potential for violence. The Rebels are good at what they do. In the day-to-day existence of a Rebel patch holder, territoriality usually means nothing more than 'just keeping your eyes and ears open.' For the past twenty-two years – in conjunction with the Warlords since 1968, and in tandem with the Grim Reapers as of 1983 – the Rebels have been the dominant force in maintaining a two-club ironclad grip on Edmonton, 'their city.'

13

Conclusion:
Retrospect and Prospect

I like speed. I like the feeling of freedom. Something speaks
to my soul.
(Anastasia Golovonova, a twenty-year-old
Russian *rocker*)

This decade of the nineties marks the first half-century of the existence of outlaw motorcycle clubs. As of 1990, there are approximately 900 outlaw clubs in North America, and the phenomenon is
now international in scope. Outlaw clubs have diffused into major
urban centres in the European countries of Great Britain, Belgium,
France, the Netherlands, Sweden, Denmark, Norway, Austria, Germany, Switzerland, and Italy, and, more recently, to South America,
Australia, and New Zealand – even in Tokyo, Japan, a group of indige-
nous bikers applied for a charter from the Hell's Angels MC ... Application denied. If you rode your motorcycle across Europe today, you
would notice that in all respects these foreign clubs are amazingly
similar to their North American counterparts. This similarity is due
mainly to the fact that the mass media, and biker magazines like
Easyriders, *Supercycle*, and *Outlaw Biker* in particular, have turned
North American clubs into an international prototype or model. This
duplication of form and content includes the basics of political structure and central activities in addition to the highly personal symbols
of leathers and Harley-Davidson motorcycle. For example, the Sofia
Bike Club of Sweden is a Harley-only organization whose members
build classic-type choppers from scratch; when their Stockholm

chapter sponsored a giant 'biker bash' in 1989, close to two hundred clubs were represented. Even more recently, as the Eastern-bloc countries explore the strange new world of democratic politics, the international biker phenomenon is riding the new wave of personal freedom there. Russian youths, known as *rockeri* (rockers), put on leather jackets and straddle their Czech-made Japwa 300s or Russian Iz Planeta 250s, then head out in informal groups to tour some of Russia's eight-lane highways. 'Almost military in their organization, the *rockeri* have a system for their midnight runs. In front is the diamond formation of scouts, the most experienced riders with the fastest bikes. In the middle are those without helmets or registrations. They ride like kamikazes and are called *smertniki* or little dead ones. Bringing up the rear are more veteran rockers' (*San Francisco Examiner*, 8 April 1990: 12)

Fifty years of perseverance justifies viewing the outlaw motorcycle club as a persistent social system, a social form that is capable of surviving in different kinds of cultural environments – provided they are western and industrialized. In a word, the outlaw biker has persisted as a social phenomenon and has become an international success story. Most law-enforcement officers that I have talked to in North America agree with my assessment that, were it not for their highly territorial nature, the number of outlaw clubs would double very easily, very quickly. As far as prospects for the future are concerned, there is every reason to believe that outlaw bikers will still be around to celebrate their centennial in the twenty-first century and toast their ancient forebears who rode Harley V-twins in the nineties. The one question that remains is why.

An outlaw motorcycle club is an experiment in utopian communalism; it is a personal grasp at self-fulfilment and a collective search for community that rides on wheels along the inner-city streets and sprawling highways of industrial society. Western industrial society has created the precipitating conditions for the emergence of many such attempts at establishing subcultural and counter-cultural alternatives. The result has been a plethora of different groups – from Beatniks, Hippies, and street gangs to surfers, religious cults, and the New Age movement – which in turn have promoted a variety of 'ultimate' activities – from personal transformation through jazz, spiritual transcendence through meditation, and manhood through fighting to the thrills of surfing or the awakening of human potential through spiritualism, channelling, crystals, rebirthing, numerology, herbalism, and holism: whatever gets you through the night. These social forms and activities are a testament to humanity's social ingenuity; but they are also an indictment of a deep-rooted discontent that appears to plague industrial society. What is the nature of the problem?

THE PROBLEM OF ALIENATION: EVOLUTION'S SIMPLE TWIST OF FATE

Technological innovations enabled humanity to advance from band society, based on primitive hunting and gathering, to modern industrialism, based on fossil fuels and nuclear fission. In a few short ten thousands of years we have gone from being scavengers to become the urban masters of the world. One necessary demand of this technological advancement was the creation of elaborate socio-politico-economic institutions in order to manage that technology. As a rule of social evolution, the more complex a social system is, the greater its need for centralized control and bureaucratic administration. The state structure that administers industrialized technology is the ultimate in complexity, centralization, and bureaucratization. One unfortunate result is that in attempting to achieve a balance between the needs of the individual and the requirements of a large institutionalized state structure, the integrity of the individual is often sacrificed. In order to establish and maintain the complex division of labour that is required, the administration of growing cities and industries necessitates the fragmentation of cultural order, traditional institutions, interpersonal relations, and symbols of identity. At its best, the technocratic establishment becomes very specialized, rational, and efficient; but it also becomes very impersonal and unemotional. It becomes necessary for the Establishment to define and administer the human being as an autonomous unit, separate from his or her environment. However, when the environment from which one is separated includes other people, one's social institutions, and ultimately oneself, we have the makings of a severe problem: alienation. In effect, this problem of alienation is the result of the individual taking on those qualities that best facilitate centralized power and bureaucratic administration: he/she is isolated, and powerless, and his/her values and identity can be fragmented and altered to suit the many different − often inconsistent and conflicting − situations an individual must face. By itself, alienation represents the ultimate irony of human technological and sociological evolution: the paradox that as humanity becomes more physiologically crowded and omnipotent, the individual becomes more psychologically alone and impotent.

Alienation is a social-psychological phenomenon. The *sociological dimension* of alienation can be defined as those social conditions that reduce an individual's ability to appreciate his/her position in a given society by precluding any meaningful participation in its practices. These social conditions lead to the *psychological dimension* of alienation: the individual's failure to bring under control a self-image, personal capabilities, behaviours, possessions, and relationships that will reflect a desirable personal identity and encompass the totality of his/her existence. Alienation is a multidimensional phenomenon in terms of both its origin and its effects. Yet the social conditions that cause, and the psychological states that constitute, alienation all reflect the basic feature of an individual's inability to achieve self-fulfilment. Isolation from meaningful social participation and the subsequent psychological experience of alienation may result in a personal search for self-authenticity. The alienated individual may seek out alternative social relationships and create 'ultimate experiences' wherein meaningful social participation and personal identity can be realized. For a man, the search may lead to the thrills of a Harley-Davidson motorcycle and the brotherhood bonds of the men that ride them.

In this study, I portray the Rebels as a product of urban industrial society, a collective social response to the conditions of alienation as they are experienced by the young men of the working class. Seeking a meaningful personal identity and a genuine sense of community, some of these men join groups like the Rebels MC, and in so doing separate themselves structurally and emotionally from the social mainstream. The Rebels provide an example of a subculture that sets itself up as an alternative, often in opposition to, and sometimes in serious criminal conflict with, the social norms of mainstream North America. What exactly does an outlaw club offer?

OUTLAW MOTORCYCLE CLUBS:
GROUP ISOLATION AS A SOLUTION TO PERSONAL ALIENATION

As a subcultural alternative outlaw-biker clubs like the Rebels create a society that provides its members with meaningful participation on three levels of sociocultural reality: personal, interpersonal and institutional.

Personal level of participation

An outlaw motorcycle club provides its members with a prerequisite to human social life, a definitive concept of self. A man who enters this subculture in search of an identity looks to the outlaw-biker tradition to provide him with long-standing values, behaviours, and symbols. What he will find are heroes and role models, a personal legacy that is consistent with what he learned on the streets was the complete man. He will find ultimate values and peak emotional experiences that he feels are worth living for as a biker. The young men who join the Rebels share a biker bond: their attraction to the prestige and power of Harley-Davidson motorcycles, machines that they customize ('chop') into highly personal statements of chrome and steel. The man who 'earns his colours' becomes a member of an élite group that struts with a high profile; on a personal level he transcends the ordinary and the mundane in his search for self. The outlaw club provides a cultural ethos, including a set of core values, that makes it possible for a member to locate and declare himself as a distinct entity within a meaningful context. The ideological foundation of the subculture accurately reflects the lower-working-class origins of its participants; the lifestyle of the typical outlaw biker constitutes a lower-working class bohemian subculture. Within the outlaw tradition a man pieces together a system of values and a behavioural style as he moulds himself into a 'righteous biker.' He will adopt attitudes and learn behaviours that gravitate around lower-class focal concerns with independence, freedom, self-reliance, aggressiveness, toughness, impulsiveness, and masculinity, all of which will be embodied in a highly romanticized image of the anti-hero. Within the context of the biker subculture these values are complementary and consistent, integrative and all-encompassing.

Interpersonal level of participation

Bonds of shared biker values bring twenty-five men together into a tightly knit social network that behaves like an extended family – they call it 'brotherhood.' Their interaction is intense and frequent, and includes a wide range of activities that are conducted within an atmosphere of camaraderie and intimacy. The sense of interdependence that develops between the club's members is the foundation of involvement; it leads to an unflinching commitment that is based on the very fundamental perception of a shared common fate. Through these social interactions a new patch holder not only pieces together a biker identity, he also has that identity confirmed by significant others who have already mastered it. The patch holder is drawn into an intimate social network of highly committed individuals that provides reinforcement for his core biker values and enables him to express himself emotionally through the formation of intense bonds of friendship. He becomes a brother to other bikers, 'guys who you know will always be there when it counts.'

The outlaw biker is not antisocial; nor can joining an outlaw club be considered a flight from commitment. A prospective patch holder may have to endure the rigours of a two-year striking period in order to earn his colours. To me this behaviour reflects a need for some form of community and commitment to persons, objects, and endeavours that will generate excitement and provide purpose. Outlaw motorcycle clubs demand a quality of personal participation such that the commitment to community is never in doubt; their survival depends on it. If a biker is antisocial and running away from responsibilities and commitment, the last place he should run to is an outlaw motorcycle club.

Institutional level of participation

Becoming a Rebel means being part of a tightly knit formal organization that includes a political structure, a financial base, a geographical territory, a chain of command, a constitution, an elaborate set of rules, and internal mechanisms for enforcing justice and compliance from within. On an institutional level of participation, the core values of being a biker and the social bonds of brotherhood are given a medium of expression through formally organized club activities; the man becomes a 'Rebel.' As a Rebel patch holder he finds the stability of a corporate identity. In return, he exchanges uncompromising commitment for the power and the pride of 'flying' the Rebel skull patch on the back of his leathers. He locates himself in the structure of a club whose activities allow him to act out 'the real me' and give him 'the freedom to be the biker I want to be.' But are there real grounds for the outlaw biker to be concerned about freedom, or is freedom a bogus issue?

Most Americans and Canadians feel that they are already free to pursue life, liberty, and happiness, in any manner they choose. They would quickly point out that outlaw clubs do not exist in eastern

European countries. Obviously, the western version of modern industrial society is not a situation of blatant oppression; advanced industrial society has learned to manipulate rather than brutalize. There is
nothing inherently evil about a technocratic bureaucracy – 'the
Establishment.' It is simply a matter of administrative complexity
creating a situation where 'commanding heights' exist – wherein the
key decisions are taken outside the social milieu of the people they
affect, by remote élites rather than by men and women in face-to-face
relationships, and in a manner that is often imposed and one-sided.
In this situation institutions regulate and the primary-group orientation is no longer relevant to an individual's existence; interpersonal
reciprocity and informal consensus reaching give way to the power
politics of competing self-interest groups, force, and conflict. In
North America, individuals have perennially used subcultural and
counter-cultural groups as social leverages in an attempt to extract
their individualism from the vice grip of bureaucratic control. The
themes of freedom and of resistance to institutional authority have a
deep psychological basis in the North American psyche. But even
hippy communes, which, along with the rest of the youth counter-
culture of the sixties, championed individualism under the slogan 'Do
your own thing,' still required structure and rules on how to do that
thing. All human behaviour reflects a very basic tension between the
individual and the underlying structure of his/her social context. In a
subculture, the problem becomes one of how to maximize individualism (a desire for personal 'freedom') within a meaningful community
(which requires some form of social structure). The extreme of
either individual anarchy or its opposite, institutional bureaucratization, will destroy the whole subcultural experiment. The question
becomes: How does an outlaw motorcycle club mediate the tension,
or dialetical opposition, between individualism-in-community and
structure-of-community in its attempt at creating a cultural utopia?

If all is well and harmonious in an outlaw motorcycle club, two
factors will mediate the dialectic between individualism and structure: *political participation* and *egalitarianism*. An outlaw club is a
participatory democracy. In the political world of outlaw bikerdom
the individual patch holder feels that he and his opinions are of
significance; at the very least, he is an active participant, not simply
a passive functionary. Members are afforded an opportunity to
initiate, evaluate, and control club policies. The formulation of club
policy is always predicated on an informal exchange of information

and opinion between the brothers, often in the club bar, that usually results in a group consensus. The formal decision making that takes place at club meetings serves to make official these informal decisions or decide matters that otherwise cannot be resolved. While all members are different in terms of their personal prestige and the political impact of their opinions, the bottom line on participation is egalitarianism; all decisions are resolved on a one-man, one-vote basis, majority rules. The Rebels MC is made up of twenty-five headstrong individuals who often factionalize in terms of diverse and conflicting opinions about what the club is all about. It is the element of political participation, 'we all get our say,' and the strong sense of equality, 'we're all brothers,' that allow an outlaw motorcycle club to accommodate the fact of internal diversity without either infringing upon the freedom of its members or, alternatively, lapsing into unbridled self-interest. Participation and egalitarianism enable the club to bridge the paradox between individualism-in-community ('the club gives me freedom; it gives me the freedom to do and be what I want') and structure-of-community ('bike clubs are more structured and hierarchical than any other organization except perhaps the military' – RCMP, 1987).

The most outstanding feature of the above three levels of participation is that they are integrated as a unit. For the individual patch holder the end result is a sense of *wholeness*. Industrial society develops a mode of existence in which specialization and compartmentalization have destroyed a sense of wholeness of self or spiritual integrity. The fact that one can or must constantly assume new identities means that, in effect, one actually does not have an identity. Life becomes an acting out of lifestyles; one's commitments remain provisional; discontent and an ongoing search for consistency come to characterize one's life, not happiness and self-fulfilment. The integration of personal, interpersonal, and institutional levels of participation provides the foundation for the outlaw-biker subculture. Effective integration transforms a motorcycle club into an urban community that is capable of counterbalancing the negatives of alienation: powerlessness, meaninglessness, normlessness, cultural estrangement (valuelessness), self-estrangement, and social isolation (Seeman, 1975: 93–4). The man who 'earns his Rebel colours' does more than accept a patch; he creates an all-encompassing lifestyle. 'It's more than a club,' according to Tramp of the Rebels, 'it's a way of life.' Outlaw bikers share with one another a common world-view, values and beliefs, norms of behaviour and bonds of trust, a distinct language style and mode of dress, and a wealth of symbolism that imparts to them a sense of solidarity that they do not extend to outsiders. According to Caveman of the Rebels, 'It's our own society.' How does this Rebel society, an outlaw-club subculture, relate to the host society?

In addition to being integrated, the boundaries of the above three levels of subcultural participation are sharply demarcated in terms of an *oppositional process*. The theme that underlies the bikers' subcultural participation is that by creating explicit personal, inter-personal, and institutional borders between themselves and the host community individual members are able to establish a calculable and meaningful existence. For example, the inter-group opposition under-lying and symbolized in much of outlaw-club behaviour, for instance, 'bikers' versus 'straight society,' leads to intragroup cohesion: in the form of the brotherhood. While the social borders established within this subcultural frame of reference theoretically restrict a member's range of behaviour, that same border-making process functions to enable members to reduce their world to knowable and appreciable proportions: 'I'd say [conventional] society stinks in a lot of respects. At least with the club I know what's happening. Whereas outside the club, I don't know what's happening. I don't know who to turn to and I don't know who not to' (Caveman, Rebels MC). Thus, members of the Rebels Motorcycle Club achieve a collective identity by separ-ating themselves structurally and emotionally from the larger soci-ety. The outlaws' perceived opposition between themselves and the host society intensifies their collective consciousness and generates a degree of internal solidarity that otherwise would not be possible. The 'separate society' contention is an emotional issue with many outlaw patch holders, but how real is it?

The world of the Rebels is never entirely removed from the larger society of which it is a part. Outlaw bikers do not hold or express any deep rejection of modern society. They are usually anti-conventional, often deviant, and sometimes criminal. But they are neither Marxists nor revolutionaries: they simply want to carve out their own niche of community and behaviours within the system as it currently exists. For all intents and purposes they use the same secondary institutions to fulfil their basic living requirements. Outlaw bikers make use of the same state-organized secondary institutions as these relate to employment, housing, hospitalization, education, social welfare services, purchases of food and fuel, and so on. A patch holder will maintain these secondary relations as long as they do not interfere with his primary relation to the club and his social relations with club members. Thus the opposition between an outlaw club and host society does not involve the creation of social institutions that replicate or replace those of the host society. That is, *the boundaries between the outlaw motorcycle club and the host society are not institutional boundaries that represent a formal break with the familiar structure of our urban society.* Rather, the opposition is grounded in an anticonventional social psychology, comprising boundaries of values and attitudes, that manifests itself in anticonventional behaviour, represented by acts of deviance and crime. What then is the nature of this social-psychological opposition that leads to deviant, and sometimes criminal, behaviour?

Regardless of whether we wish to praise outlaw bikers as heroes or condemn them as villians, we simply cannot explain the nature of their opposition in terms of the conventional stereotype of a sociopath. Despite the subcultural displays of deviance and occasional criminal behaviour witnessed by the general public, many of the values inherent in conventional society are indeed espoused by the outlaw patch holders within the framework of their 'biker society,' e.g., social solidarity, brotherhood, independence, masculinity, patriotism and individual freedom, corporate membership and co-liability, ideological participation and responsibility, and adherence to rules and regulations in a democratic organization. If there is indeed this much value and attitude overlap, wherein lie the social-psychological boundaries – source of value and attitude opposition – that lead to deviance and crime? The source of opposition lies in the fact that an outlaw motorcycle club is a reaction against the superego of technocracy – the Protestant ethic: the principle that one's work is one's life. Outlaw bikers desire to go beyond a purely rationalized sense of self and society. The core motivation for the outlaw biker is to achieve a sense of personal self that transcends the ordinary, and to live an existence that occasionally breaks the shackles that chain one to the mundane. He escapes into a highly hedonistic existence. Symbolism, rituals, the power of a Harley-Davidson, the high sensation of speed, and the eroticism of flesh are the biker's refuge from the forces of rationalization. The world-view of the outlaw biker places an emphasis on the sensually stimulating and the erotic within the social context of community. This is certainly not a rational pursuit, it is more of a visionary quest.

In total I spent approximately three years riding with the Rebels. After the members formally approved my study, I continued to ride with the club for another year and a half, during which time I carried out formal data-gathering procedures – structured interviews. As my role as an ethnographer became more evident, my role as a biker became more contrived and I began to be excluded from the brotherhood. Once again, there were no formal decisions or announcements; my contact with members simply became less frequent and less intense. As an ethnographer, my relationship to the club lost its substance and meaning and I lost touch with the innermost core of Rebel reality; I simply faded away. What I shared with these men led me to believe that I would at least maintain ties of friendship after I completed the ethnography. The enduring emotion would be one of comradeship. I was wrong. I would be like so many of the ex-members who simply drifted away, never to be seen or spoken of again. But only years later did I realize this, as Patricia (a new companion) and I rode along the Alaska Highway towards the mountains of Kluane National Park in the Yukon Territories. While riding in the wind I came to understand that it could not have turned out any other way. Yes, these men were once my brothers, but it's not the same, could never be the same. The empathy that exists between members is based on a shared common fate. It is such an intense involvement that it leaves no room for shades of grey. A brother is a man you can trust with anything because you have probably had to trust him with your life. However, the special world that had sustained our intense comradeship was gone. Like the others I was reclaimed by everyday life. I had survived. I would be myself again, or so I thought.

Appendix A: Motorcycle Club Constitutions

REBEL'S MOTORCYCLE CLUB

1 In order to be a member, an applicant must own a Harley-Davidson of at least 900 cc's. Strikers may strike with English bikes.

2 Prospective member's striking period is at the discretion of the club. Directorship shall decide when a vote is necessary.

3 Strikers pay dues for the first full month they start in. Initiation fee is $15.00, to be placed as a deposit on colours.

4 Strikers do not have to do anything that maims body, bike, or costs him money. Orders are restricted to club duties, club functions, and clubhouse.

5 All meetings will be run on a parliamentary basis. Members will be evicted for unruly conduct.

6 Quorum for a meeting is sixty percent of membership. Eighty percent for membership votes.

7 Dues are $60.00 annually, payable semi-anually.

8 On April 1st, colours will be taken if a member's bike is not on the road. On April 30th, such members shall be reduced to striking.

9 If a member's bike is not running for a period of thirty days, unless he is in jail or hospital, his colours will be confiscated. A member's bike must be running for at least one week (e.g., not fifteen minutes), to be exempt from the above rule. This period is subject to change at the discretion of the club.

10 Rebels losing privilege of wearing colours will also lose privilege of over-ruling strikers.

11 Victoria Day and Labour Day are mandatory runs. A $20.00 fine will be
   incurred if absent or leaving early, and $5.00 fine for being late.
12 Directorship gives the president authority to judge items not in the
   Constitution.
13 New strikers are to strike one month before being allowed to attend
   meetings.

SATAN'S ANGELS MOTORCYCLE CLUB

Rules and regulations

The rules of the club will be strictly enforced. If any one breaks them, they
will be dealt with by an appointed committee made up of the five original
members. There will be a special group of rules, and if broken will require
immediate dismissal. There will also be general rules. If these are broken, it
could mean either dismissal or suspension, whatever the committee sees
fit.

   Breaking any of the following Rules will be reason for immediate
dismissal:

1 Failure to pay his dues according to the section dealing with the paying
  of dues.
2 If a group or individual attacks any member, the whole club shall stand
  behind him and fight if necessary. If, however, the member is drunk and
  aggressive and purposely starts an argument, the rest of the members
  will escort him away, or step between before trouble starts.
3 No member will disgrace the club by being yellow. (The above rules will
  be put forward to applicants. If they feel they cannot abide by these
  rules and are not in favour of them, they will be denied membership to
  the club.)
4 No member will destroy club property purposely.
5 No member will take the attitude that he doesn't have to help other
  members and other members don't have to help him.
6 No member will go against anything the cub has voted for and passed.
  Meaning if we decide to have a ride and when we reach there we will
  sleep out in sleeping bags, no one will go off by himself and rent a room
  for the night unless he is sick with a cold or that sleeping out would be
  impossible for some reason. The people in charge of the ride will decide
  if he has a legitimate reason.
7 No members will get together on their own and plan something for

themselves on club rides. It will be brought up to the whole club and the whole club will participate in anything that is decided upon.

8 The club will always stay together on rides, field meets, etc., and will not fraternize with rival clubs. The only way a member will be permitted to leave the main group will be to notify the president or whoever is in charge. When the time comes that the majority feel it is time to leave we will all leave together. Anyone staying behind for a good reason will do so at his own risk and can expect no help.

9 Members will have good attendance. Must have good reason for not attending meetings or rides, such as working, sickness, no transportation, bike not running.

Dues

Dues will be $2.00 per month payable every meeting or every second meeting. Upon failure of paying dues within two weeks, members shall be suspended and turn in his crest. If within two months dues still aren't paid, the crest will be forfeited to pay them and member will no longer be considered a member. The only exception to this shall be if a member is in jail or if he is out of town for a period of time. If he is in jail, dues won't be expected, but if he is out of town dues will be paid when he returns.

Applications

Anyone wanting to become a member must go through a two-month waiting period or more. Upon voting him in, the vote of members will only be taken as an opinion. The five original members will decide whether he is in or not. To be voted in, an applicant will fill out a form and a fee of $5.00 is charged. If at the end of two months it is decided he will not make a good member, he is refused membership and his application fee is not returned to him.

Whether he is voted in or not will be based upon:

1 Participation in club affairs, rides, meetings, etc.
2 Must have a running bike worth $500.00 or over.
3 Show a sincere interest in club and bikes.
4 Will stand behind club and members.
5 Will go along with what the majority of club decides.
6 Interested in road club. Road rides come before competition events.
7 His opionion on rule numbers 2 and 3.
8 Is on the road with bike equipped for the road.

General rules

1 No girlfriends taken on weekend rides unless decided upon by membership.
2 If club calls a ride all members will attend. If a member is working, sick, bike not running, he will be excused. If a member turns up at a ride and has no bike, someone who isn't packing can pack him unless he is already packing or if his bike isn't in good enough shape to pack or if packing a rider will in some way do harm to the bike.
3 On weekend rides, a member should be able to take the time off work to attend. If for some reason it is impossible and there are over four members who can't leave till the following day, the rest of the club will wait for them.
4 Meetings will be closed except for prospective members and anyone there on business. Or, the meeting before a weekend ride, anyone wishing to attend the ride will be allowed at the meeting. Any non-member attending one of our rides will follow our rules. This goes for any other club attending our rides. If they break our riding rules, we stop and let them continue by themselves.
5 Anyone who has been kicked out will return his crest and will receive only half of what he paid for it.
6 During a meeting there will be no talking among members until they get the floor through the president. A sergeant-at-arms will be appointed and anyone not abiding by the above will be evicted.
7 No one shall pass the road captain or whoever is in charge of the ride.
8 Where we go on our rides will be voted upon by the entire membership.
9 The treasurer shall keep a clear record of all money paid in and out during the week and will balance it before every meeting. The books will be gone over once a week.
10 Everyone will attend the meeting on his bike if it is favourable weather, unless his bike is broken down or not running at the time.
11 If for some reason such as a licence suspension, a member can't ride on the road, or if his bike is not running for a long period of time, or if he is without a bike for a short time, he will turn in his crest and upon getting back on the road, the crest will be returned.
12 Everyone must have a bike. Consideration will be given to any member who is in between bikes but he must sincerely intend to get another bike in the near future.
13 It is recommended to members to have their crests fitted to their jackets with snap buttons so they can be removed without damage.

14 No one shall lend his crest or t-shirt to any non-member unless it is someone who is being packed. Once off the bike, the non-member must return the crest.

15 Around town, no members will purposely cause trouble wearing a crest, such as causing a disturbance at the clubhouse in such a way as to have cops brought in.

16 Everyone wears his crest in rides – only crests, no club jackets.

17 Anyone leaving town for period longer than six months turns in crest and is no longer a member. Can submit application when he returns.

18 Anyone missing meetings even if at work gets fined $1.00 except for guys in hospital or jail or out of town for a period of time. Two weeks' holidays not included, including applicants.

HELL'S ANGELS BYLAWS

1 All patches will be the same on the back, nothing will show on the back except the HELL'S ANGELS patch. City patch is optional for each charter. 1 patch and 1 membership card per member. Member may keep original patch if made into a banner. Prospects will wear California rocker on back and prospect patch left front where top of pocket is on a Levi jacket. FINE: $100.00 for breaking above bylaw.

2 No hypes. No use of heroin in any form. Anyone using a needle for any reason other than having a doctor use it on you will be considered a hype. FINE: Automatic kick-out from club.

3 No explosives of any kind will be thrown into the fire where there is one or more HELL'S ANGELS in the area. FINE: Ass-whipping and/or subject to California President's Decision.

4 Guns on California runs will not be displayed after 6:00 p.m. They will be fired from dawn till 6:00 p.m. in a predetermined area only. Rule does not apply to anyone with a gun in a shoulder holster or belt that is seen by another member if it is not being shot or displayed. FINE: $100.00 for breaking above bylaw.

5 Brothers shall not fight each other with weapons; when any HELL'S ANGEL fights another HELL'S ANGEL, it is one on one, prospects same as members. If members are from different charters, fine goes to California Treasurer. FINE: $100.00 for breaking above bylaw or possible loss of patch.

6 No narcotics burns. When making deals, persons get what they are promised or the deal is called off. FINE: Automatic kick-out from club.

7 All HELL'S ANGELS fines will be paid within 30 days. Fines will be paid

to that charter's treasurer to be held for the next California run.

8 One vote per charter at California Officer's meetings. For California votes, 2 no votes instead of majority, 2 no votes to kill a new charter and if a charter goes below 6 they must freeze or dissolve on the decision of California Officers' Meeting.

9 If kicked-out, must stay out 1 year then back to original charter. HELL'S ANGELS tattoo will have an in-date and out-date when the member quits. If kicked-out, HELL'S ANGELS tattoo will be completely covered or a ½ inch X through the tattoo. Of which of these is left to the discretion of the charter.

10 Runs are on the holidays; 3 mandatory runs are Memorial Day, July 4th, Labor Day.

11 No leave period except hospital, medical or jail.

HELL'S ANGELS MOTORCYCLE CLUB BYLAWS
OAKLAND, CA

President
Vice President
Secretary
Treasurer
Sergeant of Arms

1 There will be a meeting once a week at a predetermined time and place.

2 There will be a $2.00 fine for missing a meeting without a valid reason.

3 Girls will not sit in on meetings unless it is a special occasion.

4 There will be a $15.00 initiation fee for all new members. Club will furnish patch which remains club property.

5 There will be no fighting among members; a fine of five dollars will result for each party involved.

6 New members must be voted in. Two 'no' votes equal a rejection. One 'no' vote must be explained.

7 All members must have their own motorcycle.

8 Members with extra parts will loan them to members. They must be replaced or paid for.

9 There will be no stealing among members. Anyone caught will be kicked out of the club.

10 Members cannot belong to any other clubs.

11 New members must come to three meetings on their motorcycles. They will be voted on at the third meeting. Vote will be by paper ballot.

12 Any persons coming up for vote are subject to club rules.
13 To be eligible to come up for vote in the club, prospective members must be brought up for vote at the meeting by a member.
14 Anyone kicked out of the club cannot get back in.
15 When packing double, members can let girl wear patch.
16 Anyone who loses his patch, or if the patch is picked up by an officer or member, the member will pay a $15.00 fine before he gets the patch back.

PAGANS MOTORCYCLE CLUB CONSTITUTION*

Club organization
The Pagan motorcycle club is run by the Mother Club. The Mother Club has last and final say so on all club matters. Any violation of the constitution will be dealt with by the Mother Club.

Chapter organization
Six (6) members needed to start a chapter. Four (4) officers, no new chapter may be started without approval of the Mother Club.

President
Runs chapter under the direction of the Mother Club. Keeps chapter organized, makes sure chapter business is carried out and inspects all bikes before runs and makes President meetings.

Sergeant at arms
Makes sure President's orders are carried out.

Vice-president
Takes over all President's duties when the President is not there.

Secretary treasurer
In charge of minutes of meetings and treasury. No members may change chapters without the Mother Club members' permission in his area. All present chapter debts are paid and is approved by the president of the new chapter he wishes to change to. If a member has a snivel, he must use chain of command, in other words, (1) his Chapter President, (2) Mother Club member in area, (3) President of Club.

* Based on Lavigne, 1987: 174–8.

Meetings
1   Chapters must have one organized meeting per week.
2   Chapter meetings are attended by members only.
3   Members must be of sound mind (straight) when attending meetings.
4   If a Mother Club member attends a meeting and a member is fouled-up, he will be fined by the Mother Club member.
5   Miss three (3) meetings in a row, and you're out of the club.
6   Members must attend meetings to leave club and turn in his colors and everything that has the name PAGANS on it (T-shirts, wrist bands, mugs, etc.)
7   If a member is thrown out of the club or quits without attending meeting, he loses his colors, motorcycle, and anything else that says PAGANS on it, and probably an ass kicking.
8   When a member is travelling, he must attend meeting of the area he is travelling in.
9   If a vote is taken at a meeting and member is not there, his vote is void.
10 Members must have colors with him when attending meeting.

Bikes
1   All members have a Harley-Davidson 750–1200cc.
2   If a member is not of sound mind or fouled-up to ride his motorcycle in the opinion of another member, his riding privilege may be pulled by said member until he has his head together.
3   All bikes must be on the road April 30th, or otherwise directed by the Mother Club.
4   All members must have a motorcycle license.

Mandatories
1   Two (2) mandatories, July 4th and Labor Day. Mother Club may call additional mandatories if need be.

Funerals
1   If a member dies in a chapter, it is mandatory for all members in his chapter to attend funeral.
2   Chapter is in charge of taking care of all funeral arrangements, parties, police procession, etc.

Parties
1   Pagan parties are Pagan parties only. Each chapter must throw (1) party or run per year.

Respect

1 Respect is to be shown to all Mother Club members, officer members, members' personal property, bike, ol' Lady, house, job, etc. In other words, if it's not yours, 'Don't Mess With It.'
2 No fighting among each other is allowed, any punches to be thrown will be done by the Sgt. at Arms or a Mother Club member.
3 No stealing from members.
4 Respect your colors.

Colors

1 President gets colors from Mother Club member in area when new member is voted in.
2 When a member leaves club, the president of his chapter turns over his colours to the Mother Club member in his area.
3 Respect your colors, don't let anyone take them from you except the president of your chapter or a Mother Club member.
4 No colors are worn in a cage, except during funerals and loading or unloading a bike from a truck.
5 Nothing will be worn on the back of your jacket except your colors, diamond, 13 patch.
6 No Hippie shit on the front.
7 Colors are to be put on cut off denim jackets only.
8 The only member who may keep his colors if he leaves the club is a Mother Club member.

Ol' ladies

1 Members are responsible for their ol' ladies.
2 Members may have more than one (1) ol' lady.
3 Members may not discuss club business with their ol' lady.
4 No ol' ladies allowed at meetings.
5 No property patch is worn on an ol' lady. So if you see a chick you better ask before you leap.

Prospects

1 Prospect must be at least 18 years old.
2 Prospect must be sponsored by one member who has known him at least one year.
3 Sponsor is responsible for prospect.
4 Prospect must have motorcycle.
5 Prospect must ride his bike to meeting at time of being voted into club.

6 Prospect cannot do any drugs.

7 Prospects can not carry weapons at meetings and Pagan functions, unless otherwise directed by his president.

8 No stealing from prospects.

9 Prospects must attend all meetings and club functions.

10 Prospects must do anything another member tells him to do, that a member has done or would be willing to do himself.

11 Prospect must be voted in by all members of the chapter and three (3) Mother Club members.

12 Prospect must pay for his colors before receiving them.

13 Prospect's period is detemined by Mother Club member.

14 Pagans M.C. is a motorcycle club and a non-profit organization.

Appendix B:
Summary Guide and
Activity Chart for
Group Participation

The summary guide below and the activity chart that follows outline the nature of members' participation in the Rebels Motorcycle Club subculture. The range, type, and frequency of both formally structured institutional events and more informal interaction within the group's social network are documented for what is considered to be a 'typical' summer (riding season) month.

LEGEND   *   Formal – compulsory club activity
         **   Formal – optional club activity
         †   Informal – optional club activity

TYPES OF EVENTS

Weekly Club Meeting* (May 7, 14, 21, 28)
– Meeting of members to discuss club business, plan and organize activities.
– Attendance is compulsory (Rebels MC Book of Rules); informal interviews and observations indicate that there are rarely more than one or two absentees (membership – 24).
– Meetings are followed by a pool/drinking session at the clubhouse, trips to bar, or a short run.
– Attendance at after-events is optional; observations indicate a two-thirds mean participation; e.g., fifteen members counted in Rex Bar on May 14.

Executive Meeting* (May 6, 20)
- Meeting of the executive plus two board members (a total of seven individuals) to discuss executive business and plan proposals to be forwarded to the membership.
- Attendance is 'compulsory'; meetings occur on a bi-monthly basis unless an emergency meeting is required.
- Attendance is usually complete although there are no formal rules; i.e., attendance is just expected.

Victoria Day Run* (May 17, 18, 19)
- A three-day mandatory run to Amisk Lake.
- There are two mandatory runs per riding season: Victoria Day and Labour Day.
- Attendance is mandatory (Rebels MC Constitution, 1975); e.g., on the Victoria Day run all members, plus strikers.

Non-Mandatory Runs** (May 3, 11, 31)
- Either a one-day or weekend outing.
- There are usually three or four runs per month.
- Attendance is optional; however, members are required to attend one run a month (Book of Rules); e.g., on the Warburg run, there were nineteen members, two strikers, two friends of club, and six old ladies.

Boys' Night Out** (May 1, 8, 15, 22, 29)
- Activities usually include drinking at bar and/or a party at the clubhouse.
- According to the Rebels MC Book of Rules, members' old ladies are not allowed at the clubhouse or at Rebel bars. This ruling does not mean, however, that other females are not present at these events.
- Attendance is optional; however, members are generally expected to participate once or twice a month; e.g., the mean attendance for the May 8th and 22nd outings was sixteen.

Barbecue** (May 10, 31)
- Members bring steaks and/or steal a pig. The club in addition purchases two or three kegs of beer.
- Held at clubhouse.
- Attendance is optional; e.g., attendance at May 31st barbecue included twenty-one Rebels, three Rebel strikers, two friends of club, thirteen King's Crew, four Warlords, and thirteen old ladies.

Private Parties[†] (May 2, 9, 23)
- Party at member's residence.
- A non-club activity, but guests are usually limited *ex post facto* to patch holders.
- Attendance is optional; for example, there were thirteen members plus old ladies at Indian's May 9th party.

Drinking at Bar[†] (May 5, 13, 27)
- On an open night when one of the above or other activities are happening, several members are usually to be found at what has been established at that time as the club bar.
- Attendance is optional; e.g., on the dates of May 5th, 13th, and 27th, there were seven, ten, and nine members there, respectively.

FREQUENCY OF MEMBERSHIP PARTICIPATION

	Executive (board) members	Members
Total number of formal-compulsory club activities (*)	9	7
Total number of formal-optional club activites (**)	10	10
Total number of informal-optional club activities (†)	11	11
Total number of club activities	30	28
Total number of days on which there were club activities	25	23

Activity Chart

SUNDAY	MONDAY	TUESDAY	WEDNESDAY	THURSDAY	FRIDAY	SATURDAY
				1 ** Boys' Night Out	2 † Roast Pig Party	3 * Warburg Run
4 † Informal Visiting (Saint, Coyote & Striker at Blue's house)	5 † Capilano Bar	6 * Executive Meeting	7 * Club Meeting † Corona Bar	8 ** Boys' Night Out	9 † Private party at Indian's	10 ** Barbecue at Clubhouse
11 ** Run to see possible land buy	12	13 † Rex Bar	14 * Club Meeting † Rex Bar	15 ** Boys' Night Out	16 † Mech. prep. of m/c for run. Collect/pack food and equipment	17 * Victoria Day Mandatory Run to Amisk Lake
18 * Victoria Day Mandatory Run to Amisk Lake	19 * Victoria Day Mandatory Run to Amisk Lake	20 * Executive Meeting	21 * Club Meeting † Capilano Bar	22 ** Boys' Night Out	23 † Private party at Whimpy's	24 † Clubhouse pool/ drinking session
25 † Impromptu 'boogie' (8 members) Canoe trip down N. Saskatchewan River	26	27 † Corona Bar	28 * Club Meeting † Rex Bar	29 ** Boys' Night Out	30 † Mechanical preparation of motorcycles	31 ** Red Deer run to meet King's Crew MC ** Barbecue at clubhouse

Bibliography

Agar, M. 1986. *Speaking of Ethnography*. Beverly Hills, Calif.: Sage

Ayoob, Massad. 1982. 'Outlaw Bikers.' In *Police Product News* 6, no. 5 (May)

Bardwick, Judith M. 1979. *In Transition*. New York: Holt, Rinehart and
    Winston

Berger, John. *Ways of Seeing*. Markham, Ont.: Penguin

Bertothy, Ron, and Betty B. Bosarge. 1983. 'State Police Plead for Federal
    Help with Biker Gangs.' In *Organized Crime Digest* 4, no. 2

Brownmiller, Susan. 1984. *Femininity*. Toronto: Random House

Forkner, William. 1986. '"Wino" Willie Forkner: All the Old Romance Retold.'
    In *Easyriders* 16, no. 159

Henderson, Bill, and H.R. Kaye. 1968. *A Place in Hell*. Los Angeles, Calif.:
    Holloway House

Holt, Simma. 1972. *The Devil's Butler*. Toronto: McClelland & Stewart

Hughes, Robert. 1971. 'Myth of the Motorcycle Hog.' In *Time*, 8 February

Kapuscinski, Brendan A. 1988. *'Application for Warrant to Search and Seize.'*
    Attorney-General of the Province of Alberta

Keiser, Lincoln R. 1979. *The Vice Lords: Warriors of the Streets*. Toronto: Holt,
    Rinehart and Winston

Kirby, Cecil, and Thomas Renner. 1988. *Mafia Assassin*. Toronto: Methuen

Klapp, Orin E. 1969. *Collective Search for Identity*. Toronto: Holt, Rinehart
    and Winston

– 1972. *Currents of Unrest: An Introduction to Collective Behavior*. New York:
    Holt, Rinehart and Winston

Lavigne, Yves. 1987. *Hell's Angels: Taking Care of Business*. Toronto:
    Ballantine

Lofland, John. 1969. *Deviance and Identity*. Englewood Cliffs. NJ: Prentice-Hall

Maanen, John van. 1988. *Tales of the Field: On Writing Ethnography*. Chicago: Ill.: University of Chicago Press

Marsh, Peter, and Peter Collett. 1987. 'Driving Passion.' In *Psychology Today*, June

Morgan, Raymond C. 1978. *The Angels Do Not Forget*. San Diego, Calif.: Law and Justice Publishers

Reynolds, Frank, and Michael McClure. 1971. *Freewheelin Frank*. London: New English Library

Royal Canadian Mounted Police. 1980. 'Outlaw Motorcycle Gangs.' In *RCMP Gazette* 42, no. 10

– 1987. 'Outlaw Motorcycle Gangs.' In *RCMP Gazette* 49, no. 5

Seeman, Melvin. 1975. 'Alienation Studies.' In *Annual Review of Sociology* 1

Spradley, James P., and Brenda Mann. 1975. *The Cocktail Waitress: Women's Work in a Man's World*. New York: Wiley

Thompson, Hunter S. 1967. *The Hell's Angels*. New York: Ballantine Books

Visano, Livian. 1989. 'Researching Deviance: An Interactionist Account.' Paper presented at Canadian Sociology and Anthropology Association annual conference, Quebec City

Wetherington, Ronald K. 1967. *The Nature of Man*. Dubuque, Iowa: W.C. Brown

Wethern, George, and Vincent Colnett. 1978. *A Wayward Angel*. New York: Richard Marek Publishers

Wolf, Daniel R. 1990. 'High Risk Methodology: Entering and Leaving a Closed Society.' In *Experiencing Fieldwork: Qualitative Research in the Social Sciences*, ed. by William B. Shaffir and Robert Stebbins. Beverly Hills, Calif.: Sage Publications

– 1986. 'Women and the Outlaws: Hard-core Gender Dynamics.' Paper presented at the Canadian Ethnology Society annual meetings, Edmonton, Alberta

Wolf, Daniel R., and David E. Young. 1983. 'The Adaptive Significance of Intracultural Differences.' In *Culture* 3, no. 2: 59–71

Index

alienation: evolution of social condition for, 341–2; as a factor leading to countercultural and subcultural groupings, 340–1; as an industrial phenomenon, 340; leading to the search for a biker identity, 30–2; outlaw clubs as subcultural responses to, 342–7; psychological dimension of, 342; sociological dimension of, 342

alliances of clubs, 327. See also territoriality

AMA (American Motorcycle Association): as parent organization representing American motorcycling, 4; role in defining the outlaw biker, 4–5, 7, 119–20, 276–7

biker: as building an outlaw identity, 30–62; hassles and hazards of becoming, 16–17, 55; making contact with a club, 60–2; the need for brothers, 59; as a search for personal identity, 30–3; self-image as heroes of freedom and independence, 9, 56–9. See also socialization process

boogies. See economics

broad, 145–8. See also women

brotherhood: code of 96–8; formal club rules and testing of commitment, 80, 98–100; gift giving and underground economy, 68–9; mutual support ethic, 98; as a protective mechanism, 16, 97, 203–9; as a social network, 16, 81–3, 97, 100–3, 361–4; as threatened by ties to women (ol' ladies), 137–42

Canadian Airborne Regiment, battle of Rebels with, 203–9

chopper, chopping. See motorcycle (customizing)

CISC (Criminal Intelligence Service of Canada), evaluation of outlaw clubs as criminal organizations, 7–8

club bar: boycotting of by some members, 196–8; camouflaging differences between brothers,